BRADLEY

and the

STRUCTURE *of* KNOWLEDGE

SUNY series in Philosophy

George R. Lucas, Jr., editor

BRADLEY

and the

STRUCTURE *of* KNOWLEDGE

PHILLIP FERREIRA

STATE UNIVERSITY OF NEW YORK PRESS

Published by
State University of New York Press, Albany

© 1999 State University of New York

For information, address State University of New York Press,
State University Plaza, Albany, NY 12246

Production by Laurie Searl
Marketing by Patrick Durocher

Library of Congress Cataloging-in-Publication Data

Ferreira, Phillip [date]
    Bradley and the structure of knowledge / Phillip Ferreira.
        p.   cm. — (SUNY series in philosophy)
    Includes bibliographical references and index.
    ISBN 0-7914-4141-5 (alk. paper). — ISBN 0-7914-4142-3 (pbk. :
alk. paper)
    1. Bradley, F. H. (Francis Herbert), 1846–1924. 2. Knowledge,
Theory of. I. Title. II. Series.
B1618.B74F47 1999
121'.092—dc21   98-24538
                                                                CIP

10 9 8 7 6 5 4 3 2 1

For Bernard Green

— In Memoriam —

CONTENTS

ACKNOWLEDGMENTS

THIS book would not have been written without the support and encouragement of family, friends, and colleagues. Early guidance was provided by Calvin Normore and Gordon Nagel. In more recent years my interest in Bradley has been nurtured by those active within the International Bradley Society. I have immensely enjoyed their published work; but I have benefited most, I believe, from discussions with (to name only a few) Jim Allard, James Bradley, Bill Mander, Leemon McHenry, Timothy Sprigge, Guy Stock, Betty Trott, and Fred Wilson. Though I am sure they will disagree with much that I say, my own understanding of Bradley has been sharpened by their comments and questions.

My thanks also to Jane Bunker and Laurie Searl of SUNY Press (their editorial advice and good humor have been invaluable); to Oxford University Press for their permission to use quotations that might still fall under copyright protection; to Thoemmes Press for allowing me to reprint portions of my article "Bradley's Attack on Associationism"; and to *Bradley Studies*. It is with the latter's permission that portions of my articles "Perceptual Ideality and the Ground of Inference" and "Contradiction, Contrariety and Inference" appear. The cover photograph of Bradley appears through the generosity of Mrs. W. H. Walsh, Oxford.

Finally, I would like to mention the inestimable support provided by my dear friend Elisabeth Perz and my wife Jane. They, along with the rest of my family, have contributed far more than they know.

Chapter 1

INTRODUCTION

F.H. Bradley was and remains today the best known of the English idealists. For more than forty years Bradley was not only the leading voice of the British Absolutist school, he was also the most read and most influential of all English-speaking philosophers.[1] And still his influence—only dimly felt at times—persists.

Although Bradley's views are decidedly opposed to those that came to characterize the "analytic turn" in philosophy, he continues to fascinate a surprisingly diverse philosophical audience. And the reasons for this continuing interest are many; not the least of them, it would seem, is Bradley's philosophical style.[2] With subtlety and precision, his attack on an opponent's position can be ruthless. Yet, on occasion, we find the discussion approaching the poetic. And, while there can be no doubt that Bradley is capable of persuasive dialectic, to attribute his influence to mere rhetoric is to do him a great injustice.[3] On any serious reading one cannot come away from Bradley but with the impression that he is a man who, having deeply thought through the issues, passionately believes in what he says—even if from the perspective of common sense his claims sometimes seem far-fetched or extreme. There is always the feeling that no matter how removed from our ordinary conceptions or the received philosophical opinion the result may be, if the argument demands a controversial conclusion then Bradley is willing to entertain it. Richard Wollheim, in his influential monograph *F. H. Bradley*, describes him as a man who is "forced backwards, step by step, down a strange labyrinth, in self-defence, until at last finding himself in the comparative safety of some murky cave he rests among the shadows."[4] It isn't, Wollheim suggests, that Bradley is committed in advance to any philosophical program, it is that his own examination of the issues forces him to take the stand he does.

1

These sorts of characterizations have led some to call Bradley a "philosopher's philosopher." And, as accurate as such an account might be, it seems that Bradley never sees his own views as particularly problematic (insofar, at least, as we might attach this label to a position that deviates from common sense). Bradley believes that his position—although it certainly rejects the *philosophical* adequacy of common sense—is eminently reasonable and in accord with the common person's deepest intuitions. And it is, he suggests, only through their being misunderstood that his views might seem radical or extreme. Bradley never dismisses the everyday intellectual abstractions by which we live our lives as unimportant or irrelevant. They are, each of them, necessary but limited truths (what he calls "appearances"); and each, he believes, is valid and true within its own sphere. Thus when he propounds such things as the unreality of time or the self-contradictory character of relational thought, Bradley is espousing purely metaphysical theses which claim that there exist in our ordinary conception of these matters problems; and these problems, while not apparent to our ordinary consciousness, must, if they are to be overcome, submit themselves to metaphysical scrutiny.

Although there is much truth in the description of Bradley as a "philosopher's philosopher" it is also possible that such an understanding could cause us to ignore another side of his philosophical disposition. And I refer here to Bradley's elevation of "feeling" (and even "instinct") as a criterion—ultimately *the* criterion—of philosophical truth. Despite his apparent devotion to ratiocination as a means of arriving at truth, Bradley often comes down strongly on the side of what might be called "experiential knowledge," and thus he shares with common-sense a certain distrust of purely intellectual maneuvering. It is at this primary level of felt experience, Bradley believes, that final judgment on the adequacy of any theory is made. A philosophical theory is accepted (or rejected) because it "satisfies" (or it doesn't). And satisfaction, when and where it is achieved, largely results from grasping an issue from a broader perspective than purely ratiocinative means can provide.

This is, of course, an oversimplification that must be corrected as we proceed. However, we can say at this point that Bradley takes this view because he believes that it is at the level of feeling that we are most directly in contact with reality. Mere thought, or what Bradley calls "relational thinking," he sees as incapable of either recognizing or correcting its own defects and limitations. However, the fact that we can somehow apprehend these limitations at all demands that conscious *experience* be acknowledged as—in some manner—already beyond relational thought and in possession of a deeper criterion of truth and reality. We shall, in the chapters that follow, consider in detail Bradley's refusal to see this criterion as supplied by thought. For now, I would only mention that Bradley sees this experiential measure as one that is "suprarelational" and that, as presupposed by merely relational thinking, acts as critic of itself in a lesser form.

It was around this theme that the greatest controversies of Bradley's career developed. And it is also, I shall suggest, on this issue that some of the grossest misinterpretations of his views have arisen—misinterpretations that have allowed until only recently the man who was once the English-speaking world's "most eminent philosopher" to have fallen into neglect.[5] Hence, it will be my primary concern in this essay to communicate what I understand as Bradley's actual position on this point. And, although it will require the discussion of many pages to communicate the force of Bradley's philosophical vision, I would like to provide in these introductory remarks a fuller statement of the problem and the difficulties that any student of Bradley will encounter when attempting to unravel his thought.

One of the most striking aspects of Bradley's philosophy is the degree to which it concerns itself with judgment and the act of predication. Not only in his specifically logical works, but also in his more metaphysical (and even ethical) discussions, the reader is continually reminded of what it means to apprehend something, both sensuously and intellectually, as a subject and to attach to that subject a further condition that qualifies, conditions, or relates it to something else. Time and again the reader finds himself following Bradley's detailed analyses of subjects, predicates, and their various modes of relation. And virtually everything Bradley has to say about knowledge and human experience revolves around his doctrine of "judgment" or "predication."[6] (The two terms are synonomous here.) Indeed, it would not be going too far to say that the act of predication (judgment) is *the* focus of Bradley's work.

The central focus of this work will also be Bradley's account of judgment and the theory of systematic knowledge it entails. Of course, in order to make clear precisely what this act of predication (or judgment) is will require the discussion of the following chapters. However, even at this point we should be aware of the following. To be consciously aware is, for Bradley, to predicate (or assert) one thing of another. That is, to be aware at all is already to have judged, or at least to be experiencing the results of prior judgments. Bradley completely rejects the idea that consciousness begins with a conceptually bare, sensuous "given" that is subsequently wrapped in intellectual "interpretations." If the contents of experience have become part of my conscious life they are, according to Bradley, *already* related to one another through the act of judgment.

Judgment (predication) is thus with us from the beginning of our conscious existence. And, as we shall soon discover, Bradley sees the goal of judgment to be the complete qualification of the subject by the predicate. In other words, when we judge (i.e., attach a predicate to a subject) we seek to apprehend perfectly the sense in which the terms of our judgment relate to and qualify one another. And, while there is always a degree to which any act of predication (judgment) succeeds in realizing this goal, it is, nevertheless, always the case that the judgment also fails to achieve completely its end. Briefly stated, Bradley's claim is that whenever we attempt to qualify a subject by a predicate in the act of judgment we never fully manage to do so. For a variety of reasons (to be considered in the following chapters), Bradley remains convinced that articulate thought—even at the highest levels—remains essentially finite, limited, and unable to apprehend fully its object. It is Bradley's continual claim that, as a merely analyzing intellect, thought attempts to find satisfaction by making explicit to itself the structure of reality; but, in this it can achieve only relative success. No matter how elevated or advanced thought becomes there always exists, according to Bradley, a gap between it and its object. And, though what we desire in any cognitive act (the act of judgment) is a total seizing in thought and language of our object, this he sees as being, in principle, impossible.

The object of thought (reality) is always, Bradley remains convinced, entirely unique and individual; thought and language, no matter how augmented and specific are still to some extent, abstract, universal, and general; and in maintaining these characteristics it is incapable of grasping the unique individuality of its referent. Hence, to use a popular philosophical expression, we can never fully say (or more accurately, think) what we mean. And, since for Bradley there exists no direct intuition of reality that is entirely preconceptual, our knowledge of everything must always remain, to some degree, defective. This leads, however, to one of the most distinctive features of Bradley's philosophy.

For Bradley, so long as there exists conditions that are essential to the characterization of the subject in any judgment but that are not brought into the explicit formulation of that judgment, it cannot be said to be entirely true. Thus Bradley writes:

> If there is to be sheer truth the condition of the assertion must not fall outside the judgment. The judgment must be thoroughly self-contained. If the predicate is true of the subject only by something omitted and unknown, such a truth is defective. The judgment therefore, as it stands, is ambiguous and it is at once true and false, since in a word it is conditioned.[7]

We may illustrate his point, at this stage only in an approximate fashion, by the following example. When I judge, let us say, "Mary is happy" I have predicated of the subject something that does not intrinsically and necessarily belong to it. Indeed, the fact that "happiness" and "Mary" are now, through the act of prediction, brought together at all presupposes many conditions (time, place, etc.) that allow for their union but that fall outside my conscious apprehension. And this externality of conditions to the union of subject and predicate provides us with, Bradley claims, an "unstable" and hence defective assertion.

This is, in effect, a condemnation of contingent truth by Bradley. A truth in order to be fully true must, on his analysis, be universally true. True, that is, not just now under these circumstances—circumstances that partially conceal the conditions of the actual judgment—but true anywhere and always. However, when it comes to our actual judgments we find that there must necessarily attach to them a degree of contingency from which they cannot escape. Not only must there exist conditions that are external to the judgment and upon which it depends for its truth; but these conditions must remain largely unknown. Bradley is committed to the position that not only can there not exist a contingent judgment that is fully true, neither can there exist a judgment—at least as it is understood by us—that is absolutely necessary.[8] Hence, every judgment is to his mind at least partially false. And the act of asserting a predicate of a subject is, in failing to realize complete necessity and universality, always a partial failure.

It is this aspect of Bradley's theory of predication that has frequently led commentators to describe his position as "sceptical." However, what is so often missed is that all is not a loss. Despite Bradley's claim that the truth of any judgment relies on conditions that are external to it (and that thereby make the judgment subject to falsification), he still believes that judgment can, so to speak, improve its lot. Bradley is convinced that we can, in a progressively increasing but never complete manner, include the conditions that had previously remained external to the judgment. Thus, any assertion can lessen its propensity to falsification and thereby secure for itself a greater *degree* of truth. But yet he writes:

> Can the conditions of the judgment ever be made complete and comprised within the judgment? In my opinion this is impossible. And hence with every truth there still remains some truth, however, in its opposite. In other words you can never pass wholly beyond degree.[9]

This passage expresses the conviction that lay behind his doctrine of "degrees of truth and reality" (the subject of chapter 6). And we may say at this early point in our discussion that, for Bradley, although thought can elevate itself through the use of "higher" or more "developed" concepts (which, as we shall see, come about through increased "systematization"), it is still condemned to fail in its effort to show how a predicate completely qualifies its subject, and how any specific judgment actually relates to the unique reality to which it refers. Although implicitly at work in his first book (*Ethical Studies*) this view explicitly emerges in the first edition of the *Principles of Logic* and is maintained by Bradley throughout his career.[10] And it is the explication of this point that will constitute the greater part of my discussion.

I would also mention here that this aspect of Bradley's philosophy—an aspect that lies at the very heart of his system—was, during Bradley's career, rejected by a variety of critics. Realist philosophers rejected the doctrine because it denies the existence of independent facts that are externally related to one another and that are thereby capable of being either true or false.[11] Bradley's theory—a theory that sees the facts about which we judge to consist ultimately in the "one great Fact" (the universe-as-a-whole)—is diametrically opposed to any view of truth as either the relation between a state of the judging subject's mind and a wholly external object, or the apprehension of "timelessly subsisting propositions." For these writers Bradley's theory was unacceptable because it views the universe and its relation to the knowing subject in a manner that fails to do justice to what they believed is the independent manner in which subjects and objects stand to one another.

The more orthodox idealist writers, on the other hand, felt that Bradley had committed the opposite error. They argued that Bradley lets thought and its object become too independent and that he erects an unreal (and unnecessary) impediment to the attainment of the higher reaches of objective truth and knowledge. The thrust of their criticism was that Bradley allows thought and reality to fall apart to such an extent that their separation is incapable of being overcome in any act of judgment.

My claim, however, is that Bradley commits neither of these errors. Hence, one of my fundamental objectives in this essay is to consider the relevancy and force of the arguments against Bradley on this point. But in order to understand Bradley's central claim (and the attacks by his critics) we shall be forced to consider his views on a number of interrelated topics. Not only must his specific views on predication be examined, but also his controversial critique of "relational thought," his understanding of the role of "feeling" in judgment, his views on "degrees of truth" and even the nature of the "Absolute."* However, by focusing on the act of predication (i.e., the general nature of judgment) we shall maintain a perspective on Bradley's philosophy that possesses significant advantages. First, there is no issue more characteristic of Bradley's thought from his earliest work to his latest. And second, through an explication of this area of Bradley's philosophy we shall also bring into sharp relief some of the major ambiguities of the *Principles of Logic*; ambiguities whose influence—even after they are eliminated in the mature writings—still, to some of his readers, taint much of what Bradley says in his later years.

I speak here of what was known as the "doctrine of floating ideas," a theory that—although quickly abandoned—continued to cloud the understanding of many when considering the general theory of predication (a theory Bradley maintained and developed). These were seen in the minds of some as complementary theses that were indicative of a "latent empiricism." It shall be my claim, though, that the two doctrines are—if properly understood—in no way aligned, and that to see them as such is to misinterpret Bradley's philosophy. Through a thorough examination of the theory of predication as it evolves over the course of Bradley's career we should be in a better position to separate fully these issues and to come to an accurate understanding of his mature thought. But how did the doctrine of floating ideas relate to his theory of judgment or predication? And how were the two conflated in the minds of some critics?

In short, the troublesome doctrine of the floating idea is a theory in which significant or meaningful ideas are seen as capable of "floating" or "wandering" in the consciousness of a judging subject without being simultaneously affirmed as real or true. In other words, it contains a central thesis of traditional empiricism: namely, that an idea is the result of a derivative act of abstraction made on given sense data, and that this idea (which can "float" unattached) is fundamentally prior to the act of judgment and (ontologically) different from the object to which it refers. Not only on this theory does an idea become a mere representation, but it leads to a position in which the knowing subject is essentially estranged from and forever an Other to its object. Bradley's occasional comments that suggest such a view alarmed his idealist colleagues as it apparently put him in an alliance with traditional empiricist doctrine to

---

* Bradley often capitalizes "Reality," "the Real," and "the Whole" when they are used as synonyms for "the Absolute." I have followed his convention only for the term "the Absolute."

such an extent that he was suspected of perpetuating both radically dualist and sceptical theses.[12]

It is true, of course, that the doctrine of floating ideas *is* closely aligned with the position that the general thrust of Bradley's *Logic* is intent on overcoming. And it is also true that when and where such a theory raises its head it constitutes a profound inconsistency within the pages of his book. However, it is decidedly false, I shall claim, that this doctrine is implicated by the larger theory of predication (judgment) at any stage in Bradley's career. Even after the doctrine of the floating idea is purged from his philosophy, Bradley continues to believe that in every judgment (the basic act of knowledge) there exists an effort—ultimately unrealizable—to say something about reality in such a manner that it is completely and unconditionally true.

However, in light of scattered comments found in the 1883 edition of the *Principles of Logic* some readers seriously misunderstood the import of Bradley's theory of predication. For some, the reason why, on Bradley's view, thought can never accurately grasp its object is because it becomes, in his hands, *mere* thought—thought that is fundamentally different from the reality of which it is asserted. On one interpretation— the one that inaccurately characterizes his position—thought is seen as a merely formal activity that can in no manner get concrete reality within its grasp.[13] Thought, on this reading, deals with merely abstract universal concepts that when combined through the act of judgment exist in external (and ultimately irrational) relation to one another and their ultimate subject—reality as a whole.

Now, on such an interpretation the characterization of Bradley as a sceptical empiricist is accurate. However, as we shall see, such an understanding of the mature Bradley is entirely without foundation. Although he grants that there is always an aspect of thought that can be characterized as a mere "thinking about" its object, Bradley is equally insistent that in every act of judgment, thought and its object partially coincide (in the literal sense); and, that to think is to get *closer* to reality—not further from it. This is, however, a complex topic, and to appreciate this problem fully we must await the discussion of later chapters. At this stage I would merely point out that the portrayal of Bradley as either a mystic or a sceptic calls into question the identification of his philosophy with any species of traditional idealism. And, though it is usually conceded that "absolute" or "objective" idealism has at least *an* answer to the sceptic (if one is willing to accept certain of its metaphysical claims), it has been unclear to what extent Bradley's position is consistent with the antisceptical doctrine of this school.

The idealist doctrine that some of Bradley's statements in the *Principles of Logic* seem to threaten is one that views the questions of dualism and scepticism as intimately related and capable of being overcome only through a properly formulated theory of thought and its object. Although the precise meaning of this statement must remain at this stage somewhat unclear, I think it not inaccurate to say that the traditional idealism avoids the problem of scepticism because, at some level and in some sense, thought is seen as at least partially coextensive with its object—at least in the sense that subject and object, knowledge and reality are generally understood as poles or aspects of a larger unified experience within which both fall. However, in the case of Bradley, it has often been asked whether or not his theory of floating ideas and his subsequent condemnation of thought as too abstract to fully apprehend its object divorces him from this tradition. But, before considering in any detail how Bradley's theory might break with the idealist tradition, let us consider the extent to which his early work appears to be in harmony with it. Some of the most unambiguous statements of Bradley's early metaphysical views are found in the final chapter of his work on moral philosophy. And I quote at length one such statement as it provides as clear an indication of Bradley's position as could be desired. There Bradley writes:

> It is forgotten that when mind is made only a part of the whole, there is a question which *must* be answered; 'If so, how can the whole be known, and for the mind? If about any matter we know nothing whatever, can we say anything about it? Can we even say that it is? And, if it is not in consciousness, how can we know it? And if it is in and for the mind, how can it be a whole which is *not* mind, and in which the mind is only a part or element? *If the ultimate unity were not self or mind, we could not know that it was not mind*: that would mean going out of our minds. And, conversely, if we know it, it cannot be not mind. All in short we can know (the psychological form is another question) is the self and elements in the self. To know a not-self is to transcend and leave one's mind. If we know the whole, it can only be because the whole knows itself in us, because the whole is self or mind, which is and knows, knows and is, the identity and correlation of subject and object.'[14]

That there exists a commitment to an idealistic monism in this passage (and many others in *Ethical Studies*) is, I think, undeniable.[15] And when I say this I want to emphasize Bradley's belief that all experience presupposes an essential unity between subject and object, and that the con-

tents of any subject's thoughts are—while not an entirely accurate dupli-
cation of the object—nevertheless, continuous with and, at some level, of
the same stuff as it. While it is true that we find Bradley's characteristic
reservation about the finite subject's ability to experience its object perfectly (a view that always keeps him from identifying thought and reality
tout court), the degree to which Bradley rejects all versions of dualism is
striking. And this, we shall see, is a theme he is to maintain throughout his
career.[16] We find it in 1874 with the "Presuppositions of Critical History"
and in his last, posthumously published, work—an unfinished article entitled "Relations."[17] And over the course of this essay I shall supply what I
believe is compelling evidence that this commitment to such thoroughly
holistic views, although at times not fully worked out, never actually
wavers.[18] Indeed, it is one of the principal theses of this essay that any
empiricist tendencies in Bradley's *Principles of Logic* are, so far as they
actually exist, an aberration; and, I shall argue, the main thrust of the
mature work represents not only a refinement of his earlier views, but also
a continuation and development of British post-Kantian idealism.

The point we must be sensitive to, however, is this: Although Bradley
believes that the ultimate continuity between thought and its object can be
established beyond doubt (since it is a presupposition of all experience and
directly apprehended at the level of feeling), the *details* of their unity is
something that can only be progressively—and never fully—apprehended.
Ultimately, it is because thought cannot fully envisage its deeper identity
with the whole that it is condemned as intrinsically defective. And it is this
contrast between feeling (which *can* sense its identity with the whole or
Absolute) and the finite judging self that lay behind virtually all of
Bradley's harsh statements regarding predication and relational thought.[19]
But this doctrine is worked out—sometimes tortuously so—over many
volumes. And in order to develop an understanding of Bradley's larger
theory (and his commitment to monistic idealism) we must now begin to
unravel the theory of judgment and significant ideas that first appears in
the *Principles of Logic*. Before embarking on this project, though, let me
say something about the material we shall be considering.

The title of this essay suggests that we are concerned with Bradley's
theory of knowledge; and this is certainly correct. But we shall soon
discover that what philosophers today call the "theory of knowledge"
was understood by Bradley and his contemporaries to fall within the
purview of "logic." And certainly it is in Bradley's *Principles of Logic*
that we find the topics with which we shall be most concerned first discussed. However, we must remember that, while the theory we shall be
examining is first developed in the 1883 text of Bradley's *Logic*, it is
not fully articulated until 1922 when, after a lifetime of elaboration

and refinement, it receives its final—and we must assume most author-itative—formulation in the "Terminal Essays."[20] Hence, I shall have much to say about the intervening works and the apparently sceptical side of Bradley's thought as found in the works of his middle years: *Appearance and Reality* and *Essays on Truth and Reality*. Indeed, it is in these works that the shortcomings of cognitive experience receive their most exhaustive treatment. The problems dealt with in the origi-nal edition of the *Principles of Logic* are the problems that Bradley con-siders throughout his career, and it is not as though we are leaving Bradley's logical-epistemological theory behind when we consider his more explicitly metaphysical writings. Thus it is essential that we con-sider his views as developed in these other works if we are to under-stand the "Terminal Essays," which constitute the greater body of the 1922 revisions to the *Principles of Logic*. In these "Terminal Essays" Bradley makes continual reference to *Appearance and Reality* and the *Essays on Truth and Reality*; and any tolerably complete understand-ing of the final edition of the *Logic* cannot be had without some famil-iarity with these books.[21]

Based upon Bradley's own evaluation, then, we shall consider the *least* informative volume (because at times misleading) to be the first edi-tion of the *Principles of Logic*. It is here that, by his own admission, unresolved metaphysical difficulties (i.e., the floating idea) lead to what is at times a faulty account. However, it is only through an understand-ing of the position contained therein (and Bradley's reasons for repudi-ating portions of the first edition *Logic*) that we can fully appreciate the evolution of his thought and the final position he is to take.

It is my intention in this essay, then, to explicate Bradley's larger theory of knowledge as found in the two editions of the *Principles of Logic, Appearance and Reality*, and *Essays on Truth and Reality*. I shall trace the development of Bradley's views on these issues and attempt to provide a coherent account of the mature position that claims to have effected a reconciliation between abstract thought and concrete reality, between thinking subject and given, recalcitrant world. It is here, I shall argue, that we encounter what *appears* on first look to be an essentially sceptical position. However, on closer examination, we shall see why Bradley himself understands it as the only effective response to radical scepticism. Bradley, I shall argue, remains thoroughly convinced that only by declaring all knowledge to be inherently relative to the greater whole within which knowledge, will, and feeling coexist in an interde-pendent manner, can the various philosophical puzzles regarding the subject-object relation and the development of inference be found. Only by sacrificing its claim to *complete* knowledge of anything, Bradley argues, can philosophy avoid an account of the world wherein a self-refuting scepticism is the result.

It will also be my claim that, despite his rejection of certain aspects of orthodox post-Kantian idealism, Bradley's mature position remains, nevertheless, firmly within the idealist tradition.[22] And, I shall suggest, Bradley ultimately does overcome that "cheap and easy monism" that he thinks characterizes so much of the idealist literature.[23] Bradley, I shall claim, takes the traditional position and through an indefatigable effort to "push the question to the end," brings to light what he sees as the Achilles heel of idealist doctrine—the inability to reconcile fully the abstract character of thought with the concrete nature of reality as it is experienced in perception, feeling, and will.[24]

I should also, perhaps, say in these introductory remarks something about the structure of this work and the role of "feeling" in Bradley's theory of knowledge. While I begin, as do most writers on Bradley, with a general discussion of judgment, significant ideas, and inference, at numerous places in the early chapters I also make reference to Bradley's doctrine of feeling—a theoretical device that assumes a role of great importance in his account of knowledge (and an aspect of his thought which has received little attention in the work of many commentators). However, it is not until chapters 8 and 9 that this theory is treated in any detail. Now, given the role in Bradley's theory of knowledge that the doctrine of feeling finally takes, it might seem reasonable to deal with it at the outset. However, a number of considerations suggest that this is not the best approach.

The first of these is that Bradley's logical-epistemological views do not in their early appearance appeal to the idea of feeling (at least not as it is finally formulated). Indeed, the epistemological difficulties that the doctrine of feeling attempts to overcome are ones that only progressively force themselves on Bradley—and this only after his general theory of judgment and inference are quite developed. Hence to discuss the issue in detail at the outset would be to discuss a solution without the problem it was meant to solve. A second (but closely related) reason for delaying the discussion of feeling is this: any account of feeling that I might provide early on would require my making frequent reference to general logical-epistemological concepts such as "subjects," "predicates," "judgments," "ideas," and "inference." And should I appeal to these notions without having first considered in detail Bradley's understanding of them—an understanding which is, by contemporary lights, highly idiosyncratic—confusion would most likely result. Hence I think it the more prudent course to approach these difficulties in the same order as did Bradley.[25]

I would also mention here that, in addition to explicating the general theory outlined above, this essay will comment on several historical points. First, I hope it will quickly become apparent that it is a serious error to identify Bradley's "idealism" with the sort of subjectivist-empiricism to which the term has sometimes been applied;[26] second, I shall argue, that it is a also mistake to identify Bradley's thought with any variety of Bergsonian mysticism in which reality is intuited but not thought;[27] or (third) as a type of modern Spinozism in which distinctions disappear as relational thought is transcended.[28] Although each of these interpretations of his theory of experience is occasionally put forth, each, I shall suggest, can be taken seriously only by ignoring large sections of the Bradleian corpus.

More importantly, though, I hope to make clear that, despite recent efforts by analytic philosophers to "salvage" his views, Bradley's thought is greatly removed from much of twentieth-century English-speaking philosophy.[29] And, although there are, at times significant, similarities between the views of Bradley and writers like Frege, Russell, and Wittgenstein, this similarity can be (and often has been) taken much too far.[30] If Bradley is right, then a good deal of twentieth-century philosophy must be seen as either misguided or anachronistic. And I hope to show that those philosophers who are inclined to defend Bradley should, if they are to continue in their defense, be prepared to abandon some of the most cherished ideas of mainstream philosophical analysis.[31]

My principal goal, however, is to communicate to the contemporary reader the general rationale of Bradley's position. While his views remain at some distance from our ordinary understanding, they are not at all unreasonable. And I hope to show that his holism is, though unlikely to be embraced by contemporary philosophy, still suggestive of solutions to our philosophical concerns that may prove to be, in the end, unavoidable. In my concluding remarks I shall also attempt to make clearer the relation of Bradley's thought to these concerns. There I shall consider why Bradley's metaphysics cannot be accurately portrayed as either realist or antirealist, nor his epistemology as either foundationalist or antifoundationalist (at least as these terms are understood today). And, while my discussion may not win any new converts to absolute idealism, I hope that, by clarifying Bradley's position on some important issues, I can at least help to illuminate the historical darkness that has plagued English-speaking philosophy's awareness of itself for so much of this century.

Chapter 2

The Differentia of Judgment

ANY discussion of Bradley's philosophy demands that his theory of judgment be considered, not merely in passing, but in great detail. The judgment, on Bradley's view, is not just *a* function that along with others constitutes the act of knowing and the elements of logic; the judgment is *the* basic act of cognition by which we knowingly encounter reality. And, while we cannot say that experience and judgment are, for Bradley, entirely co-extensive, we can confidently assert that—as far as any *conscious* experience is concerned—the judgment is always present. Hence it is here with judgment that we must begin.

However, before directly considering Bradley's positive doctrine of judgment, something more needs to be said about the status of the 1883 edition of the *Principles of Logic*. And the first thing we must be aware of is this: despite the problematic doctrine of floating ideas, Bradley always considered the account he provided there to be essentially sound. Hence, it is not as though the student of Bradley—even if fully aware that some of his statements in the *Principles of Logic* are to be rejected or modified—can ignore this early work. Although Bradley does feel that there are inconsistencies in his 1883 discussion, he claims, nonetheless, that the overall point is made (he thought) with sufficient clarity that it should have prevented his readers from being led too far astray by the "careless" language he sometimes employs.[1] Having said this, though, I might once more emphasize the contentious nature of what we are now to consider from the first-edition *Logic*. That Bradley's position in this work is less than unambiguous is evidenced by the controversy that followed in its wake. And I shall point out how even the most fundamental definitions that Bradley provides are—if not read entirely within context—subject to conflicting interpretations. However, I do this not just in an effort to account for the various readings that commentators have provided, but also to point out that Bradley was in 1883 still somewhat unsure on at least two important issues.

As we shall consider in some detail below, there are, by Bradley's own admission, two persisting flaws in the first-edition *Logic* that he would later take great pains to correct. These were (i) the belief that some ideas can exist outside the act of judgment so as to be unaffirmed and hence "float"; and (ii) the closely related claim that the act of affirmation itself is in no way dependent upon the content of the judgment. (That is, that the act of affirmation is an all or nothing affair.) These two views—views that are absolutely inconsistent with the larger argument of the *Principles of Logic*—are completely disavowed by Bradley before the publication of his metaphysical treatise *Appearance and Reality*. However, in order to appreciate the extent to which these two theses conflict with the larger thrust of the work (and his mature view) we must first develop a general sense of judgment.

SOME "ERRONEOUS CONCEPTIONS" OF JUDGMENT

Let us begin by considering what Bradley sees as the legitimate starting point for any logical study (remembering always, though, that by "logic" Bradley means something closer to our idea of an epistemological analysis of judgment, inference and the theory of significant ideas).[2] Although it has been traditionally argued that an examination of questions in logic should begin with an examination of the "term" or "logical idea" (it being the simplest element out of which others are developed), Bradley tells us that there is no compelling reason why one should treat the elements of logic in any particular order. In the opening pages of the *Principles of Logic* Bradley tells us that the judgment, in being considered before the logical idea or inference, reflects nothing more than an arbitrary choice. And by beginning in the middle, we are informed, he hopes to "touch the ends" of the subject as well. In my discussion of the 1883 *Logic*, then, I shall begin, as does Bradley, with the judgment. However, in order to come to grips more quickly with Bradley's positive account of judgment, let us consider several things that, he is convinced, the judgment is *not*.

Judgments as Grammatical Propositions

First, we are told, the act of judgment is not to be identified with the grammatical proposition (i.e., the sentence). This is a point of great importance whose full significance we can only appreciate further along in our discussion. For the present we need merely be aware of Bradley's initial grounds for depreciating the role of the grammatical proposition in the study of logic.

Although Bradley feels that it is essentially through language that we become aware of universals as such, he still believes that the sentence often fails to indicate the real structure of our thought.[3] The actual (logical) subject of the judgment is often, Bradley claims, different from what a grammatical analysis would indicate. And this belief is substantiated, he argues, when we consider judgments such as "A is simultaneous with B," "C is to the east of D," "E is equal to F." Bradley feels that it is quite unnatural to view A, C, or E as they appear in the above propositions as being the only rightful subjects to which the predicates B, D, or F can be applied. He claims that we can also—and perhaps with greater ease—view the predicate terms functioning as subjects. ("B is simultaneous with A," "D has to its east C," "F is equal to E.") Even more illustrative, however, might be to reinterpret these propositions so they read "A and B are synchronous," "C and D lie east and west," and "E and F are equal." Although we have from a grammatical standpoint altered the relation of subject and predicate, it is plain that we have not obscured—but may perhaps have clarified—the meaning of the original propositions. Bradley also claims that since a variety of grammatical forms can be seen to express the same significant idea ("Das Schnee ist weiss," "La neige est blanche," etc.) there is something more fundamental to the morphology of judgment than is indicated by its superficial linguistic formulation. Hence, he sees the grammatical structure as a mere schematic of an underlying conceptual structure. And this grammatical structure may or may not accurately characterize what is in fact being judged.

Judgments as Combination of Ideas

Another important point to be made at the outset is this: While the judgment may or may not be accurately characterized by its grammatical formulation, Bradley believes that its conceptual structure must be seen as somehow other (in a sense yet to be considered) than the reality to which it refers. Put differently, we may say that Bradley sees the act of judgment as involving *ideas*. However, he makes it very clear that the judgment does not consist in what might be called the combination of mere ideas. In judgment we do not attempt to combine ideas by asserting a "predicate idea" of a "subject idea" either directly or indirectly (i.e., through the assistance of a third "copula idea"). The act of predication does not consist in an effort to unify individual and independent ideas in such an external fashion. If this were the case then a true analysis of judgment would trap us in a subjective idealism such that when I assert "The earth goes round the sun," I would really be claiming no more than "My *idea* of the earth goes round my *idea* of the sun." This,

however, is precisely what I do *not* mean when I make such an assertion. What I actually mean, Bradley claims, is that the *real* earth goes
around the *real* sun—and all in a manner that is largely indifferent to my
personal conception of the matter.[4] Indeed, while Bradley feels that ideas
are involved in judgment, at some point and in some way, *reality*, he
tells us, must enter into the account as well. But with this recognition
comes the further result that any significant idea—that is, the content
that is being judged—can never be a *mere* idea (understood as an independent and self-sufficient fact existing only in someone's head).

Associationism

Bradley sees as one of the most objectionable theories of judgment
and inference the "theory of the association of ideas" (or "associationism"). However, given the complexity of the doctrine, I can provide here
only the briefest statement of it principles. (See the appendix for a fuller
treatment.) Still, since it represents the antithesis of Bradley's view of judgment, I think it important to be aware of why he views it as unacceptable.

In its essentials, associationism is the theory of judgment and inference developed by traditional empiricism. Viewing the logical idea as a
mental image (or psychical state) the associationist goes on to account
for our thought processes by a theory of "mental habits." For example,
if I were to experience regularly and without exception the sight of
"snow" followed by a feeling of "cold" I would have developed within
me a "psychical bond" connecting these ideas; and I would come to
believe (solely upon my experience of their contiguous appearance) that
there exists a fundamental connection between them. And when later
presented with an impression (or idea) of "snow" I would have called
up in my mind the idea of "cold"—even if there were no such presently
existing impression. Of course, not all associations would be this
strong. If I had sometimes (but not always) experienced nausea after
tasting apples, I might come to believe that apples have the capacity to
cause sickness; but I would not believe that nausea is their invariable
result. What is important about this theory, though, is its claim that the
chain of reasoning I am engaged in is entirely mechanical and the result
of my prior (and possibly idiosyncratic) experience. There can be on
this theory tremendous variations between the associations made by
different subjects; and no chain of associations can claim any greater
validity than any other.[5]

Now, Bradley sees this doctrine as incoherent for several reasons.
(See appendix.) He believes that, not only is the idea of "preserved
images" unintelligible, so too is the associationist's account of "resemblance" between these images. Most objectionable, though, is the fact

that the theory appeals to the arbitrary frequency of conjoined psychical facts as that which establishes the ground of any inference. If *I* have experienced X followed by Y without exception, then *for me* it is legitimate to see Y as following from X with something approaching necessity. However, if *you* have experienced Y after X only sporadically, then it would be improper *for you* to make the same inference. Taking the ground of inference out of the objects themselves and placing it in the minds of individual subjects, Bradley sees the theory of the association of ideas as an unacceptably subjectivist (and sceptical) account of human thought. Associative theories such as these are, Bradley claims, "mere theories," and as such they fail to achieve the most basic requirements of a doctrine of judgment and inference.

JUDGMENT'S CAPACITY FOR TRUTH AND FALSEHOOD

While we have only touched upon these "erroneous conceptions" of judgment, the reasons for Bradley's rejection of them should become clearer as we proceed. I would mention here, though, that what they all have in common is that they treat the judgment as something that is wholly external to its object, and thus as some sort of "mental entity" that falls completely within the consciousness of the judging subject. But, as we shall see, such a vision of cognitive experience is one Bradley is completely unwilling to embrace. But what is Bradley's proposed alternative?

Although it will require the discussion of many pages to make this idea clear, I would state at the outset that Bradley sees the act of judgment as an *element* within a larger mass of experience that comprises what he calls "feeling," "will," and "thought." What will prove most difficult to follow, though, is Bradley's claim that each of these experiential components is both subjective and objective at once. Although thought, will, and feeling are seen as, in one sense, *my* thought, *my* feeling, and *my* will, in another sense they are understood as manifestations of an objective reality that is the same for all judging subjects. And trying to follow Bradley's analysis of this dual-natured experience is the difficulty that will be with us for the entirety of this essay.

However, rather than try to grasp Bradley's vision whole and complete let us begin by focusing on the sense in which cognitive experience (the judgment) is "subjective" and "mine." And this brings us to the judgment's capacity for error. Indeed, the first positive (and perhaps most obvious) point that must be made about judgment, Bradley tells us, is that it concerns itself with claims of truth and falsity; and where this fundamental condition is absent, so too is the activity of judgment. But, he adds, with this recognition we are forced to acknowledge that—

although it must not be seen as absolute—in judgment we do have, nevertheless, a difference between reality and the idea that is referred to it. We read that

> Judgment, in the strict sense, does not exist where there exists no knowledge of truth and falsehood; and since truth and falsehood depend on the relation of our ideas to reality, you can not have judgment proper without ideas.[6]

That these ideas are not mere ideas or mental representations of external facts we shall consider in detail further down. But first we must grasp the more fundamental point Bradley is making. Although we must acknowledge the existence of specific psychical states, unless these states are somehow "referred beyond themselves," they cannot, Bradley tells us, possess significance. And where there is no effort to declare something beyond what is given to have a determinate character (and thus open itself to falsification) such states are not and should not be called "judgments." The judgment's essential characteristic, then, is that it takes an idea and says of it that it is not a *mere* idea—not just a psychical state—but that somehow it forms a *continuous tissue* with the reality to which it is referred. And in the act of predication (judgment) I attempt the following: In judgment I declare that reality is, although real, in some way continuous with and not different from my idea(s) of it. Or alternatively, I am saying that while reality consists of universals such as I entertain in idea, these universals are what constitutes the real.[7]

> Affirmation, or judgment, [we are told] consists in saying, this idea is no mere idea, but is a quality of the real. The act attaches the floating adjective to the nature of the world, and, at the same time, tells me it was there already.[8]

Hence in judgment—the basic act of thought—I am asserting that the contents I cognitively apprehend are, though my *idea* of reality, still of the same character as reality. But we must remember that in judgment I can be mistaken; indeed, this capacity for error is the judgment's very differentia. Although I might believe that my idea and the reality are continuous and one, the fact that I am sometimes wrong impresses upon me that there remains (despite my belief) a fundamental difference between my idea as asserted and the real that has falsified my idea. Hence we must give some consideration as to how this can occur.

The essential feature of the judgment that allows it to be falsified by further experience has to do, Bradley tells us, with its *ideal* character. Although reality may indeed consist in the same universals as are found in the judgment, there must still exist some difference between the universal quality as it exits *in reality* and as it exists *in the judgment*. The judgment, as an idea that is affirmed as true of the largely recalcitrant reality, must (since it is falsifiable) be somehow other than that reality.[9] But what can we say about the judgment as ideal-not-real? The first thing that we should be aware of, according to Bradley, is that as ideal it is *not* a mere copy. A copy is something that, on most accounts anyway, possesses a substantive—that is, an ontological—difference from that of which it is a representative duplicate. No, Bradley tells us: the judgment is "ideal" in a different sense. And, although we cannot yet fully consider this point, we might say at this stage that the judgment is ideal-not-real because it is sensuously *abstract*.[10] Although it should not be viewed as possessing a radical ontological difference, it can be understood as being somehow "thinner" or "poorer" than what given reality provides.

But let us examine this statement more closely. If we reflect upon any conscious experience we may identify, Bradley tells us, different aspects. There is a given component that is sensuous and that strikes us as wholly concrete and real; and there is an aspect that seems to fall short in this regard. But it is just this less than fully concrete aspect of our experience that constitutes for Bradley the "ideal content" of judgment. And in this ideal content there is, when compared to the totality of our sensuous experience, something missing. It (the ideal content that is affirmed in judgment) lacks—not just the wealth of content that given experience provides—it also lacks a certain sense of "presence" or "facticity."[11] (Precisely what this means we shall consider below.) However, the second point we must consider is an important qualification of this statement.

While the aspect of our conscious experience we call the judgment is poorer than given experience in the sense that it cannot fully and explicitly duplicate its wealth of content or its existential presence, it is in another sense much richer. Whereas given experience ties down any quality or condition to its *present* factual instantiation, the ideal content of judgment refuses to acknowledge this limitation. The judgment as ideal-not-real augments, elaborates on, and extends given experience in a manner that is, though thinner in one sense, more expansive and full-bodied in another. Although stripped and purified of much of the content provided by sense, the ideal content of judgment projects into a limitless space as well as an indefinite past and future.[12] But herein it finds its liability. In attempting to grasp *more* of reality than given experience provides—in attempting to go beyond what is immediately present to sense—our ideal content (which *is* the judgment) may not be entirely accurate. We, as finite judging subjects, may extrapolate or extend reality in a manner that is, in fact, not wholly warranted. We may break the relevant connection of content in our ideal extension of the given reality in a manner that is no longer dictated by that reality itself. We may ideally develop the contents of given experience in a manner that is largely subjective in both origin and result. And thus this ideal content is falsifiable.[13]

Now, before developing this idea any further, I would like to pause and comment on a possible source of confusion here. Bradley, throughout his works, uses the term "given" in describing that which the act of judgment (thought) works upon. However, we must exercise caution in our interpretation of this term. Although Bradley speaks of "given" experience we must never think that by this term he means *merely* given. Bradley's theory of experience starts from the fact that as finite subjects we always find ourselves in the world. It is undeniable, he believes, that we are born with certain felt experiences out of which our intellectual activity arises.[14] In addition to this is the fact that whenever we judge we must begin at the point of focus that our previous act of judgment has provided—that is, we are always left somewhere by its movement. No matter where we are in our intellectual elaboration of reality, we must not forget that there is a reality that provides the material that is worked and reworked by judgment. And we must remember that judgment does not arise out of nothing. At any moment the finite subject is confronted by a mass of experience that far exceeds the bounds of any single act of assertion. Thus a "world" is understood as always hanging from my judgment; and it is this world that, in Bradley's terminology, constitutes the "given." Most importantly, though, this given is not to be seen as some sort of concept-free experience that stands in opposition to the "mental" ideas of the judging subject. To view Bradley's given in this fashion is to misunderstand him completely.

But we are somewhat ahead of ourselves with this discussion. Our only concern at this point is to discover in what sense the falsifiable "ideal content" is ideal-not-real. And, although the precise character of "ideality" (which is never merely ideal) shall prove to be one of the most elusive aspects of Bradley's philosophy, we can say at this point at least the following: insofar as an asserted content is mediate, that is, insofar as it *refers away* from its present instantiation in given experience, it is considered to be ideal and thus "different" from given reality. And it is just this mediate character that makes it liable to error. But let us consider this mediate and ideal character of judgment more closely.

Bradley tells us that, while the difference between given sensuous experience and the ideal content of judgment is not absolute, there is a difference nonetheless. The sensuous given, although it has an ideal or universal *aspect*, is not primarily ideal. As suggested above, it has something that our asserted contents do not possess (or more accurately, only partially possess). Sensuous experience conveys, Bradley believes, a sense of *reality* (what he calls the "infinitude of relations") that does not fully penetrate into all aspects of our conscious lives. And, while the act of judgment is what brings this sense of concrete reality into our explicit conscious awareness, the sense that there *is* a concrete whole is not the result of thought's (i.e., the judgment's) activity. Hence the ideal activity of judgment is understood as standing over against a fuller sense of concrete reality. And, though these two aspects of our experience are not to be seen as absolutely different, they are still distinguishable. And it is just this difference between given recalcitrant experience and the mediate idea that makes the judgment "ideal-not-real" and thus subject to error.

But again, we must be careful not to interpret this difference as a difference in kind. As we shall see, the essence of this difference lies with the fact that reality is *complete*. It is, to use Bradley's term, "individual." Our ideas in judgment, however, can never possess this complete individuality; to greater or lesser extent they are abstract, incomplete, and refer beyond themselves for their fuller significance. But the abstract contents that they are will turn out, in the end, to be the *same* contents that belong to reality (albeit in a sensuously poorer form).[15] Thus Bradley's theory should not be understood as a "representationalist" theory of knowledge—at least as this theory is commonly understood. These are, however, aspects of the doctrine we are not yet prepared to consider fully. And in order to avoid confusion we must first examine several other distinctions.

SUBJECTS, PREDICATES, AND COMPLEX IDEAS

The distinction between the ideal and the real in experience that has now been introduced will occupy our attention for the rest of this chapter. Indeed, it holds so central a place in Bradley's philosophy that we must struggle for some time if we are to avoid misunderstanding and error. But rather than embark immediately on an extended discussion of these matters I would like to provide a fuller, even if provisional statement, of the larger theory of judgment we are trying to understand; and to this end I would like to consider Bradley's rather unusual conception of subject and predicate in logical assertion. However, as a first step in understanding Bradley's concept of a logical predicate, I must say something about his doctrine of complex ideas.

Complex Ideas

While there is much that must for the moment remain unexplained, we need next consider how for Bradley the significant idea (ideal content) that is affirmed in judgment is always one that possesses a *complex* content. Although it is true that we can, through an act of intellectual abstraction, think away much of what is presented to us in perception or imagination, it is almost always the case that we carve up given reality in a manner that identifies certain attributes as *belonging together*—as consisting of a *single* though internally complex phenomenon.[16] And it is just the activity of identifying such unified (though internally complex) phenomena and asserting them as real that constitutes for Bradley the act of judgment. But, I would insist here on a point already raised: It is wrong to view the judgment as consisting of the conjunction of separate ideas. It is not true, Bradley informs us,

> that every judgment has two ideas. We may say on the contrary that all have but one. We take an ideal content, a complex totality of qualities and relations, and we then introduce divisions and distinctions, and we call these products separate ideas with relations between them. And this is quite unobjectionable. But what is objectionable, is our then proceeding to deny that the whole before our mind is a single idea; and it involves a serious error in principle. The relations between the ideas are themselves ideal. They are not the psychical relations of mental facts. They do not exist between the symbols, but hold in the symbolized. They are part of the meaning and not of the existence. And the whole in which they subsist is ideal, and so one idea.[17]

For example, when I judge "The wolf eats the lamb" I am not dealing with two wholly independent ideas ("wolf" and "lamb") that are somehow conjoined by the copula ("is eating"). If we claim that the concepts of "wolf," "eating," or "lamb" are independent ideas that we later somehow connect through the act of judgment, we are, on Bradley's view, just going against the obvious facts. We are told that what it is in such a judgment that I abstract from the given situation and develop as an ideal content is something that *already* contains the internal diversity that is expressed by the grammatical subject, copula, and predicate. But what could possibly be Bradley's motivation for such a claim? Not only does he see the alternative as leading to insuperable difficulties, Bradley seems to hold this position because he feels that the presence of internal diversity in an ideal content is something that is quite natural and obvious. If we look at the wolf do we find, he asks, a simple self-same identity? No. If we look at the lamb can it be found? Or the "is eating"? Again, no. Thus, when speaking of this problem, Bradley tells us:

> We have the idea of a wolf and we call that one idea. We imagine the wolf eating a lamb, and we say, There are two

ideas, or three, or perhaps even more. But is this because the scene is not given as a whole? Most certainly not. It is because in the whole there exist distinctions, and those groupings of attributes we are accustomed to make. But if we once start on this line and deny the singleness of every idea which embraces others, we shall find the wolf himself is anything but one. He is the synthesis of a number of attributes, and, in the end, we shall find that no idea will be one which admits any sort of distinction. Any content whatever, which the mind takes as whole, however large or however small, however simple or however complex, is one idea, and its manifold relations are embraced in a universal.[18]

According to Bradley, the fact that all ideas can be seen to possess internal diversity illustrates the arbitrariness that infects any effort to say that one idea is complex while another is simple. The true criterion of *an* idea would seem to be merely "that which the mind takes as a whole." Thus "the Battle of Waterloo"—if considered by a single act of mind—would constitute a single logical idea. And we could go on indefinitely.

The presence of internal diversity is, then, no argument against the singleness or unity of the idea. (Indeed, it just illustrates that any concrete notion of unity *demands* a diversity that can be unified and one.) And this internally complex idea is what Bradley and his fellow idealists call an "identity-in-difference." When using this phrase Bradley only means to call attention to the fact that all ideas (at least as actually used in judgment) possess some degree of internal diversity that is systematically interconnected. And whenever the judgment is present we are really doing nothing more than apprehending an identity-in-difference that is then asserted as continuous with the reality that extends beyond the sphere of our immediate experience.[19]

Now, the fuller relation between the act of predication and an identity-in-difference we shall examine in some detail in chapter 4. However, at this stage I would only mention that a great deal will ultimately rest on this point. Unless we are willing to concede to Bradley the claim that a single idea can have an internally complex content, his entire analysis of logical subjects and predicates falls apart. Hence, while the present treatment of this topic is brief, we must not view this doctrine as unimportant.

Subjects and Predicates

Avoiding for the moment unnecessary controversies, let us now direct our attention to Bradley's claim that, since the logical idea whose reality is affirmed in judgment is a complex entity (the internal differences of which are schematically expressed by the grammatical utterance), we may treat these complex ideas as themselves *predicates*. "The wolf eats the lamb," "Jones is a good man," "This is red": These are all, on Bradley's account, complex ideas that—since the mind takes their content whole and at once—must be viewed as incapable of any real reduction to a mere collection that is somehow reassembled in judgment. The true predicate in judgment, then, just is the complex idea as is (usually but not always) expressed by the *entire* grammatical proposition. But if Bradley sees these complete propositions as constituting the true predicate in judgment, *what*, we must ask, is this idea being affirmed of? Just what is the substantive *subject* to which our predicate-*qua*-sentence becomes both predicate and adjective?[20]

Although I must immediately qualify this statement, it would not be wrong to say that the subject of which the ideal predicate-*qua*-proposition is affirmed is always, for Bradley, *reality-as-a-whole*. And it is in this sense that he speaks of judgment as referring to a reality that is "beyond the act." But such a view left unqualified can lead to tremendous difficulties. At the heart of Bradley's theory is the claim that the reality and the idea that is asserted of it are, while in one sense different, in another continuous and one. (Should he deny this his asserted ideas become mere "representations" or wholly "mental" contents referred to an external and alien reality.) Thus Bradley is forced to say that the reality that is the "ultimate subject" of judgment must be both inside and outside the judgment at once. That is, although reality-as-a-whole is the ultimate subject in judgment, this reality must also be one that appears or is present to us.[21] And this leads us to the notion of the "special" or "limited" subject.[22] What Bradley calls the "special subject" of any judgment must be seen, then, as the *juncture* at which the larger (presupposed) reality presents itself to us in perception. It is, we may say, the *point of focus* upon which we attach our complex predicate-*qua*-sentence—a point that may be (and often is) represented by the grammatical subject in the sentence, but that, as we have already considered, may not be grammatically expressed at all.[23]

But let me illustrate this idea by considering our previous example. In "The wolf eats the lamb" this complex predicate idea is attached to a point of sensuous experience (either perceived or imagined) in such a manner that I extend my present perception while simultaneously declaring this extension to be part and parcel of the reality before me. There is in the judgment no sense of a break in continuity between presented fact and ideal extension—the one leads into the other. And when we consider this sentence ("The wolf eats the lamb") as a unified predicate idea, we must, Bradley claims, view its subject as reality-as-whole. However, in this example reality-as-whole appears to us *through* the wolf. And, though we are certainly justified in calling "wolf" the "special" (or "limited") subject, we must never forget that it is always reality-as-a-whole that both special subject and special predicate (in their continuity) are referred to.[24]

But let us consider one more point before continuing with other matters. In the judgment "This road leads to London" we find that the special subject "this road" is the point of perceptual (or imaginary) focus that we have isolated, and that the special predicate ("leads to London") is seen as both continuous with and characteristic of the point of reality that our subject term has identified. Although the assertion "This road leads to London" can be seen as a single and unified idea, one aspect of this complex idea ("this road") is more than merely ideal—it is also perceptually real.[25] Hence, while reality (the ultimate subject) lay beyond the act, it should not be seen as doing so completely. Rather it should be seen as *reaching into* the judgment and *appearing* as the limited subject of the assertion ("this road"). Reality can be seen, then, as both within and beyond the act at the same time. The reality selected by the special (or limited) subject of the judgment is, we might say, the "tip of the iceberg" (with the submerged portion of the iceberg representing the rest of reality). Hence the special subject is best seen as reality's "representative." The reality of which it is the representative is always, though, the ultimate subject—reality-as-a-whole.

I might summarize here by saying that when the proposition is affirmed we assert the continuity of (*a*) an unspecified reality (reality-as-a-whole) with (*b*) the explicit subject term of the proposition (often but not always the grammatical subject), which is itself further characterized by and continuous with (*c*) the predicate term of the proposition (which is often but not always the grammatical predicate). Indeed, in any judgment we are asserting S(R)P. Or, in other words, "Reality, being what it is, P can qualify S and together they both qualify the larger reality which is their condition."[26] What is truly important here, though, is the idea that the judgment consists in an affirmed *continuity* of conditions. That is, "This road leads to London" asserts as an uninterrupted tissue the elements of content that are both within and beyond the explicit act of consciousness that comprises the judgment.

CONTENT AND EXISTENCE

We have now considered some fundamental aspects of Bradley's theory of judgment. We have examined the differentia of all judgment (its ability to be true or false), and we have considered Bradley's often misunderstood claim that in judgment the ultimate subject is reality-as-a-whole. However, the discussion thus far has been merely in outline. And in order to grasp the fuller import of Bradley's doctrine we must now consider in greater detail some of the ideas we have thus far only touched upon. It is to this end, then, that I would like to next examine Bradley's distinction between what he calls the "content" and "existence" of experienced objects. As we shall see, this distinction is central to Bradley's metaphysical vision and represents a distinctive element in his style of philosophizing. And, though its clarification shall confront us with considerable difficulties, it must not (for this or any other reason) be avoided. Through an understanding of these elements we shall come to grasp more fully Bradley's notion of the significant (i.e., logical) idea that, as we have already suggested, can ultimately be identified with the judgment itself. But let us consider Bradley's own words here:

> In all that is [we are told] we can distinguish two sides, (i) existence and (ii) content. In other words we perceive both *that* it is and *what* it is. But in anything that is a symbol we have also a third side, its signification or what it *means*.[27]

Leaving aside the aspect of symbolism for the moment (it is examined in chapter 3), let us consider the first two distinctions. It is obvious, Bradley tells us, that the things we experience *exist*—that is, they have a specific and unique presence in the world of fact that cannot be extracted and held in isolation. Put differently, we may say that there is some aspect of every object that presents itself as *unique* and incapable of abstraction out of its existential conditions. But in addition to this existential uniqueness, all objects possess contents that are (or may be seen as) *identical* in their various instantiations. That is, experienced objects have a qualitative side that seems to be essentially different from the "that" of their existence. Qualitative distinctions do not depend on their locatedness or precise instantiation in order to be what they are. They are not unique; rather they are universal. However, this does not mean that these aspects are wholly isolable; "the two are," Bradley writes, "inseparable."

> That anything should be, and should not qualify and give character to anything [we read], is obviously impossible. If we try to get the 'that' by itself, we do not get it, for either we have it qualified [by a 'what'] or else we fail utterly. If we try to get the 'what' by itself, we find at once that it is not all. It points to something beyond, and cannot exist by itself as a bare adjective. Neither of these aspects, if you isolate it, can be taken as real, or indeed in that case is itself any longer. They are distinguishable only and not divisible.[28]

Of course, most of us would not find it difficult to conceive that, let us say, a specific shade of color now before us could occur elsewhere. And many would even claim that this color could also be grasped, if only

via an act of intellectual abstraction, as not being instantiated in any particular time or place. It would seem that only if content and existence
were inextricably wed and incapable of being divided—even in thought—
might we legitimately deny these distinctions. However, according to
Bradley these distinctions *are* ultimately abstractions. Not only must the
"that" always have *some* content, any bare "what" always has at least a
tendency to become instantiated and to find a "that" for itself. Although
it is of the very nature of thought (as opposed to "reality") to consist in
a "what" which has been partially torn away from its "that," we might
say that this "what" always seeks to overcome its abstract separation
from the given "that" and discover for itself its *other* instantiations (i.e.
further "thats"). And it is through the ideal elaboration (in judgment) of
the sensuous given that this tendency develops.

Content and existence, of course, appear in everything there is, and
thus there is nothing extraordinary about claiming the simultaneous
presence of these conditions. But what is significant here is Bradley's
claim that the cognitive grasp of a content-existence complex—a phenomenal object—entails that there exists a *residue* of content that
escapes the limits that would impinge upon it should its momentary
existence determine its boundary.[29] I would also emphasize that focused
perceptual experience (which in being focused is cognitive) is itself what
gives rise to this content-existence rupture. As Bradley writes:

> The content of the given is for ever relative to something not
> given, and the nature of its 'what' is hence essentially to tran-
> scend its 'that'. This we may call the ideality of the given
> finite. It is not manufactured by thought, but thought itself is
> its development and product. The essential nature of the finite
> is that everywhere, as it presents itself, its character should
> slide beyond the limits of its existence.[30]

Thus it is with this excess or residue content that we discover the
beginnings of the idea (or "ideal content"). We find that in the very act
of focused perception there exists a consciously grasped universal quality that spills over the boundaries of the given object. And we should
also recognize that any apprehension of fact already contains this "ideality." However, we are warned that we should not view this division as
something that is merely the result of the percipient subject's activity.

> There exists [Bradley writes] a notion that ideality is some-
> thing outside of facts, something imported into them, or
> imposed as a sort of layer above them; and we talk as if facts,
> when let alone, were in no sense ideal. But any such notion is
> illusory. For facts which are not ideal and which show no
> looseness of content from existence, seem hardly actual.[31]

Now, there are two points that, I think, need to be emphasized here. The first is that to experience a division between content and existence is not an option that the judging subject may exercise at his or her discretion. To be conscious of "facts" at all is to judge; and to judge is to engage in an "ideal elaboration" of the given. The second point I would emphasize is this: Even though this content-existence rift is everywhere before us, we must not forget that the sliding away of content from existence is a condition that, although an essential feature of all cognitive perception, is not wholly acceptable. It creates, if you will, a *tension* in experience—a *problem* to be overcome.[32] And, so long as there exists a sense of this content-existence split, the subject finds the object as somehow defective. Just as the "that" (existence) always demands a "what" (content), the "what" that points beyond the perceptual "that" demands for itself some sort of concrete instantiation. And it is through our effort to ideally create a *larger context* for the orphaned content that we provide it with solace.[33] Thus in an effort to heal the division between content and existence, one expands one's articulate awareness of the object upon which one's attention is directed. And in this manner the assertor hopes to overcome the isolation of the perceived object through the *extension* of its content into other contexts and different settings. By creating this enlarged context—by expanding one's perspective we might say—the perceptual object is no longer isolated and its severed "what" has to some extent found relief.[34] It has managed to find a larger context and further "that" in which it can (at least temporarily) find rest.[35]

But how, it may be asked, can an ideal—a thinking—extension of the perceptually given real provide such satisfaction? Although any tolerably complete answer to this question must be postponed until chapter 4, we can say at this stage that, for Bradley, thought—even in reaching beyond given perceptual content—can still be concrete. And in order to follow Bradley here we must remember what was previously said about given perceptual experience. On Bradley's account, though we find ourselves at any moment confronted by a largely intractable reality, the contents as they exist in that given reality and in our judgments are essentially the same. There is no line or point of demarcation that allows us to say "this is the given (and real) content," and "this is the thought (and merely ideal) content." Experienced content is experienced content. And the only difference that can be found between given contents and asserted contents is this: Given contents are usually sensuously richer and carry with them an imprecise sense (supplied by feeling) of the "infinitude of relations" that underlay them; the contents of our ideal elaborations in judgment are usually sensuously poorer. However, the contents as asserted are (almost always) *intellectually* more concrete in that the merely felt infinitude of relations that gives the sensuous object its "facticity" or "presence" is, in the judgment, made explicit and conscious.[36] Now the felt infinitude of relations (by which is meant the object's "thatness") is never completely contained in judgment. And thus we are forced to say that the judgment is, on account of this shortcoming, "abstract." Still, we must not forget that, while the asserted content fails to carry with it the full sense of "thatness" that our larger experience provides, by giving up its preoccupation with immediate perception, the judgment can seek a *more* (intellectually) concrete and expansive experience than mere sense can provide.

> In becoming more abstract [Bradley informs us] we reach a wider realm of ideas; which is thus not sensibly but intellectually concrete. What is abstract for one world is concrete in the other.[37]

Thus our expanded intellectual ideas can, according to Bradley, explicitly approximate, to greater or lesser degree, the given and implicit sense of concretion and infinitude that is immediately before us in the given object(s). And, as we shall consider in later chapters, the very reason we judge is, on Bradley's account, that we may consciously duplicate in cognitive experience that which we feel must be the case. Though we somehow feel it, we cannot yet explicitly think it. And, so long as this discrepancy between thought and feeling exists we are condemned to intellectually elaborate and expand our experience through judgment. However, before considering this point in greater detail we must attend to other matters.

Chapter 3

SYMBOL AND SIGNIFICANCE

WE must next consider a point of some importance for Bradley in the first-edition *Logic*, and this is the relation between the psychical image and significant idea. But before proceeding to this topic, a few words are in order regarding the relation between significant ideas and judgment proper, because it is here that the great confusion of the first edition of the *Principles of Logic* is to be found.

Although in my discussion of "floating ideas" I shall be forced to consider the "reactionary" view that sometimes creeps into Bradley's discussion of 1883, throughout the previous chapters I have treated the significant idea and the *affirmed* significant idea as one and the same.[1] In other words all meaningful ideas have been treated by me as entailing the judgment. Now, this is precisely the position Bradley emphatically puts forth from shortly after the original publication of the *Principles of Logic* to the end of his career. (And it is also the position that is largely present throughout the 1883 *Logic* itself.) However, that Bradley explicitly states otherwise (at a number of points) has not gone unnoticed. I am all too aware of those occurrences in the 1883 edition where the doctrine of the unaffirmed or floating idea raises its head.[2] But, for simplicity's sake, a single account of judgment has been (and will continue to be) provided. And only after a general picture of judgment has been developed shall we consider the problems that befall Bradley's theory when he treats as plausible the floating idea. For the present, though, we may assume that with our apprehension of an experienced content as significant we have asserted the continuity of that content with the reality out of which it is selected—in other words, that we have judged. However, in order to clarify this point, we need to consider more fully just how these "ideal contents" exist within the judgment, and why these significant ideas must not be understood as mere psychical facts or mental images.

PSYCHICAL IMAGE AND LOGICAL IDEA

In order to understand the significant idea, then (and hence the judgment itself), we would be advised to examine the fate of the psychical particular or mental fact that lacks an "overreaching" content. Bradley's attitude towards any theory that claims for the mere psychical image the ability to *refer* (or otherwise "mean") is concisely stated when he writes:

> If an idea *were* treated as a psychical reality, if it were taken by itself as an actual phenomenon, then it would not represent either truth or falsehood. When we use it in judgment, it must be referred away from itself. If it [the psychical particular] is not the idea *of* some existence, then, despite its own emphatic actuality, its content remains but a "mere idea." It is a something which, in relation to the reality we mean, is nothing at all.[3]

Two points may be noticed here: First, "mere ideas" (i.e., ideas as psychical images or mental states) completely lack the capacity to be falsified. Whatever *images* we might possess are wholly self-contained—at least as images—because an image or psychical state is just that experience in which content and existence *retain* their unity. However, only through the extrusion of a specific content from its psychical instantiation—only through the suggestion that the content found *here* in this psychical image also applies *elsewhere* to things not present—does the possibility of error arise. But no such liability belongs to the idea as image.

And this brings us to the second point. As a mere psychical state (in which the "what" and "that" have not fallen apart) the idea also loses its capacity to *mean*. Meaning, Bradley tells us, depends upon an image's ability to refer beyond itself. And an idea that can't mean is, according to Bradley, not really an idea (in the logical sense) at all. Thus Bradley rejects the psychical particular—the mental fact in which content is inextricably bound to existence—as being of any concern for logic. From the perspective of philosophical logic, Bradley tells us, meaning (or significance) can never be the same as the psychical state that might be coincident with it. "The idea in judgment," we are told, "is the universal meaning; it is not ever the occasional imagery and still less can it be the whole psychical event."[4] Indeed, the factual existence of any idea, we are told, is largely irrelevant when it comes to its meaning. And, as a temporally located fact that is "stuck within its own four corners," it is meaning*less*. Bradley writes:

> The ambiguity of "idea" may be exhibited thus. *Thesis*, On the one hand no possible idea can be that which it means. *Antithesis*, On the other hand no idea is anything but just

what it means. In the thesis the idea is the psychical image; in
the antithesis the idea is the logical signification. In the first it
is the whole sign, but in the second it is nothing but the symbolized.[5]

In the thesis the idea does not mean (or refer) because it does not—
being a mere image—project or extend beyond itself. In Bradley's
antithesis as described above the idea is nothing but the content shorn
of its immediate existence such that it may seek (if not always find) *other*
instantiations in the greater reality that hangs from present perception.
It is that ideal content which has gone *beyond* present perception in a
manner that allows it (for all we know at the time) to be proven false.
And this loosened content is not the mere imagery. (*That* is content still
married to immediate existence.) It is the nonimmediate, *ideal quality*
that extends away from immediate, sensuous instantiation (in either
imagination or perception) that constitutes an idea's significance. And
this same ideal quality moves into a realm that is mediate and (compared
to present perception) essentially subsistent.[6] But there are always two
sides to any significant fact. And this brings us to Bradley's conception
of the "symbol."

Now, Bradley's discussion of the symbolic image has within it several
points that are likely to mislead the reader who does not take the greatest of care. On the one hand every significant idea is said to be significant
only so far as its factual existence is disregarded. And, as has already been
suggested, Bradley is committed to the existence of nonpsychical (in the
sense of being nonimmediate and nonsensuous) ideas as essentially constituting the ideal realm of meaning with which logic deals. But we must
not forget that these ideal contents are somehow *continuous with* and
attached to the real as it presents itself in given perception. Or, put differently, significant ideas are always accompanied by some sort of perceptual content that may be seen as the *symbol* of the larger meaning
which is *symbolized*. And if we say that an image or psychical fact is
meaning*ful*, we can only be understood as saying that it stands in the
relation of symbol to a nonsensuous significant idea (the symbolized).
However, Bradley continually warns us against taking the image, or any
other symbolic fact, as constituting meaning. We read that

> A symbol is a fact which stands for something else, and by
> this, we may say it both loses and gains, is degraded and
> exalted. In its use as a symbol it forgoes its individuality, and
> self existence. . . . A fact taken as a symbol ceases so far to be
> fact. It no longer can be said to exist for its own sake, its indi-
> viduality is lost in its universal meaning. It is no more a sub-
> stantive, but becomes the adjective that holds of another, But,

on the other hand, the change is not all loss. By merging its own quality in a wider meaning, it can pass beyond itself and stand for others. It gains admission and influence in a world which it otherwise could not enter. The paper and ink cut the throats of men, and the sound of a breath may shake the world. We may state the sum briefly. A sign is any fact that has a meaning, and meaning consists of a part of the content (original or acquired) cut off, fixed by the mind, and considered apart from the existence of the sign.[7]

Bradley is careful to point out that a symbol—although it can be seen as a psychical image (but not a mere image)—must be understood as having significance only so far as it gets beyond its mere existence as a fact. To "mean" or be "significant" the symbol must transcend its psychical existence. However, we must be clear as to what the fuller relationship between symbol and symbolized is. Although psychical facts (images) functioning as symbols may seem as somewhat disconnected from the ideal contents they refer to, that which has become a sign or symbol can also be seen as an *element within* the larger significant idea to which it points. And, even though a symbol possesses a transcendent side that extends beyond its concrete factual existence, the meaning that extends beyond the immediate sign is also somehow connected to that sign; it shares a point of *identity* with the symbol of which it is the meaning. But the specific sign (as either an image or word), may, on Bradley's account, vary tremendously.

Although imagery (as a sign) always accompanies our thinking, the specific sign-image itself is capable of being accompanied by a great deal of irrelevant material;[8] and hence the precise image, which at any moment functions as our symbol, cannot be said to be meaningful except so far as it shares with the actual (ideal) meaning a common quality or point of identity. Even though it contains the essential universal (which is the essence of our meaning), it often contains a great deal of other material under or behind which our true universal meaning is hidden. To illustrate this point, Bradley writes:

> We have ideas of redness, of a foul smell, of a horse, and of death; and, as we call them up more or less distinctly, there is a kind of redness, a sort of offensiveness, some image of a horse, and some appearance of mortality, which rises before us. And should we be asked, Are roses red? Has coal gas a foul smell? Is that white beast a horse? Is it true that he is dead? we should answer, Yes, our ideas are all true, and are attributed to the reality. But the idea of redness may have been that of a lobster, of a smell that of castor-oil, the imaged horse may have been a black horse, and death perhaps a with-

ered flower. And *these* ideas are *not* true, nor did we apply
them. What we really applied was that part of their content
which our minds had fixed as the general meaning.[9]

The point here is that, although the symbolic image itself shares a
point of identity with that to which it refers (and hence means), it cannot be said to *be* that meaning. The most that could be said is that it is
a *part* of the meaning that has been artificially isolated through a process of abstraction. However, it would be more accurate to say that the
symbol is meaning*ful* because it shares (in the literal sense) a content
that reaches out beyond the specific image-*qua*-symbol to those other
subsistent occurrences of the universal idea.

Let us consider Bradley's own example to illustrate this point.
"Death" as a meaning has been symbolized by us, let us suppose,
through the image of a withered flower. And this dead flower that we
hold before our mind must be understood as but a moment in the integrated nexus (identity-in-difference) of dead things. We have focused on
one *aspect* of this systematic unity (all dead things) and through it we
look beyond to all those other things that are connected to our flower
through an identity of content (dead horses, dead people, dead birds,
etc.).[10] We may say that our symbolic image is meaningful, then, because
we have fixed an aspect of its content and extended that content so as
to include it in a larger universal nexus in which it participates as a difference held together by a conceptual identity. It is this ideal (and mediate) content, then, that constitutes the essence of our meaning and
that—through its separation from its immediate existence (its "thatness")—is made subject to falsification.

THE IDEAL REALM OF MEANING

Although the way in which Bradley characterizes the significant idea
changes somewhat during his career, let us make no mistake that
Bradley always views the nonpsychical (subsistent) idea as being necessary to any coherent account of meaning. In the first edition of the
Logic we read:

> An idea, if we use idea of the meaning, is neither given nor
> presented but is taken. It can not as such exist. It can not ever
> be an event, with a place in the series of time or space. It can
> be a fact no more inside our heads than it can outside them,
> And, if you take this mere idea by itself, it is an adjective
> divorced, a parasite cut loose, a spirit without a body seeking
> rest in another, an abstraction from the concrete, a mere pos-
> sibility which by itself *is* nothing.[11]

But why cannot an idea *exist* as such? We must not forget that an individual fact is located; it has a precise place in the spatiotemporal nexus. And, although such a characteristic is applicable to the psychical image, this locatedness is, for Bradley, the antithesis of logical meaning. As an approximation to the notion we are trying to capture we might say that the significant idea is the concrete identity relation that binds together or runs through diverse phenomena. Thus it is transtemporal and transspatial; it has no one location. And, though this is a reasonable place to start in our characterization of the significant idea, such a characterization is flawed. The problem is that a significant idea, conceived in this manner, appears to be a self-sufficient and independent entity. But this is wrong. Since there are myriad conditions both above and below any significant idea that are necessary to its significance, we cannot view these ideas as being self-sufficient or independent in any strong sense.

But, in order to illustrate this difficulty, let us consider the following significant idea: "the fourth game of the 1959 World Series." Here we have an idea that—while it describes an event that has boundaries of a sort (it began at a precise time on a precise date)—the *meaning* of the idea-event cannot, for Bradley, be so easily pinned down. And this can be seen, I think, if we realize that the "the fourth game of the 1959 World Series" itself presupposes an entire nexus of meanings—"baseball," "Los Angeles," "the USA," "championship games," "national pastime," "hot dogs and beer" (and, of course, many others). And without these additional ideas, the concept "the fourth game of the 1959 World Series" has, on Bradley's account, *no* meaning. All significant ideas are parasitic upon others. And if we were to attempt to clearly identify the boundaries of any significant idea we would find that we cannot. Continually we would be forced beyond the concept with which we began.

Hence, it is perhaps best to view the significant idea as hierarchically *nested* within a larger domain of meaning-fact that intersects it in an inexhaustible manner. And, while with this comment we are thrust into the heart of Bradley's metaphysics, we can say that (even in the 1883 *Logic*) every idea—as an idea—ultimately demands (in order that its significance be complete) the *entire universe* as its elements or moments. And no matter what the point of focus, no matter what limited perspective we take, what we always mean when we speak, or what we always try to say in judgment, is our idea in its fullest significance or truth. Thus, what we mean by "the fourth game of the 1959 World Series" is—although we can never fully think it—a unique event, the precise and unambiguous determination of which would entail a description of every relation between every existent fact in the universe. Why? Because the positive content of the event in question is permeated and determined by precisely this infinity of relations. And, though when we speak of *the* meaning of an idea we refer to those spheres of significance that are nearest to it, what we *ultimately* mean—no matter what we actually manage to say—is the truth. And the truth for Bradley is (in the end) nothing less than *the whole*. There exists for him a permanent (i.e., "eternal") order of qualities, relations, and events that is not only the presupposition of our every conscious experience, it is also this same permanent order that makes every individual thing what it is. And it is this idea of the whole that—despite its particular focus—constitutes the ultimate intent of any meaning.

Thus we may consider once more the provisional definition of the significant idea offered above. When we grasp any significant idea we are in fact grasping the structure of reality itself, as seen through this or that of its internal elements. To fully understand the significance of "my tired old car" or "my lovely wife" or anything else is to *think the Absolute* beginning with the entity or event in question. And, while I may only think of a limited portion of the universe when I think of "the fourth game of the 1959 World Series" (any significant idea must begin with its *local* conditions), in the end all significant ideas refer to that whole that makes them what they are.

SYNTHESIS AND ANALYSIS

Before concluding this chapter we must consider how the doctrine of floating ideas conflicts with the theory of judgment developed thus far. However, before discussing this difficulty I would like to consider a further aspect of Bradley's theory of judgment. And, while my treatment must be brief, I hope by considering this aspect of judgment what we have already considered might make better sense. Specifically, we must now examine Bradley's doctrine of abstraction as both the analysis *and* synthesis of experience.

We must not forget that the first phase in the formation of the significant idea (and act of predication) is the selection of a content from given experience. And coextensive with this act of selection is a loosening of the selected content from its given, instantiated existence. The second phase, though, is the ideal extension of this loosened content. In this act of ideal extension (or "elaboration") we thus "reattach," to use Bradley's term, our selected content to the reality that is "beyond the act." That is, when we affirm the existence of our loosened predicate idea, we apply it to areas of reality that are not given. What is important to realize, though, is this: What I have described here as two phases are not really two at all. Or put differently, *already* in the initial act of selecting a content there has occurred an ideal extension of that content (and hence judgment). And, while it is certainly true that we may, feeling dissatisfaction with our initial result, immediately move forward in thought, searching for a fuller and more complete reunification of our orphaned content with the larger reality from which it was taken, there is never before our mind an act of *mere* selection. That is, we never select a content without simultaneously affirming that content as *real*.

That there could exist such a "mere selection" is, of course, at the heart of the doctrine of floating ideas (which we shall consider in a moment). However, that Bradley was already committed to the simultaneity of selection and affirmation of content in the 1883 *Logic* is evidenced by his discussion of the relation between analysis and synthesis in judgment. As Bradley tells us:

> Take an act of analysis in which A becomes (A)bcd. The elements in the result come to us as separate, but this very separation involves a relation. *They are distinguished by virtue of a central identity*, and they stand thereby in some kind of relation with one another. But this relation is synthetical. It did not exist [for us] before the operation, and has resulted from it. Thus the analysis, whilst analyzing, has shown itself synthesis. Now take an act of synthesis. We have A-B, B-C, and from this we go on to produce A-B-C. We have got to a relation which before was absent; but our process is also an act of analysis. For A, B, and C are now related within a visible whole; these terms and their relations are the constituent elements of the whole A-B-C. And yet, *as* these members, they did not and could not exist till that whole was realised. Thus the synthesis has analyzed while it seemed to conjoin. Summing up the above we may say it so. Analysis is the synthesis of the whole which it divides, and synthesis the analysis of the whole which it constructs. The two processes are one.[12]

Now, while this passage does not explicitly say that in our initial selection of a content from the mass of given experience there is a simultaneous affirmation of that content as real, it does tell us that the general movement of thought is both analytic and synthetic at once. And what Bradley says here does commit him to the view that in the act of predication (explicit assertion) our deepening recognition of diversity within a selected content entails its being simultaneously attached to other instantiations of itself (even though this might go unnoticed by us). And conversely, if in our judgment we focus on the identity of a given content with something that is not given, there occurs a simultaneous analysis (and thus internal differentiation) of that which is before us. But if we bear in mind Bradley's claims that (*a*) there is no clear line

of demarcation between the "perceptually given" and its "ideal elaboration," and (b) the contents of given perception are permeated by the
results of prior judgments and themselves are "ideal," it is hard to see
how comments like these cannot be taken as supporting the idea that the
very act of "selecting a content" itself involves an affirmation of that
content in judgment.

Now, we shall return to this problem further down. But let us first
examine more closely the sense in which Bradley sees analysis and synthesis as—though simultaneous operations—different. He provides us
three senses in which we might distinguish these intellectual operations:

(i) *The material from which they begin is different.* When we analyze
we look to our given contents and go on to differentiate them further. In
analyzing "we operate upon an explicit whole and proceed to its invisi-
ble inside."[13] In synthesis, however, we begin by focusing on the differences that, as differences, are not seen as members of the whole to which
they belong. In synthesis we concentrate, not on seeing the detail within
the separate elements, but with unifying these elements within in a larger
identity; and this is an identity that is not recognized before we judge.

(ii) *The result is different.* The movement of analysis and synthesis
can also be seen in the result of the new judgment. Where the judgment
grasps previously given differents under a broader concept, the process
is synthetical. Where it results in new differences not previously noticed,
it is analytic.

(iii) *The operations differ in what we are conscious of.* Analysis and
synthesis, though two sides of the same operation, will not always be
consciously apprehended as such. Frequently when we analyze we do
not keep the synthetic development in sight. And when we consciously
combine elements we do not necessarily pay attention to the fact that
there is occurring an analysis of this newly apprehended whole. When
we analyze (to take that first) we often forget, by the time we reach our
new elements, the unity with which we began and the fact that they are
differences *of* this unity. Or (second) when we synthesize given differents
these differences are often forgotten by the time we arrive at our new
synthetic unity. It is usually only when we philosophically reflect on
these operations that their interdependent character becomes evident.

SELECTIVE AND ELIMINATIVE ABSTRACTION

Now, the simultaneity of analysis and synthesis may also be appreciated
by considering the difference between Bradley's "selective abstraction"
and the "eliminative" theory embraced by certain species of empiricism
and realism ("nominalist" and "conceptualist" doctrines). Whereas for

the eliminativist theory the selection of qualities out of the given is a *mere* selection that results in an idea containing less content (fewer "marks") than that out of which it has been abstracted, for Bradley, to select (abstract) is also to *extend* our conception of reality starting from its base in the sensuous present. Whereas on the eliminativist account our ideas become only poorer (because more abstract), on the Bradleian analysis we find that our experience becomes simultaneously enriched. But let us consider in greater detail why this is understood to be the case.

We must remember that on Bradley's account *thinking*—the affirmation of a selected content as real—is, while in one sense engaged with abstract ideas, in another, the mechanism by which we more fully and completely experience reality. And, while any detailed treatment must be postponed, we should still be aware that Bradley does not see immediate *perceptual* experience as providing us with perfectly individuated objects. As we shall see, it is *feeling* (a detailed examination of which must await chapters 8 and 9) that conveys to us our sense of the "infinitude of relations" and "complete individuality" that the objects of perceptual experience claim. And it is only when perceived contents have been worked over—that is, brought into fuller and more systematic relations with the rest of reality through judgment—that what we *feel* to be the case can be explicitly *thought*. Put differently, Bradley sees thought (the judgment) as an indispensable component in our explicit grasp of the specificity of any state of affairs. By progressively bringing the contents of perception within broader and more systematic contexts, the merely felt individuality of the experienced object becomes explicitly apprehended *as* individual. Of course, after we have judged, our given perceptual contents carry with them the results of our assertions; that is, they reflect a relative individuality that prior judgments have developed within our awareness. But this given particularity never just appears to us in a concept-free fashion.

We should also notice that this conception of thought as a means by which we might experience more concretely given reality is one that is diametrically opposed to the doctrine that sees concept formation as a process during which we merely ignore differences and notice similarities. Such a view (I am thinking primarily of Locke here) demands that as our concepts become broader and more "denotative" they become *emptier* and contain less detail than either the original perceptual or conceptual experience from which they were derived. For example, in order to arrive at the concept "deer" I must on this theory (*a*) experience a number of relevantly similar animals; (*b*) hold before my mind only their points of similarity while ignoring their differences; and (*c*) fix these points of similarity by some means (usually by naming them). And when the resulting concept is compared to the original perceptual data there is a great loss of concrete detail. Consider also the concept "mammal." In order to arrive at this concept I must (on the doctrine of eliminative abstraction) follow the same steps. And, just as in the previous example, I must include within my concept (mammal) only those similarities that existed between the previously developed notions upon which the abstractive function was directed. Just as the perceptual experience of different deer was richer than the concept derived from them, so too must the individual concepts "deer," "human," "whale," "lion," and "cow" possess a richer internal content (i.e., more "marks") than my new concept "mammal." *This* concept can only possess such marks as "warm-blooded," "vertebrate," "gives live birth," and so on. It is for this reason, then, that we say that the "intension" (the conceptual marks) decreases as the "extension" (the actual entities referred to) increases. And it is also for this reason that "thinking" on this theory always takes us *further away* from the concrete individuals that perceptual experience provides. On Bradley's view, though, precisely the opposite occurs .[14]

> The distinction and separation, which appears first in judgment, implies, as we have seen, both analysis and synthesis. The perceived exclusion of one element by another involves their relation, and hence their unity in an embracing whole. . . . [Analysis and synthesis] are two sides of one process. And it follows from this that *the increase of one must add to the other.* The more deeply you analyze a given whole, the wider and larger you make its unity; and the more elements you join in synthetic construction, so much greater is the detail and more fully the differentiation of that totality.[15]

Bradley believes that in the normal course of consciousness we focus our attention and thereby extend the present perception by either seeing more detail within what is given, or including the given as an element within a larger whole.[16] And it is, on his theory, an act of *intellect* (in conjunction with feeling and will) that allows us to apprehend objects as individuated in the first place. Indeed, it is Bradley's claim that the conscious apprehension of both universal and particular is the result of a thought process (ideal elaboration) that is both analytic and synthetic at once. According to Bradley, experience does not begin with "concept-free" atomic particulars that are artificially bound together by subsequent thought relations. To apprehend the elements of sense as somehow particular and individualized is already to see them within the context of assertion. (And, likewise, to analyze an intellectual datum is not to pull apart what consists merely in idea.) On Bradley's account, experience of both particulars and universals arises simultaneously.

Let us summarize our discussion thus far as follows: In order to consciously perceive (or think) something we must focus our attention on it. That is, we must *select* (abstract) an element from our larger felt experience. And in this selection the rupture between content and existence arises. However, in the loosening of content from existence—which *is* the act of selective abstraction—conscious experience transcends the moment and goes beyond the limits of present perception. And, while consciousness might appear to lose hold of reality by ignoring much of the given sensuous content, it in fact gains enormously. It is only by loosening the content from the existence (which sense and imagination force upon us) that a broader perspective than that found in the immediate data may be realized. Through this act of abstraction we extend and elaborate on given perception in a manner that allows us to connect one occurrence of a quality with others in a larger vision of reality. And thus we are through selective abstraction involved in the articulation and determination of our presupposed and, to greater or lesser extent, unconscious *Weltanschauung*. Through the loosening of the "what" from the "that" we are always going on to discover and make conscious a fuller "that." And thus the act of judgment—beginning with selective abstraction—is understood as integral to the making conscious to ourselves that reality which only dimly appears in our immediate sensuous experience.

THE FLOATING IDEA

I would bring this chapter to a close by saying something more about the "inconsistencies" of the 1883 *Logic* to which Bradley himself so often refers. And the problem that the first edition of Bradley's *Principles of Logic* poses can be understood in light of our previous discussion of the continuity between the real and ideal aspects of experience. Simply put, the question that must be asked of Bradley is this: "Just how strong (or continuous) on your theory is the point of contact between the ideal content in judgment and the content as found in sensuous presentation?" If Bradley is to be seen as rejecting the intrinsic dualism of representationalist theories—and if he in any way is to be seen as continuing in the post-Kantian tradition of idealism—his response must be "very strong, indeed."[17] However the student of Bradley who ignores all later works (including the 1922 edition of the *Principles of Logic*) might detect a different answer to this question and come to see Bradley in a very different light than that which I have provided thus far.[18] But let us consider the issues that—by Bradley's own admission—led to a faulty account of judgment in his 1883 *Logic*.

Throughout the first two chapters I have described Bradley's views on judgment and the significant idea in a manner that is consistent with his mature position. I have avoided any troublesome quotations; and where Bradley's own words required some sort of qualification I have attempted to provide it. However, the fact remains that there are statements in the first edition *Principles of Logic* that, according to Bradley himself, are in error. For example, we cannot forget that Bradley sometimes claims in the 1883 *Logic* that the actual subject (which is always reality-as-a-whole) falls *completely* outside the judgment.[19] Also problematic are occasional comments made about the nature of perception. While at many points Bradley clearly states that all perception is "ideal" (and hence not that which conveys to us a sense of an object's complete particularity), there are other points at which he seems to oppose ideal thought to the pure particularity of the given percept. Perhaps most difficult, though, are the occasional comments about "supposal." We must realize that the issue of floating ideas concerns not just ideas held in isolation. It concerns any (apparent) assertion that is put forth as a *mere* supposal. For example, the doctrine of the floating idea says not just that I can entertain the idea of, let us say, "the present king of France" (as either limited subject or predicate) without attaching to it a further idea ("The present king of France is bald" or "Henri is the present king of France"). This is not the real issue. What lies at the heart of the doctrine of the floating idea is the general view that it is possible to entertain any significant idea without finding for it a *categorical* basis. Or, what is the same thing, "affirm that idea as true of the real given in perception." And whatever the reasons may have been, such remarks—as occasional as they might have been—create enormous difficulties when we try to reconcile them with what appears to be the larger thrust of Bradley's argument.

The problem might be restated as follows: With the espousal of the unaffirmed significant idea, Bradley is committed to a position that ultimately reduces these ideas to some sort of "mental stuff" that is (ontologically) different from what is given in perception. But if thoughts and perceived facts are truly of a different order then there can exist no continuity between them in any significant sense. And, as Bradley is to later clearly see, if it were the case that we *could* abstract (or "fix a content") from of the sensuously given in a manner that does not simultaneously affirm this content as continuous with the perceptually given real, then the "what" (content) of our judgments must be one that is *absolutely* ideal and thus *merely* "mental." And such a purely ideal content would stand in complete opposition to the real, which, we should recall, has a perfectly unified content and existence. If a content can be abstracted without being affirmed, then this is to be in possession of a "what" without going on to postulate a further and fuller "that." It is to analyze without a simultaneous synthesis; and it is to view the "real" as *only* found in the sensuous present. In other words, if there can exist an unaffirmed idea, then the continuity between the content of the perceived real and our ideal extension is an artificial one, and it represents a difference between idea and reality that is not one of degree but one of *kind*.[20] But, if this is truly Bradley's position then, in the end, there would be very little difference between his theory and that of the nominalist-conceptualist whose doctrine he spends so much time attacking.

While it is somewhat premature to discuss Bradley's theory of inference, I would also mention that the doctrine of the unaffirmed or floating idea has disastrous consequences here as well. Indeed, Bradley later came to realize that should he allow that our ideas may be significant without their simultaneously being affirmed as true (in judgment), then he is not only committed to some sort of representational theory of thought, but he has lost the very thread upon which his account of rational inference develops. As we shall see, crucial to Bradley's doctrine of inference (even in 1883) are the claims that (*a*) we are justified in inferring one judgment from another because the contents that appear in premises and conclusion are continuous with one another; and (*b*) that these contents are not the mere fabrications of the judging subject's fancy; they reflect the structure of reality itself. Hence, should Bradley allow that some contents might be entertained by the mind without simultaneously being affirmed as real or true, he has admitted (again) that these significant ideal contents might be merely ideal. But in making this admission Bradley has severed the logical idea from the contextual guidance that he understands given reality as providing. Only if he insists that all our significant ideas are affirmed as continuous with the larger reality out of which they are abstracted can he maintain this contextual interpenetration and guidance for the idea in its inferential development. And it is only by appealing to this continuity of the significant idea with reality that inference can be understood as a nonarbitrary movement in thought.

But why is Bradley sometimes led to claim that we can abstract out of given experience an idea that is "held in suspension," free from affirmation? While Bradley himself later claimed that he *had* no good reason for saying this, we might better understand his difficulty by considering the following propositions. "If you ask him for a loan, he will refuse," "All trespassers will be shot," "If the Nazis had won World War II, we would all be speaking German," and "The square circle is an impossibility." The received view (then and now) claims that we may *suppose* a good many things without affirming them as true (which in this context means, as having "existential import"). For example, we may imagine (suppose) that Hitler had won the Second World War; and we may, based upon this supposition, infer a further result. But what we must recognize here is that a theory of pure supposal—a theory that claims we can reason about things that have no real existence—is completely at odds with the account of judgment described thus far. We have said time and again that, on Bradley's view, to hold an idea before the mind is to affirm that the idea forms a continuous tissue with the real as given in perception. But if this is, indeed, the essence of Bradley's theory of judgment, how does he deal with assertions like those cited above?

While we must await the discussion of chapters 4 and 5 to treat of this problem fully, we may for now say that a partial solution put forth in 1883 is found with Bradley's differentiating the judgment from the sentence. Hence, when we assert "The square circle is an impossibility" we are, Bradley tells us, actually asserting that "The nature of reality is such as to exclude the simultaneous presence of squareness and roundness in the same object" (or some such thing). And a similar approach is taken when he deals with judgments like "If you ask him for a loan, he will refuse." We are really saying here, Bradley informs us, that "Jones's character is such that when asked for a loan he always refuses." "All trespassers will be shot" also asserts what Bradley calls a "latent condition of the real." And thus, even though there may never be an act of trespassing, it can still categorically assert something about the real that comes to us in perception.

The mere propositional fragment is also easily dealt with by Bradley. For example, if I were to say only "The desert sun" I am *not* holding an unaffirmed but intelligible idea before my mind; I have in fact judged but with an incomplete grammatical expression of that judgment. What I *thought* was surely something like, "The desert sun is hot" or perhaps "The desert sun has been the cause of death for the ill-prepared traveler" (or some other complete affirmation). Thus by differentiating the actual judgment from its superficial linguistic expression, and by realizing that many of these linguistic expressions are incomplete approximations to an underlying assertion, these difficulties—at least most of them—are solved.

But still there are recalcitrant examples about which (in 1883, anyway) Bradley seems unsure. Certainly we can intelligibly entertain the idea of a "minotaur" or "the present king of France." And surely we can go on to use these ideas in propositions like "Pity any man who encounters the minotaur" or "The present king of France is bald." But, if this is the case, how can it be said that all significant ideas must be found within the context of the judgment, *and* that judgment itself is the affirmation of a continuity between an ideal content and the real as it presents itself in perception? If the intelligible assertion of any idea demands that it be seen as both real and continuous with perceptual experience, how can "minotaurs" and "the present king of France" (in 1998) fit into this theory? This is the problem. And, since in 1883 Bradley had apparently not thought through the implications of the floating idea for his larger theory, he decided to simply claim that "Yes, some significant ideas—those that are clearly about 'unreal' things—can be intellectually entertained without going on to affirm their real existence in judgment." Not knowing (at this stage of his career, anyway) what to do with the idea that—although significant—could not possibly be "real" this seemed a quick, if not entirely satisfactory, solution.

Now, precisely when Bradley grasped the degree to which this doctrine conflicted with his larger theory of judgment and inference, we do not know. However, when Bernard Bosanquet published his *Knowledge and Reality* in 1885, Bradley's account was criticized on several heads.[21] And, whether under the influence of Bosanquet or just through a more careful consideration of his own position, Bradley soon completely retracted his commitment to the unaffirmed idea. Indeed, by 1893 (the year that *Appearance and Reality* was published) virtually every trace of the doctrine of the floating idea had been purged. And, by whatever means, Bradley soon became aware that the doctrine of the unaffirmed idea introduced a profound inconsistency into his work, and either his theory of judgment (and inference) must be dramatically altered or the floating idea must go. But how does Bradley solve the difficulty described above?

As we shall see in the next chapter, Bradley already in 1883 had a well-developed theory by which he could account for experienced contents that are not immediately perceived. This was not the real difficulty. However, Bradley's ultimate solution to the problem of floating ideas was simply to expand his conception of "reality."[22] Ultimately, Bradley was to claim that physical reality (usually lower case) is not exhaustive of Reality in the fullest sense (usually upper case).[23] While all are continuous, Bradley believed that there are "many worlds" other than that which we call the "physically real"—the world that appears in external perception. And, even though there are ideas that might resist affirmation in the real *physical* order, they can be found to have existence in one of these other realms. This is not to say that these worlds are "merely possible"—on the contrary. Unless they are actual, and unless they are somehow continuous with the existing world (physical reality) as we know it, the theory of judgment and inference would have to be modified. But this Bradley was never willing to do.

In everything written after 1883, then, Bradley makes it very clear: There is *never* an act of mere abstraction in which the idea abstracted from given experience is not also "reattached" to that reality in an act of constructive synthesis (or predication). And there is never a judgment that involves a "mere supposal." Reality-as-a-whole is still understood as the ultimate subject in judgment. And the limited (special) subject is still the explicit point at which that reality appears. However, now the *continuity* between the real and the ideal is unambiguous. Thus, for Bradley, the content of the real as it comes to us in feeling and perception is one and the same content as it appears in assertion. And there is now no possibility of interpreting him as advocating an ontological divide between the perceptually real and the ideal contents of thought.

In addition, Bradley no longer sees the *force* of assertion as something that is the same in all judgments. He now begins to argue that logical affirmation is not a mechanical act that even-handedly attaches an ideal content to the real as found in perception. Rather, he now sees varying *degrees* of necessity attaching to judgments; and this necessity can itself be seen as the degree of affirmation that accompanies any judgment.[24] When a judgment is so deeply penetrated by the context within which it is made that to deny the judgment is to deny the context itself (reality-as-a-whole), such a judgment can be seen as possessing an assertive force that greatly exceeds that of an assertion that stands at arm's length from this reality. But the fuller implications of this doctrine we are not yet in a position to consider. First we must examine Bradley's theory of the individual judgment—the subject of the following chapter.

Chapter 4

The Classification of Judgment

In the previous chapters we followed Bradley in his claim that all judgment must be directed toward the real that is given in perception. There we saw that the distinctive characteristic of predication is the assertion of a continuity of condition(s) between given perceptual experience and the explicit content of the judgment such that this "ideal extension" might be falsified. But the description of judgment developed thus far is incomplete. Since it is obvious that many of our judgments do not *directly* qualify the perceptually given, we must now consider the sense in which an assertion that is not immediately concerned with the contents of sensuous experience can still meet the requirements of this definition. How, we must ask, do the numerous judgments that do not explicitly develop the contents of perception attach themselves to it? And in what sense can they still be said to constitute a "continuous tissue" with reality as given?

Some Logical Distinctions

In order to facilitate our discussion of these questions we shall follow Bradley in his consideration of some of the traditional distinctions that logicians have made in their discussion of the judgment. Although we shall soon discover that his analysis of the traditional species of judgment bears only slight resemblance to any that were commonly entertained, their consideration provides common ground between Bradley and earlier logicians as well as the point of departure for his discussion. Over the course of the next two chapters, then, we shall examine Bradley's doctrine both in relation to what philosophers have called the "relational" aspect of assertion (this classification characterizes judgment as categorical, hypothetical, or disjunctive), as well as the "quantitative" (this consisting in a description of judgment as either singular, universal, or particular).[1] But we must be aware that the purpose of this discussion is not just to understand how these types of assertion conform to the general description of judgment that we have been developing. While it is necessary to grasp the manner in which Bradley brings all judgment forms under his account of predication, far more important is his radical claim that, despite superficial appearances, *no* judgment can (in the end) express fact, whole and complete. And with this doctrine clearly stated we shall have before us the central theme of Bradley's theory of knowledge: all acts of predication fail to realize their end. And that end is the unqualified assertion of truth.

Although the continuing explication of this doctrine will require yet many pages, it might be of value to indicate in advance the limited goal we are trying to achieve in this chapter. Simply put, the claim we are trying to understand is this: No judgment, Bradley argues, can be "categorical" if by that term we mean *adequately* expressive of independent fact. All judgment, on the Bradleian analysis, will show itself as hopelessly general and incapable of denoting the given real in its unique particularity. And all efforts to achieve this goal—either through determinate idea or by designation—will prove ineffective. Ultimately, Bradley will characterize all judgment as not only general (and thus universal) but also as hypothetical and conditional.

I would immediately add, though, that while all judgment is seen as hypothetical, it is not merely so for Bradley. As we have already learned, judgment is always *about* fact; it is always *of* reality—and in this sense will possess a categorical intent. In the end, Bradley will maintain the (apparently) paradoxical position that all judgment is *both* categorical (since about fact) and hypothetical (because conditional).[2] And, as we shall see in chapter 5, for Bradley, there will ultimately be no substantive difference between the traditional distinctions of categorical, hypothetical, and disjunctive judgments other than the degree of adequacy to their subject that each possesses. Predication will succeed or fail—that is, the judgment will be true or false—to the extent that it explicitly comprehends its intended subject (and approaches necessity). And, contrary to the more common analysis, the singular categorical judgment (which has usually been understood as being the least subject to falsification by further experience) is, on the Bradleian view, seen as the most unfit to bear the title "true." In the final analysis it is understood as a merely conditional judgment of a very low sort. And it occupies, we shall discover, the lowest of rungs in the hierarchy of truths.

To begin our examination of judgment forms, then, we should realize that the received scheme of logical classification that Bradley knew, although little changed from what it had been for centuries, was suddenly undergoing scrutiny by philosophers of diverse orientations. With the publication of Mill's *System of Logic* in 1843 the philosophical foundations of logic became the topic of heated debate.[3] And amongst the most discussed issues in Great Britain at the time was the general question of the relation between categorical and hypothetical assertion (the two broad classes of propositions that comprised the accepted schemes).

On the categorical side we find those judgments that purportedly express fact, and that can be further divided according to "quantity." Thus we find logicians speaking of categorical assertions as either particular, universal, or singular. Ignoring for the moment the negative species of each, we find as a particular affirmative judgment examples such as "Some men are mortal," as universal affirmative, "All men are mortal," and as singular affirmative "Socrates is mortal."[4] The hypothetical side of this division (which was often included as an appendix) consists in explicitly conditional and disjunctive judgments. Examples of the former are "If A is B then it is C" or "If you ask him he would refuse"; and of the latter, "A is B or C" or "The signal light is either red or green."[5] On this view the categorical affirmative judgment—either particular, universal, or singular—is understood as a proposition that possesses "existential import." And based upon this understanding, the various relations of implication between contraries and subcontraries were developed.

Although the idealist writers of Bradley's day had many problems with this scheme, it is (fortunately) for our purposes unnecessary to follow their criticisms in any detail.[6] We need only be aware that there was a project at work which sought to reorganize and reinterpret these divisions in light of their own (the idealists's) metaphysical views. And an important aspect of this project involved the reformulation of the nature and relation of hypothetical and categorical assertion.[7] The universal affirmative, if it were not an enumerative or collective judgment, was on this new account understood as analyzable into a hypothetical,[8] and thus to make no claim as to the specific existence of its elements as affirmed. And the particular affirmative, to consider it next, was seen as always ambiguous: sometimes it was capable of being construed as universal, at other times as singular.[9] However, in spite of any controversy these analyses engendered, there was (before 1883, anyway) little concern over the claim that *some* judgments should still be called "categorical" in that they were unambiguously about fact. And neither was there disagreement that the most obvious candidate for the factual or categorical judgment was the singular affirmative assertion. "My sweater is red," "The sink is stopped-up," "Irene is older than Louise"; each of these, it was generally agreed, was, if true, *entirely* true of some state of affairs.[10] The categorical assertion says "X exists" and it says so without reservation.

It affirms the reality of its elements and declares that as asserted it is directly true of that reality. And, given this requirement, the nonexistence of those elements will affect the truth of any such assertion.

THE HYPOTHETICAL JUDGMENT

Now, Bradley has a good deal to say about the categorical status of the singular affirmative assertion. However, the most effective way to approach his thought on the subject is through a consideration of the *universal* affirmative. And the first point to be made here is that he sees the universal affirmative judgment as both conditional and, in most cases, hypothetical. Bradley approaches this analysis in two steps.

First, he impresses upon us that the unquantified categorical assertion is really a universal affirmative. In "Animals are mortal" we can mean either of two things. Either we mean that there is a collection of existing things (or things that have existed in the past) in which some sort of contingent relation between "animal" and "mortality" is present; or we can view the assertion as it is more normally used. In this more usual case we must interpret it as saying "*All* animals are mortal" (and not in any merely collective or enumerative sense). Under normal circumstances, Bradley tells us, when we assert "All animals are mortal" we mean not only those animals that have existed in the past or which presently exist in *rerum natura*; we also make a claim about any future (and currently nonexisting) animals. Indeed, we very often use the unquantified categorical judgment to affirm a relation between conditions that do not—and sometimes cannot—exist in the physical order even though, it should be said, we are still affirming the real existence of some unstated condition).[11] And we must be very clear that we differentiate this use of "all" from that which merely means a collection such as might be found in "All the examinations have been marked" (a use that is obviously not universal in the above sense).

Second, once Bradley establishes this difference between the collective and true universal assertion (and his argument is really an appeal to ordinary usage here) he goes on to tell us that the less ambiguous way of interpreting the universal affirmative is to view it as hypothetical. When we say "All animals are mortal," "we *mean*," Bradley writes, "'whatever is an animal will die,' but that is the same as *If* anything is an animal *then* it is mortal."[12] We are asserting, he claims, a *connection between universals* such that if something possesses the qualitative distinction "animal" it will also possess that of "mortality"; and we are asserting this (in many cases) without the slightest hint of existential implication for the explicit consequent and antecedent in our hypothetical proposition. Hence we read:

> In universal judgments we may sometimes understand that the synthesis of adjectives, which the judgment expresses is really found in actual existence. But the judgment does not say this. It is merely a private supposition of our own. It arises partly from the nature of the case, and partly again from our bad logical tradition. The fact that most adjectives we conjoin in judgment can be taken as the adjectives of existing things, leads us naturally to expect that this will always be the case. And, in the second place, a constant ambiguity arises from the use of "all" in the subject. We write the universal in the form "all animals" and then take it to mean each actual animal, or the real sum of existing animals. But this would be no more an universal judgment than "A B and C are severally mortal." And we *mean* nothing like this. In saying "All animals," if we think of a collection, we never for a moment imagine it complete; we mean also "whatever besides may be animal must be mortal too." In universal judgment we never mean "all." What we mean is "any," and "whatever," and "whenever." But these involve "if."[13]

Although this analysis of our use of "all" might make a great deal of sense considered in itself, one must immediately ask what the implications for such view are for the general theory of judgment developed thus far. Indeed, bearing in mind the results of the previous chapter, might it not be legitimately asked here how such claims regarding the nonexistence of the explicit subject and predicate terms can be consistent with a theory of judgment that views predication as the ideal self-development of the object before us in *perception*? Is not this interpretation of universal assertion one that runs against the grain of a theory that sees perceptual experience as possessing a fundamental role in *all* judgment? These are not, I think, questions we can afford to ignore; and we must now consider Bradley's response to them.

The answer that Bradley provides here (and that is found throughout his works) is simply that in judgment—unless there exists a specific reference to the time of predication in the content—the *present* existence or non-existence of elements is irrelevant to the truth or falsity of the judgment. This is because we are always asserting about the *logical* present; and this must be understood as but another expression for the universe-as-a-whole (something that is fundamentally outside of time). As we should recall from the discussion of the second chapter, the ultimate subject of all judgment is, for Bradley, precisely such an all-inclusive reality (the Absolute). And, indeed, every judgment best exemplifies its true form if expressed with some sort of prefix like "Reality is such that S-P"; or alternatively, "Reality is such that if P, then Q." And to illustrate Bradley's point here, let us consider the judgment "All trespassers will be shot." Here we have an assertion that can be immediately construed as "If there are trespassers then they will be shot." And, Bradley would tell us, if it is an actual judgment, it is an assertion of a continuity of condition between the content of the judgment itself and the given real. (And it is only on this basis that it is subject to falsification by real.) But how can this be the case when it doesn't say that there *are* or that there ever *will* be trespassers? How could we possibly understand this as an assertion of a continuity of condition within given reality?

In answer to this Bradley tells us that, what we are really asserting in such a case is a "latent condition of the real." And the *actual* condition which we envisage in the judgment could perhaps be restated as "The guards on the estate are poised and ready to deal with trespassers in the harshest of manners, that is, by shooting them." In other words, the factual content that it asserts is a very complex one regarding the general condition of the estate, its owner, the guards, and a great deal more. And the truth or falsity of the judgment will rest entirely on whether or not these existing conditions are such as to contain that which is latent within them (e.g., trespassers being shot).[14]

Since we are now only introducing Bradley's views on judgment forms, I must ignore the many objections that might spring to mind here. And, at this stage, I would continue our discussion of the universal affirmative assertion by pointing out that Bradley understands it as asserting a far more inclusive content than does any merely individual proposition. When, for example, I judge "Water boils at 212 degrees Fahrenheit," I am, on Bradley's view, making an assertion that (implicitly) refers to all of time and all of reality.[15] Although there are still many unstated and essential conditions to the truth of this assertion (e.g., "at one atmosphere of pressure"), its truth is still understood to be more encompassing than what might be put forth in "*This* water boiled at 212 degrees Fahrenheit." In this singular assertion there is at least the suggestion of a mere conjunction between attributes, whereas in the universal affirmative (our hypothetical) we have what is understood as a necessary connection between them.[16]

Now, what goes into the apprehension of necessary connection we cannot consider in any detail until chapter 5. And our main concern in this chapter is to understand how Bradley sees the categorical assertion as itself a very low-level conditional judgment whose difference from the openly hypothetical assertion is one of degree rather than kind. But in order to understand exactly why this is the case will require the discussion of yet many pages; and hence we shall now proceed to consider Bradley's views on the categorical judgment.

THE INDIVIDUAL JUDGMENT

Bradley's treatment of the categorical—or as he prefers to call it the "individual"—judgment is to be found in the second chapter of the *Principles of Logic*. In the original text of 1883 we find Bradley dividing categorical (or individual) judgment into three classes. Bradley discusses what he calls "analytic judgments of sense," "synthetic judgments of sense," and an unnamed "third class" that includes those judgments that, although not conforming to the definitions of the first two divisions, are still understood as unconditional assertions about facts (at least of a sort). But before considering these species of categorical judgment, let me mention that, for Bradley, these distinctions are relative distinctions only; and if forced into absolute divisions they do not hold up. As we shall see, they are used to illustrate what ultimately is a difference of degree and not of kind. Thus, not only is the difference between these three species of categorical judgment hopelessly blurred, but, Bradley argues, so too is the rigid distinction between categorical and hypothetical assertion itself. And, with this in mind, let us proceed to a brief discussion of the peculiarities of each form of individual judgment.

The Analytic Judgment of Sense

The most basic form of individual (categorical) judgment is, for Bradley, the "analytic judgment of sense." This judgment is (roughly) taken to be an analysis of that which is given in present perception in that the logical (i.e., special or limited) subject and predicate of these judgments are always explicitly and overtly present to sensuous experience.[17] Examples that Bradley provides include "There is a wolf," "I have a toothache," and "That bough is broken."[18] This species of categorical judgment is said to be "merely analytic" because it does not affirm the existence of any ideal content that is not immediately given. Although the specific subject and predicate might not be wholly contained in the judgment (it could never be so contained according to Bradley), there is no explicit *additional* content imported into the assertion that might be construed as an outright inferential construction.

But in order to grasp this first distinction within the threefold division of individual judgment, let us consider the following example. If while standing on the roadside I assert "This road is paved with bricks" (assuming that the bricks are visible), I have made an analytic judgment of sense. I have not extended the content in any explicit manner. However, if instead I say "This road leads to London" (assuming "London" is not within my perceptual awareness), I have gone beyond that which is explicitly present. And this is the essential difference. The analytic judgment of sense must, of course, ignore a great deal of presented fact.

But, though it must ignore, it does not visibly extend or augment the given content. While content and existence are understood still to have fallen apart to some extent, the "pointing beyond" itself that this rupture entails is such that it is not developed into an explicitly different content. In other words, the analytic judgment of sense is that species of judgment that (so far as this is possible) does not attempt to transcend present perception. It is, in Bradley's terminology, "merely adjectival" in that it focuses on and articulates an aspect of given sensuous experience.

I would also mention here that, while the use of designating terms such as "this," "here," and "now" will create a special set of problems, we can for the moment ignore these difficulties and consider the analytic judgment of sense in which they occur as being entirely consistent with the definition of judgment we have considered thus far. Let us consider Bradley's example "This bird is yellow." Of this judgment Bradley says:

> It is not the bare idea symbolized by "this bird" the grammatical subject of which we go on to affirm the predicate. It is the fact distinguished and qualified by "this bird," to which the adjective "yellow" is really attributed. The genuine subject is the thing as perceived, the content of which our analysis has divided into "this bird" and "yellow," and of which we predicate those ideal elements in their union.[19]

The analytic judgment of sense is, then, the paradigmatic case of a judgment in which the proposition functions as a unified predicate term that is affirmed as being a true analysis of that which is given in sense experience. In effect, the judgment claims that what is given before us in perception exhibits a continuity of content that differentiates itself into "birdness" and "yellowness"; that is, given experience consists in an identity-in-difference containing these features.

But we must not overemphasize this idea of resting with given content. As we should recall from the discussion of the previous chapters, not only does the bond of predication imply an identity-in-difference between those contents as expressed by the articulate proposition, it also implies that these contents share a bond with other entities that are not explicitly present.[20] We must never forget that *all* contents are for Bradley universals—universals whose contents spill over the boundaries of present perception. And, although an analytic judgment of sense may not *overtly* import a different content into our judgment (as would "This bird came from Africa"), still, all contents must be understood as transcending the given perceptual experience in which they are found. For example, if I judge "This tree is green" while perceiving a green tree (or its representation), I am asserting an existing continuity of content between the tree as it exists in my experience and elsewhere (in different times and places). Since all judgments, on the Bradleian analysis, assert the reality of universals there is a definite sense in which we must say that even the analytic judgment of sense is more than "merely analytic." It, like all judgments, is synthetic in that it proclaims the existence of an identical factor in the tree before me and those examples of "greenness" and "treeness" that are not present. However, even bearing this in mind we can see how the notion of the analytic judgment of sense is wholly compatible with the general idea of judgment in that it (i) does not overtly import a nongiven content; while (ii) remaining an ideal extension of the given that is subject to falsification.[21]

The Synthetic Judgment of Sense

Moving on to the synthetic judgment of sense, we can say of it that, although starting from what is present in sensuous experience, it goes beyond the given content in an *explicit* manner. And in this judgment the inferential construction starts to become overtly developed. "This road leads to London," "Yesterday it rained," and "Tomorrow there will be a full moon" are amongst the examples Bradley provides.[22]

In this class of judgments it is claimed that there is an element of content that, although constituting an identity-in-difference with perceptual experience, is not *directly* given at all. The explicit content of the judgment is, at least in part, an elaboration or extension (usually indicated by the predicate term in the sentence) that only shares a point of contact with sense presentation—hence the appellation "synthetic." Here we are unambiguously constructing a reality that attaches itself to the adjectival articulation of the presented real through an identity of content.[23] The synthetic judgment of sense has, we might say, one foot in and the other outside of the present perceptual experience. Bradley tells us that

> Synthetic judgments thus cease to be merely adjectival, and they express a series of unique events by indirect reference to the real which appears in unique presentation. They are connected by an inference with the content of this appearance, and so far are directly related to perception. But their ideas are never referred as adjectives to the presentation itself. They are attributed to the reality, which both shows itself there, and extends itself beyond. The content of our perceptions, and the content of our ideal constructions are both the adjectives of *one reality*. They are both appearances, which both (unless our assumptions are false) are valid and true of the real world.[24]

For example, in "This road leads to London," we might have before us a perceptual complex that does not explicitly contain any content that characterizes the city of London (or, perhaps, even a "leading to"). In our synthetic construction, however, we take part of the given perceptual content (that indicated by "this road") and we assert an identity of content between (a) the actually given road; (b) our ideal road which is a continuation of the given content; and (c) some aspect of the city of London that is continuous with our ideal road. We are claiming, in effect, that the precise content of "this road" is such that it is continuous with "London." We are creating a worldview such that "this road" does, indeed, form a continuous tissue with our inferential extension.

In explicating the synthetic judgment of sense Bradley tells us that a "link" must be found between what is given ("this road") and that content that is not immediately present (in this case, "London"). Hence he writes:

> That link is found by establishing a point which is the same in both, and is the same because its quality is the same. The "this" contains a complex of detail, either times or spaces (or both) in series, which we may call c.d.e.f. The idea, on its side, contains a series of particulars a.b.c.d. The identity of c.d. in each extends the perception c.d.e.f. by the ideal spaces or times a.b. and the whole is given by synthetical construction as a single fact a.b.c.d.e.f.[25]

To apply this to our example, let us consider c.d.e.f. to be the perceptual content that is before us and part of which can be described by the phrase "this road." Now, although this perceptually given content may contain a great deal more than what we select and characterize as "this road," this must largely be ignored. However, *within* the concrete content that we have selected and identified by "this road" are specific elements of content that upon further analysis indicate, let us say, a particular sort of superhighway. Now, when we begin to analyze this given perception (which itself involves an unpacking of our knowledge of such superhighways) we start to realize that only the city of London, for example, has this unique type of road leading into it. Thus we are led to postulate a.b.—our idea of the city of London; and as part of its content c.d.—this type of superhighway that we know is only found extending from London. The entire ideal content a.b.c.d. is a complex predicate idea that we might characterize as "road leads to London." Thus c.d. (our London-specific superhighway) is the bridge that is found in present perception and that—through a synthetic analysis of its content—suggests to us that this given perception be ideally elaborated by the predicate "road leading to London." We should also not forget, though, that in making this judgment the whole series is simultaneously referred to the greater reality that is presup-

posed and (partially) indicated by the given perception from which the
ideal content (c.d.) was originally selected.

The difference between this overtly synthetic judgment and the analytic judgment of sense, then, is merely that the complex quality that
functions as the special predicate in the analytic judgment of sense is
held to be part of the explicit perceptual content while here it is not. This
does not mean, though, that the synthetic judgment of sense contains an
ideal elaboration which is wholly synthetic. As we saw in the example
above, the synthetic construction is always (or should be, anyway) based
upon an analysis of what is given in sense. Although the explicit content
of our logical predicate ("London") is not explicitly given in perception,
it does lie *hidden* there, and an analysis of the overt presentation brings
this forward in our synthetic elaboration. There must exist something
about this particular road that provides for us a clue that can be inferentially developed into a "leading to London-ness." We might say, then,
that a "leading to London-ness" is *implicitly* present because through an
analysis of what is given we are lead to connect it with what isn't.[26]

We shall consider this mechanism in greater detail further down. But
at this stage we need only be aware that the difference between the analytic and synthetic judgments of sense is—when considering their reliance
on ideal development—merely one of degree. We should also realize that
not only is this process a simultaneous analysis and synthesis common to
both species of judgment, it is, on Bradley's view, also the basic mechanism by which (as we shall see) all explicit inference operates.

The "Third Group"

Let us now consider the nameless "third group" of individual judgments discussed by Bradley. This third group (which remain unnamed)
are identified as those judgments that have for their predicable, ideal
content something that is not immediately given in perception at all.
Indeed, in one sense their content is something that cannot even be said
to be a "thing" or "event." And these consist of judgments that deal
with (often controversial) subjects that are, as Bradley puts it, "never a
sensible reality in time."[27] Included in this class, we are told, are assertions about such things as the "history of man or a nation," or those
judgments about such "nonsensibles" as "god" or the "universe."
Amongst the examples that Bradley offers are "God is a spirit," and
"The soul is a substance."[28]

Now, according to Bradley, what would make this last class of judgments categorical or existential is that, like their synthetic siblings, they
make a continual—albeit indirect—reference to and possess, through a
series of ideal connections, a point of identity with that which *is* given

in perception (or they at least try to do this). Hence, even though in an indirect way, these judgments must still be seen as referring to individually given fact. And, should it be the case that the content indicated by either the subject or predicate term does not exist, we would be forced to reject the judgment as false.[29]

Although Bradley tells us that the line that separates this third class and the synthetic judgment is "unstable," this group of judgments can be recognized by the fact that neither the limited subject nor special predicate ideas (which together function as a complex predicate referred to reality) shares a point of common content with what is given in perception. It is thus only through a network of ideal connections (possibly many stages removed) that our assertion is "linked with" or "attached to" presented fact. For example, if I assert "The settlers of the New World were very courageous" while seated in my study, I would probably find no element of content as explicitly articulated in the proposition present to external perception. However, what *is* given (the walls, books etc.) would—through an analysis of content—be seen to possess a point of identity with other universals that would (sooner or later) exhibit an identity of content with the explicit content of the judgment "The settlers . . ."

We might say, then, that a "third class" judgment is a synthetic judgment that attaches itself to other synthetic judgments that at some level manage to fasten themselves to perceptual experience. There is something about my present perceptual experience that forms an ideal bond with something that is partially within and partially external to it; this would be our first synthetic judgment. And this judgment, in turn, forms an ideal bond with something that is, although wholly absent from my *direct* perceptual experience, connected to it by the synthetic assertion that functions as an intermediary.[30] It is, however, always perception that provides the point of stabilization and orientation.[31] Bradley clearly expresses this view when he writes:

> [On the one hand] The real . . . transcends the presentation; and invites us to follow it beyond that which is given. On the other hand, we seem to find contact with reality and to touch ground nowhere, so to speak, outside the presented. How then is a content to be referred to the real if it cannot be referred to the real as perceived? We must answer that the content is referred *indirectly*. It is not attributed to the given as such; but, by establishing its connection with what is presented, it is attributed to the real which appears in that given. Though it is not and cannot be found in present perception, it is true because it is predicated of the reality, and unique because it is fixed in relation with immediate perception. The

ideal world of spaces beyond the sensible space, and of times
not presented but past and future, fastens itself on the true
actual world by fastening itself to a quality of the immediate
this. In a single word continuity of content is taken to show
identity of element.[32]

There are, I think, two important points in this quotation that need
to be emphasized. One is that present perception is always the point of
reference for all ideal elaboration in judgment. It somehow provides a
ground for experience that cannot be ignored. The other point is that
our ideal elaboration (based on perception) is not arbitrary. It is "fixed
in relation with immediate perception" and has an "identity of element"
with the content as given. In the synthetic extension of present perception we are providing an inferential elaboration or construction that is
not a mere construction; it is seen by Bradley as an analysis of the given
content that (to consider our previous example) says, "*this* road is not
just any road but is one the very nature of which contains a 'leading-to-
London'." And should we go on to develop a third-class judgment (such
as "London remains the center of European financial markets") we do
so upon the basis of the presupposed nexus of knowledge that permeates
the given perception and provides the constraints according to which all
ideal elaboration must proceed.[33] Hence, although we are effecting a synthetic construction that is, perhaps, many steps removed from the given,
this synthesis is one that is justified by the fact that it constitutes a precise analysis of the actual—even though hidden or implicit—nature of its
perceptual content.[34]

The difference, then, between the analytic judgment of sense and the
third-class assertion is just that, in the latter, this analysis is at a deeper
level. Both the explicit subject and predicate concepts of our third-class
judgment can be said to be even more deeply hidden in given experience
because they involve the synthetic-analysis of an idea that itself is only
implicitly present in the sensuous content. For instance, if we judge "Lon-
doners have always been industrious" while standing before our erst-
while road, we have an assertion that—although its genealogy can be
traced—has gone entirely beyond the explicit perceptual content as given.

We must not forget here that perceptual experience is permeated by
the universal nexus of meanings that is always present, and that every
meaning, according to Bradley, contains many submeanings. And neither should we forget that this meaning always exists both above and
below us in any assertion. Not only does every meaning possess submeanings, but any meaning can, on the Bradleian analysis, itself be seen
as an element within other more expansive meanings. Indeed, it is just
this interconnection between meanings that constrains us in our ideal

development of the perceptually given fact. For instance, the judgment "This tree is a conifer" (an analytic judgment of sense if made within the presence of a conifer) contains interconnections with other meanings such that it will not allow us to develop it in certain directions (e.g., "This tree was elected mayor of Cincinnati"). Why not? An answer to this question will bring us to a significant aspect of Bradley's theory of knowledge. And given the importance of this doctrine in his philosophy, we should, perhaps, consider more closely the structure of inferential development. But, before we discuss inference proper, let me provide some cautionary remarks regarding this threefold division of the individual judgment that Bradley provides in his *Principles of Logic*. The motivation behind the examination of these three types of individual judgment is here, I should mention, largely historical. Although they occupy a great deal of Bradley's attention in the 1883 edition of the *Principles of Logic* these divisions are (not surprisingly) entirely absent from his later works.[35] Bradley became concerned that—although not incorrect—they could be misleading; and thus thought that they were better dropped from his account. Hence, it would be useful if we briefly examine the ways in which one might go astray if these distinctions are viewed too rigidly.

There are three points here that should be made. First, to distinguish between two classes of judgment—one called "analytic," the other "synthetic"—could obscure the fact that all judgment is, for Bradley, *both* analytic and synthetic. (My discussion has, it is hoped, placed sufficient emphasis on this point that no further comment is required.) The second point I would make is this: Bradley presents his examples in terms of differences between grammatical propositions without emphasizing the fact that even though what we *verbally* assert might be construed as an analytic judgment of sense, we could, while making such a verbal assertion, be in possession of a judgment that belongs to one of the more explicitly inferential classes. In other words, this terminology obscures the fact that the grammatical formulation may, indeed, hide the true logical form of the judgment. And lastly, this division suggests that the distinction between given and nongiven contents is clear and precise. Even if we are sensitive to the fact that all judgments are both analytic and synthetic, and that the overt grammatical expression of the isolated judgment is often misleading, any usefulness that the distinction possesses is one that revolves around the notion of a content that is perceptually present and one that isn't. But, as Bradley was later to insist, not only does this invest external perception with far too much importance, it is impossible to identify any precise point at which "perceptual" and "nonperceptual" (i.e., "conceptual") experience begin and end. Discussing the matter in these terms could, therefore, (particularly in connection with what Bradley says about the existence of unaffirmed ideas) leave the reader with the belief that perception and conception, "ideal" and "real," "given," and "inferential" are terms that represent something more than relative distinctions. But, as I have already argued (and as he himself was to insist many times after 1883), to attribute such a view to Bradley would be to fail to understand his logical/epistemological doctrine.

THE INFERENTIAL NATURE OF JUDGMENT

It should be by now apparent that any consideration of Bradley's theory of judgment cannot rest wholly within itself. As suggested above, not only are synthetic judgments of sense and the nameless "third class" largely inferential, so too (albeit to a lesser degree) is the more rudimentary analytic form. Indeed, given Bradley's claim that *the* distinctive characteristic of judgment is its ideal elaboration of perceptual experience that is subject to falsification, we must acknowledge that even the most basic cognitive act that conforms to such a definition must, in some sense, be "inferential." Realizing, though, that we must confine ourselves here to the inferential aspect of judgment proper, let us consider more closely what, according to Bradley, constitutes the constraining factor in the ideal development of given experience.

As already suggested, the first and most important point that must be made about Bradley's view of inferential development is that it is not an arbitrary or fanciful process. Contained within any judgment are layers of significance that provide enormous restrictions and constraints on our ideal elaborations. And, ultimately, both the narrowly focused analytic judgment of sense and the overtly inferential "third class" assertion should be seen as the recognition or discovery of systematic relations that exist within the real.[36] We must not forget that when we first perceptually apprehend something as complex as (for example) a "road" we are in possession of a great deal more than bare concepts. "This is a road" is always a judgment whose content not only spills over its boundaries but it is (as is every judgment) one whose *context* penetrates and conditions this content. Every judgment has, then, not just *a* content, but a *precise* (and pervasive) content that reaches back into its history. However hidden and implicit, this deeper web of significance is always present. And it is because of this contextual interpenetration, Bradley claims, that the content of the "object itself" can dictate the direction in which any inferential development must proceed. Indeed, on the Bradleian analysis such a necessitated development arising from the object is the very differentia of inference. "Every inference," we read

> . . . is the ideal self-development of a given object taken as real.
> The inference is "necessary" in the sense that the real object,
> and not something else, throughout develops its proper self,
> and so compels or repels whatever extraneous matter is hos-
> tile or irrelevant. And the inference is "universal" . . . in the
> sense that it has an essence as opposed to a particular accom-
> paniment of more or less irrelevant detail. Every inference is,
> in other words, something beyond its "this," "here," and
> "now." It contains a "reason why," a "principle," a
> "because," and a "must." As against the resistance of the irrel-
> evant or hostile, we have seen that its self-development may
> entail and may show the character of compulsion.[37]

Now, Bradley is certainly aware that we can (and often do) make
very bad inferences. He is also entirely willing to concede that there can
exist a transition between ideal contents that is not at all necessitated (or
only to a slight degree). But what distinguishes the bad inference from
the good inference (or more accurately the better from the worse) is the
thread of *relevancy* and *necessity*. If we expand an ideal content in an
appropriate and relevant manner, that is, if we follow out the lines of
identical content that the object itself provides, then we are (to greater
or lesser degree) inferring. However, if on the other hand we ideally
develop our object in a manner that is insensitive (and thus distorting of)
this presented content, our ideal movement is within the realm of the
"merely subjective." Whenever what is either irrelevant or arbitrary
enters into our progressive synthetic-analysis of experience then we have
left the domain of inference proper and are confronted by what may be
called, for lack of better term, "imagination."[38]

We must not forget that Bradley sees every judgment as presuppos-
ing and made within a specific context.[39] "There is," as Bradley tells us,
"always a great deal more *in* the mind than can ever be *before* it." And
it is this felt totality of content that provides us direction in our inferential development of an assertion. The act of judgment focuses upon a
specific area of our larger given experience (which is both in and before
the mind); and it is through this selection that experience moves from
the presupposed and implicit to the explicit and articulate. Judgment we
might say is the light by which we illuminate first this, and now that,
area of the larger experience that exists beyond the confines of our present conscious awareness. And, although judgment proper resides
within this specifically illuminated experience that we have selected, its
boundaries are not rigidly defined; the context out of which it comes
always provides a "feeling base" for what follows. Indeed, when
Bradley speaks of the "given" out of which we selectively abstract a con-

tent, he is referring to nothing other than this larger sense of the world—
the world that we possess both consciously and unconsciously and with
which we are engaged in a continuous process of articulation, refinement, and expansion.[40] There is, to consider our previous example,
something about the given "this road" which—should we look closely
enough—is *already* permeated and conditioned by a "leading to London." And it is a sensitivity to this interpenetration of explicit content
by that which is not directly perceived—that which is implicit—that provides the guiding hand in our ideal elaboration of given experience. If we
are insensitive to this interpenetrating content then surely, according to
Bradley, we do not infer, we merely create "castles in the air." But
should we allow the content itself, as permeated by our presupposed
world, to dictate the direction in which it will develop we have before us
the inferential process *par excellence*.[41]

But what about the bad inference? What if we don't let the "object
itself" guide our ideal elaboration? While we are not yet ready to pursue
in any detail Bradley's notion of error, we can at present still consider
the following. If I assert (for example) "This plant is a *Ficus lyrata*"
while in the presence of a *Dracaena fragans*, I have asserted an identity
of content between the given and the ideal world of meaning-fact that
does not hold—at least not fully. It cannot be too strongly emphasized
that in analyzing the given content I am also (simultaneously) synthesizing or constructing a larger conscious worldview. And in each case I am
attempting to effect an ideal bond between those characteristics that are
perceptually given and those that—although absent—are nonetheless
part of the continuous fabric of knowledge that is shared by all judging
subjects and which constitutes the underpinnings of any assertion. Now,
in this instance (in judging this tree to be a *Ficus lyrata*) I have attempted
to effect such an ideal bond, but my fuller experience has repelled it.[42]

In the objective world of meaning-fact (based upon a long history of
shared experience), "*Ficus lyrata*" means, amongst other things, "possessing large fiddle shaped, dark green leaves" and "being a nonflower-
ing member of the fig family." But "*Dracaena fragans*" means, amongst
other things, "possessing long slender green leaves" and "bearing fra-
grant flowers in the wild." Although it is true that there are many submeanings to both of these predicate concepts that are common property
between them, those that are most characteristic of the terms in question
are not. Common to both is the fact of their "being a plant," "having a
photosynthetic metabolism," "cellulose based cell structure," and so on.
Indeed, we could go on at great length describing those contents that are
legitimately possessed by both. But the "green" in each case is not precisely the same shade; the "cell structure" is somewhat different as well.

Hence, my judgment fails to mesh fully with the larger realm of meaning-fact within which it falls, and thus is false—even if not entirely so.[43]

Although we can only touch on the issue at present, the reason why even our false assertions are capable of possessing a partial truth (see chapter 7) is because every judgment presupposes the entire world of meaning-fact. Even in an assertion that shares far fewer common elements than in our example above, there always exists something within the complex content of the asserted judgment-idea that does manage to attach itself to given reality.[44] When I make any judgment (e.g., "This tree is a *Ficus lyrata*") I am, while directly referring to the classificatory scheme of flora and the significance with which each term has been invested, indirectly appealing to a great deal more. Indirectly I am referring to the conditions of existence of this scheme. And this consists in, immediately, the world of biological science, and at a further remove, virtually *every* logical meaning. And because of this complex and hierarchically organized content—a content that, for Bradley, exists both in the asserted proposition and in the given reality—there always exists some element of overlap between the false assertion and the fact with which I attempt to identify it. Even if I were to assert "There is a white rabbit" while actually viewing the vague grey outline of a crumpled piece of paper in a darkened alley, still, Bradley claims, there is an element of commonality (and thus truth) between my assertion and the actual object. (In this case, it would probably a partial identity of shape and color between the rabbit-idea and the paper.)

Bradley's argument here, as always, rests upon the inability of any meaning to be self-referential and self-contained. Any logical predicate we might consider always, Bradley tells us, refers beyond its own boundaries in order to maintain significance for itself; and any meaning that is discovered there will itself be found to possess a further reference (and so on). It is this nexus, then, which—although almost entirely presupposed and only partially within of our present conscious awareness—still constitutes the grid against which any judgment either fits or doesn't. And when we judge wrongly it is this network of meaning that makes us wrong and that refuses to incorporate—or at least partially refuses to incorporate—the judgment into its web without (sometimes significant) modification.[45]

This ideal realm of significance, we must say is, on Bradley's account, always present. And, although not necessarily apparent on the first look, it is that *for which* we look when we feel dissatisfaction with our present judgment. It provides that clue or hint as to the real significance of what perceptual experience provides. And as always present it supplies the thread of relevancy by which we elaborate and expand any judgment. What is explicitly before us is always permeated by what is implicit and presupposed. The unraveling and conscious development of this realm of presupposed meanings is thus the mechanism of inference itself and the basis of an ideal development in judgment; and it makes judgment (as opposed to imagination) that which we are *compelled to think*.[46] "Perhaps we need not judge," Bradley tells us, "but if we judge we lose all liberty."[47] And, as inadequate as these comments are to the larger subject of inference, we must leave the matter for now lest we lose sight of our more immediate goal.

Chapter 5

SEARCHING FOR CATEGORICAL TRUTH

WE have now come to what is, perhaps, the most distinctive thesis in Bradley's philosophy. After considering the several species into which Bradley analyzes the individual judgment we must now consider why he believes them all incapable of being fully categorical, or of what is the same thing, expressing independent fact. And, though we shall not be in a position to consider the matter in any detail until the following chapter, I would like to offer a few comments here as to why Bradley sees this project as significant.

Simply put, the problem is that should the individual judgment be capable of stating fact categorically—that is, whole and complete in its unique individuality—then there would exist no means by which inferential development might be justified. The existence of wholly independent facts would *sever the bonds between them*—bonds that are ultimately the only basis upon which inference may proceed. In addition, the existence of fact complete unto itself would imply, Bradley believes, the externality of thought to its object. Given and unique fact, understood as existing external to and alongside other such facts, would make of thought a merely abstractive function that could only deal with empty universal concepts. Although "thinking" on such a view might have some pragmatic value, in no way could it be seen as the legitimate means of realizing the individuality of our intended object. And, with this brief statement of Bradley's need to reject the perfectly categorical judgment, let us now proceed to examine his more detailed rationale.

Bradley's attack on the individual judgment (which focuses on the analytic judgment of sense) can be divided into three different arguments.[1] These I shall call (i) the incompleteness argument, (ii) the distortion argument, and (iii) the uniqueness argument. In the end, however, we shall see that all rest on the same metaphysical claim—namely, that reality is a singular, integrated whole; and finite thought, while it must presuppose that reality is such a whole, is still incapable of making the individual nature of any aspect of that whole fully explicit and articulate.

INCOMPLETENESS

What I have called the incompleteness argument is, perhaps, the best known of Bradley's attacks on the individual judgment and thus it offers the most appropriate starting point. In its barest outline the claim is that in order for a truth to be categorically true—that is, adequately true to the fact it claims to be about—we must get the *complete* fact into our judgment.[2] But, due to the finite nature of judgment and the infinite character of its object, this is impossible. Hence, no true categorical judgment exists.

In order to make clearer this claim we might break it down into the following premises: (*a*) For any truth to be categorical it must be the whole truth about its object; (*b*) Judgment—the bearer of truth—is necessarily finite; and (*c*) The object of truth (judgment's referent) is necessarily infinite; and (*d*) therefore: No truth can be categorical. And as a corollary: To assert any truth categorically is to assert falsely.

Probably the only one of these statements that could be viewed as uncontroversial is (b). Certainly (c) involves an enormous metaphysical claim. (This point we shall consider in chapter 6.) Somewhat less controversial, perhaps (but certainly open to attack), is premise (a). This claim we shall examine in a moment. First, however, I would like to examine some further implications of Bradley's position.

Central to this argument is, of course, the infinite nature of judgment's referent, and Bradley describes this by saying that the object as it exists in our judgment is "conditioned" by what lies beyond it. But his claim, we must remember, is not just that our categorically asserted fact is conditioned. It is the much stronger claim that our fact has conditions that are, although external to the fact as asserted, still *essential* to its being what it is. We can never get all the fact into our judgment because all the fact entails its external, but still necessary, conditions. Wherever we look, even if we think we have reached the end, there will always be more. But if this is true then it is not just that we assert subject to a condition; rather, *every categorical assertion rests upon unknown conditions*. However, this makes the truth of the judgment as asserted vulnerable. Should these unknown conditions come to light they *may* falsify my assertion. (Or at the very least they may cause me to modify it or put it forth with reservation) And if any unknown condition falsifies my assertion then I certainly am not in possession of a categorical *truth*. Neither can I be said to possess categorical truth if I am forced to modify my assertion. We must remember that it was not the modified assertion that I put forth as true.[3] And, should I still assert my truth but only subject to reservation (which means upon the basis of explicit conditions; e.g., "If X, then . . ."), I am not in possession of a *categorical* truth.

Let us consider the judgment "Sally is happy." Ignoring for the moment the question of which Sally the judgment designates, let us ask the following of this judgment: Can it be always applied to our friend Sally? Is Sally happy when loved by her children? All right. What about in the face of desertion by her husband, or the loss of her job? It would seem doubtful that the truth of the assertion would still hold here. It is always the case, Bradley tells us, that when confronted by differing circumstances the original judgment would be, if not completely retracted, then at least modified.[4] Hence, the judgment taken *as such*—that is, on its face—cannot be accepted as true. But what happens to the notion of "categorical" assertion here? Certainly we must realize that the fact we have actually asserted is not the fact as it exists. We have asserted but a piece of a complex situation that—should we know more about it—might cause us to withdraw the claim. As Bradley tells us:

> The analytic judgment is not true *per se*. Asserting as it does, of the particular presentation, it must always suppose a further content which falls outside that fraction it offers. What it says is true, if true at all, because of something else. The fact it states is really fact only in relation to the rest of the context, and only because of the rest of that context. It is not true except under that condition. So we have a judgment which is really conditioned, and which is false if you take it as categorical. To make it both categorical and true, you must get the condition inside the judgment. You must take up the given as it really appears, without omission, unaltered, and unmutilated. And this is impossible.[5]

This claim rests, of course, on the metaphysical assumption of an ontological monism. And, though we shall consider Bradley's defense of this view in the later chapters, we should note that he sees any one fact (such that we can even speak of a single fact) as so interpenetrated and determined by its relations to all other facts, that the very singling out of it from its conditioning context leaves us with a mere fragment of the fact as it actually exists.

Another assumption here is that any truth in order to be true must be so necessarily and universally. If we cannot at any time and in any place assert "Sally is happy" then this alone, Bradley suggests, betrays the assertion's conditional nature. Failure to be true always and everywhere entails an "if" and reveals the judgment as, in fact, hypothetical. Although Bradley is entirely willing to concede (indeed, to insist) that we can and must, at the level of pragmatic concern, treat facts as though they were independent and sufficient unto themselves, at a deeper level we must presuppose that all is connected, and that outside of their somewhat arbitrary limitation in judgment, the "facts" exist in an utterly interdependent manner. But this is to say (once more) that in judgment, although we are *trying* to qualify fully this or that fact, in our efforts to realize this qualification, we find no end. To qualify fully a single fact in judgment would, for Bradley, entail bringing in all its conditions; but since these conditions are infinite, our attempt to qualify adequately any one fact is, in principle, incapable of being realized.

Only if there exists some state of affairs the *entirety* of which could be explicitly asserted—while leaving out no necessary conditions to its existence or elements of its meaning—might we be in possession of a truth that is wholly categorical. However, Bradley is convinced that no such unconditioned, externally related facts (and hence truths) exist. While the analytic judgment of sense *appears* to present fact whole and complete, this appearance betrays its lack of self-sufficiency when we examine the structure of predication. Indeed, in identifying any determinate quality in judgment we have, according to Bradley, already left the confines of the given and have, however implicitly, begun to reconstruct synthetically the spatiotemporal nexus that reaches beyond the present and that ultimately provides the context through which the analytic judgment of sense achieves intelligibility. Does not the judgment "This apple is red" itself demand an implicit reference to "nonred" (the system of color) as well as the existence of the vegetable kingdom? And would not the sense of the judgment be lost if such a reference did not exist? Bradley's answer is most emphatically, Yes; and any belief that the "facts" we assert in the analytic judgment of sense (or any judgment) can be confined to the given present consists in a wholly inadequate analysis of our experience.

> The real which appears within the given [Bradley tells us], cannot possibly be confined to it. Within the limits of its outer edges its character gives rise to the infinite process in space and time. Seeking there for the simple, at the end of our search we are still confronted by the composite and the relative. And the outer edges themselves are fluent. They pass forever in time and space into that which is outside them. It is

> true that the actual light we see falls only upon a limited area;
> but the continuity of element, the integrity of context, forbids
> us to say that this illuminated section by itself is real.[6]

Now, we might notice that many critics have insisted that a fundamental mistake occurs here. "Just because we don't get *all* of the fact
into our judgment," it has been argued, "doesn't mean that what we do
get into it is not entirely accurate and true; and it is a simple fallacy to
claim that just because I don't know all of the truth I know none of it.
It would be the same as to say that because I am not familiar with all of
the works of Beethoven that I, therefore, know none of them." But the
first thing to note about this objection is that it misrepresents Bradley's
claim. Bradley is not claiming that in our failure to grasp the entire truth
we don't know the truth *at all*. We do possess knowledge; and of this,
he claims, there can be no doubt. But it is one thing to say that we have
knowledge, and quite another to assert that this knowledge is anything
like certain or complete. This, however, is exactly what the pretense of
the categorical assertion amounts to.

Bradley insists that we have real (as opposed to merely phenomenal)
knowledge; this claim lies at the very foundation of his philosophy. But,
even though we are in cognitive possession of the real, this does not
mean that our knowledge is without defect. We do have knowledge but
that knowledge is—in part, at least—"adjectival." And it is adjectival (as
opposed to substantive) because it consists in only an aspect—a partial
vision—of the object that it is about. Thus, it must always assume an
enormous amount of significance that is not part of the explicit content
of the judgment in order for that judgment to be intelligible at all. And,
Bradley tells us, given that what knowledge we do explicitly possess
exists in such a dependent relation to what we don't, such knowledge
can never be called "categorical" in any usual sense of the term. The
incompleteness of any judgment, Bradley argues, rests with the fact that
what we do know cannot, in principle, be self-contained. Its essential
nature is always "disrupted" by a reference beyond itself to something
that is not fully present in the judgment. As we are told, in any object of
our assertion

> The reference of content to something other than itself lies
> deep within its internal nature. It proclaims itself to be adjec-
> tival, to be relative to the outside; and we violate its essence if
> we try to assert it as having existence entirely in its own right.[7]

The only way the above objection could be made good, Bradley
claims, would be by showing that what we know of any fact is whole
unto itself and in no way "infected" by such relativity to what exists out-

side its own four corners. But, again, this he believes is impossible. And, while Bradley's strongest defense of this claim was not to come until the publication of *Appearance and Reality* (some ten years after these words were written), we might also consider his treatment as it originally appeared in the 1883 *Principles of Logic*. Continually stating his desire to avoid detailed and explicit metaphysical argument, Bradley—realizing the role that the "monistic assumption" plays in his logical theory— often provides his readers with a statement of his metaphysical convictions. The following is typical:

> The reality we divined to be self-existent, substantial, and individual; but, as it appears within a presentation, it is none of these. The content throughout is infected with relativity, and, adjectival itself, the whole in its elements are also adjectival. Though given as fact every part is given as existing by reference to something else. The mere perpetual disappearance in time of the given appearance is itself the negation of its claim to self-existence. And again, if we take it while it appears, its limits, so to speak, are never secured from the inroads of unreality. In space or in time its outside is made fact solely by relation to what is beyond. Living by relation to what it excludes, it transcends its limits, it joins another element, and invites that element within its own boundaries. But with edges ragged and wavering, that flow outward and inward unstably, it already is lost. It is adjectival on what is beyond itself. Nor within itself has it any stability. There is no solid point of either time or space. Each atom is merely a collection of atoms, and those atoms again are not things but relations of elements that vanish. And when asked what is ultimate, and can stand as an individual, you can answer nothing. The real can not be identical with the content that appears in presentation. It forever transcends it, and gives us a title to make search elsewhere.[8]

We might, I think, better understand this statement if we recall the discussion of chapter 2. There we saw that in every explicit assertion there is always a severance of the "what" from the "that." By its very nature, Bradley argues, the explicit content of any assertion points beyond itself to the larger context of experience out of which it is selected (abstracted) and upon which its significance rests. But, since this underlying base of experience cannot, in principle, be wholly included in any one assertion, it exposes the reliance of what is explicitly present (our content as judged) upon that which is implicit and presupposed. And once this dependent relation is grasped, Bradley claims, we shall give up immediately any belief that our assertions can be unconditionally—that is, categorically—true.

DISTORTION

The next attack that we shall consider, Bradley's distortion argument, can be summarized as follows: Given that reality comes to us as an integrated unity of differences that interpenetrate and condition one another, the act of selective abstraction in judgment can do nothing but introduce a disfiguration into this differentiated unity. The given whole upon which abstraction works, and out of which explicit judgment arises, can never be accurately brought into our conscious assertion; and this is because to select out of this whole is already to distort the nature of anything in it. Since the limited nature of the finite judging mind is such as always (at some point) to cut off the connections of content that exist between the present focus of our attention and their existence beyond that focus, we are left with a cognized object that has had its actual character *altered*. Indeed, Bradley tells us that the content as it exists outside the judgment—in reality—reaches into and is an intimate part of that content that is explicitly before us. But in the individual judgment this intimate connection of content is, to some degree, always suppressed. And this exclusion of content from the explicit assertion is sufficient to introduce a distortion into the content which is internal to the judgment at hand. Hence, we read:

> As soon as we judge we are forced to analyze, and are forced to distinguish. We must separate some elements of the given from others. We sunder and divide what appears to us as a sensible whole. It is never more than an arbitrary selection which goes into the judgment. We say "There is a wolf," or "This tree is green"; but such poor abstractions, such mere bare meanings, are much less than the wolf and the tree which we see; and they fall even more short of the full particulars, the mass of inward and outward setting, from which we separate wolf and tree. If the real appears as X=a b c d e f g h then our judgment is nothing but X=a, or X=a-b. But a-b by itself has never been given, and is not what appears.[9]

Now, this way of putting the matter is liable to tremendous misinterpretation, and shortly we shall comment on how this misunderstanding might arise. However, for the moment we might say that the problem, on Bradley's view, is that in the given fact there is not only a great deal more than what we have in our selected content (the incompleteness problem), but what we have left is itself altered (distortion).[10] It has been altered, and is thus distorting, because what we do possess no longer reflects or shows its intrinsic *connectedness* to that which conditions and interpenetrates it. In our abstracted ideal predicate this element of interconnectedness and continuity, to some degree, always falls out. And whenever the object of our judgment fails to show its integral continuity with everything else it involves a modification of the actual fact, and hence introduces an element of falsification.

Even assuming that we could (*per impossibile*) get all of our presented content into the judgment proper, we would still have the problem that this content does not exist in the judgment in the same manner as found in the given whole. (Much of this is not contained in judgment proper but in what Bradley calls the "feeling base.") And, as we shall see when we examine the "relational form" in chapter 6, when we assert (for example) "This shirt is red," the intrinsic unity and interpenetration of the redness and the shirt as found in our fuller experience are not the same as they exist in the explicit judgment;[11] something, according to Bradley, is missing. Where before the given content was sensed as one of a piece with its context, in explicit predication this seamless continuity is missing;[12] and hence, any judgment's presentation of *unconditional* fact must be seen as faulty. Of this continuity of content Bradley writes:

> It was *in* the fact and we have taken it out. It was *of* the fact and we have given it independence. We have separated, divided, abridged, dissected, we have mutilated the given. And we have done this arbitrarily; we have selected what we chose. But if this is so, and if every analytic judgment must inevitably so alter the fact, how can it any longer lay claim to truth?[13]

The point, it must be remembered, is that the elements we predicate are not *as such* to be found in the present, feeling-based, perception.[14] But it is precisely this "as such" that an assertion must capture if it is to be categorically true. As asserted "we falsify the fact" and hence we must take a harder look at the claim to truth of any categorical judgment. Even if we are to leave standing a class of judgments that should go by this name, we must not for a moment, Bradley tells us, believe that they are categorical because they adequately state the facts as they truly exist.

We might also notice that the argument from incompleteness and that from distortion are difficult, if not impossible, to distinguish at times. Continuity has been left out; but does this make our judgment faulty because incomplete or distorting? It would appear idle to insist on either description.

> The fact which is given us [we read], is the total complex of qualities and relations which appear to sense. But what we assert of this given fact is, and can be nothing but an ideal

content. And it is evident at once that the idea we use can not possibly exhaust the full particulars of what we have before us. A description, we all know, can not ever reach to a complete account of the manifold shades, and the sensuous wealth of one entire moment of direct presentation.[15]

Although Bradley would later comment that he was in the first edition of the *Principles of Logic* too inclined to attribute the richness of given experience to perception, the point as made is still essentially sound. Reaching into the content of present perception are those elements that tie it into the broader context of experience.[16] Some of this makes its way into explicit judgment—much, however, does not. And, unless all of it can be included, we have distorted the content as given.

It is at this point, though, that we must pause. As always we must be on guard against misinterpretation. The possibility of attributing to Bradley a position he does not (and could not) hold is once more before us, and is, in this instance, great. And the danger is, here, I suggest, of attributing to Bradley some species of what I shall call "vulgar" or "popular" mysticism.

The position of the commonplace mystic is one that emphasizes the abstract nature of thought and its tendency to "mutilate" given reality—a reality it sees as essentially ineffable. And, given Bradley's comments regarding the distorting effect of thought on given experience, it is quite possible to attribute to him some such doctrine. Although Bradley's position bears a certain resemblance to purely intuitional and mystical theories, this resemblance is, I suggest, only superficial. The two positions differ on an issue of fundamental importance. And the difference I refer to lies with the sense in which Bradley claims for the given or presented experience a richness that the results of discursive thinking come short of. We must never lose sight of the fact that any "richness" found in our larger experience (and out of which we select a content for ideal development) is, for Bradley, largely inarticulate and "merely felt." Although we do possess a *sense* of our object as unique, individual, and intimately bound to the totality of existence, it is a sense that, as merely felt, cannot satisfy the demands of conscious assertive experience. Conscious assertive experience will only be satisfied, Bradley tells us, with the explicit recognition of its object on its own terms—that is, *as conscious*. And, indeed, it is precisely this lack in the presupposed felt background that motivates us to judge at all. Although we might be said to possess an "extraconceptual" grasp of the perfectly real, this grasp is one which is thought's complement; and it is never explicitly present within conscious awareness (even though it is thought's ideal—its ultimate aim—

to make it so). But to say this is not to say that ultimate reality is "ineffable"—at least in the sense that certain accounts of mysticism would suggest. Indeed, the garden variety of mysticism maintains two theses that Bradley must reject. First, it claims that the perfectly real (the unique and individual) can be experienced in a conscious knowing manner via some sort of "pure intuition" in which the distorting influence of thought has ceased; and second, it maintains that all thinking is—because merely abstract and merely general—distortive .

Bradley's position can be said to differ from theories of "pure intuition," then, on the following points: (*a*) the experience of contextual interpenetration (and any sense of objective uniqueness that may result) does not present itself as a fully *conscious* experience that is somehow before us in a prelinguistic, preconceptual manner.[17] This sense of the unique is an only partially conscious experience that the activity of judgment attempts to continually bring into a fuller awareness; and (*b*) it is not through the *suppression* of thought that we reach the unique and individual. It is only through a progressive series of conscious judgments that we rise to its heights. Hence, contrary to popular accounts of mysticism, thinking and the experience of actuality (reality-as-it-truly-exists) are seen by Bradley as cooperative activities.

UNIQUENESS

Having cautioned the reader against attributing to Bradley any antirational form of mysticism, let us now go on to consider what is, perhaps, the most dominant line of attack on the categorical pretense of individual judgment. Although I must immediately qualify this statement, I might indicate the thrust of Bradley's argument here by saying that due to the abstract nature of thought and language we always fail to get our object explicitly within our linguistic-conceptual grasp. "Here we are safe," "I have a toothache," and "This orange is bitter" are, each of them, expressions that, although directed toward unique and individual occurrences, can in no way capture that uniqueness. These assertions could be put forth by any number of individuals on any number of occasions. And thus we might summarize Bradley's claim here as follows: (i) The referent of every judgment is a unique individual; (ii) Every asserted truth (judgment) is to some degree abstract and general; (iii) To be categorically true a judgment must uniquely apply to its referent; and (iv) therefore: No judgment can be categorically true.

Of course, one might want to counter Bradley's argument by claiming that there is a suppressed premise here to the effect that "It is impossible for a general truth to designate uniquely its referent." While perhaps conceding the truth of the premises (i) through (iii) one might still attempt to rebut Bradley by rejecting this further suppressed assumption. And, indeed, the most common counterattack on Bradley could be stated as follows: "Although our assertions may be merely general, we can and do uniquely designate our referent through the presence of the unique contents of sense. It is patently absurd to claim that when I say 'This orange is bitter' I do not know which orange I am referring to. By holding the unmistakably unique contents of perception alongside of the articulate proposition no error as to which orange I am referring to could occur."

Bradley would agree, of course, that when we say "This orange is bitter" we *mean* this unique orange and no other; we *mean* that individual thing that holds a specific place in the parade of all time that is complete and absolute.[18] "*This* orange" is, indeed, what we *intend* when we use the word "this," or "here," or "now," or any other indexical term. But what we mean (i.e., intend) and what we actually assert must be understood—on any interpretation, Bradley insists—as two entirely different things. We read that

> In every judgment, where we analyze the given, and where
> as the subject we place the term "this," it is not an idea
> which is really the subject. In using "this" we do *use* an idea,
> and that idea is and must be universal; but what we *mean*,
> and fail to express, is our reference to the object which is
> given as unique.[19]

Although there is a sense in which we *are* in contact with a "this" that we know to be unique, the uniqueness that is given and that we attempt to capture in assertion becomes a mere "thisness"—a general idea of presence—when it is transformed into conscious judgment. The "this" (as opposed to "thisness") is that *felt* sense of the whole that, when held against our abstract assertion, provides us with the (false) impression that we have said (or thought) exactly what we mean. What we mean is utterly unique and wholly individual. But, for Bradley, since that uniqueness consists in the totality of relations that a thing possesses we could not (in principle) think this out in an explicit manner. Although we do have a felt sense of this unconditioned and unique totality, when we attempt to make this indeterminate feeling explicit through conscious reflection, our felt, unique "this" is largely stripped of its "that" (existence), and thus always comes up short of complete individuality. While our assertion is capable of exhibiting some *degree* of individuality, it is a degree that always falls short of the perfect individuality and uniqueness that is presupposed within the feeling base of experience. And thus, "here," "now," and "this" are, when they assume their role in explicit judgment, utterly incapable of accomplishing the task that is asked of them.[20] As Bradley tells us:

> You cannot at once translate feeling into judgment and leave feeling untransformed; and what is lost in translation is the positive uniqueness you demand. The "this," as you use it, becomes general, and, though it does not become negative wholly it becomes essentially negative. You insist that "this" is not "that," though to each you give only a sense which is general. But the "this" which you feel and which you mean, does not trouble itself about a "that" since, it is positively itself. And since your truth fails and must fail to contain this positive meaning, your truth is defective and self-condemned.[21]

To be a content within conscious judgment just *is* to be abstract. And abstract, not because merely general; there can be a tremendous amount of particularized and systematized content internal to any assertion. Rather, the judgment is always abstract because incomplete and less than fully individual. And even though we are capable of grasping a *sense* of our ultimate meaning, it is of the very nature of conscious assertive experience that what we ultimately mean can never be fully said, thought—or for that matter—even perceived.

Now, this point plays a tremendous role in Bradley's theory of knowledge. And there are two ways in which he works this argument to his ends. Bradley goes to great lengths in the *Principles of Logic* to illustrate that judgment cannot be about "mere ideas." If judgment were the mere combination of abstract concepts (such as are expressed by the isolated grammatical proposition) then it would be hopelessly general in its reference and utterly incapable of expressing fact. No combination of *abstract* universals can ever result in the *concrete* particular, Bradley insists. And if categorical judgment exists it is only because judgment does not consist in any mere combination of such ideas. If there is to be found a categorical judgment it is only because judgment attaches itself—is continuous with—that sense of felt concreteness (the intrinsic unity of the "what" and "that") that resides in the deepest recesses of feeling and that reaches into perceptual experience. However, after persuasively arguing that the judgment must always contain a reference (either direct or indirect) to the sense of uniqueness that is given in felt experience, Bradley then goes on to claim that—even granting this—the judgment still cannot achieve its goal of precise characterization of existential fact. No matter how you interpret the judgment, Bradley claims, it will always show itself incapable of adequately denoting the unique object or event that we try to capture in our individual propositions.[22]

Bradley's case is, I think, most easily made if we consider the mere proposition rather than the perception-bound judgment to be the basic unit of thought. Certainly if we consider abstract words as they are combined in a sentence as constituting the judgment there is a level of generality present that is obviously incapable of adequately characterizing the assertion's unique referent. "Today is Tuesday" is a proposition that—although it means a precise and unique day when asserted—can in no way begin to express the actual day's uniqueness. It could honestly be put forward on any number of days and be felt to be equally true. But, at the same time as it is true in one place, it is false in another. And the same can be said of "Now it is noon," or "I am in pain." While the concrete time that I attempt to designate by the term "now" is in actuality a unique moment in the history of the universe (as is the "I" who is in pain unique), the sentence "Now it is noon" could be uttered at any time by any one (given that it is always noon somewhere) and be construed as true or false, depending on local circumstance.

Bradley also tells us that it is hopeless to attempt to overcome this difficulty by specifying a particular time series or spatial location.[23] For example, saying "Now—on September 14, 1996—it is here in Philadelphia, Pennsylvania 25 degrees Celsius" I am still left with a merely general designation. It is not logically impossible that there could be more than one time series in which a date referred to by this phrase occurs. And the same could be said about the locale. It is not in principle impossible that throughout the history of the universe there might have been (or will be) more than one location that is designated by the phrase "Philadelphia, Pennsylvania." Thus Bradley claims that if the judgment is only what language makes of it (the isolated sentence) then surely it can never adequately designate its intended object.

"But," it may be objected, "Bradley is using here an argument to which he is not entitled. Characteristic of both our own and Bradley's theory is the claim that it is *not* the mere proposition or sentence that constitutes the judgment. Ignoring our view (that of designation) for the moment, we might say of Bradley's that, on his own principles, it is acknowledged that the concrete elements of sense experience are part of the content affirmed in judgment. Thus, it would be utterly inconsistent of Bradley to reject the judgment as inadequate to its object because it conveys only the bare generalities of language. Granted, mere speech cannot adequately denote its object; however, speech grasped in unison with perception is the very mechanism by which concrete reference occurs. And the specificity of reference that the bare sentence cannot capture must be admitted if we are to claim that perceptually laden judgment is the actual unit of meaningful thought and the basis of all speech."

Now, on any consideration of Bradley's theory an objection such as this is the first that comes to mind. And, indeed, given Bradley's view that it is not the bare sentence but rather the perceptually impregnated judgment that constitutes the basic unit of thought, this protest at first seems to the point. "Just how," we must ask, "can Bradley condemn judgment as inadequate to its perceptual object if that object is understood to be integrally tied up with the act of judgment itself?" The answer, Bradley would claim, is to be found by examining just what it is that is truly present within the perceptual content of the judgment. And when we do this we realize that even as bound up with its perceptual base the judgment still fails to capture its intended object. But how can Bradley defend such a view?

Although there is a point to this objection, in the end it fails to have an effect, Bradley claims; and this is because, even while insisting that perceptual experience is a constitutive element in judgment, there still exists a level of internal generality within perception such that perception too fails to uniquely designate its intended object. In the end, the abstractness of the judged content is—although capable of varying degrees of concretion—still subject to the same damning criticism made of the isolated sentence. Even granting that the judgment immersed in perception is more than merely general and partially capable of designating its object (through its internal and systematic coherence), the principle complaint, Bradley believes, still holds.

The heart of Bradley's claim here is that no matter how much you include within the conceptual-perceptual experience that is judgment, there will always be a remaining distance between what you have managed to "get inside" the judgment and what you mean. What you mean is something absolutely individual and unique. But what even the perceptually impregnated judgment does not capture is this uniqueness. The perceptual content of every judgment necessarily involves a splitting apart of the "what" from the "that" such that the sense of experienced uniqueness from which the judgment begins (and to which it attaches itself) can never be said to be contained *within* the perceptual content. Thus, for Bradley, if while (a) reading the headlines on today's paper (which expresses a major historical event); and (b) having full awareness of my physical location, as well as the precise hour and minute; and (c) possessing in conjunction with this a rich and diverse visual and auditory input, I then bite into an orange and assert "This orange is bitter," I have still—even allowing for this perceptual content within the judgment—not tied down this experience to a unique point in space and time. It is not impossible, Bradley claims, that this precise cognitive-perceptual experience could be duplicated at another time or in another place. And, even on the assumption that this judgment has not yet been duplicated elsewhere in the past, we are still confronted by an open-ended future.

> Even if you could predicate the whole present content [we read], yet still you would fail unless you asserted also both the past and the future. You cannot assume (or I, at least, do not know your right to assume) that the present exists indepen-dent of the past, and that, taking up one fragment of the whole extension, you may treat this part as self-subsistent, as something that owes nothing to its connection with the rest. If your judgment is to be true as well as categorical, you must get the conditions entirely within it. And here the conditions are the whole extent of spaces and times which are required to make the given complete. The difficulty is insuperable. It is not merely that our understandings are limited, that we do not know the whole of the series, and that our powers are inadequate to apprehend so large an object. No possible mind could represent to itself the completed series of space and time; since, for that to happen, the infinite process must have come to an end, and be realized in a finite result. And this can not be. It is not merely inconceivable psychologically; it is metaphysically impossible.[24]

Bradley is, of course, the first to admit that *practically* we should not have the difficulty of confusing this judgment with another; or even that it would occur at another time or place in the history of the universe. His claim is the logical and metaphysical one that there is no way that we could guarantee that it couldn't. He is also convinced that every actual fact we attempt to describe in judgment (and whose actual description would constitute the categorical judgment as traditionally understood) is truly a fact—that is, an individual state of affairs—solely upon the basis of its relations to everything that has, does, or will exist. Although I shall state the matter in a way that will require some qualification, we might say that it is the *totality* of a fact's relations that constitute its uniqueness;[25] and this totality can never, in principle, be brought into the finite judgment. And, even though Bradley says that this uniqueness is summed up in the immediately experienced (felt) object, he is adamant in his claim that this uniqueness does not fully manifest itself within the perceptual content of the judgment that accompanies the larger experi-ence.[26] In order to make this felt union of the "what" and "that" fully transparent to consciousness we would have to assume a (literal)

"God's-eye point of view"—a view of eternity, so to speak. Only thus could we explicitly realize the actual individual and thus wholly categorical nature of our object. And, no matter how far we go, as long as we are discussing *a* judgment that is made by *a* finite knower, the difficulty is insuperable. To be a finite knower itself entails a beyond that is not explicitly contained within any individual act of knowledge such a being could possess. And thus, for a judgment to be *a* judgment entails that it refer beyond itself to something that is not (and could not be) wholly contained within it. While we often believe that we have said— or at least, explicitly thought—what we mean, this occurs only because we have failed to differentiate between that which constitutes the judgment as explicitly apprehended and our implicit meaning. For Bradley, though, the two must be distinguished.

The difficulty in understanding Bradley here can, I think, be put as follows. On the one hand, we are told that there always exists within our experience a point of direct contact with the real; there is always present a felt unity of existence and content that provides the experiential foundation upon which all else is built. But, on the other hand, we are also informed that this experienced unity of content and existence can never be fully apprehended in explicit thought; indeed, that perfect unity is, for Bradley, not even found in perception per se. The "this"— our sense of a perfectly united "what" and "that"—exists for Bradley neither within explicit assertion nor our conscious concept-laden perceptions. The "this," our experiential sense of the "eternal object," resides, Bradley believes (post 1883, anyway), within the furthest reaches of what he calls "feeling." And though it manifests itself partially within both the intellectual and sensuous sides of our being, its appearance in either sense or thought is never complete.

Although Bradley certainly does acknowledge (indeed, insists) that some degree of individuality and uniqueness *is* carried over into the judgment, it is never, he believes, enough; it is never that complete individuality of our object as it exists, either within our larger felt experience or in a reality that might transcend it.[27] Our experience of *that* individuality—although it partially appears within the perceptually immediate object—ultimately resides within the felt totality of experience that constitutes the backdrop and condition of our judgment. And Bradley's claim here is that there exists no reasonable interpretation of either *a* judgment or *a* perception that would allow us to include this backdrop within the limited judgment or perception itself. But to say this is not enough. It must be admitted, I think, that this aspect of Bradley's doctrine poses as many questions as it answers. And until we achieve some clarification on these points some crucial aspects of Bradley's theory of knowledge will evade us. Hence, it is to the more detailed consideration of these issues that we now proceed.

THE PROBLEM RESTATED

We might recall from our discussion in the opening chapters that, for Bradley, there are two fundamental difficulties to be overcome in any theory of knowledge. First, there is what (for lack of a better phrase) we might call the "problem of distance" between subject and object; and second, there is the question regarding the relations which exist between experienced objects. Bradley believes that on any coherent account of knowledge there must be given an explication of the relation between the knowing mind and its object such that what the mind cognitively apprehends *is* the object itself—even if in only fragmentary form. And, in addition, for any account of reasoning to be intelligible, some sort of interconnection between the objects known must be theoretically provided for. If the first condition is not met, then we are left with a merely representational conception of knowledge in which thought and reality are wholly estranged (and which is subject to complete sceptical deconstruction); and if the second cannot be realized then there exists no rational basis for (nontautological) inference in our philosophy. But Bradley believes that should perceptual designation be accepted as an adequate means by which to establish uniqueness of reference in judgment, two results, neither of which he can allow, would follow. These are (*a*) thought becomes wholly external to its object with its principal activity consisting in an abstracting function superimposed on given individual facts; and (*b*) inferential development is based either upon the unpacking of "nominal essences," or the putting forth of tenuous empirical hypotheses that rest upon the unjustifiable (on its own terms) assumption that "the future will resemble the past."[28]

To consider the latter first: Bradley is convinced that if the universe consists in independently existing, unique facts, then there can exist no justifiable basis for the ideal development of these facts in judgment and inference. If the given objects of perception are independent and self-sufficient particulars, then we are committed to hold that many (if not all) of their relations to other such entities are both external and essentially indifferent to their determination as objects of knowledge. But with this move we have, Bradley believes, radically subjectivized the process of inference.

We must always remember that if the given facts are capable of being perceived in their independent particularity, then whatever *con-*

nections we understand as existing amongst them must be seen as merely "mental" and entirely "subjective" superadditions. And whenever our assertions go beyond the bare, perceptually given, facts we are forced to admit the merely subjective nature of our inferential constructs. (And, of course, any assumptions regarding the future behavior of the universe goes well beyond the given facts.) This would be the case, it is argued, because, to declare such facts to be wholly independent of one another is to internalize their determinate nature; it is to say that any individuality or uniqueness they might possess is non-relational and completely self-contained.[29] But by making uniqueness completely internal to the individually given objects, and by holding that they possess this uniqueness and determinate individuality in a manner that is indifferent to other such objects, we are forcing ourselves into the admission that there is nothing in the *objects themselves* that would justify inferring something about one upon the basis of another. We are, to state the problem otherwise, denying the existence of *universals*, the only entities that can provide a rational ground for movement within thought.[30]

And, regarding the question of thought's externality to its object, we might say the following: If it is true that the object as given in perception is wholly unique and individual then thought must be understood as playing no part in this uniqueness. Thought thus becomes an absolutely external Other that—because of its necessarily abstract character—can only produce inadequate copies of the given object.[31] On this view thought becomes (at best) a pragmatic tool that allows us to either state collectively large numbers of individually given facts that have already appeared, or to form "nominal definitions."[32] If uniqueness and individuality are already in the facts as they first appear to perception, in no way can *thought* bring us closer to their precise determination—their truth.[33]

For Bradley, then, any doctrine that proclaims the givenness of the completely determinate fact must end in a dualistic and self-refuting scepticism. And he believes that if one is to provide a justifiable account of judgment and inference, the absolute independence and self-sufficient individuality of any experienced entity must be rejected. Judgment and inference can only be logically justified, Bradley is convinced, if there exists some *intrinsic bond* between—not only the knowing subject and its object—but also between what we infer and the ground out of which this process develops.[34] And any theory that allows either thought or perception to explicitly possess a wholly unique and self-subsistent fact has, he insists, cut this bond and thus finds itself in a cul-de-sac from which there is no exit. But let us now take our bearings and consider what lay ahead. With our examination of Bradley's attack on the individual judgment what is, perhaps, the most significant phase in our explication of his theory of knowledge is now complete. And the next step in our journey must be to consider in detail how these pretenders to categorical truth (individual judgments) relate to the more openly hypothetical forms of assertion. For a tolerably complete grasp of Bradley's position we must come to better understand why the individual judgment, exposed as abstract and conditional, must take its place on a scale of truth somewhere *below* the explicitly hypothetical and disjunctive forms.

But, while a consideration of these higher judgment forms is essential, there remains in our path an obstacle that must first be cleared away. This difficulty (and it is no small one) we described at the close of the previous section as the problem that surrounds our apprehension of uniqueness and individuality; or, it may be otherwise stated, it is the difficulty we encounter when we attempt to account for the *criterion* of truth by which the shortcomings of the individual judgment can become known. On the one hand, Bradley claims that no judgment can express the unique and individual character of its referent. However, on the other hand, the recognition of any judgment as inadequate to its object presupposes that we are in possession of a standard by which this failure to measure up can be experienced. Thus, not only must we come to some understanding of the scale of judgments (which Bradley believes constitutes a hierarchy of adequacy for judgments as truth-bearers), we must answer the question "Just what is this standard or criterion of truth, and in what sense do we posses it?'

THE IDEALITY OF PERCEPTION

I must say straight away that our answer to these questions is here only provisional. The fuller consideration of these problems must await the discussion of later chapters. Still, we must at this point provide at least a limited understanding of the difficulty. And to this end we must first realize why it is that neither mere sense nor the more elevated perception can provide, for Bradley, the measure by which our assertions are understood as defective.[35]

While the discussion as found in the *Principles of Logic* sometimes emphasizes what we may call the experiential (as opposed to the intellectual) aspect of the criterion of knowledge, Bradley makes it very clear—at least in his later works—that when describing our ultimate standard of truth in that text he is *not* discussing perception.[36] While he never gives up the claim that perceptual experience implicitly con-

veys a sense of uniqueness, Bradley leaves no doubt that he sees perception per se as both universal and ideal, and thus not itself the true
source of our sense of the unique subject to which our predicates
attach in judgment. Already in the first-edition *Principles of Logic* we
find Bradley saying that

> No perception ever . . . has a character contained within itself.
> In order to be fact at all, each presentation must exhibit ideal-
> ity, or in other words transcendence of self; and that which
> appears at any one moment, is, as such, self-contradictory.[37]

Postponing for the moment any consideration of how perception
involves contradiction, let me reiterate that, for Bradley, *no* perception
can be self-contained and individual (which is to say unique). Thus,
whatever experience we have that provides us with our sense of the
unique, this experience should not be seen as falling within the domain
of the perceptual—at least not fully. Now, what does provide us with
any sense of uniqueness and individuality Bradley ultimately describes
as resting in the "feeling base" of experience (the explicit topic of chapters 8 and 9). However, the topic of feeling is a complex and controversial one, and we must approach it slowly, only after having cleared up
several possible sources of confusion. For now we need only realize that
all judgment is understood as working upon an immediate experience
that somehow informs us that—at some level—it contains a perfect
unity of content and existence. This felt experience possesses, Bradley
believes, not only a diversity of content but also a vague sense of completeness or wholeness in that there is not yet a rupture between "what
it is" and "that it is." And there is something about this fundamental
ground of experience that, for Bradley, always remains perfectly concrete. But perception per se, we must realize, is not the same as this
larger experience. Perception, we shall soon learn, is really sensuous
immediacy as it has been worked over by the assertive consciousness.
And, as such, it is, we may say, "cognitive" throughout. In the *Principles of Logic* we read that

> As soon as you have made assertions about what it [feeling as
> it manifests itself in the 'this'] contains, as soon as you have
> begun to treat its content as content, you have transcended its
> felt unity. For consider a 'here' or 'now', and observe any-
> thing of what is in it, and you have instantly acquired an ideal
> synthesis. . . . You have a relation which, however impure, is
> at once set free from time. You have gained a universal
> which, so far as it goes, is true always, and not merely at the
> present moment; and this universal is forthwith used to qual-
> ify reality beyond that moment.[38]

We might say, then, that the perceptual object, as it is identified in judgment, finds itself part of a nexus of significance; it now *means* something in that it has a reference beyond itself—a reference that claims that its full reality cannot be experienced solely through its immediate apprehension in the disappearing "now." This side of perception we may call, then, its "mediate" aspect; and without it perceptions must remain meaningless and incoherent.

What I would emphasize at this point, though, is the following: If the given data of sense were not worked over by judgment, then we would have no perceptions. Such sensuous data Bradley identifies by a number of names: "sensuous immediacy," "mere feeling," and the "merely felt" are the most common. But perception, we should understand, must be differentiated from any sort of given sensuous immediacy. And this is because, what is merely immediate in sense is for Bradley the *most* problematic form of experience we possess and far below the level of cognitive perception. What some may find surprising, though, is that sensuous immediacy—in being merely immediate—is the most defective experience we have because the most *ideal*. And, though this comment might strike some as strange (since we have said that to be ideal is to be falsifiable), Bradley's position is not hard to follow.

We should realize here that, since the contents of mere sense are continuously disappearing, they provide extremely distorted experiential contents. Sheer immediacy often suggests that an object "is" and that an instant later it "is not" (or at least that its nature is radically different). By forever disappearing within the ever-changing "thatness" the existence-content complex as found in sheer immediacy provides us with an experience that distorts the pervasive nature of its universal "whatness."[39] In other words, sensuous immediacy might be said to possess the opposite defect from that which we find in explicit cognition. There, in conscious assertion, we have contents that are, to some degree, "existenceless" and thus they "refer beyond themselves." In sheer immediacy, however, though our content is intimately wed to its existence, it is, nevertheless, a content that is artificially cut off from its full and actual comprehension ("whatness"). Since sensuous immediacy is limited to the disappearing "here" and "now," it cannot provide the completer sense of a universal quality that, extending beyond the present, permeates and conditions other "thats."[40] Sensuous immediacy, in other words—at least as *we* are forced to experience it—distorts the true character of universals.

Of course, Bradley must allow for an experience that recognizes this defect in sensuous immediacy (and any subsequent perception or cognition). And this experience he came to call "feeling." As we shall later

consider in some detail, in our most primitive experience it is the conflict between sensuous immediacy and our fuller feeling that motivates
us to judge. And, though our judgments are certainly "*ideal*" when compared to the fullest feeling base of experience, and though too they
always fall far short of perfect concreteness, the judging consciousness,
is in fact, an advance over our merely sensuous experience. Despite its
(judgment's) containing a falling apart of content and existence of all it
apprehends, we must say that it is still much *more* concrete than mere
sensuous experience. Hence the judgment, while it poses certain problems at one level of our lives, is itself a solution to the universality and
abstractness of mere sense.

Hence we may summarize here by saying that the imposition of the
act of selective abstraction (judgment) in which the unified "what" and
"that" of the object to some extent fall apart is hardly one that merely
denigrates a more immediate, and on some theories more "accurate,"
form of experience. We must say that judgment, while it might appear
to introduce a distortion into the experienced object by rupturing its
"what-that" unity, in fact constitutes a profound advance in our merely
sensuous apprehension of reality.[41] Even though Bradley sometimes
refers to the act of predication as the "provisional estrangement" of content and existence, we must always be aware that the ideally recon-
structed experience of judgment is immensely more concrete (and thus
real) than that from which it begins.[42] To be sure, what we apprehend in
judgment is defective (because limited). However, the defects found
within conscious assertion pale when compared to mere unmediated
sense experience.[43] Imprisoned in the disappearing "here" and "now"
this mere sensuous feeling constitutes that which judgment must first
overcome in realizing its goal. And the truth of what is immediately
experienced in sense is, we might say, only to be found through the
assistance of conscious assertion.[44]

THE SYSTEMATIC UNIVERSAL

The inability of perception to provide us with a complete sense of the
unique and individual constitutes an important element in Bradley's
theory of knowledge. And the reasons for this should become clearer
when we consider Bradley's understanding of universals and particulars.
But we may approach his thought on this topic only if we bear in mind
several points that we have already discussed. These are: (i) universals
are essentially identities; however, (ii) all identities are identities-in-dif-
ference; and (iii) the act of judgment itself is nothing other than the cognitive apprehension of an identity-in-difference.

Now, as we have said repeatedly, the content in any judgment involves a partial falling apart of itself and its existence, and thus it exhibits what Bradley calls "ideality." But, even though the content of every judgment must involve the rupture of the "what" from the "that," we must never forget that, on Bradley's analysis, the abstract and ideal character of any judgment (which reflects this split) is always a matter of *degree*; and that every judgment is, to some extent, capable of exhibiting a content that overcomes its inherent abstractness and generality by showing itself as participating within the one nexus of objects and events which is reality. That is, by *contextualizing* themselves all asserted contents begin to overcome their proclivity to be merely general notions. While we are forced to say that no judgment can fully duplicate the sense of the unified content and existence that immediate experience conveys, each judgment is, according to Bradley, *more or less* adequate to its actual object.

This notion can be better grasped, I think, if we consider more closely the nature of the true universal as understood by Bradley and as developed thus far in our discussion. A true universal is not for Bradley (we should recall from chapter 3) a self-same and empty identity. It is not derived through the process of eliminative abstraction; and thus it is not a mere quality that somehow subsists in isolation from concrete instantiation. A true universal, Bradley tells us, is nothing other than a determinate *system*. It is a unified and integrated complex of terms—an "identity-in-difference." A true universal—as a system—is, then, a *whole* within which every partial aspect makes a difference to the being of every other aspect. And such a universal is, Bradley insists, always (relatively) *concrete* in that it exhibits this sensitivity of part to whole (and vice versa). Indeed, it is just this systematic interpenetration of parts and whole that, we are told, constitutes both the notion of "concreteness" and that of "system." However, we must also understand that any whole—any system—would be *entirely* concrete and exhibit no trace of generality or abstractness only if it were a *complete* system. This point is crucial in any understanding of Bradley's theory, and we shall consider it in further detail in a moment. However, to better appreciate this claim let us first say something about the particular and how, for Bradley, it relates to universals-*qua*-systems.

Not only does Bradley believe that we often misconstrue the actual nature of the universal by viewing it as a merely abstract quality or type, but equally distorted is the particular as it appears in many philosophical theories. The true particular—the "concrete particular"—is merely an *aspect* or *element* of a concrete universal (an integrated system); but it is an aspect that reflects its membership within this system, and that thereby exhibits the nature of the whole in its particularity. Being conditioned by its place within the whole, it too is concrete and may exhibit internal diversity or function, we may say, as a "system within a system." Indeed, for Bradley, universal and particular—properly understood—are terms we use to portray the relations that exist between systems that are hierarchically nested. When one systematic identity (which is an identity-in-difference) is internal to another it functions as a particular; and that system that is the more comprehensive (and within which this subsystemic particular exists) functions as the universal. Indeed, we may say of any system (concrete universal) that if it functions as an element within a broader, more-encompassing system, then it can be construed as a concrete particular. And the only system that could not assume the role of the concrete particular, then, would be *the* system—the universe-as-a-whole. Thus, we must on the Bradleian analysis understand "particular" and "universal" as entirely relative terms.[45]

There is, however, an important aspect about any system that must be immediately noticed. As we have remarked above, *all systems are defective* insofar as they (*a*) are less than all-inclusive; and (*b*) exhibit indifference amongst their internal elements.[46] These factors (which when described positively Bradley calls "comprehensiveness" and "coherence") will be considered in detail in the next chapter. For now we need merely understand that the sort of systematic apprehension that, for Bradley, constitutes the judgment will always be limited because it is disrupted by a reference to a larger reality that is external to it and that it cannot include.[47] We must not forget that since every judgment consists in an act of selective abstraction it must ignore (presuppose) a great deal of context. And, since judgment must both select and focus on "this" (and not "that"), it must always have external to it conditions upon which it ultimately depends for its meaning and to which it implicitly refers. Thus, what we select out of the mass of immediate experience is a systematically organized perceptual-conceptual content that is "ragged" at its edges. It is ragged because its content suggests its presence elsewhere; it indicates, without explicitly showing, a further "that" in which it seeks rest, but which, in principle, it can never fully realize.[48] And, since any experience of a limited system (judgment) must contain a rupture between its "what" and "that," we are forced to acknowledge that—not only does it point beyond itself to a larger context in which its content might find its fuller instantiation, but—internally this same content exhibits a degree of *generality* or *abstractness*. Because of this internal looseness that exists between content and existence in every judgment (even when understood as an integrated system), the judgment takes on the characteristics of a *sort* or a *kind*.[49] That is, so far as our judgment fails to include its complete contextual conditions, it functions as an empty, abstract universal. Thus in being less than all-inclusive and less than unique, the systematic content of any judgment—although it is partially concrete—betrays its general character; a character that is capable of being duplicated elsewhere and that necessarily falls short of the ideal of complete determination—perfect individuality and uniqueness.

Chapter 6

CONTRADICTION AND THOUGHT

WE have now learned that every judgment is an act of systematic apprehension. Indeed, on Bradley's view the judgment just consists in our conscious grasp of an integrated unity of perceptual-conceptual elements selected out of our larger felt experience. But we have also learned that every judgment is, to some degree, defective. Any act of systematic apprehension (judgment)—since it is ideal—continually "overreaches" itself. And this overreaching, we have seen, consists in the judgment's unstated reference to the greater context within which it is made and upon which it is parasitic. But the fact that all judgment depends for its fuller specificity and meaning upon conditions that lay beyond its boundaries demands that we look more closely at the effects this has on its *internal* elements. Specifically, we must now consider how Bradley sees the internal elements of every assertion as—to some degree—standing in bare conjunction and exhibiting contradiction. And after we have examined Bradley's notions of contradiction and contrariety we shall go on to consider their role in what is one of the most frequently discussed aspects of his philosophy—"relational thought." As we shall soon discover, in being relational, thought is plagued by an irremedial defect. And once more we shall find that—while thought may progressively realize its end—full satisfaction is something that is forever beyond its grasp.

CONTRADICTION

We might begin here by considering the judgment "John is honest." Considered solely as a grammatical proposition, the truth of this judgment would depend on which John I mean and precisely what sorts of behavior count as honest. And, as we have seen, though the perceptual content of this (or any) judgment provides a higher degree of specificity than is expressed by the mere proposition (the grammatical form of the

97

judgment), we should recall that the internal content of any judgment
still cannot uniquely determine its referent. The various conditions that
go to make the "John" whom I intend a unique individual are never
fully present before my mind when I judge. And neither can it be that
any precise definition of "honesty" is fully and explicitly known at the
time I make such an assertion. What this means for Bradley, however, is
that the basis upon which I combine my special (or limited) subject
"John" with the special (or limited) predicate "is honest" is inadequate.[1]
Indeed, since so much of what would properly bring together "John"
and "honest" in my assertion is *missing*, the relation that exists between
these terms is, Bradley tells us, ultimately one that is "merely conjunctive." And, as we shall see, whenever predicates stand together in the
relation of mere conjunction (as all must ultimately do) we are left with
what Bradley calls "contradiction."[2] Thus we read:

> What is real must be self-contained and self-subsistent and
> not qualified from the outside. For an external qualification
> is a mere conjunction, and that, we have seen is for the intel-
> lect an attempt of diversities simply to identify themselves,
> and such an attempt is what we mean by self-contradiction.
> Hence, whatever is real must be qualified from itself, and that
> means that, so far as it is real, it must be self-contained and
> self-subsistent.[3]

Now, before I develop this notion of contradiction as conjunction
there are several assumptions here that I should first mention. We must
always bear in mind that, for Bradley, *reality cannot be contradictory*.[4]
Indeed, the difference between what is understood as ultimately real and
what is not (that is to say, "appearance") is most often stated by Bradley
in just these terms. The real, we are told, *is* real precisely because it contains no contradiction or inconsistency.[5] Its diverse aspects and differentiated elements are such as to always be both wholly intelligible and
completely necessary. Although we must postpone any discussion of
why Bradley believes that the real must possess these characteristics, our
examination of contradiction cannot get off the ground unless we are
aware that he believes the internal structure of reality to always possess
a "reason why" and a "because" that would—if we could apprehend
it—provide complete satisfaction to our fundamental need to know.

We might further notice that the act of predication is one that has
as its goal the making explicit of this necessary relation or "reason
why." When I judge that "John is honest" I want to show, either myself
or others, that within the real universe "John" and "honest" form a continuous tissue with one another. And so far as my judgment is *true*—
which is to say, so far as it provides any sort of intellectual satisfac-

tion—the necessary continuity between the larger universe of experience, "John," and "honesty" will be made self-evident.[6]

But we must also remember that Bradley believes all judgment to be only more or less adequate to its object. The grammatical proposition "John is honest" can not only refer to different "Johns" and differing sorts of "honesty', it can also contain differing degrees of internal detail and systematic coherence. Indeed, it is precisely this varying degree of internal systematicity that conveys to us the *relative* adequacy of the assertion. But—and this is the important point regarding contradiction—no matter how much internal systematicity is present, at some point my explicit apprehension of the precise adjustment to one another of the predicates "John" and "honest" (as well as their adjustment to the reality beyond the act) will come to an end. At some point the explicit notion of "John" that I envisage is at its limit; and the same can be said for my understanding of "honesty." While my grasp of who and what "John" is may intellectually mesh with my articulate notion of "honesty," there inevitably comes a point where my insight into the detailed interconnection between these notions stops. And at this point—should I fail to further adjust my terms to one another—the mechanism of "bare conjunction" (and thus contradiction) makes itself felt.

We might better understand Bradley here by considering the following metaphor. We might consider the limited subject and special predicate in judgment to be like gears in a machine. We might further imagine each to possess a set of teeth that fit into one another. And the more complex and matched the interface between the two gears the more adequate we can consider their connection to be. While an interface between smooth-surfaced wheels that relies solely upon friction might get the job done (under certain conditions, anyway), precisely machined and tightly matched gears would certainly be more effective (unless, of course, occasional slippage was a requirement of the mechanical system). However, we must always realize that even the most complex and tightly matched interface still consists in a relation between what are different gears—gears that are not of a piece. There remains, no matter how effective their actual fit, a certain gap between them that could (in principle) always be improved—that is, some refinement and deepening of their adjustment could always be effected.

Of course, this is just a metaphor and we must not be misled by it. The point, though, is this: no matter how adequate our conception of the relatedness of things is it can always be improved. It can always be improved because the factors that constitute the adjustment of subject to predicate in reality itself are (ultimately) infinite; and thus there is no end to the degree of adequacy that any relation of "fit" can have for us. But what does this tell us about contradiction? Although in a moment we shall have to differentiate between overt contradiction and the sort of implicit tension every judgment contains, the mechanism is, according to Bradley, ultimately the same. The normal progress of knowledge is such that we are always seeking a more refined sense of fit between subject and predicate in judgment. We are forever attempting to deepen our systematic insight into the continuity that exists between the larger universe, the limited subject and the special predicate.[7] But when the demands of our fuller experience are not met by explicit assertion we experience contradiction.

> Take any object [Bradley tells us] and you find that, as it is, that object does not satisfy your mind. You cannot think it as real while you leave it just as it comes. You are forced to go outside and beyond that first character, and to ask, What, Why, and How. You must hence take your first object as included with something else in a wider reality. There is thus a demand so far, we may say, for comprehension. On the other hand you want to know the object itself and *not* something else. Therefore, while going beyond the object, you must not leave it but must still follow it. If you merely conjoin it with something outside that is different and not itself, this in principle is contradiction.[8]

What I understand Bradley as saying here is that we are always dissatisfied with brute facts. We experience dissatisfaction whenever we fail to see the object of our awareness as immersed in the larger system of reality and as possessing precise (and necessary) relations to other objects. Of course, this dissatisfaction is always present to some degree. However, when we go on to overcome this (relative) isolation we must make sure that we contextualize or systematize our object in the appropriate way. The special subject of any assertion always possesses a precise and determinate content. Thus when I go on to attach a special predicate to the subject, it must be the *right* predicate. That is, the predicate must be a legitimate extension and elaboration of the variegated content that comprises the special subject.

For example, if I say "Susan Smith is knowledgeable" I must not just view Susan Smith as externally related to some merely abstract notion of "knowledge." Rather, I must see her as possessing a specific sort of knowledge—a knowledge that is the sort that *this* "Susan Smith" would possess. If "Susan Smith" is an accountant and I make this judgment bearing in mind her knowledge of accounting, the predicate "is knowledgeable" will possess a certain fit—it will function as a concrete extension of "Susan Smith"—and thus be experienced by me as (relatively) satisfactory. However should I find myself in the company of sub-atomic particle physicists discussing the behavior of quarks, the term "knowledgeable" takes on a somewhat different sense. In this context I might judge "Mary Jones [the physicist] is knowledgeable" and—though there will certainly exist elements of "is knowledgeable" that are the same in the two instances—the special predicate "is knowledgeable" must also exhibit specific differences that make it the sort of knowledge that particle physicists in general, and Mary Jones in particular, possess. And, while to attach to the special subjects "Susan Smith" and "Mary Jones" exactly the same special predicate concept would provide us with a certain degree of intellectual satisfaction, certainly more could be achieved by tailoring these special predicates to their subjects.

"But how," it may be asked, "can this be construed as contradiction? Surely," one might object, "there is a profound difference between asserting 'P is Q' and 'P is both Q and not-Q.' And Bradley has apparently told us nothing here. Throughout the history of logic 'contradiction' has meant the ascription of mutually exclusive or opposing predicates to the same subject. And it does not seem as though Bradley's doctrine has addressed this notion at all."

Although Bradley's answer will require further elaboration, I would at this point say that there is, for Bradley, ultimately no difference between "P is Q" and "P is both Q and not Q." If we are dissatisfied with the latter proposition we are dissatisfied precisely because its terms can *not* stand in anything more than conjunctive relation to the special subject. And so far as "P is Q" exhibits this externality between special subject and predicate it too will constitute for us a contradiction. Though it must always be a matter of degree, when we are making an ordinary assertion we are claiming that there exists a certain predicative relation between the explicit terms of the judgment. And this relation, we are told, is ultimately to be understood as the relation of identity-in-difference between special subject, special predicate, and the reality that is their condition. It is the presupposition of all assertion, Bradley tells us, that the special subject and predicate in judgment are both distinct and yet combined; and that it is reality itself that provides the ultimate ground of both this distinction and union.[9] Even though *we* may not be capable of fully apprehending this ground, within the real, it is always there. And it is there, we must assume, in a manner that is perfect and complete.[10] Thus, when we judge we are always seeking the ground or basis upon which diverse terms (or predicates) can be legitimately brought together—that is, we are seeking their *actual* identity (or, more accurately, identity-in-difference) as it exists in the noncontradictory whole.[11]

For Bradley, it is just the contrast that exists between our necessary presuppositions as to the nature of the real and our explicit judgment that forces thought onward. We think and rethink our object because there is a *failure* of fit between what we must believe reality to be like and what we have before us in conscious assertion. And the failure of fit to which I refer here comes about primarily because the terms within the assertion are undeveloped. That is, when special subject and special predicate are viewed in an excessively abstract and general fashion, not only are we liable to find these terms collapsing into bare conjunction, we are left with an assertion that is simultaneously true and not true. And this for Bradley is a case of contradiction.

But let us consider an example. If we take the judgment "Dynamite explodes when a match is put to it" we have an assertion that is, because undeveloped within the assertive consciousness, subject to falsification. And this can easily be seen if we consider that, while under normal conditions putting a match to freshly compounded dynamite will result in an explosion, should the dynamite be soaking wet, then certainly an explosion will not occur. Thus we find the failure to include conditions—that is, the failure to make fuller and more concrete our assertion—can leave us with a judgment such as "Dynamite both will explode and will not explode when a match is put to it." (Or alternatively "It is both true and false that 'Dynamite explodes when a match is put to it'.") And what we have illustrated here is just that, so far as we take our conditional assertions—assertions whose truth or falsity depends upon external factors—as categorically true, we shall fall into inconsistency and conflict. As Bradley tells us,

> The Law of Contradiction tells us that we must not *simply* identify the diverse, since their union involves a ground of distinction. So far as this ground is rightly or wrongly excluded, the Law forbids us to predicate diversities. Where the ground is merely not explicit or remains unknown, our assertion of any complex is provisional and contingent. It may be valid and good, but it is an incomplete appearance of the real, and its truth is relative. Yet, while it offers itself as but contingent truth and as more or less incomplete appearance, the Law of Contradiction has nothing against it. But abstracted and irrational conjunctions taken by themselves as reality and truth, in short "facts" as they are accepted by too many philosophers, the Law must condemn. And about the truth of this Law, so far as it applies, there is in my opinion no question. The question will be rather as to how the Law applies and how far therefore it is true.[12]

It is significant to note here that as long as our truth "offers itself as but contingent the Law of Contradiction has nothing against it." Bradley's point is, I believe, that there is a certain attitude that we may take toward any judgment that, if maintained, will prevent our assertion from becoming openly contradictory. This we may call the "conditional" or "provisional" attitude in judgment. We might understand it as that openness to the fact that our predicates *are* conditioned and that the "reason why" of their combination is never capable of coming wholly before us. And, so long as we are willing to continually augment and modify the interface between special subject and predicate through the inclusion of their conditions, we shall find ourselves progressively more satisfied that our judgment is accurately capturing the real. It is only when this continual supplementation and modification ceases—that is, it is only when we declare our judgment to be *unconditionally* true and refuse to look for its deeper conditions—that the relation between subject and predicate begin to betray themselves as "merely conjunctive." And it is just this insistence—the insistence that our truth is categorically true—that develops into an open clash of terms. If the significance that attaches to both special subject and predicate is held static, then ultimately we shall find our terms collapsing in a manner that exposes the absence of a ground or reason why they should be connected as they are.

But what can this "collapse" be? According to Bradley the discomfort that an overt contradiction brings is nothing other than the discomfort that results from holding together two ideas that do not have the requisite fit. (It would be like feeling the movement of two gears whose teeth were cut in different fashions.) And, although there can exist a difference in the extent to which terms do not accommodate one another, in the end, the mechanism is the same for the overt contradiction and the merely inadequate categorical assertion. With this in mind, then, let us go on to say that, while there is always a point at which our present apprehension of the ground of connection between terms fails, we need not fall into *overt* contradiction. If we are willing to ideally develop both special subject and limited predicate so that they become better fitted and more systematic, then we need not feel the jarring effect that a dogmatic categorical assertion would bring about.[13] However, the case is different when we put forth our truths as unconditioned. When we insist that the facts are just as we have them in our judgment we betray an unwillingness to supplement the conjunctive relation between our terms and to further refine their adjustment to one another. But this is just to ignore the demands of our larger experience, and, sooner or later, the conflict between felt wholeness and categorically asserted fact will force us to move forward by augmenting and extending our knowledge.

To further illustrate this let us consider the judgment "My painting is beautiful." For Bradley, the special subject is a term that always has a complex content. And, as we have previously learned, "My painting" can be understood as a phrase that systematically organizes a number of perceptual-conceptual experiences. Its meaning is one that can never be exhausted by a finite list of characteristics. It cannot be exhausted because as a significant idea in the judgment it is (at least for me) for-ever undergoing expansion and modification. "My painting" as a living idea is continually relating itself to other ideas and thus is always (for me) refining its significance. And in its development it is quite possible that it will be forced to deal with—that is, systematically incorporate—a number of different qualities and relations. Thus, as the meaning of "my painting" develops we might find that it is not only "beautiful" but also "expensive', "a good investment', "something I've wanted for a long time," and so on. However, it is also quite possible that one of the predicates that will experientially attach itself to "my painting" is "not-beautiful" (or "ugly"). But then an analysis of "my painting" will show, in addition to the other predicates, that "My painting is both beautiful and ugly" (or "It is both true and false that my painting is beautiful").

As the subject is ideally developed different predicates show them-selves as attaching to it. And (at least on the surface) some of these pred-icates may appear as wholly incompatible. "My painting is both beauti-ful and not beautiful (or ugly)" is an assertion that puts forth inconsistent predicates as belonging to the same subject. On most accounts, of course, we would be inclined to say that "My painting is *either* beautiful *or* it is not-beautiful." Certainly, it may be argued, "beautiful" and "ugly" are incompatible and thus only one or the other can be legitimately put forth as characterizing our subject. But, Bradley would respond, this is not nec-essarily true. Only if we treat this assertion as narrowly categorical—that is, only if we believe it to be unconditionally true in a manner that ignores its context—(and if we refuse to develop this supporting context), would it seem that one of these "incompatible" predicates must go. However, if we are sensitive to the conditioned nature of the judgment, and if we are willing to progressively incorporate these conditions into the explicit form it takes, then the most (apparently) antagonistic of terms can be brought together. While it is true that "My painting is beautiful and not-beautiful" leaves us uncomfortable, when it evolves into "My painting is beautiful by daylight and not-beautiful by incandescent light" we begin to realize not only a fuller and more concrete concept but also greater sat-isfaction. And, though the terms "beautiful" and "ugly" may not be capable of residing in, as Bradley puts in, the "same point," the refine-ment and expansion of each allows them to progressively overcome any repulsion to one another they might have seemed initially to possess.

CONTRARIETY

Now, we have already discovered what Bradley's views are on the categorical judgment. However, in order to follow him in his discussion of contradiction we must consider a further point. For Bradley, the distinction between contradictory and contrary must be rejected. And, if we bear in mind that any predicate can only be a predicate as it is used in an actual judgment, we can see why he insists on reducing all contradictories to contraries. Since, for Bradley, all judgment concerns itself with a *positive* content, there can be no such thing as "mere" or "bare" denial.[14] When we deny something in the judgment we always do so on the basis of an "excluding content" that is itself positive (even if unstated and unknown). "Not A" can only be "Not A" because it is something else instead. And, according to Bradley, any theory that denies this has failed to understand just what the judgment is. This view was espoused by Bradley from the beginning. First articulated in the *Principles of Logic*, we read that

> The contradictory idea, if we take it in a merely negative form, must be banished from logic. If Not-A were solely the negation of A, it would be an assertion without a quality, and would be a denial without anything positive to serve as its ground. A something that is only not something else, is a relation that terminates in an impalpable void, a reflection thrown upon empty space. It is a mere nonentity which can not be real. . . . It is impossible for anything to be *only* Not-A. It is impossible to realize Not-A in thought. It is less than nothing, for nothing itself is not wholly negative. Nothing at least is empty thought, and that means at least my thinking emptily. Nothing means nothing else but failure. And failure is impossible unless something fails; but Not-A would be impersonal failure itself.[15]

We must always bear in mind that, for Bradley, if we are to think at all we must judge; and to judge means to assert that a positive quality characterizes reality. Even the negative judgment which doesn't tell us *what* something else is in explicit terms, must effect its denial on the basis of a positive ground. All negation, he insists, (and thus all contradiction) excludes only upon a positive basis; and hence what is not-A must for Bradley, be B, or C or whatever.[16]

> What are 'opposites' [Bradley says] except the adjectives which the thing cannot so combine. . . . Hence we have said no more than that we in fact find predicates which in fact will not go together, and our further introduction of their 'opposite' nature seems to add nothing.[17]

"But," one might respond, "even if we concede to Bradley that the contradictory is really better understood as the contrary, surely there must exist contraries that necessarily exclude one another. Surely," it might be said, "we can not say of a subject that it is both 'organic' and 'inorganic,' 'living' and 'dead,' 'knowable' and 'unknowable.' And surely there are *some* qualities that cannot be combined." But to such an objection Bradley would say No. And, given our examination of paintings and dynamite, his response can be easily anticipated. While Bradley would be the first to admit that some combinations of terms are more compatible than others ("extended" and "heavy" as opposed to "opaque" and "transparent," for example), he insists that even what on first glance appears to be the most blatant incompatibility can, if we look deeply enough, be understood as capable of predicative union. For Bradley—and the importance of this cannot be overestimated—*there exists no such thing as intrinsically contradictory or contrary predicates.*[18] If our terms are truly logically significant ideas that occur in an actual judgment, then—assuming the proper ideal development of both special subject and special predicate—they are always capable of being combined. And, ultimately, all special subjects and predicates must be understood, not as contraries, but *differents.* Hence Bradley tells us that

> There are no native contraries, and we have found no reason to entertain such an idea. Things are contrary when, being diverse, they strive to be united in one point which in itself does not admit of internal diversity. And for the intellect any bare conjunction is an attempt of this sort.[19]

The notion of contrariety arises, Bradley tells us, whenever diverse qualities are united—or at least when an attempt is made to unite them—on an inadequate basis; that is, because we have not developed the point in which we attempt to unite them they clash or conflict. "Beautiful" and "ugly" are, for example, conditions that cannot occupy a "single point"; and if we fail to differentiate the point in which they are brought together—if we fail to develop the ground that accommodates one predicate to the other—then surely they will conflict. However, if we expand the basis upon which they exist as contraries (as we did with our consideration of the painting under differing light conditions), this conflict can be seen to diminish. Although originally problematic, when the point or basis for the union of each predicate is expanded (by refusing to treat it as categorical), then each predicate can find a place in a larger reality and thereby avoid the conflict with what would become its contrary on a less adequate and narrower view of its ground. Bradley tells us that

'Opposites will not unite, and their apparent union is mere appearance.' But, [he continues] the mere appearance really perhaps only lies in their intrinsic opposition. And if one arrangement has made them opposite, a wider arrangement may perhaps unmake their opposition, and may include them all at once and harmoniously. Are, in short, opposites really opposite at all, or are they, after all, merely different?[20]

Bearing this in mind let us consider more closely the difference between a blatantly contradictory assertion and a normal judgment. When I judge (for example) "This painting is both beautiful and not-beautiful (or ugly)" we have on the surface a glaring contradiction. "Not-beautiful" seems to be the direct denial of "beautiful" and thus we have asserted what are mutually exclusive predicates. But what about "Harry is dishonest"? Why should these predicates ("Harry" and "dishonest")— even if taken as categorically true—be more compatible and capable of greater predicative continuity than "beautiful" and "not-beautiful"?

Bradley's answer is that, in the end, the problem we find in "My painting is both beautiful and not-beautiful" is also present in "Harry is dishonest." In both cases it is the *absence of a ground* between the terms that we find objectionable. Indeed, if the notion of "Harry" that I possess is not of a certain sort, let's say that "Harry" is my newborn baby, it could quite easily be the case that "Harry is dishonest" would strike me as *more* problematic than "My painting is beautiful and not-beautiful." And what we must always remember here is that the grammatical proposition tell us very little about the nature of the predicates as actually asserted. Every predicate, we must not forget, is a living predicate; it is a term that has for us a complex intension and systematic content.[21] And wherever there is a lack of ground between terms—as there must always be for our understanding—there is at some level an experienced contradiction.

Of course, it is true that some terms, given the way they are ordinarily used, carry with them a proclivity to be easily combined. And it must be admitted that, given our usual usage, some terms are less likely to be found together. However, we must not forget that, as Bradley sees it, any term can be brought together with any other *if* their ground is sufficiently developed. And, to return to our earlier point, it is not so much an intrinsic repulsion between terms that provides us with our sense that something is wrong; rather, it is our treatment of an assertion as wholly categorical (i.e., true without qualification), and our refusal to develop the ground between its terms that invariably leads to that intellectual dissatisfaction we refer to as "contradiction."

We may summarize here by saying that, as it exists in reality, the predicate is always a different and not a contrary. However, the judgment is an act that attempts to make explicit and fully conscious the relations within our larger (felt) experience of the differentiated real. Through (a) the abstraction of the subject and predicate terms from given experience; and (b) the affirmation of these terms of reality, the judgment attempts to recombine in explicit form the implicit connection that is presupposed by our fuller (felt) experience. But herein lies the problem. Judgment "affirms in a single point" what it *feels* in a wider context. Based upon felt experience—an experience that consists in the collective judgments of prior thought, a wealth of inarticulate sensation, and more—there exists a vast network of relations: relations that are inexhaustible and that constitute the actual ground of connection between our terms within the judgment. When we qualify A by B what we mean is "A is B because reality is such as to effect their integrative identity (in difference) and mutual qualification of one by the other." However we never in any one judgment explicitly "think', "say," or "perceive" these conditions in any complete manner. Our subject and predicate are brought together on a basis which is at some level that of "mere conjunction." It is brought together on less than a wholly adequate basis because as finite subjects we must necessarily abstract from a larger experience. And in this act of selective abstraction much must be omitted.

> Standing contradictions [Bradley tells us] appear when the subject is narrowed artificially, and where diversity in the identity is taken as excluded. A thing cannot be at once in two places if in the 'at once' there is no lapse, nor can one place have two bodies at once if both claim it in their character as extended.[22]

Just as "My painting is beautiful and not-beautiful" was too narrow to include the lapse of time and the differences in lighting that our expanded version used to overcome the contradiction, so too does any unsatisfactory judgment construe its object too narrowly. And herein, according to Bradley, lay the great danger. When we treat the conditional assertion as categorical we are condemning ourselves (sooner or later) to experience the sort of intellectual dissatisfaction that the experience of mere conjunction provides. Thus, should we desire to avoid this conflict, we must always be sensitive to the hypothetical and conditional character of all our assertions, and engage in, so far as we are able, the progressive development of their terms.

Let us conclude our discussion of contradiction, then, by pointing out that the unconscious presupposition of every judgment is always that *there is no irrational connection*. Every real unity of subject and predicate has a "because" or a "reason why" according to Bradley.[23]

Having said this, though, we should also notice that this doctrine is both the solution of one problem and the source of another. On the one hand it explains how the apparently contradictory nature of a combination of terms can be understood as not really contradictory. Given Bradley's metaphysics the appearance of contradiction in our judgment merely shows that *we* have failed in our explicit assertion to adequately specify the conditions of the union of subject and predicate. In other words, we have failed to think through what we mean. However, the belief that it is the noncontradictory nature of reality that provides the resolution of conflict in our thought, also forces us to face what some might see as unpalatable consequences. If reality is perfectly coherent it is because there exists within reality an intelligible ground for the union of its diverse aspects.[24] But the assumption that ultimate reality is coherently unified throughout carries with it a rather harsh estimation of our cognitive powers. It carries with it the condemnation of all judgment as "defective" because, as has been repeatedly emphasized, we can never make good in our explicit judgment what we implicitly believe about reality. If in this presupposed background there exist qualifying conditions that can never be fully included in the judgment, then, so far as they remain external we are left with a "bare conjunction" between subject and predicate. And this, as we have seen, is, for Bradley, the essence of contradiction. But in order to fully explicate this notion we must consider the doctrine of "terms and relations" as developed by Bradley through the course of his career and it is to this that we shall now turn.

Terms and Relations

Bradley's theory of relations is a natural extension of his views on contradiction. It also constitutes one of the most extensively discussed (and misunderstood) aspects of his philosophy. And, while there are many different approaches to Bradley's understanding of relations, we must restrict ourselves here. Our primary concern must be to understand how the rigidly defined term that exists in external relation to other such terms ultimately leads to an infinite regress and what Bradley calls "self-contradiction."

In the third chapter of *Appearance and Reality* Bradley provides in miniature what is to be the dominant theme of the rest of the work—the self-contradictory and unreal nature of anything that presents itself to us in the guise of "qualities" (or "terms") and "relations."[25] However, it must be remembered that Bradley understands there to be two kinds of relations—internal and external. The former is the relation in which our terms are somehow adjusted to one another such that a change in one entails a change in all; the latter is the relation in which our terms are indifferent to one another. And, while recent commentators have emphasized that Bradley condemned both external and internal relations as ultimately incoherent, we shall soon discover that internal relations are seen as defective because—try as they may—they cannot escape an externality of content. The internal relation—which is really a relation in the process of overcoming its relational nature—is condemned by Bradley—only so far as it is infected by externality. However, before considering how an internal relation can be (indeed, necessarily is) so infected, let us be clear about what we are referring to when we use this language.

I would begin by saying that whenever Bradley speaks of "terms" (or "qualities") and "relations" he is speaking of our intellectual apprehension of reality. That is, he is discussing how we must *construe* reality rather than how reality actually exists in its completed form. And since the mechanism of terms and relations is an intellectual mechanism, we must see it as belonging to the structure of judgment. Now we should also take care not to see our terms in judgment as (*a*) the ultimate subject (reality-as-a-whole); and (*b*) the predicate-*qua*-proposition. Since reality-as-a-whole (the ultimate subject) is never fully before us in judgment, it cannot really function as a "term" in Bradley's sense. Thus what functions as terms in the discussion below are the *special* subject and the *special* predicate. And, keeping this in mind, let us listen to Bradley's own words on the subject of "externality" between terms. In his essay entitled "Relations" he writes:[26]

> What should we mean (I will ask first) by a relation asserted as simply and barely external? We have here, I presume, to abstract so as to take terms and relations, all and each, as something which in and by itself is real independently. And we must, if so, assume that their coming or being together in fact, and somehow actually in one, is due in no way to the particular characters of either the relation or the terms. From neither side will there be anything like a contribution to, or an entrance into, the other side—or again to, or into, that union of both which we experience as a relational fact. Undeniably the fact is somehow there, but in itself it remains irrational as admitting no question as to its 'how' or 'why'—or if you insist on a reason, that would have to be sought neither in the terms nor the relation, but in a third element once more independently real and neither affecting, nor again affected by, either the relation or terms. This, I suppose, is the way in which relations have to be understood, if you take them as external merely and as ultimately and absolutely real.[27]

Simply put, the viewpoint of external relations is one that appre-hends things as existing in a manner that is essentially independent of and indifferent to other things and the relations that (purportedly) relate these things. If one term in an external relation undergoes change, there just is no reason, on this view, for the other term (or terms) to change. Since the terms are self-sufficient unto themselves any alteration of a term's character would effect a change only for that term. Hence, *inde-pendence* and *self-enclosedness* characterize the term that stands in external relation to all others.

As for the "relation" aspect of the external relation, we must say the following. Although there admittedly is a relation that is understood as existing between terms, it is very difficult, Bradley tells us, to say what it could be. We seem to be forced either to claim that the relation is a "third thing" or that it is nothing. (We shall consider this in more detail in a moment.) However, neither account is satisfactory. But before we consider exactly why Bradley believes this to be the case we should remind ourselves that—since we are talking about a structural charac-teristic of all assertive experience—we just don't have any choice whether or not to employ the mechanism of qualities (or terms) and rela-tions. And, while there are certainly grades of relational thought—the more internal the relations are, the higher the thinking—the relational form is inescapable.

> You can never, we may argue, find qualities [or terms] with-out relations. Whenever you take them so, they are made so, and continue so, by an operation which itself implies relation. Their plurality gets for us all its meaning through relations; and to suppose it otherwise in reality is wholly indefensible.[28]

To think, Bradley tells us, is to distinguish and to unite.[29] But to dis-tinguish is to apprehend a term *as* a term and to unite is to place that term in a relation to another term. However, even though we must think according to the relational form, this basic structure of all thought is *ultimately* incoherent; that is, we can never think out in a fully satisfac-tory way anything that is construed in this manner.

Although to think at all is to think within the mechanism of terms and relations, a presupposition or condition of this thinking is the belief that reality itself is *not* relational. And this belief is forced on us contin-uously by the feeling-base that supports relational thought. It (the feel-ing base) is that experiential whole out of which all terms arise and against which their adequacy is judged. But given that feeling carries with it the conviction that there is no indifferent or external relation between things—given that feeling forces us to assume that reality is a seamless and non-relational whole—we are driven to think and rethink, to modify and remodify, our vision of the world in an unending fashion. According to Bradley, this just is the human condition, and from it there is no escape. Hence we read:

> But any such irrationality and externality [as the relational form] cannot be the last truth about things. Somewhere there must be a reason why this and that appear together. And this reason and reality must reside in the whole from which terms and relation are abstractions, a whole in which their internal connection must lie, and out of which from the background appear those fresh results which never could have come from the premises. The merely external is, in short, our ignorance set up as reality.[30]

Yet, we are told that,

> While the diversities [that we apprehend] are external to each other and to their union, ultimate satisfaction is impossible. There must, as we have seen, be an identity and in that identity a ground of distinction and connexion. But that ground, if external to the elements into which the conjunction must be analysed, becomes for the intellect a fresh element, and it itself calls for synthesis in a fresh point of unity. But hereon, because in the intellect no intrinsic connexions were found, ensues the infinite process.[31]

I would add, however, that the news is not all bad.[32] While we are condemned to walk an infinite path in our journey to the Absolute (the object of every judgment) real progress can be—and is—achieved according to Bradley. Knowledge *is* capable of elevating itself to a higher ground and of becoming truer, more real, and more satisfying. But how can this be? We have, it should be noted, already provided a partial answer to this question. We have said that so far as thought can become "systematic" it is capable of overcoming contradiction and inconsistency. And what we shall now attempt to do is further refine this understanding by showing how the various forms of relational thought represent varying degrees of systematic insight and internal coherency.

The lowest form of relational thinking, and thus the least systematic, would be that which moved entirely in an external manner. Thought that (*per impossibile*) moved entirely according to externally related terms would be, for Bradley, the antithesis of systematic (i.e., true) thinking. Hence, when we speak of the relational form as involving relations that are "merely external," we should realize that we are talking about a sort of thought that is only a theoretical construct. It represents, if you will, the lower limit of thinking and its rigid and mechanical movement can hardly be seen as actual. Nevertheless, the general problem of the relational form may be put as follows: When we think we identify (and isolate) areas of experience through the medium of language. In "This bird is yellow" we identify two terms that stand in the predicative relation. However, so far as the terms "bird" and "yellow" are apprehended as independent and self-sufficient, the relation of predication remains puzzling. We sense, largely through the assistance of the feeling base, that these terms *are* somehow rationally connected; but when we try to think this relation through we are confronted with the following difficulties. A wholly independent "bird" or "yellowness" (that is a "bird" or "yellow" that were completely external) would not allow the relation (initially at least) to penetrate—that is, to actually relate them. But then either the relation is nothing—in which case it can't relate—or we must view it as a "third thing." Rejecting the understanding of the relation as nothing, let us consider how viewing it as a third (or somehow objectified) entity might help us in our effort to understand what the external relation is.

Any relation in order to be a relation must be, it would seem, a "something"; that is, it must, in some sense "exist" between the terms. (As suggested above, if the relation is nothing then surely it can't relate because it doesn't exist.) But if it is a "something" that manages to relate its terms, and if it is different from the terms it relates, then the question arises as to how this different something itself "connects" or "relates" to the terms? Of course, we could go on and postulate a *new* pair of relations that relate the relation to the terms, but this results in an endless series of "relations" that, having become external and objectified, are still in need of a relation to relate them to the new relations and eventually to the original terms. Thus, if we view our terms and relations as wholly external we are forced, when we try to give an account of them, into an infinite fission. And these relation, now like terms themselves, are in need of relations to connect them on one end to the original term, and on the other to the original relation (now itself objectified into a relation).[33]

We may restate the situation as follows: When the original relation has been construed as a thing it is sensed that the relation R does not relate our original terms in a satisfactory manner. The relational whole has been turned into a *triad* of terms (in relation) that can be expressed as either:

$$R^1$$
$$T^1 \quad T^2$$

or, since R has now become objectified, as:

$$T^3$$
$$T^1 \quad T^2$$

However, this set of terms requires in turn a *new* set of relations (R^2 and R^3)

$$T^3$$
$$R^2 \quad R^3$$
$$T^1 \qquad T^2$$

in order to relate to the original terms (T^1 and T^2) our old relation (R^1), which has now become a term (T^3).

But, as should be obvious, the problem remains. When the original relation R is objectified—that is, when it is made into a discrete entity that attempts to reunite T^1 and T^2 in a satisfactory manner—there still exists a gap. Terms T^1 and T^2, which are related by a now explicit R^1 (or if you prefer to call it T^3 in order to illustrate its now conceptually concrete and termlike nature), are still terms that stand in an indifferent and merely external relation to one another. In other words, the effort to explicitly understand how our relations relate our terms has been—so far as the relations are merely external—a complete failure; and in attempting to remedy this failure by postulating more relations (now having become objectified) to relate the relations that relate the terms we merely make it a more complex failure. In short, although we might say (or think) more in terms of the *number* of concepts (terms) that we bring into consciousness, these concepts—by staying at the most rudimentary and unsystematic level—fail to do any real work. It is as though thought and speech consisted in an endless babble that gets no closer to its original intention than if it had never spoken.

While not much of an improvement, there is another strategy by which we might attempt to save the wholly external relation. This account anticipates the theory of internal relations by theorizing an act of *penetration* by the relation into the term itself. If I insist that the relation between terms must somehow relate by reaching *into* them, then we find one of two things occurring. Either our terms themselves are disrupted by the penetrating relation in a manner that still generates the infinite regress, or our terms pass completely into the relation itself and disappear.

To consider the notion of "disruption" first. If we view our relation as penetrating its terms, then we shall find that there now exists an aspect of each related term that is continuous with the relation. But, if this is the case, how (we must ask) can we still hold that the terms are *not* the relation, and that they still have their own identity? Of course, we might say that the relation and the terms are *partially* continuous and that the relation only penetrates an "aspect" or "piece" of each term, and that the terms have another aspect that is different (and by which each term differentiates itself from the relation). But with this solution we find that the relation breaks up the unity of the terms; and thus we are forced to find a new "connecting link" (relation) between the elements of each original term that has now been disrupted. That is, we must now discover how the aspect that is continuous with the relation is related to the aspect that is not. But this presents the same problem as considered above. We are (still) led on to an infinite regress of terms and relations because the side of each term that is continuous with the relation needs to be connected to the side or aspect of the term that is not.

If, however, we insist that our relation is not "nothing" but refuse to disrupt the unity of our terms, we shall (should we persist in this attitude) find our terms *disappearing* into the relation. Bradley tells us that

> An actual relation . . . must possess at once both the charac-
> ters of a 'together' and a 'between', and failing either of these,
> is a relation no longer. Hence our terms cannot make a rela-
> tion by passing themselves over into it bodily. For in that
> event their individuality, and with it the required 'between',
> would be lost. All that we could have left would be another
> form of experience, no longer relational, which qualifying
> directly our terms would have ceased to be terms. On the
> other hand, if, to remain themselves, our terms retain their
> characters as individuals, there is no legitimate way (we have
> seen) to their union in fact. We are without the 'together',
> which (like the 'between') is essential if any relation is to be
> actually there.[34]

While we must for the present ignore any discussion of non-relational experience, we can say that Bradley's rejection of the self-sufficient term— a term that would stand in external relation to other such terms—consists in the fact that we cannot think through this form without destroying either the nature of the term or the relation. As we are told above, the actual fact of a relation's relating consists in its being both a "between" (a "something") and a "together" (a "something" that *connects* our terms). However, the notion of external relations forces the destruction of one or the other of these aspects. If we insist on the "between" we turn our relations into things that don't relate and we are forced to postulate new relations. If we insist on the "together" our terms begin to dissipate, and before our eyes they become the relations. But if the terms become the relations what is left to relate? By generating such an infinite regress Bradley hopes to show that so far as our thinking does move according to the machinations of external terms in relation, we shall be involved in an intellectual squirrel cage of the sort described. And, as we shall see in chapters 8 and 9, it is only insofar as our thought manages to rise above this mechanism that it can begin to attain intellectual satisfaction.

But, as considered above, this picture of the merely external relation is only a theoretical construction. It represents the extreme of unsystematic thinking and has probably never existed. The account of the relational form that more closely approximates how we must think is that which deals with "internal relations." And in considering it we shall have a better picture of what actually occurs in relational thinking.[35]

Now, in approaching the internal relation we find that, to a large degree, our work has already been done. Virtually every discussion of "system" and "unities-in-diversity" that we have examined in previous chapters have been accounts of the "internal relation."[36] Hence, at this point we may briefly remind ourselves that any internally related term is just a term as it actually exists in a systematic relation to other terms. We might further say that an internal relation is a relation that is (relatively) sensitive to the terms it relates.[37] It holds them together in a union such that a change in one term is, to some degree, reflected in both the relation itself and in the other term. And a perfectly internal relation would be just what we have described as a perfect "system" or a complete "identity-in-difference." A group of terms that was totally and perfectly integrated could be said to have its elements standing in complete internal relation to one another, and to be so interpenetrating that any change to any part would immediately reverberate throughout the whole.[38]

The perfectly internal relation would be (*per impossibile*) a relation that does not force into rigid distinction the identity of the terms it relates. It acknowledges the fact that the terms related are not radically distinct, but that they really constitute a single, though internally diverse, entity. The "together" is the "between," and the "between" the "together"; and this because the perfectly internal relation has given up on the notion of absolute identity that characterizes the self-same terms and relations of our previous examples. Hence, it is not a question of "how" the terms relate or "why" they are what they are. A perfectly systematic identity-in-difference is a whole that is not plagued by an external Other and thus no questions arise as to the "reason why" or "because" (either of the system as a whole or the internal distinctions it contains).[39] But, having said this, we must realize immediately that the *completely* internal relation is also a merely theoretical construct. Although ultimate reality (the Absolute) may be understood as being superior to and above relations (all the while including them), the relational form that we must employ in our thinking grasp of this reality is one that can never fully overcome indifference and externality between the terms it identifies. And, while the internal relation manages to take the special subject and predicate and view them as systematically related, there is still a point at which this mutual adjustment of terms—

both to one another and the reality beyond—breaks down. There is still a point at which they too exhibit rigidity and externality to one another. (Internally related terms are just not *as* rigid and limited as the externally related term.) Thus, the *perfectly* internal relation (by which is meant the relation that really gets beyond the relational form) is something that can never be realized in our assertive experience. When we speak of internal relations, then, we are speaking of the *degree* of systematic unity and interconnection any terms might possess.

But let us consider these ideas in terms of an actual judgment. Consider, for example, "This bird is yellow." I can say here that so far as my notion of "bird" and "yellow" are interpenetrating and adjusted to one another—to that degree—they are internally related. And so far as these terms are internally related to one another the relation of predication (the judgment) can be understood as a success. However, as we considered in our discussion of contradiction, there always comes a point where my understanding of "bird" and "yellow" come to their limit. There is a point at which the fit—which *is* their internal relatedness—stops short. And, even though this fit might be incredibly complex, and even though it might be so complete that every change in my understanding of the term "yellow" immediately reflects itself in my understanding of "bird" (and in particular "*this* bird"), still, this sort of sensitivity between terms must—at some point—come up short.

We should remember that, for Bradley, it is possible for the terms of a judgment to have relatively expanded or contracted boundaries; that is, both the comprehension and the coherency of their systematic content can vary. And when the expanse of our ideally constructed reality is great the boundaries of the subject and predicate terms can be seen—if they are truly internally related—to overlap (so to speak) and accommodate one another. Even though they fail to capture fully the sense of many-in-oneness that exists in the feeling base from which they are abstracted, they, nonetheless, exist in such a manner that an adjustment in one requires an adjustment in the other; and thus they no longer stand in a relation of sheer indifference. However, what makes these terms still relational is the following: first, there exits some aspect of explicit content in either or both terms that is *not* sensitive to a change in one of the terms to which it is related; and second, no matter how sensitive they become to each other there will *always* exist conditions of their unity and mutual implication that are left out. And here we come to the crux of the problem.[40]

The problem with the internal relation, then, is that at some point it too exhibits mere abstract difference between itself and that which opposes it (other terms). Take any judgment or theory or concrete perception; take any limited experience and make it as coherent and as comprehensive an "identity-in-difference" or "many-in-one" as you like. Still, Bradley would insist, it must exist in the medium of judgment and as such it consists in a selective abstraction taken out of a larger arena of experience. Hence, at its boundaries, it will be abruptly cut off from that which falls outside it.

We could take, for example, the most elevated religious experience, or mystical insight or, perhaps, the experience of a great work of art. And we could completely grant to the advocate of internal relations that the experience is one that is truly systematic, and that its internal parts or aspects mirror one another in such a manner that a change in one brings about a change in all. However, Bradley would claim that we are still talking about *a* religious experience, *a* mystical insight, and *an* aesthetic perception. In other words, each is *a* whole and not *the* whole. And thus the point at which the systematic concept, theory, or artwork is seen to end (or have a limit) is the point at which—despite its internal many-in-oneness—it *stands in merely external relation to the rest of experience.* Bradley's claim, then, is that there is no such thing as a combination of terms and relations—even internal relations—that is purely, wholly, and perfectly internal.[41] And, once more, in saying this he is emphasizing that *thought*, no matter how closely it approaches its object, can never do so fully. It can never fully duplicate its object because—in order to be thought—it must select out of a reality that is (necessarily) greater than itself. Should thought ever overcome this limitation, then it would no longer be thought but would be reality itself. And this, of course, Bradley sees as an impossibility. Indeed, if there is one aspect of Bradley's thinking that stands out and is truly characteristic it is that thought can never "commit suicide." And Bradley's Absolute is always one in which difference is maintained.

Of course, *if* our experience were exhausted by the thinking side of our being, then, Bradley tells us, things would be different. As we read:

> If the diversities were complementary aspects of a process of connexion and distinction, the process not being external to the elements or again a foreign compulsion of the intellect, but itself the intellect's own *proprius motus*, the case would be altered. Each aspect would of itself be a transition to the other aspect, a transition intrinsic and natural at once to itself and to the intellect. And the Whole would be a self-evident analysis and synthesis of the intellect itself by itself. Synthesis here has ceased to be mere synthesis and has become self-completion, and analysis, no longer mere analysis, is self-explication, and the question how or why the many are one and the one is many here loses its meaning. There is no why

or how beside the self-evident process, and towards its own differences this whole is at once their how and their why, their being, substance, and system, their reason, ground, and principle of diversity and unity.[42]

But Bradley goes on to tell us that this is never the case. Intellect is not reality and the division of the "what" and "that" is a permanent feature of our experience. No matter how much we may wish otherwise there is no escape from the existential side of our being. And thought, confronted by the perfect union of content and existence (as found in feeling), can only approximate such perfect coherency and systematicity.

"But does not all of this mean," it may be objected, "that the vision of relational experience that operates according to the wholly external relation is really the correct one? Has it not been admitted (particularly in the discussion of contradiction) that *all* systematic concepts are limited and that at some point *all* concepts exist in a relation that is *merely* conjunctive? And is not mere conjunction precisely what the doctrine of external relation portrays? Is it not the case that the 'supplementation' and 'expansion' of special subject and predicate in judgment involve nothing more than the fission of objectified relations working to relate the relations? And has Bradley not thus provided us with an account of thought that makes of it nothing more than a regressive treadmill that never gets us closer to its object?"

While such questions are not without foundation, I would point out that they have missed a significant aspect of the theory as discussed thus far. On Bradley's theory, even though we are condemned to indefinitely expand and accommodate our terms to one another, and even though the unity of content and existence as it comes to us in feeling can never be fully duplicated in our judgment, this ideal expansion, correctly carried out, *does* constitute an advance over the (relatively) inferior state that existed prior to it. Even though the ideal expansion of the object according to the relational form is partially defective, we must never forget that it is also partially successful. When we think systematically we are not just holding together a mere aggregate of terms conceived in external relation. When I judge, for example, that "Bach's Brandenburg concerti have an uplifting effect on the human spirit" I am dealing with concrete concepts whose complex internal content—although admittedly imperfect—nevertheless *does* reflect a profound degree of adjustment to both itself and what lies beyond. And it is just this sort of adjustment that constitutes increased systematicity and thus the advance of thought.

This leads us, however, to the topic of chapters 8 and 9. And, even though we have not yet given the topic our full attention, we should understand even here that Bradley sees underlying every judgment—every relational complex—a "feeling-base" out of which the terms of our judgment are abstracted and against which our ideal development of predicates is evaluated. Now, we have already learned that it is in feeling that we sense the complete wholeness that we are attempting to duplicate in judgment. And in the movement of relational thought the originally felt unity of our terms has, in one form and to some extent, disappeared. What was given (the felt many-in-oneness) has become, through the machinations of relational thinking, although a systematic apprehension of the real, a systematic apprehension that is imperfect and that has some of the characteristics of a mere aggregate of terms held in external and indifferent relation.

But the feeling-base always remains as the backdrop of any assertion. And this persisting feeling—with the assistance of intellect and will in a fuller experience—functions as a hovering criterion for all assertion. Feeling, we must remember, remains after relations have been abstracted out of it. And when we judge, our fuller feeling-based experience (which includes and transcends intellect and will) asks, "How completely and how thoroughly have you duplicated my universe?" And, indeed, some judgments *do* better satisfy the demands imposed by this felt experience. They better satisfy this felt criterion because they contain *more* of it, and they contain it in a manner that more perfectly duplicates its "reason why" and its "necessity." And, in order to appreciate this point more fully, let us now consider some aspects of Bradley's doctrine of Truth.

Chapter 7

COHERENCE (OF A SORT) AND ERROR

WE now have before us a general view of Bradley's theory of judgment. And in this chapter I shall attempt to answer some of the questions that our account has raised. First, we must consider the sense in which all acts of predication—although ultimately failing to express their intended meaning—can still be said to progressively capture the real. Or, put differently, we must now consider how Bradley sees every judgment as being both partially true and partially false, and as possessing a "degree of reality."[1] To achieve this understanding we must examine in greater detail Bradley's idiosyncratic (by today's lights) notion of coherence. And the discussion of much of this chapter will focus on this idea. But this is all in preparation for the discussion of chapters 8 and 9. Following our examination of truth as coherence we must face up to one of the pressing metaphysical questions that Bradley's theory suggests: namely, how it is that "feeling" can supply the criterion of the real (according to which every judgment's relative truth is measured) without committing itself to some species of solipsistic subjectivism. But before confronting in detail the metaphysical problems this question raises, let us first consider more closely Bradley's doctrine of degrees of truth and reality.

THE IDEALITY OF TRUTH

The discussion up to this point, although it has covered many aspects of the act of judgment, can, from another perspective, be understood as a sustained discussion of Bradley's doctrine of truth. If we recall our opening comments on the nature of judgment, we shall be reminded of what is the differentia of judgment for Bradley: its liability to error. All judgments, we should recall, are susceptible to error because they are not—at least not fully—that reality to which they refer. And, though we shall soon be forced to discuss the fuller metaphysical implications of such a claim, for the moment we need only remind ourselves that the judgment is, for Bradley, ideal; and in this consists its fundamental character as truth as opposed to reality. A truth in order to be such, then, must be capable of being falsified. But, curiously, at the same time any truth is *truer*—that is, it realizes its ideal—only so far as its propensity to error has been purged. But how is this achieved? The answer we have already considered. A truth becomes less prone to falsification by including within its boundaries the conditions that make it true; that is, by becoming more systematic and comprehensive. As Bradley tells us,

> Truth is an ideal expression of the Universe, at once coherent and comprehensive. It must not conflict with itself, and there must be no suggestion which fails to fall inside it. Perfect truth in short must realize the idea of a systematic whole.[2]

We have also learned, though, that the "perfect truth" to which Bradley refers here does not and cannot exist (at least not for any finite subject). Perfect truth cannot exist because if it were perfect it would no longer be truth but would have become reality.[3] Perfect truth could not exist *as* truth because in order to be perfect it would have to have fully reunited the elements of content and existence—the "what" and the "that." But, as we have spent so many pages considering, it is characteristic of thought (the truth-bearer) *not* to possess these elements in complete unity. As Bradley tells us on so many occasions, should thought (*per impossibile*) completely overcome its ideality (its content-existence rupture) it would certainly have adequately grasped its object, but as thought it would have committed a "happy suicide."

> Thought [we read] essentially consists in the separation of the 'what' from the 'that'. It may be said to accept this dissolution as its effective principle. Thus it renounces all attempt to *make* fact, and it confines itself to content. But by embracing this separation, and by urging this independent development to its extreme, thought indirectly endeavors to restore the broken whole. It seeks to find an arrangement of ideas, self-consistent and complete; and by this predicate it has to qualify and make good the Reality. And, as we have seen, its attempt would in the end be suicidal. Truth should mean what it stands for, and should stand for what it means; but these two aspects in the end prove incompatible. There is still a difference, unremoved, between the subject and the predicate, a difference which, while it persists, shows a failure in thought, but which, if removed, would wholly destroy the special essence of thinking.[4]

Truth (which must manifest itself in the judgment) must always be ideal. But what we must now consider is how some judgments can be less ideal and more real than others. We must remember that *truths are not on the same level* for Bradley. Although all judgments are understood to be at least partially true, some judgments contain so little truth that they are barely recognizable as judgments. However, on the other hand, some judgments are so broad and systematic, so deeply implicated in our every experience, that their denial would result in self-contradiction and inconsistency. These would, of course, represent the extremes of truth and falsity. But, what makes the one truer, and hence more real, than the other is that it is (i) more coherent, and (ii) more comprehensive. Hence, we must now examine how, according to Bradley, these two criteria function as indicators of a judgment's relative immunity from falsification and its degree of truth and reality.

COHERENCE

We must always bear in mind that what Bradley means by "coherence" has very little to do with the way the term is used today. Still, for the reader who has followed the discussion thus far, Bradley's notion of coherence should not be difficult to understand. And, though this statement will require qualification as we proceed, we may say that essentially what a judgment coheres with is *experience as a whole*; and further, this coherence is present only to the degree that any single assertion is systematically necessitated by the larger nexus of experience that it presupposes. And conversely, so far as a judgment lacks this character it lacks coherence.[5]

In order to grasp Bradley's rather unusual conception of coherence let us first remind ourselves of some important characteristics of the judgment. We might recall that what we ultimately mean in any judgment is the unique and individual referent of which the assertion is made. And this we might call, even though it is somewhat of a misnomer, the *real* meaning of the judgment. This real meaning is the wholly contextualized and utterly specific object that receives its uniqueness and specificity by holding a precise position in the one order of things and events that is the universe-as-a-whole. And, it is because the uniqueness of our referent entails the whole order of facts that, in an ultimate sense, Bradley believes all judgment to refer to the "one Great fact." We must never forget that, for Bradley, the ultimate subject of every judgment is reality-as-a-whole.

We should also recall a point from chapter 5. The *actual* meaning—that is, the meaning that *we* do in fact possess in any judgment—is never the *real* meaning; at least if by this latter term we mean the intended reality itself. The "actual meaning" is always ideal in that it is a truncated and distorted version of what we intend. Of course, we may legitimately say that the actual (or ideal) meaning partially *coincides* with the real meaning. But what we manage to get into our judgment (the actual meaning) will always fail to measure up in that it (*a*) lacks certain features that are there in reality (i.e., in the real meaning); and (*b*) it adds (or at least overemphasizes) aspects that should not be present. In other words, the meaning as apprehended *by us*, will always bear to some degree the work of the "subjective and irrelevant."[6]

What we really mean, then, is the perfect individual that stands in a precise set of relations to everything else. What we actually possess, however, is a fragment of this unique reality that is characterized by a degree of abstract generality, distorted significance, and internal contradiction. The point to bear in mind here, though, is that abstractness, lack of harmony and the presence of irrelevancies can vary. For example, when I assert "Mary's recent car accident has left her less able than she was" I have in mind a person named "Mary" and a "car accident" that, as they exist in my judgment, contain only a finite and limited amount of detail. And at some point my explicit idea of Mary, her accident and the resulting disability becomes indistinguishable (in principle if not in fact) from some other Mary, another car accident, and another sort of handicap. Put differently, my *idea* of Mary and her disability could, because of its inherent abstractness, equally apply to some different Mary and some different disability. And further, the point at which this occurs not only varies between individuals (who might make roughly similar assertions) but it also fluctuates within my own consciousness from moment to moment.

The generality of my (relatively) systematic apprehension is, we should also remember, distorted in that it tells me both too little and too much. No matter how detailed my grasp of Mary's disability there will be some things that escape me.[7] Even if the fuller intension of the ideas "Mary" and "car accident" are ignored, much of the specific detail of her current level of disability cannot be included in any one judgment (or series of judgments for that matter). There exists in my ideal meaning—my subjectively biased and limited apprehension—an understanding of "Mary's disability" that is certainly exaggerated in some ways and understated in others. And since this level of distortion will vary each time I make assertions about her disability, we can conclude that we are always dealing with a matter of *degree* when we speak about "diverging from the real meaning."[8]

We shall pick up this thread—this idea of "degree"—in a moment, but first let us pursue this notion of coherence by recalling an earlier point that Bradley is relentless in driving home; and this point is that *all judgment involves an act of selective abstraction out of a larger mass of experience.* Or put differently, all judgment presupposes a world within which it falls and of which it has but a limited view. As Bradley sometimes puts it, there exists a great deal more *in* the mind than can ever be *before* it. And we may say that it is precisely this relation between what is before the mind and what is in it that constitutes, for Bradley, the relation of coherence.

Now, it is not too difficult to say what is "before" the mind on Bradley's analysis. What is before the mind, we are told, is always this or that specific judgment and the ideal (i.e., actualized) meaning it has for us. What is "in" the mind, however, is somewhat elusive and a bit more difficult to describe. We might say that what is "in" the mind is (at least) the totality of our experience of the universe. And we might further say that it is with this integrated system of experience that our present judgment either coheres or doesn't.

We shall refine this notion when we examine Bradley's doctrine of feeling. But for now we may view this totality of experience as being divided into two elements that, although distinguishable, are continuous. First, there is the "ideal world" (in the sense of being "thought") that I have developed over the course of my life, and which can be said to constitute my *intelligible* universe. It is "intelligible" because it has already come before me in the act of judgment (and is undergoing modification through a continuation of the process). However, in addition to this there is that aspect of what Bradley calls the "feeling mass" that—although continuous with my intelligible world—has for me never fully become the object of explicit and overt predication.[9] It is in the furthest reaches of the feeling mass that we find content and existence completely united, and it is this level of feeling that has (from the beginning) provided the material out of which all judgment flows and into which it returns.

Although there are difficulties here to which we must soon return, we should for the present at least recognize the following. It is this larger felt "universe" (which combines both intelligible and sensuous components) that persists beyond the periphery of any momentary conscious awareness and that constitutes the "system" with which any judgment either coheres or doesn't.[10] And, since every explicit judgment presupposes a broad (actually infinite) nexus of meaning and is, in fact, but a partial selection out of it, the implicit (i.e., presupposed or unselected) portions exert a continual force and guiding influence. This guiding influence (coming from both "ideal" and "real" elements) is, then, what is *in* the mind; and it functions, depending upon what level of depth within the feeling base we are considering, as both the proximate and ultimate criterion of any explicit assertion. Now, we must await the discussion of the next chapter in order to understand the differences between what Bradley calls "immediate experience" (which functions as the proximate critic) and the felt presence of the Absolute (the ultimate standard). But we may provisionally say that it is the relation of "fit" between the overt assertion of any moment and this presupposed world of experience found in feeling that provide any judgment with its degree of truth.

Ignoring for the moment any deeper metaphysical problems, let us attempt to understand better the essentials of this relation by considering the following example. Let us imagine a group of baseball aficionados sitting around discussing the history of their game. And let us further imagine one of them to assert that "The fourth game of the 1959 World Series was a good one for the Los Angeles Dodgers." Now the key point in coming to understand the coherence relation as understood by Bradley is that every term in the judgment reaches into the infinite nexus of objective relations (past, present, and future) for its significance. Every meaning has nuances and connections that themselves lead on to further significant detail. And thus we must say that the meaning of our assertion is one that has a precise structure and articulable form. However, we must not see this structure as the result of mere human convention. And, indeed, it is entirely accurate to say that this structure of significance is, for Bradley, the structure—not of our own subjective creation—but of the experienced universe itself.

Of course, this universe can never be experienced "at once" and "immediately" in a single conscious assertion. But, nevertheless, it is, Bradley believes, always *there*. It is somehow *in* our minds and thus forms the conditioning context out of which any judgment arises and against which the coherence (or fit) of any assertion is measured. We sense (if we are at all knowledgeable about our subject) a degree of fit for an assertion based on its relative acceptance or rejection by the presupposed (felt) nexus of judgments that—although out of the explicit, focused gaze of consciousness—still provide the "world" into which the new assertion will either smoothly integrate or uncomfortably clash. In this case, it would appear, we would have an example of a relatively good fit. As anyone who is familiar with the "world of baseball" knows, the Dodgers were in the 1959 World Series, they did win the crucial fourth game; and, since it is generally understood that to win the World Series is part of the ultimate Good of baseball, there attaches to this assertion a high degree of acceptance by the presupposed world that is its basis.

We should also understand how any judgment that possesses a good fit or high degree of coherence goes on to corroborate a great many other judgments that are at a further remove. We can easily follow this idea if we bear in mind that, on the Bradleian analysis, the significance of any assertion reaches out in all directions. Any assertion possesses meaning only by holding its place in the timeless nexus of significance. And whenever we assert there are reverberations that extend into many of the different areas of the universe that our assertion presupposes. For example, the term "fourth" implicates our system of number; "game" reaches out to those activities that, by and large, are characterized by the goal of "winning" and (usually) a spirit of play; "world series" finds its meaning only in relation to that vast series of judgments that constitute the sport of baseball, and so on. And the judgments that are implicated at one remove themselves involve others. For example, the system of judgments that comprise the "world of baseball" themselves suggest, through a series of overlapping meanings, "the major leagues," "the New York Yankees," "New York," "the United States," "a colony of Great Britain in the seventeenth and eighteenth centuries," "the British Colonial Empire," and so on. As was discussed in chapter 3, there are always levels of significance both above and below any judgment. And these intersecting meanings provide the "atmosphere" within which all assertion is made. And we might further notice that this atmosphere of significance cannot be reduced to a set of conventions or agreements amongst judging subjects. When we carry through our analysis of any meaning we shall eventually encounter recalcitrant and given meaning-facts that have been "invented" by no one.

The judgment presupposes, then, this universe of significant experience, and it is always a selection out of its greater wealth of content. And when we selectively abstract (and thereby assert) we are involved in a reorganization of this content as it forms our conscious world; that is, by modifying and recombining the contents of experience in assertion we are forever trying to realize the impossible task of transforming the ideal meaning (that is, the meaning "for us") into the real meaning (the meaning "for everybody"). Progressively, and sometimes at great expense, we transform this ideal meaning so as to make it indistinguishable from the real, which is both its ground and its highest aspiration. There is, of course, much that remains to be said regarding the relation between the undeniably ideal, isolated assertion and its real ground present in feeling. However, before confronting the metaphysical difficulties that this theoretical analysis forces upon us, let us return to our example and consider some further ways in which an assertion may be accepted or repelled by the larger world of experience that provides its context. Instead of an example of a "good fit" let us now consider what would occur if one our baseball aficionados were to assert "The fourth game of the 1959 World Series was a good one for the Los Angeles Angels."

Now, for anyone who knows the history of baseball, such a judgment would probably be rejected. There would exist a grating or friction between this judgment and the larger body of significant experience that makes up its conditioning context. (This friction would be present, if not for the individual who makes the judgment, at least for knowledgeable listeners.) Given the presupposed world of baseball that, we are assuming, would be common to the participants in our conversation, the judgment now offered would—at least as formulated—be repelled by the larger scheme of meaning that is, either consciously or unconsciously, common property amongst those involved in the discussion. And that the judgment was made at all indicates one of two things. Either (a) the assertor did not share with his or her audience—at least not to the same degree—the set of presuppositions that constitute "the world of baseball"; in other words, he or she was ignorant (to a degree at least) of both the real and ideal meanings of his or her terms; or (b) his or her actual meaning was not adequately conveyed by the grammatical utterance.

If we consider (a) first we might imagine one of the participants informing the assertor that part of the very meaning of the term "Los Angeles Angels" is "a baseball team that did not join the major leagues until 1960." (And thus that they could not possibly have played in the 1959 World Series.) Of course, with this information brought to light the "error" or "falsity" would have been exposed and a retraction of the judgment—now repelled by the larger fabric of experience—would be expected. We might, of course, easily imagine a further unpacking of meaning to follow. It is easy to imagine that once it was brought to the assertor's attention that part of what was meant by "the 1959 World Series" was "the world championship of baseball played between the Chicago White Sox and the Los Angeles Dodgers" the judgment might be rejected as completely (i.e., practically) false and identified as an error. If this were to happen our misinformed historian would in all likelihood grasp the lack of coherence between the assertion and the larger body of knowledge he or she partially shared with the others, and the assertion would be withdrawn (or at least modified).

Indeed, after being chastised for this error we might imagine our historian to say something like the following: "I had always heard that the 1959 World Series was between the 'White Sox' and 'Los Angeles'. And, based on my knowledge that the team that is now called the 'California

Angels' was once called the 'Los Angeles Angels' I thought that when a reference was made to 'Los Angeles' it was a reference to the 'Los Angels Angels'. And this belief was further substantiated by the fact that I had never before heard of the Dodgers playing the White Sox (even though I knew that the White Sox and Angels had played on many occasions). But now I see my mistake. Although I thought that 'Los Angeles' meant the 'Los Angeles Angels', I only looked at the superficial evidence and was thus led into error. Had I thought about the deeper meaning and had I kept before my mind the fact that the World Series is always played between one team from the National League and one team from the American League, and that both the White Sox and Angels belong to the American League, then I would have realized that 'Los Angeles' could not have meant the 'Los Angeles Angels'." And with this realization our imaginary assertor would have effected a transformation, a refinement and deepening, of his or her actual meaning (i.e., his or her intellectual universe), which has now become more closely identified with the real meaning (reality itself).

Something like this would, I think, be a likely reaction should such an assertion be made against what we know as the "world of baseball." But, let us also consider (*b*), which we described as a judgment not accurately conveyed by its grammatical expression. We could also imagine (perhaps not quite so easily) our assertor to unpack this judgment by saying something like the following: To the claim that he or she was wrong about the Los Angeles Angels and the 1959 World Series our baseball historian might respond by saying "No, I meant what I said. The fourth game of the 1959 World Series *was* a good one for the Los Angeles Angels because the poor play of Chicago first baseman Ted Kluzewski that day tipped the balance in favor of those in management who wanted to trade him, and this allowed the newly formed Angels to pick up his contract. This was good for the Angels because, as any Angel's fan knows, Kluzewski was instrumental in the early success of the franchise. He was a real crowd-pleaser and a strong team leader whose presence greatly benefited the newly formed Los Angeles Angels baseball club."

Although this example might appear a bit contrived, it does, nevertheless, illustrate two points that have appeared in previous chapters and that still merit our attention. First, we are reminded that the grammatical form that any judgment takes is merely schematic. What is actually meant is clearly far richer than can easily be conveyed by a single proposition. And second, we are also reminded that, not only may every judgment explicitly contain a diversity of content that is richer than what is grammatically expressed, but, in being selective, it presupposes a context that is richer still. That is, all judgments are ideal; and as such they are always subject to condemnation by the real, but not fully apprehended, meaning. We should not lose sight of the fact that no matter how much is apprehended within the judgment, it will still fail to express its intended (real) meaning and thus will always, to some degree, be in error.[11]

COMPREHENSIVENESS

We shall have more to say on the question of error is a moment. However, before attempting to unpack Bradley's claim that even the grossest error contains an element of truth, let us consider the other aspect of any truth bearer (judgment)—its comprehensiveness. Up to this point we have merely discussed coherence as roughly equivalent to what we have called the "fit" between the present assertion and the presupposed system of experience. We must now move forward and discuss this fit as one of systematic implication and comprehensiveness. As we shall soon see, for Bradley, any judgment's coherence is, in the end, just equivalent to its comprehensiveness. And in a very real sense comprehensiveness should be understood but as another way of looking at the coherence relation.

The idea of comprehension is, if we keep in mind what has gone before, really quite simple. As we have already seen, a concept (or term) is, for Bradley, not a self-same (and empty) idea that is derived by abstractive generalization upon given sense experience. A concept is our subjective apprehension of an internally diverse phenomenon; it is the systematic binding together of differents that, though they exist in the real world, come to exist for us through the act of predication. To have the concept "red" is, for Bradley to use that concept in a judgment.[12] And this the minimal apprehension of a concept like "red" would come in the form of "This is red" or "A red thing is here" (or something along these lines). We must remember that with the rejection of the floating idea (the unaffirmed concept) all significant ideas must be understood as existing in judgment. When we express an elaborate or complex assertion we are expressing an elaborate but single idea; and when we possess a simple idea we are engaged in a simple judgment.

However, what we must always bear in mind is that all judgments must presuppose and select from what is, according to Bradley, ultimately *the* idea (the Absolute). All concepts, as components in judgments, can be seen, then, as subconcepts of the one whole of which they are partial aspects and limited expressions. Why is this so? Because, as we have repeatedly pointed out, every idea is, for Bradley, parasitic upon others for its meaning; and they, in turn, are parasitic upon yet further ideas. And, in the end, we find that every significant thought implicitly appeals to all.[13]

We should also realize, though, that every idea we possess—every idea as it resides in the conscious experience of a finite knower—has a "range" or "comprehension." That is, it has a varying number of differentiated elements that it binds together in its conceptual grasp. And thus some judgments can be said to have a broader "reach" or cover a greater "expanse" than others. For example, "This hurts"—at least as it would be normally made—is an assertion that focuses on a very narrow range of experience. It considers only the unspecified present and it characterizes that present by the vague notion of pain. (Whatever it is that makes the "this" what it is is left outside the judgment proper.) But, consider "Water boils at 100° Celsius under one atmosphere of pressure."[14] Here we have a judgment that contains within its own four corners the universal quality "water," the activity of "boiling," the system of "temperature," and the idea of "atmospheric pressure."[15] And in such an assertion our conscious awareness attempts to hold together a vast range of experience such that we see (nonperceptually, of course) these various elements in (relative) systematic unity.

The point I would like to emphasize here, though, is that when we speak of "higher" and "lower" (and more or less true) we are always talking about the coherence and comprehensiveness—the inclusive systematicity—of our assertion. For example, when Bradley analyzes the outwardly categorical assertion as a low-level hypothetical he is claiming, in effect, that what makes this judgment a poorer truth than the overtly universal affirmative is that its element do not constitute a closely knit system. When I say "Mary is happy" (which can legitimately be construed as "If Mary then happy") I have before me a relation between universals—universals that do not exhibit a necessary and interpenetrating connection. Rather, they stand in what is largely a conjunctive and external relation. When I assert "Mary is happy" what makes "happiness" an appropriate predicate to "Mary" is not something intrinsic to either term; rather it is the conditions that are external to the judgment that effect their relatedness.

But, when I assert "All men are mortal" I am apprehending, under most circumstances anyway, an interrelation between "manness" and "mortality" that is far stronger. Here I am grasping the interpenetration—the deeply set and multifaceted intersection—of universals such that when I have one the other must be present as well. These are comprehensive predicates whose systematic interconnection is so thorough that they are reinforced by many more at a further remove. And it is the incorporation into the assertion of this broad network of meanings that not only prevents the judgment from being overturned, but that provides it with its character as truth. Hence, the hypothetical universal affirmative "All men are mortal" will have the capacity to be tru*er* than the categorical—but actually low-level conditional—assertion of the same content (e.g., "This man is mortal").

And it is for the same reason that the disjunctive assertion is seen to be higher still. If we do entertain an assertion that is truer (or higher) than a hypothetical universal affirmative, it is only because that judgment is even more systematic. This would occur, of course, when we have before our minds an apprehension of a necessary connection between universals as they manifest themselves amongst their various instantiations. "All triangles are rectilinear" is a powerful (universal affirmative) assertion. But "All triangles are rectilinear *and* are either scalene, isosceles, or equilateral" is even stronger. Here we have an insight into the interpenetration of meanings that is even more concrete because more systematically determined. Here we see that "triangularity" and "rectilinear" are necessarily related and *in just these forms*.[16] The important point to remember, though, is that in the case of the true disjunctive assertion there is a reaching into experience that is more concrete and systematic because more coherent and comprehensive. And it is this that provides it with an even greater entrenchment within the nexus of meaning.

We may say, then, that some judgments reach into the system of significant experience in a far more ambitious manner than others. And, because of this greater reach (comprehension), a universal assertion—as either hypothetical or disjunctive—possesses what we may call a greater "exposure" or "risk" than does the narrowly focused categorical judgment.[17] It is more exposed because it has brought itself before the court of experience in a far more expansive manner. "Water boils at 50° Celsius under one atmosphere of pressure" immediately confronts an enormous mass of experience, experience that, in this case, instantly repels it and says, "No, this will not do." When we consider "This hurts," however, we have a very different situation.[18] Here we have an assertion that is not so ambitious and that—although it may be repelled at this moment—could very well be accepted in the next. But in saying this we have reminded ourselves of an extremely important point.

To say that any assertion is "true" is to say that the *assertion itself* carries with it (or bears) this characteristic. However, in the case of our narrowly focused categorical assertion what makes it true is not within the judgment's own boundaries as an assertion. The conditions that allow "This hurts" to be assertable today but not tomorrow always lie outside that explicit judgment. But, since these conditions do not belong to the assertion itself, we see that it lacks some fundamental characteristic that any truth must possess.[19] Not only does it fail to contain within itself that which makes it true, but we may also say that it lacks the "stability" that would prevent its falsification. But this is utterly unacceptable to Bradley as a characteristic of truth. To be "true" is to duplicate as closely as possible the nature of the real (i.e., to *become* that real). And to be real, Bradley believes, is for something to be what it is *necessarily*. Hence truth and necessity are closely linked in his theory. And to speak of merely "contingent truth" is, as Bradley puts it, to mistake our own ignorance for fact. Bradley believes that any judgment must in order to be true be *forced*; and it is only those judgments that, because they have an expansive comprehension and a broad-base engagement with the entire nexus of meaning, are capable of being forced by the larger system of reality. Their truth comes about through a higher degree of integration within the larger system of experience and because of this the more comprehensive judgment will always be the more coherent.[20]

CONTINGENCY, NECESSITY AND LOGICAL STABILITY

From the preceding it should be clear that a contingent truth is, for Bradley, not much of a truth at all. And if we recall the discussion of the categorical judgment (chapter 4) we shall see that we have already considered the defects of the contingent assertion. In relying for its truth upon conditions that are largely external to the judgment the categorical assertion is (from the atemporal perspective of logic anyway) both true and false at once. "Mary is happy" is, although true when she receives an award for her professional achievement, false when she is physically abused or assaulted.

Another way of stating the case is to say (again) that the contingent truth lacks *logical stability*. And by the use of this phrase we mean that any categorical-contingent assertion does not have the ability to maintain itself as true against changing circumstances. Given one set of conditions, the judgment is in harmony with the real; give a different set, its truth is blown to the winds. The categorical judgment, supported by its external conditions one moment and (as a truth) crushed at the next, entirely lacks the ability to maintain itself as a truth in the face of change. However, with the more expansive judgment forms we find our assertions locked in to the larger system and thus progressively approaching "timelessness" in their truth. Indeed, as we progress up the ladder of judgment forms we see our assertions becoming so stable that, at the top anyway, we find judgments whose denial would upset the entire system. These judgment are thus "necessarily true"; but, not because they are tautological (on the contrary).[21] Like everything else for Bradley, necessity has its degrees. And when we are in possession of an assertion that is so deeply implicated in existence that its denial upsets the basis of its assertion it is, in what is for him the only meaningful sense of the term, "a priori."

In saying this, however, I would remind the reader of a point made earlier. Even though some judgments are necessarily true (because of their comprehensive engagement of reality), this necessity is itself something that—as apprehended by us—is a matter of degree. No matter how deep our apprehension of a necessary truth might be, Bradley believes that there is always *more* that can be grasped. And the reason why there is "more" is that we are finite knowers while the object of our knowledge is infinite. And we could overcome this condition only if (*per impossible*) thought had brought about its own demise through a complete identification with and perfect apprehension of reality.

EVIDENCE AND COMPREHENSION

Perhaps one of the more effective ways to conceive of the notion of degrees of truth is to consider the notion of "evidence" and its relation to assertion. This is because, in the end, when we talk about bringing an assertion's conditions into its borders we are referring to integrating, in some fashion or other, its evidential base into our meaning.

We must remember that the judgment is, for Bradley, a consciously apprehended identity-in-difference. It is the systematic grasp of reality that contains as its internal elements (its terms) other systems. We should also recall that on the theory of selective abstraction (as we have described it in chapter 3) thinking in broader more general terms does not take us further away from the real—rather it brings us closer to it. And when we make a universal assertion such as "All mammals are warm-blooded" we are *not* expressing the results of a conceptual analysis wherein we find "warm-bloodedness" to be part of the nominal definition of "mammal." Rather we are expressing the result of our own synthetic-analysis of reality in which large tracts of prior experience are recombined and viewed from different perspectives. The concept "warm-bloodedness," for example, is not to be understood as the apprehension of an empty and abstract universal quality. We are better advised, Bradley tells us, to view this universal as a systematic binding together of a number of experiences in which the actual universal's exemplifications have come before us. Every concept has as its (ideal) internal meaning, then, our experience of its various concrete manifestations.[22] And, every concept—so far as it is a significant concept and not an empty, unmeaning picture or noise—incorporates this experience, this evidential base, as part of its ideal meaning. And it is for this reason that the more universal (the hypothetical and disjunctive) assertions are said to "engage" reality in a more comprehensive manner.

But let us approach this idea from the opposite direction by considering the case in which there is little or no evidence incorporated into the assertion. We may pursue this line by considering the case of the willful lie that turns out to be true. Let us assume that Mr. X, a disgruntled and alienated worker, decides that the way to get even with his harsh employer is to create trouble in the following manner. Mr. X informs the tax authorities that Mr. Y (his employer) is guilty of tax evasion, and that an investigation of his business dealings will bring this to light. (We are assuming, of course, that Mr. X has no evidence upon which to base this assertion, but only cares to have an investigation launched so as to harass Mr. Y.) However, let us further imagine that when the tax authorities investigate Mr. Y's business they do discover, indeed, that Mr. Y has been involved in just the sort of illegal activities that Mr. X— without any evidence—has alleged. The question we must confront, then, is "In what sense if any was Mr. X's assertion about Mr. Y's illegal activity *true*?"

Although there are those who would insist that such a scenario provides us with a true proposition, at this late stage I do not imagine that the reader who has followed our discussion would have too much difficulty in understanding the sort of response that Bradley must provide. If our imaginary Mr. X actually said "Mr. Y is involved in a massive tax evasion scheme" without any evidence—and if this assertion was a willful lie—then not only can his "assertion" not be true, but it can not even be viewed as an "assertion" or "judgment" (but only part of one). We must not forget that, on Bradley's account, a judgment affirms a condition as continuous with the real that comes to us in perception. It declares that the condition expressed by the proposition is, indeed, continuous with the larger reality out of which it is abstracted. And if Bradley's general account of judgment is correct we are forced to acknowledge that the actual judgment made at the time Mr. X lied to the authorities must have been something like "I shall create a good deal of trouble for Mr. Y by lying to the tax authorities" or perhaps "They are believing this deceitful statement I am now making." Thus we should be very clear that, on Bradley's view, it is impossible to knowingly assert a lie.

The point to be made, of course, is that, for Bradley, *evidence* is a crucial constituent of any assertion. And what we have called the "conditions" of any assertion may be viewed as the "evidence" or "reason why" we assert something as true. When it (evidence) is lacking our assertion begins to take on the categorical (i.e., contingent) form. And without a strong internal evidential base an assertion is easily over-turned and falsified. But what does it mean to say that an evidential base is "internal" to an assertion? First, we must remember that the judgment is a perceptual-conceptual act, and when Bradley speaks of the concrete experiential base that is part of the ideal meaning of any term he is referring to this fact. But we must always bear in mind that perceptual and conceptual content are not precisely equivalent. Although there is always present a perceptual (or sensory) ground to any assertion, what we may call the conceptual "depth" can vary enor-mously within a judgment.

As an illustration of this principle let us consider the difference between the judgment "Caesar crossed the Rubicon" as uttered by a schoolboy and a mature scholar—a specialist in Roman history. Whereas the superficial *perceptual* content of each assertion may at the moment the judgment is made be roughly equivalent, the *conceptual* content must be dramatically richer when being uttered by someone who has devoted a lifetime of study to Roman history. For the school-boy the name "Caesar" might bear only the significance of a paragraph he has read in his history text, or perhaps what his instructor said one day during class. Hence there exists within the ideal meaning of the term "Caesar" very little depth as it exists within his consciousness. How-ever, when the term "Caesar" springs from the lips of a mature scholar it is pregnant with an awareness of the ancient world, the relations between Greek and Roman civilization, the evolution of Roman law, the dynasty of the Caesars, and the various intrigues and campaigns that eventually led to their downfall. These are all (on what is legitimately called a supraperceptual basis) part of—not only the real meaning—but the actualized ideal meaning when put forth by a mature mind. And it is this awareness that constitutes the conceptual depth of the assertion.

With varying degrees of depth and intensity, with a contracting and expanding comprehension, the scholar will bring before his mind that wealth of detailed knowledge that makes up his intelligible uni-verse and, more specifically here, his knowledge of Julius Caesar. On a good day he might have within his intellectual grasp not only an awareness of Caesar and his idiosyncrasies but also, let us say, some peculiarity of Southern European geography such that he could arrive at a yet deeper understanding of the significance of Caesar's crossing the Rubicon. On a bad day, let us imagine he is lecturing to a class while suffering from a cold, his powers may be dimmed; and, although he knows that he could, if he felt better, call upon the wealth of information that constitutes his knowledge of Caesar, this day he is "blocked"—he can remember little and cannot make the sorts of connections he would normally make.

What is important for us to grasp, however, is that this sort of varying conceptual depth and richness—this *conceptual* inclusion of the evidential base—is always present. And it is precisely this conceptual concretion that ultimately constitutes the extent to which our assertion is immune from falsification. When our assertion consists in a comprehensive and systematic vision it attaches itself to the real in a manner that has great stability and only a slight liability of being overturned. However, when it is narrowly focused and limited in its penetration of the reality out of which it arises its propensity to err is great. Hence, it is on this basis that Bradley is led to claim that two appearances (judgments) can vary in the degree to which they capture reality and thus be true.

But this brings us back to the notion of variation in concretion between ideas (judgments). In *Appearance and Reality* we are told that

> We must notice here the higher development of concrete internal unity. For we find an individuality, subordinating to itself outward fact, though not, as such, properly visible within it. This superiority to mere appearance in the temporal series is carried to a higher degree as we advance into the worlds of religion, speculation, and art. The inward principle may here become far wider, and have an intenser unity of its own; but, on the side of temporal existence [i.e., mere perception], it cannot possibly exhibit itself as such. The higher the principle, and the more vitally it, so to speak, possesses of the soul of things, so much the wider in proportion must be that sphere of events which in the end it controls. But, just for this reason, such a principle cannot be handled or seen, nor is it in any way given to outward or inward perception. It is only the meaner realities which can ever be so revealed, and which are able to be verified as sensible facts.[23]

Bradley believes that as we progress up the scale of judgment forms (with the higher forms characteristically found in science, philosophy, religion, and art) we are just progressing up the scale of what we may call the "real" as opposed to "apparent" (i.e., sensuous) concreteness of any experience. But what constitutes this conceptual concreteness? We have used, as does Bradley, a variety of expressions throughout this essay to refer to this idea: the "reunification of the what and the that," the conceptual apprehension of the "this," "systematicity," "coherence and comprehensiveness." These are all terms that are meant to convey the fact that there *is* a difference that can be found amongst superficially similar ideas. And, although this is a less than obvious (because not overtly sensuous) fact of our experience we are trying to understand, let us at least consider the following.

Given the limitations of the human perceptual mechanism it does not seem at all controversial to claim that we cannot hold before us on a detailed perceptual basis the wealth of prior (sensuously based) experience that constitutes our evidence for asserting that "such and such is the case."[24] The purely perceptual content of an assertion would seem to be that which currently occupies our sensory field in the moment the judgment is made. But, if we are limited by the sensory organs (and perhaps the picturing ability of the imagination) in what we may perceptually work into any assertion, some other sort of content must be present. Even so simple a grammatical utterance as "If you ask the bank for a loan it will refuse" seems to be one that can exhibit enormous variations in depth of comprehension—even if made under roughly the same perceptual conditions.

But let us consider this idea further. Assume, for example, that seated at the dinner table with you is your teenage son and your accountant. Both utter "If you ask the bank for a loan it will refuse." And let us make the further, and not unreasonable, assumption that their perceptual content is when making this assertion roughly the same. Now, if under these conditions we compare the assertion as put forth by the teenage son (whose grasp of finance extends not much further than the price of cigarettes and concert tickets) and the accountant, then we must acknowledge that the grounds for saying what is grammatically the same thing are enormously different. Whereas the accountant's utterance holds in a unified vision his experience in financial matters as well as, let us assume, a personal knowledge of the idiosyncrasies of the bank's loan officers, it is unlikely that the son's assertion could bring to bear anything remotely resembling this lot of experience (all of which constitutes "evidence" or "internalized conditions"). And, if it were not the case that the same fact could be grasped with varying degrees of concretion and necessity then there would be no greater significance to our experience than that which mere perception or mere linguistic form could provide. But can we truly believe that when a seasoned astronomer gazes at the heavens his apprehension is on the same level as a young child's? Could the words "Caesar crossed the Rubicon" really mean the same thing for the schoolboy and the scholar? Certainly Bradley's view is that they cannot.

To summarize our result here we may say the following: For Bradley our ideas (judgments) are just summary restatements of huge tracts of experience. Although we cannot *visibly* (i.e., perceptually) reinstate that experience, we can do so in idea. And the simple fact of the matter as understood by Bradley is that our judgments are concrete, are systematic, and are true just so far as they (nonperceptually) *do* reach into—not only *our* past experience—but into what he believes is the *one* experience in which we all participate: that of the Absolute. And, though we shall have more to say about the relation between individual and "supraindividual" experience when we discuss Bradley's doctrine of feeling in the next chapter, for now we need only remind ourselves that any ascending scale of judgment forms, any gradient of truth and reality, depends upon this notion of the concrete idea that, although attached to perceptual experience, cannot be said to consist in it.[25]

TRUTH AND THE WHOLE

Though we have spent many pages considering the theory in a variety of ways, the idea we are trying to develop here is simply that, for Bradley, *the Truth is the whole*. (There just is no simpler way to put the matter.) And to the degree that we can *conceptually* bring that whole before us in judgment is the degree to which we have accessed reality and are in possession of Truth.

> To be more or less true, and to be more or less real [Bradley tells us], is to be separated by an interval, smaller or greater, from all inclusiveness and self-consistency. Of two given appearances the one more wide, or more harmonious, is more real. It approaches nearer to a single, all containing, individuality. To remedy its imperfections, in other words, we should have to make a smaller alteration, the truth and the fact, which, to be converted into the Absolute would require less rearrangement and addition, is more real and truer. And this is what we mean by degrees of reality and truth.[26]

This is, of course, not an idea that is new to us. It has been with us throughout our discussion, and we need only review what has already been said to see how this is so. When we discussed the relative degree of ideality in judgment, we encountered the doctrine of degrees of truth and reality. We saw in this discussion that, so far as our act of conceptual apprehension is able to include within its four corners, not only its "whatness" (its general character as a content) but also its "thatness" (its specificity as this or that unique example), only so far is our judgment capable of being true. Indeed, "thatness" was described as nothing other than this aspect of specificity and individuality. And, since, on Bradley's theory, we must assume that in the reality itself the "what" and "that" are perfectly conjoined, reality can be understood as successfully apprehended by us only to the degree that these aspects are united in our judgment.

We have also learned that an absence of "thatness" results in mere abstract generality, and that the way to overcome this generality is through the inclusion within our judgment of the context that makes our referent the unique individual it is. We incorporate "thatness" into our apprehension by seeing our content, not as a merely abstract kind, but as *this* occurrence of its kind. We bring together the "what" and "that" when we see the content as, although identical in one respect, different in others. Put differently, the "what" and the "that" are reunited in judgment so far as we can apprehend them as being *systematically exemplified* in experience. Although we must always take care not to confuse the judgment with its mere grammatical formulation, we may say that "I live on Main Street" is far more abstract (and less true) than "I live on Main Street in the borough of Kutztown"; and that the latter assertion contains a greater degree of unity between content and existence. But in saying this we are back to the idea of system and comprehensiveness. The ability to designate accurately—that is, truly to bring into conscious awareness the uniqueness of our intended object—is wholly dependent upon our ability to include with its boundaries the context within which our object falls. And, as we have now learned, this context may be construed as its evidential base. But this is to say no more than that our judgment is successful only so far as it is comprehensive or all-inclusive. The greater the comprehension or range the higher the level of both truth and reality it can be said to contain.

But let us also consider this idea in relation to Bradley's theory of contradiction and relations. Once more we find that a judgment is understood to be ensnared in contradiction and to be merely relational to the degree that its conditions are external to the act. Bradley summarizes this notion when he writes:

> Truth must exhibit the mark of internal harmony, or again, the mark of expansion and all-inclusiveness. And these two characteristics are diverse aspects of a single principle. That which contradicts itself, in the first place, jars, because the whole, immanent within it, drives its parts into collision. And the way to find harmony, as we have seen, is to redistribute these discrepancies in a wider arrangement. But, in the second place, harmony is incompatible with restriction and finitude. For that which is not all-inclusive must by virtue of its essence internally disagree; and, if we reflect, the reason of this becomes plain. That which exists in a whole

has external relations. Whatever it fails to include within its own nature, must be related to it by the whole, and related externally. Now these extrinsic relations, on the one hand, fall outside of itself, but, upon the other hand, cannot do so. For a relation must at both ends affect, and pass into, the being of its terms. And hence the inner essence of what is finite itself both is, and is not, the relations which limit it. Its nature is hence incurably relative, passing, that is, beyond itself, and importing, again, into its own core a mass of foreign connexions. Thus to be defined from without is, in principle, to be distracted within. And, the smaller the element, the more wide is this dissipation of its essence—a dissipation too thorough to be deep, or to support the title of an intestine division. But, on the contrary, the expansion of the element should increase harmony, for it should bring these external relations within the inner substance. By growth the element becomes, more and more a consistent individual, containing in itself its own nature; and it forms, more and more, a whole inclusive of discrepancies and reducing them to system. The two aspects of extension and harmony are thus in principle one.[27]

Although there is little here that is actually new, I would emphasize Bradley's characterization of the concrete systematic whole as the "individual." And the point he is making is, I think, simply this. To be an individual is to be self-sufficient. But, no system, no apparent individual, can truly be individual (in the strongest sense) until it is all-inclusive and no longer makes reference beyond itself. And, unless and until it has reached that point, it is still subject to internal disruption and contradiction. We might restate this by saying that no matter how concrete an idea is, it remains always a *selected* idea that—through its inability to grasp the entirety of experience—leaves something "outside" or "behind." However, that which is internal to a concept cannot just ignore what remains external. Through an identity of content there is a continual passing beyond itself by the idea that we entertain. As Bradley tell us, *all* of reality is immanent within any idea. And its immanent content (which may be called the idea's "implications") will just not lie still.

We have described this immanent reality, this implicit content upon which our explicit assertion depends for its meaning (but which it fails to include), as the "presupposed world" or the "feeling mass" out of which we always select in any act of judgment. And since it is only because of the hovering presence of this larger world that our assertions are capable of being condemned as defective, we must soon consider in greater detail just how Bradley understands the judging subject to stand in relation to it. First, however, I would like briefly to discuss the problem of error and some attacks that are often made on coherence theories of truth.

ERROR

The subject of error is a large one and it has already occupied a good deal of our attention. However, given that we are explicitly dealing with the notions of coherence and degrees of truth, there are two further points that I would like to make here. The first is that, for most purposes, Bradley is entirely willing to concede that we must treat truth and error as absolute. That is, we must in our daily practice act as if there were no such thing as degrees of truth. A judgment is, under ordinary circumstances, usually held to be either entirely true or entirely false; and this is, Bradley believes, completely acceptable.

Having said this, though, Bradley warns us that the requirements of ordinary practice do not always provide theoretical truth and intellectual satisfaction. And when we begin to concern ourselves with greater consistency in our thought we are forced into the doctrine of degrees of truth and reality. I would like to discuss Bradley's conception of error, then, through the consideration of the following passage as I think it clearly brings to light his doctrine as we have been developing it throughout this essay.

> Error [we read] is truth, it is partial truth, that is false only because partial and incomplete. The Absolute *has* without subtraction all those qualities, and it has every arrangement which we seem to confer upon it by our mere mistake. The only mistake lies in our failure to give also the complement. The reality owns the discordance and the discrepancy of false appearance; but it possesses also much else in which this jarring character is swallowed up and is dissolved in fuller harmony.[28]

The attentive reader should notice here a strong resemblance between this conception of error and that of contradiction developed in the previous chapter. We may recall that we contradict ourselves, and in so doing are in error, when we fail to bring predicates together on an adequate basis. And what we should also notice here is that error, as understood by Bradley, possesses precisely the same character as, and is itself always, a contradiction.

Perhaps this idea can be more easily conveyed by considering the following example. "Charles I died peacefully in his sleep" is a judgment that, on most accounts, would be construed as a blatant error and as decidedly false (given that Charles I actually died on the scaffold). But in analyzing this false assertion there are several points that we must bear in mind. First, the individual who makes the judgment is actually qualifying the real universe by these predicates. He believes that there is a real person known as "Charles I," and he also believes that there is an actual mode of death that is more or less captured by the phrase "died peacefully in his sleep" and that this latter notion is somehow continuous with the former. Second, we should consider Bradley's claim that the Absolute does, indeed, "own these predicates." And in saying this Bradley is expressing his conviction that *whatever* we assert has some sort of reality. When we say "The sky is chartreuse" we are dealing with *real* predicates that—individually considered—have their place in reality. And when we look at the special subject and predicate terms in "Charles I died peacefully in his sleep" we shall notice, again, real predicates being truly affirmed of reality. Our error consists only in the inadequate basis upon which they are brought together.[29]

At this point we would do well to remember that the conceptual-perceptual experience that we call "Charles I" has a vast network of relations above and below it. And so too, of course, does "dying peacefully in one's sleep." Thus the problem with false assertion is merely that we do not understand—to a sufficient extent anyway—what these precise webs of relations are. If we really knew the meaning of the term "Charles I" we would realize that "died on the scaffold in 1649" was part of its real meaning. And, for that matter if we really knew the meaning of "died peacefully in his sleep" we would know that it was not applicable to "Charles I."[30] What we have done when we falsely assert, then, is to bring together predicates on an *in*adequate basis. Both "Charles I" and "dying in one's sleep" are real predicates that characterize the reality to which they are applied and of which they are asserted. Of course, had we dealt with our concepts more concretely this error could not have arisen. If we had a truly concrete—that is, coherent and comprehensive—understanding of "Charles I" we could not possibly have made such an erroneous ideal development of our special subject. A concrete development, we should be aware, must be historically correct. That is, it must include just those conditions that made Charles I who he was; and amongst these is his precise mode of death.

But the fact remains, Bradley tells us, that we are always dealing with less than fully concrete notions. When we judge we are, to some degree, always involved with notions that are too abstract, too general, and less than fully specific. As Bradley puts it, when we wrongly assert

We have not only loosened 'what' from 'that', and so have made appearance; but we have in each case then bestowed the 'what' on a wrong quality within the real subject. We have crossed the threads of the connexion between our 'what's' and our 'that's', and have thus caused collision, a collision which disappears when things are taken as a whole.[31]

Perhaps we might more easily grasp this notion by employing a metaphor here. Most of us have had, I think, the experience of looking into a microscope and of viewing the specimen below the lens when it is both in and out of focus. When it is out of focus we sometimes see lines of connection which, at that point, appear to be continuous and solid with another part of the object we are viewing. However, as we turn the focusing knob things begin to change before our eyes. What had previously appeared as continuous segments of our specimen now appear, not only as disconnected, but even on separate planes within it. And detail that was absent on the first look has now appeared and provided us with a view of an articulate and detailed object that, a moment before, appeared much less complex. If we had been asked to describe the object as seen through the eyepiece of the inaccurately focused microscope, we would have made connections of content, that is, we would have asserted as continuous, certain segments that a moment later we would have said were separate.

Now, though this is only a metaphor, the mechanism of error in judgment is not, I think, too different from that which we have just described. Both special subject and limited predicate are *there* in the real universe; but the basis upon which we have brought them together is faulty.[32] (They are, we might say, "out of focus.") However, this is, we should recall, a characteristic of not just the false judgment. As we have already considered, Bradley is firmly convinced that all judgment suffers from this defect. It is only a matter of degree; and it is not at all a clear at what point—on a practical level anyway—we would be inclined to call some judgments "true" and others "false."

I would end this brief discussion of error by pointing out the following: It is not for no reason that someone would be led to assert "Charles I died peacefully in his sleep." Amongst the truthful (albeit implicit) aspects of the claim are (i) that Charles I was a human being; and (ii) that, therefore, he did die. Hence, the ideal extension of Charles I in this manner is, up to a point, completely legitimate. We might also notice that "dying peacefully in his sleep" does contain as part of its concrete meaning "how some English monarchs have died." And, indeed, there could very well be a legitimate synthesis—a working back from this aspect of the special predicate—that motivates one to attach this idea to that of "Charles I." It could be that the person who judges "Charles I died peacefully in his sleep" is trying to synthetically reconstruct a piece of history based upon two actual experiences. These might be, for example, his reading about the life of Charles I (short of his manner of death) and a statement someone made about the death of a later Charles. As Bradley tells us, "Error is truth when it is supplemented." And, we need only supplement the above judgment in order to find for it a smooth acceptance into the greater web of experience. "Charles I died on the scaffold in 1649, but Charles II died peacefully in his sleep."[33] Caught in the single nexus of meaning—a nexus that we may understand as the precise structure of the Absolute—we judge; and given our finite perspective we necessarily fail to grasp all the connections that go to make up the structure of our object. Hence, we err. And, Bradley would insist, we *always* err. But our error is never complete—it is always a matter of degree.

THE ATTACK ON COHERENTISM

At this stage I would like to briefly comment on Bradley's doctrine vis-à-vis the many attacks that have been made by twentieth-century philosophers on what they have understood as "coherence theories" of justification and truth. And to begin I would mention that, not only does Bradley see the relation of coherence—at least as we have described it thus far—as that which ultimately *justifies* any judgment, this justificatory relation is also what constitutes for him the degree of *truth* that accrues to any proposition. Hence the ideas of justification and truth cannot for Bradley be isolated. On his view, truth just consists in the relations of concrete implication that experience as a whole brings to bear on this or that judgment. And, though his own idea of coherence stands at a great remove from contemporary conceptions, Bradley still sees fit to describe the relation that holds between the asserted content and the rest of experience by this term.

Despite the differences that exist between Bradley's own and contemporary accounts of coherence, I think it useful to consider the common objections to such theories. Not only shall we develop a better sense of Bradley's conception of coherence, we shall also come to better appreciate the failure of contemporary philosophers to address the sort of coherentism that writers like Bradley endorse. Hence let us consider what are commonly called (i) the infinite regress objection; (ii) the input objection; (iii) the alternative coherent systems objection; and (iv) the primacy of logic objection. Not all critics of coherentism put forth all of these objections; and some of them overlap.[34] However, we shall soon see that, though each attack has a valid point to make, each has failed to address the theory of justification and truth as actually put forth by Bradley.

The Infinite Regress Objection

This objection says, in effect, that coherence cannot be ultimate; that is, it cannot provide true justification for any belief nor can it give the nature of truth. If it did, we would never arrive at any thing we could call *knowledge* (since there is nothing sufficiently substantive upon which to anchor our beliefs). But in order to understand this criticism we must consider how it is that the "foundationalist," the critic who makes this objection, views the relation of coherence and the question of justification.

Let us consider the following: Whenever we ask ourselves, "What justifies our belief in X" we most probably shall appeal to a further belief Y that functions as a "reason" or, in some sense of the term, "evidence" for our embracing X. And, when asked why we believe in Y we shall cite yet a further reason. Now, whenever a belief is justified by a further belief in this manner we may call that belief "nonbasic" or "inferential." And when we try to understand what justifies such an inferential chain of belief it seems that there are four alternatives open to us. Either (a) we must view the inferential chain of belief as terminating in just another inferential belief, thus leaving the chain, so to speak, "free floating"; or (b) we must see each of our beliefs as inferentially justified by others *ad infinitum* (with no termination in sight); or (c) we must understand the chain of belief as moving in a circle. That is, we appeal to Y as the justification of X and Z as that which justifies Y; but when asked what is our basis for believing Z we put forth X. However, seeing all of these accounts of justification as problematic, the foundationalist seeks a fourth option. He seeks (d) a "basic" belief—a belief that is not itself justified by ordinary inferential means—but that is somehow "self-justifying" (usually by a special relation to the external world). But, the objection runs, should we appeal to coherence as that which provides justification, we are surely engaged in reasoning that is viciously circular. Hence, coherence cannot provide us with an adequate criterion for the justification of belief (let alone truth). Either, we are told, there are noninferential "basic beliefs" upon which all knowledge is justified, or knowledge *has* no justification. And we need not deal with the alternative means by which philosophers have described the basic beliefs that (purportedly) bring the regressive chain of justification to a halt. Some philosophers believe that basic beliefs can only be known through a process of direct intuition of the noncognitive given experience, others say that a basic belief is basic if it is "caused" by external reality, and yet others tell us that basic beliefs can only be apprehended by us on an a priori basis.

Response to the Infinite Regress Objection

Ignoring the question of whether or not such "basic beliefs" could be intelligibly described at all, we need only concern ourselves here with the fact that the very idea of "linear" justification that leads to the problematic regress is one that is wholly alien to Bradley's account of justification and truth. (Bradley's own doctrine, we should now understand, is "nonlinear" or "systematic.") The linear conception of justification (that which this objection presupposes) sees coherence as a relation of formal consistency between one proposition—we shall again call it "X" and identify it as a "nonbasic" belief" and another proposition "Y" (which could be either a nonbasic or a basic belief). If proposition X can be derived from proposition Y via "accepted rules of inference" then it can be said to "cohere" and be "inferentially justified." But we need only point out (again) that Bradley's conception of coherence runs far deeper than any notion of mere formal consistency or logical deducibility.

Whereas the proponent of noninferential justification for basic beliefs must at some point rest his claim on either an unjustified belief in the reliability of the causal mechanism, a merely subjective "intuition," or of "self-evidence" (all of which being subject to dismissal by the sceptic), Bradley's's position need not rely on such a flimsy basis. For Bradley, justification is present so far as the denial of the assertion would upset the system that makes the assertion possible. And, given that some assertions are so deeply entrenched that their falsification would preclude the possibility of any experience for anyone, Bradley has provided us with an account of justification that does not force us to rely on the existence of noncognitive intuitions (whose existence is dubious), or on a conception of the causal relation that is external to our experience and hence ultimately unverifiable.

The Input Objection

This objection tells us that coherence is a matter of the internal relations between the beliefs that constitute the larger belief system of the judging subject. And, it is further claimed, these relations of coherence are in no way dependent upon the relation between the belief system and the external world. Hence if, as some coherence theories claim, coherence is the sole basis of empirical justification, it follows that a system of beliefs might be fully justified, even though completely out of touch with the world.

Response to the Input Objection

We should notice here that this objection can only be made against what is called a "pure" theory of coherence. (Bradley's own doctrine must be seen as quite "impure.") Such a pure theory sees "thought" and "perceptual experience" as distinct, and understands the coherence relation to be that which obtains only between the thought components (beliefs) in our experience. And the idea is that since thought and our noncognitive experience are distinct (and ultimately externally related to one another), it is a theoretical possibility that our "thinking" could consist of a totally self-consistent universe that remains, potentially anyway, unaffected by our larger perceptual experience.

Now, even though this objection is frequently made against coherence theories of truth, I am not sure that anyone has actually espoused such a doctrine. (Certainly no writer in the idealist tradition has ever held this view.) And I hope it is evident by now that such an objection could not touch Bradley given his commitment to the idea that every belief is grounded—directly or indirectly—in sensuous experience. If the objection has any force at all it must, I think, be this: It would seem that the coherentist must be able to say that our "observational beliefs"— that is, our judgments that bear directly upon the given contents of sense—must be (roughly) the same for subjects who are exposed to the same empirical input. And I say this because, if it were the case that different subjects who were exposed to the same empirical input could construe this input in radically different ways, then surely there is no reason to suppose that all judging subjects would—even if they achieved maximal coherency within their belief systems—construe reality in the same fashion. Put differently unless there is something about our observational beliefs that is a priori, and unless that a priori content can somehow dictate the direction in which nonobservational beliefs will develop, the project of coherentism seems in for a difficult time. But since these points are best discussed in response to the "alternative coherent systems objection," let us proceed to it.

The Alternative Coherent Systems Objection

It is often said that any belief system must, on the coherence theory, be itself epistemically justified only through relations of coherence that are internal to it. But if this is true, then the presence of "coherence" within a belief system will never allow us to choose between *different* systems of belief (at least if each is equally justified by its internal coherence relations) so as to pick out that which is *true* (or at least the *most* true). Since on some contemporary conceptions of coherence, there will always be many systems of belief (possibly infinitely many) that are—while equally coherent—different and incompatible, no nonarbitrary choice between belief systems can be made, at least not on the basis of coherence.

This is probably the single most important objection to any coherence theory of justification or truth. And in order to understand its importance, let us consider again what was said in response to the input objection. For coherentism of any sort to work we must be able to say that (i) all subjects must bring to empirical input the same (more or less) conceptual apparatus; and (ii) that this conceptual apparatus must have the capacity to guide the inferential development of empirical input in such a way that—so far as our beliefs exhibit coherence and comprehensiveness—they will coincide. That is, a *maximally* coherent belief system must, on this doctrine, be the same for all judging subjects. However, if it be granted that there is no "guiding thread" at the level of observational belief (or later within the domain of nonobservational beliefs), then the possibility of radically different, and ultimately incommensurable, belief systems is a real one. But how does Bradley deal with this problem?

Response to the Alternative Coherent Systems Objection

In essence, Bradley's response to this difficulty is via a series of transcendental arguments. That is, Bradley claims that any coherent experience must presuppose (at the level of feeling) a number of things about the structure of reality. While Bradley does not try to deduce "categories," he does argue that all judging subjects must assume both that the contents of experience stand in precise and invariable relations to one another and that the universe that comprises them is *one*. (If this can be established then the idea of "alternative conceptual systems" begins to look like an impossibility.) And Bradley further argues for the necessity of a single *true* conceptual system by pointing out that all recognition of differences entails that those differences be brought under a unified set of concepts. If we talk of different "spaces" or "times," the very recognition of them *as* different recognizes a bond of unity and thus synthesizes them into a single systematic vision. And the same can be said about different "conceptual systems."[35] To recognize a different belief system *as such* would presuppose, on the Bradleian view, a point of common ground and shared identity. But with this recognition one must give up the idea that the belief systems are different in any fundamental sense.[36] It is only on the assumption that knowledge is just "in the mind of the subject" and that it "copies" an external object that the objection can be maintained. But, as we have spent so many pages discussing, Bradley's conception of judgment utterly rejects this radical split between knowledge and its object. And, for Bradley, there can only exist "alternative conceptual schemes" so far as these schemes are *incoherent*—i.e. false.[37]

The Primacy of the Logic Objection

It is sometimes said that, although coherence is a useful test as to the truth of this or that judgment (which we test to see if it is coherent with already known truths), it cannot provide us with an account of the nature of truth because it doesn't reach deeply enough into our experience. Coherence must presuppose the laws of logic in order to exist at all. Thus we are forced to conclude that the laws of logic are themselves immune from the test of coherence. And thus we know that *they* are true on some other basis (this usually being "self-evidence" or "correspondence").

Response to the Primacy of Logic Objection

While this objection seems less serious than those already considered, some have seen it as decisive. Here again, though, the critic presupposes important metaphysical views about the nature of truth and attacks a straw man that has little if any force against Bradley's actual position. As we have already seen, Bradley's notion of coherence is not that of formal consistency. That which either coheres or doesn't is not the bare grammatical proposition; rather it is the perceptual-conceptual entity he calls the judgment. And, although Bradley would be the first to agree that—in one sense—the laws of logic *are* ultimate, he would insist that our awareness of their truth could only be known via an appeal to the criteria of coherence and comprehensiveness. If we bear in mind that Bradley's notion of coherence rests upon the idea of a harmonious and comprehensive fit between various elements of a larger conceptual-perceptual mass of experience, the ultimacy of logic objection seems to fall to the ground. These laws of logic themselves are but descriptions of what constitute "a good fit" (coherence); they are, if you will, codified claims that reality *is* coherent. And, as such, they can hardly be called "prior to" and "immune" from the test of coherence. Any estimation as to the truth and falsity of a judgment that expresses these laws itself must proceed according to the sense of fit that either does or does not come about when we weigh the meaning of that judgment against the larger fabric of experience.

COHERENCE, IDENTITY, AND CORRESPONDENCE

Before moving on to consider the all-important relation of "feeling" to judgment I would like to comment briefly on the claim that is sometimes made regarding the actual nature of Bradley's theory of truth. It has occasionally been suggested that his theory of truth is not a coherence theory at all, but either an unusual version of "correspondence" or an "identity" theory.[38] And, since these claims are not without basis, I would like to offer the following observations.

It could be said that since Bradley views all truth as ideal—that is, as something suffering from a content-existence rupture—and since the real is understood as enjoying a perfect unity of these elements (such that the degree to which our ideas reflect this unity is the degree to which they can be called "true"), we are left with an understanding of the relation between judgment and reality that is surely best characterized by the term "correspondence." And, it might be continued, this is further corroborated by what Bradley says about the feeling-base of experience. If it is true that felt experience consists not only in the totality of my prior judgments (which may be said to constitute my intelligible world) but also an excess of content that extends far beyond anything I have ever encountered in thought or perception, then surely this "excess" constitutes an unintellectualized surd. And since coherence is, and must be, a relation between mere *ideas*, the relation in which my judgment stands to its object can only be called "correspondence."

Now, this is not an unreasonable objection. However, we must see why it is that Bradley rejects it, and why he is always inclined to see his own doctrine as best characterized by the term "coherence." And there are two considerations here: (i) Bradley does not believe that what we have in our perceptual-conceptual apprehension of the real is a mere copy; rather he believes that we experience the object itself, even though our grasp of it must be partial, incomplete, and infected with irrelevancies. The object of perception-conception in judgment is understood to be the *object itself*—even if in a limited and (to some degree) "mutilated" form. Hence, Bradley sees the content as it appears in the mind to be the *same* content as it is in the object. But, if this is the case, one must wonder what it is the judgment is supposed to correspond to? Given that virtually all correspondence theories see the judgment as some sort of representation or duplicate of an object that is itself wholly nonconceptual, it seems difficult to regard Bradley's account of truth as a species of correspondence theory. And the only way that one could maintain such a view is if one were to persist in the (erroneous) interpretation of Bradley's theory of experience that finds given perception as the source of the perfectly unique and self-sufficient object. On this view thought and reality fall apart to such a degree that our thinking becomes a mere "thinking about" the object. But, as we have seen, such a reading of Bradley is entirely in error.

But what about "identity theories"? Here the claim carries much more force. And, indeed, one *could* legitimately interpret Bradley's doctrine along these lines. (Of course, the details of the identity theory would be all-important.) It is true that Bradley sees the mind of the judging subject as partially coincident with its object in true assertion. (And all assertion, as we have learned, is true to some degree.) That is, so far as any assertion possesses truth the mind of the assertor has *identified with* or (literally) *become* the object. And if this is what is meant by an "identity theory," then certainly Bradley's theory would qualify as such.[39]

I would also mention that construed as an identity theory, Bradley's doctrine seems to overcome some of the powerful objections that have been raised against such views. For example, it has long been considered the death-blow to all accounts of truth as "identity" to point out what this means for false judgments. On most accounts the false judgment, in order to be intelligible at all, demands that there exist *something* (some kind of "false fact") that the assertor's mind identifies with when the proposition is asserted as true. However, what could this "false fact" be? If a true assertion is true just because it involves a coincidence between the mind and the object known, what can we say the mind is identified with when we judge falsely?

Bradley's answer may be found when we recall what he says about error. As considered earlier, it is Bradley's position that even the falsest of assertions contains some truth. That is, in some way the terms of the judgment must be partially identified with their object. And the difference between the assertion that possesses a high degree of truth and one that possesses a lesser degree is the basis upon which these terms are brought together (the inclusion of the terms's conditions). But, having already discussed this point, I shall not consider it further. I only mention the identity theory because I think that Bradley's own concept of truth seems to come close to what some proponents of this view have in mind. And Bradley's doctrine also seems to provide a plausible way in which some of the fundamental objections to these theories might be met.

But whatever we call Bradley's theory of truth, there are some important points to bear in mind. While we have yet to consider this aspect of his theory in any detail, we must remember that Bradley believes the universe to be essentially *experience*. He also believes that every content—even though it may not have been thought of or experienced by *me*—has been experienced (he does not say "thought") by someone or something.[40] And he utterly rejects any experience transcendent "thing-in-itself" that might constitute ultimate reality and that could serve as the real criterion of truth. But, given the fact that the ultimate referent in any judgment is something that is experienced—and given that it is of the same order as the content within my judgment—Bradley is inclined to call this relation between what is before the mind (the judgment) and what is in the world (the object) "coherence." And, so long as we are careful to distinguish Bradley's doctrine from those contemporary versions of "coherentism," we shall not be wrong to use this term to characterize his own theory of truth.

Chapter 8

FEELING AND KNOWLEDGE (i)

WE are now approaching the end of our discussion, and still one of the most controversial aspects of Bradley's philosophy—his doctrine of feeling—remains to be examined. Here we find Bradley advocating a position that was rejected, not just by his realist and empiricist critics; it also found less than a sympathetic audience amongst some of the orthodox idealist writers. Indeed, in his doctrine of feeling we find Bradley propounding a conception of the criterion of knowledge that is, if not entirely new in the development of monistic idealism, at least a restatement so original as to be found suspect by many. Still, Bradley sees this move as the most reasonable way out of some pressing philosophical difficulties.

In what follows, then, we shall be forced to make the following distinctions. (i) First there is what Bradley calls "mere feeling" and the "merely felt." Strictly speaking, this is any felt experience that is less than all-inclusive. However, I shall illustrate Bradley's meaning here by focusing on sensuous immediacy. Sensuous experience, in being continually disappearing, constitutes for Bradley the narrowest type of feeling and most clearly illustrates the problematic nature of the merely felt; (ii) next, there is Bradley's widely discussed conception of "immediate experience." As we shall soon discover, this is *not* to be identified with the merely given sensuous present. Immediate experience is, for Bradley, quite rich in that it contains, not only our given sensuous awareness, but also much of our intellectual and volitional lives. Although often understood as a kind of preconceptual confrontation with reality, we shall soon learn that it is best understood as the unified experience of the various sides of our being. And lastly (iii) we shall be forced to examine Bradley's conception of "feeling" in a sense that appears to transcend even immediate experience. Here we find a form of feeling that, though it is continuous with my own, cannot truly be said to be "mine" but not "yours.". And in discussing this most inclusive form of feeling we shall be forced to consider how Bradley understands the Absolute's experience of itself.

While these various distinctions must be seen as continuous—they are all aspects of the "feeling base"—this last form will be crucial for Bradley's theory as it provides the route by which he hopes to establish the objectivity of judgment. And, though it is not the most primitive form of experience we possess, I think we might most profitably proceed by considering first Bradley's conception of (ii) immediate experience. As we shall see, immediate experience is certainly felt; but, in the end, what we feel as immediate experience must be, though greater than our sensuous existence, something less what we are ultimately capable of apprehending.

"IMMEDIATE EXPERIENCE"

But what *is* Bradley's understanding of immediate experience? We may first say that it is a form of experience that, though it includes our assertive awareness as an element, it goes well beyond its boundaries. Whereas the assertive (relational) consciousness always provides us with explicit objects (or experiential complexes) that are at some point discrete and discontinuous, in immediate experience things are different. In immediate experience we are somehow aware of a larger unified world with which the object identified in judgment is continuous and to which it belongs. In his *Essays on Truth and Reality* Bradley writes:

> Immediate experience is not a stage, which may or may not at some time have been there and now ceased to exist. It is not in any case removed by the presence of a not-self and of a relational consciousness. All that is thus removed is at most, we may say, the *mereness* of immediacy. Every distinction and relation still rests on an immediate background of which we are aware, and every distinction and relation (so far as experienced) is also felt, and felt in a sense to belong to an immediate totality. Thus in all experience we still have feeling which is not an object, and at all moments the entirety of what comes to us, however much distinguished and relational, is felt as *comprised within* a unity which is itself not relational.[1]

Now, there are a number of points in this passage that demand our attention. First is the idea of the omnipresence of immediate experience. Bradley is explicitly rejecting here the idea that we have immediate experience only when our minds are undeveloped or otherwise immature and that this form of experience is something that we subsequently outgrow. While Bradley is willing to acknowledge that there has existed in the life of each of us a stage that can be called "mere immediacy"—a stage that is with us when we are young but that later disappears—his own conception of immediate experience is not captured by this idea. (Mere immediacy, it would appear, is sensuous experience accompanied by a severely limited assertive consciousness.) We must always remember that when Bradley uses the term "immediate experience" he is referring to our direct and unmediated grasp of certain experiential contents. And this sort of direct apprehension is, he believes, something that is always with us.

Bradley's idea of immediate experience may also be introduced by contrasting it with our limited assertive awareness. In the relational or assertive consciousness, we should recall, I focus on this or that aspect of my larger experience. However, when I focus on an aspect of experience—when I cognitively determine it within my field of awareness—I make it an object. But the object as it comes before the relational consciousness is always limited. In judgment, we should recall, I only select so much from the larger feeling mass; only a portion of what I sense as the fuller object of my awareness comes within my focused cognitive grasp. And, as we have now seen, within the relational consciousness there exist gaps and discontinuities. Although there exists a degree of continuity between terms, at some point this continuity breaks down. Not so, however, for immediate experience. And when Bradley tells us that it is "non-relational" he wants to force upon us the idea that in immediate experience we have an awareness that—though containing internal distinctions—is essentially *seamless*. Whereas any judgment (relational awareness) will always exhibit discontinuities and gaps between its internal elements, immediate experience is, first and foremost, the felt continuum that supports our assertive consciousness. And without this felt continuum we could never sense the discontinuity that our relational awareness contains.

Of course, when I do judge, it is just the contrast between what is explicitly before the mind in judgment and what remains in this fuller immediate experience that provides me (sooner or later) with the sense that my assertive experience is defective. Through the juxtaposition of the relational consciousness—my present judgment—and its conditioning context of immediate experience, there is forced upon me a sense that the former is somehow incomplete and distorted. (See chapter 5.) And, though it is this fuller immediate experience that betrays my relational consciousness as defective, it is this same immediate experience that provides much of the material through which this defect can be progressively (though never completely) overcome.[2] Since the relational consciousness is always built upon something fuller than it can itself provide, I always have a sense of the object that is greater than what I have managed to get into my explicit assertion. And it is the ongoing supplementation of the relational consciousness by the material supplied by immediate experience that constitutes thought's advance.[3]

But this brings us to another important (and often misunderstood) aspect of immediate experience. Immediate experience not only provides us with ongoing sensuous data; it also functions as a reservoir or container for the data that is being continually integrated into our larger intellectual world.[4] As Bradley tells us:

> The felt background, against which the object comes remains always immediate. But, on the other hand, its content may to some extent show mediation. Parts of this content may have been elements included in the object, and may have at some time been internally distinguished into relations and terms. However nonetheless now, *this relational content forms part of the felt background.*[5]

Immediate experience, then, is not just sensuous in nature, rather it would appear that Bradley sees it as consisting in our present sensuous awareness as it is conditioned by our prior intellectual experience. Although immediate experience contains a diversity of content that is far greater than what our relational consciousness has produced, we may still say that it is in immediate experience that the *results* of this relational consciousness are—along with their sensuous and volitional complements—preserved. That is, it is in immediate experience that the persisting web of significance that conditions this or that explicit assertion resides, and where any assertion's meaning or significance is made directly available. In short, we may say that it is in immediate experience that there exists the ever present concrete context—sensuous, intellectual, and volitional—that makes any significant object what it is for us.

For example, my assertive (judging) apprehension of a piece of bread has as part of its implicit meaning that it "nourishes." I may not overtly *see* this in the sensuous data; nor might I have the idea of nourishment explicitly before my mind. But still, I may in the next instant recognize this meaningful aspect of the contents of either perception or imagination because immediate experience keeps these meanings at, so to speak, my "experiential fingertips." And this principle is, Bradley believes, constantly at work. On Monday I may witness Jones brutally beat his dog. (Of course, in my witnessing this event I judge something like "Jones is cruel to animals.") On Tuesday I see him acting benevolently toward his girlfriend's cat; but still I *feel* suspicious. And this felt uneasiness may be accounted for by the fact that there is directly experienced by me a meaning—a further significance—that attaches itself to my recognition of "Jones." This meaning may be partially the result of my prior intellectual activity; and it may in addition to this, contain elements never before brought into my relational awareness. The important point, however, is simply this: though this significance may or may not be explicitly and instantaneously brought into my conscious awareness, it conditions and colours what *is* explicitly before my mind, and it provides me with a sense of, in this case, who and what Jones really is.[6]

"Transcending" Immediacy

Now, there is a potential confusion here that we must at this stage warn against. One of the first obstacles to overcome in coming to grips with Bradley's theory of feeling is his sometimes idiosyncratic (and highly context-sensitive) use of terms. And of all the terms used by Bradley, the most misleading is, I think, "immediate experience." Whereas for most philosophical writers the term "immediate experience" means something like "that which is present here and now in sense experience," or "the direct object of our conscious awareness"; for Bradley, we should understand, the term often possesses a rather different meaning.

Although Bradley sometimes employs the terms "immediate" and "immediacy" in their more usual philosophical sense, he also has what we may call a technical usage. And, on Bradley's technical usage of "immediate experience," the idea carries with it the sense that there are many things we know—not because they are currently being conceived by us in judgment—but rather because we implicitly or intuitively grasp them.[7] For example, in a conversation with an old friend I do not explicitly hold before my mind the idea "This is John with whom I am speaking"; rather that "This is John" constitutes what we may call a "background assumption" of my more focused awareness. And, though my focused assertive awareness is continuous with its larger sensuous, intellectual, and volitional ground, it is not the same thing as it. And so too are these wholly sensuous differences that, though they are beyond the range of my cognitive awareness, are, nevertheless, there as elements within my larger experience. Indeed, it is just my focused assertive experience, when considered in *isolation* from its felt conditioning context, that constitutes what Bradley calls the "relational consciousness." And, on Bradley's theory, when the mind focuses on an experiential datum—when it discriminates at all— it takes an element from the immediate "feeling base," and casts it into the relational form (thereby, of course, placing it within the larger framework of ideas). Strictly speaking, though, any idea that has been so isolated by judgment is on Bradley's view no longer "immediate." It has at this point been made an object of our awareness; and, as such, it loses its purely immediate character. Hence, we must say that, for

Bradley, it is just those contents of experience that lie *outside* our explicit assertive experience that are most entitled to this moniker. But, as Bradley freely admits, this idea of immediate experience, while providing a solution to some fundamental difficulties, itself gives rise to a problem. As we read:

> The difficulty may be stated by asking, How immediate experience itself can become an object. For if it becomes an object, it, so far, we may say, is transcended, and there is a doubt as to how such transcendence is possible. On the one hand as to the fact of immediate experience being transcended we seem really certain. For we speak about it, and, if so, it has become for us an object. But we are thus led to the dilemma that, so far as I know of immediate experience, it does not exist, and that hence, whether it exists or not, I could in neither case know of it.[8]

We must realize here that by calling the experience that extends beyond our explicit and focused awareness "immediate," Bradley has backed himself into something of a philosophical corner. Since anything of which we can speak is, on this rather peculiar definition, no longer immediate per se, we must acknowledge that there exists on this theory no explicit awareness of our domain of discourse. But if we have no such awareness, if immediate experience is something for which we have no direct evidence, how can we speak of it at all?

Bradley's answer to this question rests upon a transcendental argument of sorts. While we do not possess any overt evidence that there exists a merely felt "knowing and being in one" that extends beyond and is, in one sense, other than the object of our explicit awareness, we may still confidently rely upon its existence by noticing what are the *conditions* of that which we do explicitly apprehend. Should we reflect upon the fact that both the given contents of sense and any object discriminated in my assertions may have significance only if there is something like the direct awareness that Bradley calls "immediate experience," we shall have, he believes, all the evidence required for our justified belief in its existence.[9] Assume at any point, Bradley tells us, that the thinking subject is *not* immersed in a nexus of significant experiential contents (which are not the object of explicit awareness), and you shall find that the given object that appears in judgment is without meaning. And if we are to assume that the perceptual apprehension of, let us say, a crust of bread, can mean something like "is edible" or "nourishes" we must, he claims, postulate some condition within our larger experience that is capable of possessing this fuller sense of the asserted object.[10]

Intellect and Will

We have up to now said that immediate experience comprises my larger intellectual universe (so far as it extends beyond the explicit focus of judgment) and my present sensuous experience. There is, however, more to what Bradley calls immediate experience. As we read:

> In my general feeling [i.e., immediate experience] at any moment there is more than the objects before me, and no perception of objects will exhaust the sense of a living emotion. And the same result is evident when I consider my will. I cannot reduce my experienced volition to a movement of objects and I cannot accept the suggestion that of this my volition I have no direct knowledge at all. We in short have experience in which there is no distinction between my awareness and that of which it is aware. There is an immediate feeling, a knowing and being in one, with which knowledge begins, and, though this in a manner is transcended, it nevertheless remains throughout as the present foundation of my known world. And if you remove this direct sense of my momentary contents and being, you bring down the whole of consciousness in one common wreck.[11]

While emotion and will are not usually discussed in epistemological treatises, I think that something must be said here about Bradley's conception of their role in our cognitive experience. At the very least we should recognize that Bradley sees both our larger intellectual world and its sensuous ground as thoroughly combined with our emotional and volitional being in immediate experience. And we must realize that immediate experience is for Bradley more than merely sensuous, merely intellectual, or merely volitional. Rather, immediate experience is the concrete *union* of these various sides of our being. And it is a union in which the whole is greater than the sum of its parts. In immediate experience the abstract nature of our intellectual universe is to a great extent overcome by its continual admixture with our sensuous being. And both intellect and sense are in immediate experience made even more concrete through their being supplemented by volition. Our intellectual and sensuous being is, then, continually conditioned by an awareness that they are (individually) not the totality of what we experience. And through the omnipresence of will there is maintained within our immediate experience an awareness, however implicit and merely assumed, that there is an *end* toward which our intellectual and sensuous being is directed.

But just what, according to Bradley, does the immediately experienced will seek? Although only the briefest of answers is possible here, we may say that, according to Bradley, what each of us wills, ultimately, is truth, goodness, and beauty.[12] These are, of course, only general terms used to indicate the complete fulfillment of the various sides of our nature. And Bradley is the first to admit that as the will is concretely manifested in any individual's immediate experience, something far less than the true, the good, and the beautiful is found. But, by telling us that will is an essential feature of immediate experience, and (more importantly) by insisting that at its furthest reaches we all must will the same thing, Bradley is emphasizing here that it is only through the presupposition of a universal end (the Absolute) that our relative ends can make sense; and further, the absolute ends that are assumed by the various sides of our being are, he believes, not contingent or arbitrary.[13] Of course, we may be almost entirely unaware of these presuppositions—these a priori ends. However, it is Bradley's firm conviction that we must not only believe certain things to be true of reality, we must also *desire* certain ends if we are to function at all as cognitive subjects.[14] And we may understand here that Bradley's argument for the existence of these a priori conditions is always the same: assume at any point that agents do not share such common ends that can be progressively (if not perfectly) realized, and you bring down in ruin the whole of conscious experience. Indeed, if it were the case that human experience is driven by purposes that are only coincidentally the same (if at all), we would, Bradley believes, be lost in a sea of intellectual and perceptual confusion. And should we try to conceive of an experience in which the common ends of truth, beauty, and goodness (or some such universally embraced goals) were not at work, the behavior of others would remain for us fundamentally unintelligible.[15]

The Comprehensiveness of Immediate Experience

Before moving on to consider the other forms of feeling mentioned at the beginning of the chapter, I think it worthwhile to say something more about immediate experience and its relation to the "relational consciousness." And the points I want to insist upon here are these:

(i) Bradley's understanding of experience is not one that sees our finite awareness as first confronted by an alien Other that we thereafter intellectually "interpret." From the beginning of our conscious existence the judgment is (albeit in rudimentary form) present. If we are consciously aware of a world at all, we have affirmed a continuity of content between what appears to our awareness and what we must believe exists beyond our finite apprehension. What this means, though, is that there are no preconceptual facts that are wholly non-ideal and that could be consciously perceived prior to our assertive awareness. But this leads to a further point.

(ii) If we cannot be consciously aware of a preconceptual given that is subsequently interpreted by judgment, any rigid line between our assertive (relational) consciousness and immediate experience is artificial.

While it is true that Bradley does distinguish the relational (thinking) and non-relational (felt) aspects of experience, we must take care not to pull apart these aspects of what is a larger unified experience into two rigidly distinct entities. As we read:

> Everything which is got out into the form of an object [relational awareness] implies still the felt background against which the object comes, and, further, the whole experience of both feeling *and* object is a non-relational immediate felt unity. The entire relational consciousness, in short, is experienced as *falling within* a direct awareness. This direct awareness is itself non-relational.[16]

Time and again, we are told, the relational consciousness "falls within" this immediate totality. And repeatedly we hear that our non-relational immediate experience "includes" the relational consciousness that somehow "transcends" it. Indeed, we are also told by Bradley that to separate in thought immediate experience and relational awareness at all is to engage in a potentially misleading abstraction. To speak of immediate experience as one thing that is discontinuous with and in opposition to another is to see immediate experience only as an object standing in relation to another object. But as we have already learned, immediate experience, when it has been so objectified, is no longer immediate, and we have misunderstood its actual nature.[17]

This suggests, then, that the relational consciousness should not be seen as some sort of mental superaddition that covers over a wholly noncognitive sensuous ground. (Indeed, given what Bradley says about both mere sense and perception, this seems an impossible interpretation.) Rather, I think, we are better advised to understand immediate experience as somehow containing *all* sides of experience. And, so far as we must differentiate the relational consciousness from the fuller sphere of immediate experience, we should see it as comprising only the focused and discriminating awareness of the presently affirmed idea. Though I might judge "The cat is on the mat," a moment later I think to myself "The cherry is on the tree." But, when I am thinking of cherries and trees, *where* has my thought of cats on mats gone? I think we have missed Bradley's meaning if we see it as somehow preserved in some purely intellectual universe called "the relational consciousness"—a consciousness that somehow hovers above a concept-free sensuous ground. And when we are told that the "relational content forms part of

the felt background," it seems quite reasonable to take Bradley as claiming that this "relational content" returns from whence it came: immediate experience.[18] And residing there it constitutes part of the larger experience that conditions this or that explicit assertion.

We should also realize the following about those contents that fall
within immediate experience but that are seen by Bradley as "relational."
Strictly speaking, a content is understood as relational only if it (a) is
presently before our minds as a component in judgment; or (b) has previously appeared as an explicit component in this or that assertion. This suggests, then, that contents that are somehow sensed by us but that have
never become part of our explicit awareness in judgment are non-relational. And it is in this sense, then, that immediate experience per se can be
seen as noncognitive. However, there is a further point that demands our
notice here. Though this should become much clearer after we discuss the
other forms of feeling, I would mention at this stage that "non-relational"
does not, for Bradley, mean "non-ideal." As we shall see, any experiential
content (including sensuous and volitional contents) so far as they are
exclusively "mine" will be seen as Bradley as ideal; and as such they will
exhibit a falling apart of content and existence. But in order to follow
Bradley on this matter, let us now consider the idea of "mere feeling."

"MERE FEELING"

With some understanding of Bradley's idea of immediate experience in
hand, I would now like to consider what I identified at the beginning of
this chapter as "mere feeling." As stated in my opening remarks, Bradley
tends to identify as "merely felt" any aspect of non-relational experience
that is less than all-inclusive. (And, as we shall see, even our immediate
experience is, in one sense, merely felt.) However, in order to communicate what I understand as Bradley's intention here, let us focus for the
moment on sensuous immediacy. Though certainly part of the "feeling
base," it should be seen as the narrowest form of felt experience. And
unless we understand why such feeling is different from the rest, confusion is the possible result.

Feeling's Internal Flaw

At many points in Bradley's writings, the emphasis is placed upon
the defects of the relational consciousness. However, what is often not
taken into account is that the relational consciousness is itself seen by
Bradley as a *development* out of a more primitive experience, and a
solution to problems that are found therein. Simply put, relational
thinking is ultimately understood by Bradley as an effort to overcome
the defect of mere feeling. As Bradley tells us:

Feeling has a content, and this content is not consistent with itself, and such a discrepancy tends to destroy and to break up the stage of feeling. The matter may be briefly put thus—the finite content is irreconcilable with the immediacy of its existence. For *the finite content is necessarily determined from the outside*; its external relations (however, negative they may desire to remain) penetrate its essence, and so carry that beyond its own being. And here the "what" of all feeling is discordant with its "that," it is appearance, and as such it cannot be real. This fleeting and untrue character is perpetually forced on our notice by the hard fact of change. And, both from within and from without, *feeling is compelled to pass off into the relational consciousness*. It is the ground and foundation of further developments, but it is a foundation that bears them only by a ceaseless lapse from itself.[19]

But what can Bradley mean when he tells us that "feeling is inconsistent with itself," and that it is "compelled to pass off into the relational consciousness"? I shall answer this question in a moment. But I would reiterate here that any experience that has this liability must be seen as falling short of feeling in the broadest sense. And, though we must recognize that there are other types of feeling that share this liability, sensuous immediacy is the most obvious.

Consider, for example, how a sensuous content presents itself to our awareness. An object is directly apprehended in sense. But in the moment a sensuous content presents itself it begins to disappear. As merely felt, then, the sensuous content slips out of our experience an instant after we have contacted it. (This is its "ceaseless lapse.") And it is in an effort to *preserve* this disappearing content that we judge. Through its incorporation into our larger intellectual universe (this incorporation taking place, of course, through the activity of judgment), the given but vanishing content is transformed—preserved within the larger intellectual world that is maintained within our immediate experience.

Something in our experience (precisely what we shall consider further down) tells us that what is given in sensuous awareness is unacceptable. And it is here that the motivation to judge—the desire to engage in relational thinking—is found. The *mere* immediacy and impermanence of sensuous content clashes and jars with something—some yet *fuller* form of experience—that allows us to sense its truncated and distorted character; and the activity of judgment is, in effect, an effort to supply that which vanishing sensation cannot on its own provide. I directly encounter an object; let's say a tree. However, I am somehow aware that the full reality of what I apprehend lies beyond what is given. Hence, it is through the act of judgment that I transform the sensuous and disappearing content into one that is relatively permanent. By "working over" the given contents of sense in thought I transport them from the self-destructive sphere of mere sense into the eternal ideal universe—an ideal universe that is maintained by me in my immediate experience.

We have, of course, already discussed at some length the sense in which Bradley sees our idealized assertions as defective. Whereas the ideal reconstruction of reality that takes place in judgment and inference may be defective in the sense that its contents are not grasped in their complete existence, the sensuous immediacy of mere feeling appears to be defective for the opposite reason. Sensuous immediacy—in being merely immediate—truncates and distorts the contents of my larger experience. In sensuous immediacy I have before me contents that, while in reality are *continuous* with other instances of themselves, appear in their immediacy to stop short at the boundaries of the disappearing object. For example, in my merely sensuous apprehension of something that is "red" I fail to see the fullness of this content. By sensuously experiencing only *this* "red" as it appears in *this* immediate presentation I have failed to experience "red" in its full comprehension. My immediate experience (which, we must remember, contains my larger intellectual universe and more), tells me, however, that "red" exists here *and* beyond in a multiplicity of ways.

While idealized conception is problematic in that it suggests that I possess mere thoughts—thoughts that have no real existence—mere feeling implies, it would seem, an opposite, but equally one-sided, error. The sensuous immediacy of mere feeling suggests that there are objects that are *self-contained* and not at all continuous with and dependent upon other objects. For example, by suggesting to me that the shade of red I experience in one rose cannot be identical to and continuous with the red I apprehend in another, the merely felt sensuous presentation has cut the threads by which reality maintains for me its unity. The merely felt presentation suggests, then, that these reds are merely similar, and that their apparent identity is but a fabrication of thought not contained in the objects themselves.[20] But this suggestion, according to Bradley, is a falsification of what our larger felt experience imposes on us. And when our larger experience does betray the sensuously immediate data as defective, the first step we undertake is the transformation of the merely immediate sensuous present into what now becomes (relatively) more stable perceptions.

But let me emphasize here that it is the "disruption from without" that is the source of instability. Sensuous immediacy is experienced as defective and in need of ideal elaboration in judgment because it is felt to be less than all-inclusive. It is a mere fragment of our larger experience. And were it not for the presence of this larger experience, its defective character could not be recognized. However, we shall soon consider that, in one sense, my immediate experience is also a mere fragment. (It is a fragment of the Absolute's experience.) And given that it, too, is less than all-inclusive, we shall see that, though infinitely more stable than the disappearing data of sense, immediate experience exhibits (in the end) the same shortcoming. But before pursuing this topic, let me say something more about the role of perception.

Perception Revisited

This talk of the disappearance of sensuous immediacy brings to our attention problems that were, perhaps, not sufficiently noticed in our earlier discussion. In particular, the question of perception is one that, I think, may now require some further consideration. And in order to deal with any potential confusion here, let me reiterate the following about Bradley's views on perception.

Perception per se is, for Bradley, the point at which the feeling base of experience works its way into our relational awareness. And, Bradley tells us, this identifiable juncture between feeling and the relational consciousness we may call the "this." On the one hand, the "this" contains that implicit sense of concrete specificity that is continually intruding upon our assertive awareness. On the other hand, though, the relation between the "this" and judgment proper must be properly understood. According to Bradley (post 1883), our sense that the object of our conscious experience is ultimately unique and specific does not come to us as a perception. Indeed, whenever I focus on the "this" I actively transform feeling into a *perception*. However, when that which I feel as unique is captured by my selective attention, I bring it into the confines of the relational consciousness; and as a component within judgment, my felt sense of specificity becomes, to use Bradley's term, "idealized."

But we should recall here what has already said about the transformation of sensation in judgment. When we become explicitly aware of this or that sensuous datum, that datum both loses and gains. Our sensuous experience gains, we may say, in that when worked over by thought it is brought into the universe of ideas, which is permanent. No longer are the contents of sense lost in the instantaneous and disappearing "now." And, though Bradley sometimes writes in the 1883 *Logic* as if there is some great loss taking place through the activity of judgment, we must take care here to understand precisely what that loss might be. We should realize that—so far as the disappearing data of sensuous immediacy is concerned—there is only gain. And when Bradley speaks of a loss he is referring to the fact that—when compared to its felt apprehension in our larger experience—our idealized perceptions will appear to have lost some of their concreteness and specificity.

I would insist here, though, that this complete sense of concreteness and specificity does not belong to perception per se. That is, if we consider a perceptual datum in isolation from the larger felt experience that is its ground, it takes on a more or less abstract and general character. And, though our perceptions are a more concrete than the merely felt sensuous given, they must be seen—as must any asserted content—as failing to exhibit the level of concreteness that our larger felt experience possesses. What the idealized perception cannot fully capture, then, is the concreteness of sense as supported by the *entirety* of my felt experience: sensuous, intellectual, and volitional. And, though this felt sense of specificity is partially preserved in perception as it appears in this or that judgment, there is still the sense that the content that has appeared is less than what our deepest feeling tells us it must be.

We may summarize here, then, as follows: While perceptions are much more concrete than what is sensuously immediate, they are less than wholly specific and unique. And thus as an ideal component within our awareness, perception has partially succeeded and partially failed to achieve its end—the perfect characterization of its object as uniquely itself and no other. It succeeds in that it transforms the contents of mere sense into members of the permanent ideal order of experience. It takes a sensuous content and sees it (to some degree) *sub specie aeternitatis*. But perception fails, too, in that its effort to see the contents of sense in this light always falls short—far short—of what our fullest experience assumes. Perception can only give us relative particularity and uniqueness. However, our fullest sense of the universe understands every component within it to be—in and through its relations to all that exists—uniquely itself.

IMMEDIATE EXPERIENCE AS CRITERION

We have now seen that Bradley understands immediate experience as providing us with a felt sense of the unity of all things; and we now also understand that it is in this immediate experience that we maintain our larger experiential universe and directly possess the various meanings that the relational consciousness presupposes. In addition to this, we now understand that residing within our immediate experience is an implicit sense of that which we ultimately desire. However, besides providing this concrete ground for the relational consciousness, immediate experience functions in yet another capacity. And let us turn once more to Bradley in order to introduce this further role. In his *Essays on Truth and Reality* we read:

> Immediate experience, however much transcended, both
> remains and is active. It is not a stage which shows itself at
> the beginning and then disappears, but it remains at the bot-
> tom throughout as fundamental. And, further, remaining it
> contains within itself every development which in a sense
> transcends it. Nor does it merely contain all developments,
> but in its own way it acts to some extent as their *judge*.[21]

Now, most of the ideas in this passage (e.g., the omnipresence of immediate experience, and its capacity to retain the results of relational thought), we are now familiar with. But one idea that we have not yet considered is that which Bradley mentions at the end. Immediate experience, he tells us, functions, in some sense, as the *judge* of all that comes before the relational consciousness.[22] Hence we must ask in precisely what sense does immediate experience function in this capacity? And why, we must further inquire, does Bradley say that it is only "to some extent" that it assumes this role? These are, I suggest, all important questions in any discussion of Bradley's theory of knowledge. And in attempting to answer these questions we shall find ourselves confronted by some of the most perplexing and enigmatic aspects of his philosophy. But before confronting the more difficult answer Bradley provides, let us consider a quicker (but ultimately inadequate) response that is some-times attributed to him.

It has sometimes been suggested that, since we know that one's intelligible universe is maintained in what Bradley calls our felt "imme-diate experience," we may see this immediate felt experience as provid-ing the grid against which any present assertion can be measured. If an assertion fits smoothly into the background of immediate experience, we may say that it "coheres" (more or less) with what has gone before. And thus we might be inclined to think the judgment that easily integrates into its immediately experienced context is a judgment that, in cohering, is true, while one that jars, or in some sense fails to be easily accommo-dated, is false. Certainly there is nothing in this way of putting things that conflicts with the theory we have developed over the course of the preceding chapters. Yet, as suggested above, this way of looking at things is, for Bradley, too simple.

Indeed, we have already learned that Bradley's criterion of coher-ence is not to be understood as mere consistency between a present assertion and the larger intellectual and sensuous world that we main-tain within immediate experience. Even though my present assertion may tightly mesh with my immediate experience, I could see this sort of coherence as guaranteeing the truth of my present assertion, only if I can assure myself that my immediate experience is itself not subject to falsification by something external to it. What this means, though, is that unless Bradley can find a way to establish the objectivity of immediate experience, its effectiveness as the critic of this or that judgment remains dubious. And if we recall from chapter 7 our discussion of the various problems that plague coherentism, we shall realize that there is nothing here that precludes the possibility that my immediate experience—so far as it is merely *my* experience as one finite centre amongst others—is somehow quite distorted and thus incapable of functioning as a reliable (i.e., objective and truth-promoting) critic.

Bradley is, of course, enormously sensitive to this difficulty. And in order to follow his thinking here, we should recall that, even if my present assertion is perfectly consistent with my immediate experience, it will still at some level be sensed as relatively defective; and this is because, even when taken in its full extent, my immediate experience is parasitic upon a *deeper* sort of feeling that betrays it as, to some degree, merely mine; at some level it apprehends that it is less than fully comprehensive. And, no matter how expansive it may have become, there always remains a residue external to it. My immediate experience, while it provides the hovering sense of a "universe" or "world" against which any assertion is measured, is not itself the whole of reality. Immediate experience is (to reiterate) *my* experience—*my* intellectual, sensuous, and volitional being. And so far as merely mine (which means here "mine-not-yours") its objectivity is open to question.

A LARGER SENSE OF FEELING

When Bradley discusses the limitations and shortcomings of relational thought, he always tells us that it is "feeling" (in some sense) that allows us both to recognize those shortcomings and move beyond them. Indeed, we are continually told that it is the felt non-relational whole that supplies us with the measure according to which thought's primary defect is recognized. And, further, it is this same feeling that somehow provides the material that allows us to overcome, at least partially, this defect. Hence, our result so far is as follows: What Bradley often calls "mere feeling" (the limited sensuous presentation of the "now") is continually augmented and transformed by the relational consciousness. However, the defects of the relational consciousness are themselves being continually corrected by our more inclusive immediate experience. That is, in immediate experience we sustain a sense of the universe that is infinitely larger that what mere feeling or the focused relational consciousness can embrace. And it is in this sense, then, that feeling as immediate experience is the "judge" of both mere feeling and any assertion as it comes before the mind. But, though Bradley certainly sees immediate experience as the *proximate* judge of truth and reality, it cannot function as its *ultimate* critic. Given that immediate experience is conditioned by something greater than itself, we must recognize that its ability to function in this capacity is limited, and that there must be accessible to us a deeper criterion of truth and reality. But what could this criterion be?

Immediate Experience and Finite Centres

In order to follow Bradley's thinking on this issue we must first come to understand something of what he says about the partially ideal nature of immediate experience. And we may best approach this topic by considering his larger subject of experience—the "finite centre."

> Immediate experience . . . we have seen is a positive non-rela-
> tional whole of feeling. Within my immediate experience falls
> everything of which in any sense I am aware, so far at least as
> I am aware of it. But on the other side *it contains distinctions
> which transcend its immediacy.* This my world, of feeling and
> felt in one, is not to be called 'subjective', nor is it to be iden-
> tified with my self. That would be a mistake fundamental and
> disastrous. Nor is immediate experience to be taken as simply
> one with any "subliminal" world or any universe of the
> Unconscious. However, continuous it may be with a larger
> world, my immediate experience falls, as such, strictly within
> the limits of my finite centre.[23]

This and similar passages are, I suggest, of enormous importance in coming to grips with Bradley's theory of knowledge. And we should consider closely the following points:

(a) Immediate experience is, for Bradley, non-relational; not only does it provide the sense of unity and a continuity that relational thought (judgment) must always fall short of, but it also comprises differentiated contents that have never appeared in explicit assertion.

(b) We should realize too that any conception of "self" and "other" (not-self) is a distinction that is derivative upon immediate experience. "Self" and "not-self" are, we may say, distinctions that fall *within* and thus belong equally to immediate experience. But this leads us to a third and all important point.

(c) Although any cognitive determination of "self" and "not-self" must fall within my immediate experience, there is a larger sense of my finitude—an experiential sense of self—at work here. This larger sense of self (even though any cognitive determination of "self" and "not-self" is internal to it) is what Bradley calls a "finite centre of experience." And most important for our purposes is Bradley's claim that my immediate experience falls "strictly speaking within my limits as a finite centre." Now, in itself this hardly seems controversial. Bradley is merely saying here that immediate experience is, in some sense, "my experience." What this means, though, is that immediate experience—so far as it is merely mine—is not *all* of experience. Immediate experience has limits or boundaries, and perhaps most importantly *viewpoint* or *perspective*. But this, I suggest, is of great significance.

What we must recognize here is that every experiential content that falls within my boundaries as a finite centre presupposes a greater world that extends beyond it. Or, to put the matter differently, feeling as immediate experience must be seen as continuous with a form of feeling even larger than itself. But just what can be said of such a larger feeling? I think that what Bradley wants to emphasize here is simply there exists experiential contents that, although connected to my experience, must fall outside "me"—even when considered as a finite centre. Since my immediate experience must fall within with my limits as a finite centre, there are, it must be admitted, *some* realities that have been part of neither my intellectually constructed universe nor the given sensuous base from which that intellectual world has arisen. But this takes us to the brink of what constitutes, I believe, the ultimate theoretical difficulty in Bradley's philosophy.

When an experience is said to be *my* experience (whether sensuous, intellectual, or volitional) it is limited and thus *perspectival*. But so long as an experiential content remains perspectival, so long as it experiences the universe from a "point of view"—even a "felt" point of view—it remains the possession of one centre of experience and not another. (This is true even of contents that we understand as belonging to the "not-self" in judgment and contents that, though immediately experienced, never explicitly manifest themselves in conscious assertion.) Put bluntly, if a content is part of immediate experience per se—if it falls within *my* boundaries as a finite centre—it must, to some degree, be experienced from the "here" and "now" of my experiential viewpoint (again, even if we say that viewpoint is only felt). Absolutely crucial to Bradley's doctrine, however, is the idea that the contents that are superficially perspectival, at some level of feeling break through this limitation. Somehow what I immediately experience must be understood as reaching *beyond* the experiential limit that I possess as a finite centre. And thus what *I* feel becomes—at the deepest levels—continuous with and the same as what *you* or *anyone else* feels. And, though it remains in most of us largely unconscious, it is in the deepest recesses of feeling that we as individuated subjects step beyond the boundaries of our circumscribed personal identity and participate in a universe that is (somehow) the possession of all. We must conclude, then, that the feeling state that is called "immediate experience" is not ultimate. It is, in one sense, the manifestation of an experience that is deeper, that is all-inclusive, and that is in no way "disrupted from without." And, though this deepest form of feeling is perfectly continuous with my immediate experience, and, in a manner of speech, may be said to reside therein, the two must be distinguished.

I would emphasize here that Bradley sees such a bedrock level of feeling as absolutely necessary to his theory of knowledge. Indeed, if he does not insist upon this ultimate continuity of experiential contents between all finite centres, he has lost the thread by which referential objectivity can be maintained. If Bradley does not metaphysically allow for what we may call the "transcendence of experiential finitude"—the overreaching of the boundaries of a finite centre of experience—then any content experienced by that centre becomes a merely subjective state. It becomes, in the end, a mere representation of a reality whose existence has been theoretically expunged from the sphere of finite awareness. But to completely circumscribe our experience—to concede that my knowledge, perception, or feeling is *merely* mine" is to provide the sceptic with all he or she needs to win the day.

IDEALITY AND FEELING

I would like to bring this part of our discussion to an end by considering once more some points made in chapter 3. There we learned that the distinguishing characteristic of thought is its ideality. And ideality, we should recall, belongs to an experiential content just so far as its existence, its various instantiations, are absent from our awareness.[24] But these are ideas with which we are now quite familiar. What may not be so evident, however, is this: On Bradley's theory ideality is proportionate to the narrowness of experiential focus. And it is for this reason that we must see the merely sensuous datum as less concrete (i.e., more ideal) than a datum that has been transformed into a perception by the judging consciousness. It is also this same narrowness—this failure to be all-inclusive—that can condemn any experience as ideal-not-real. Our relational awareness is considered to be defective, not because it is an abstract mental representation of an object that is ontologically opposed to it; but rather its defect is a result of its ideality—its *limited* systematic apprehension of some experiential content. And the relational consciousness overcomes its ideality, then, just so far as it manages to view its object from a broader and more inclusive viewpoint.

But what, we must now ask, does this tell us about the various forms of feeling we have examined in this chapter? Certainly it tells us that our relational awareness is more concrete than mere sense. But what is perhaps less obvious is that, since the presence of ideality is proportionate to absence of all-inclusiveness, even our immediate experience must remain, in some respect, ideal. Sometimes Bradley openly embraces this idea. However, at other times he suggests that our immediate experience—the experience that is coextensive with the finite centre per se—is wholly non-relational and completely concrete (i.e., non-ideal). But when such suggestions are made, they seem to betray a central ambiguity in Bradley's thought.

We must not forget that for an experience to be *perfectly* concrete (i.e., wholly non-ideal) it would have to be all-inclusive. And this follows simply because anything less than an all-inclusive (Absolute) experience is subject to the external disruption of which Bradley so often speaks. But to say that an experience is "mine" is to suggest that it has an empirical content that is apprehended from a specific spatiotemporal location. And any such content—sensuous, intellectual, or volitional— *must* be disrupted by that which is external to it and thereby exhibit ideality. Hence, if a content is wholly non-ideal, it must have lost its empirical-perspectival character. What this seems to mean for Bradley's larger doctrine, though, is that, strictly speaking, immediate experience can be called wholly non-relational and completely non-ideal only in the sense that it is *continuous* with an Absolute experience. And this is because it is only an experience that has transcended the perspectival character of experiential immediacy that could be said to have overcome *all* traces of the merely ideal and merely relational.

But, if stripped of such character, in what sense is it "mine" and not "yours"? "How," to put the question more directly, "can I as a finite (i.e., perspectival) centre experience the Absolute—even at the level of feeling?"[25] Bradley's answer, so far as I am able to follow him, is that it is not so much that *I* immediately experience the Absolute in its perfectly concrete and non-ideal nature. So far as my feeling of the Absolute is *my* experience (even at the level of immediate experience) the Absolute's character is partially misapprehended. Rather we are forced to postulate as the most fundamental experience the Absolute's experience of itself. But since my immediate experience is both continuous with and parasitic upon this deeper experience, the most philosophically accurate way to put the matter is simply to say that the Absolute thinks and feels *through* me. In other words, it is the *condition* of any finite centre's experience that there exists an Absolute experience of which our feeling as this or that finite centre is but a limited and partial manifestation.

And it is for this reason Bradley tells us that we can only apprehend the Absolute in a "general fashion." Though we may understand it as the ultimate condition (and presupposition) of our finite experience, anything more specific than this results in a perspectival and hence bastardized apprehension. Hence, we must say that so far as any wholly non-relational and wholly non-ideal feeling falls within my experience, it is, strictly speaking, not merely my experience: it is rather experience *qua* experience, and the possession of the Absolute itself.

Chapter 9

FEELING AND KNOWLEDGE (ii)

FEELING AND DIALECTIC

Although we must develop further Bradley's understanding of the relation between finite experience and the Absolute, I would like to briefly digress here to consider again the topic of inference. As we have already seen, integral to Bradley's theory of experience is the distinction between the real and the ideal (a distinction we have encountered in a number of guises). But unique to Bradley amongst idealist writers is his willingness to confine one side of the distinction to that which is essentially discursive and finite.[1] While Bradley is the first to admit that at some level we experience the universe in a manner that is direct and complete, he is loathe to call this experience either a merely "thinking" or merely "sensuous" one. Both thought and sense are, for Bradley, but partial aspects of what includes and goes beyond them—our larger felt experience of reality.[2]

Bradley's choice of terms in describing that which he believes our deepest experience of reality to be is not, however, without reason. He elects to use neither the term "thought" nor "sense" to describe our fullest experience because each carries with it, he thinks, an inescapable suggestion of the merely finite and merely subjective. Now, the short-comings of a wholly sense-based theory of inference we discussed in chapter 2. (See also the appendix.) And Bradley's condemnation of asso-ciationism need not detain us here. But what about his relation to the idealist tradition? How does Bradley understand the claim that thought itself contains the seeds of inferential advance?

Bradley is, of course, well aware that when the great idealist authors spoke of the "dialectical advance of thought" it was not their intention to subjectivize what they believed to be ultimately real. But still, it is all too easy, Bradley believes, for a hostile critic to put such an interpretation onto this term. And, while the use of the term "thought" by some of Bradley's predecessors appears to have had as its motivation the desire to emphasize an unbroken *continuity* between subjective experience and objective reality, Bradley feels that this language can mislead. It is Bradley's belief that by using "thought" to cover both the subjective and objective aspects of our larger experience the differences between these elements are obscured.

But Bradley's commitment to maintaining the explicit distinction between subjective, ideal experience (either sensuous or intellectual) and objective reality has another result for speculative idealism. Although it was rather late in his career before the idea took its final form, Bradley comes to argue that the usual account of inferential advance fails to explain adequately either how contradiction within finite experience develops or how it is overcome.[3] The theoretical account of the relation between experiential finitude and its criterion was, Bradley believes, the Achilles heel of all previous expressions of idealism. And, although he accepts the general claim that finite experience moves through a dialectical sequence wherein its modes of apprehension are modified ("negated") and then modified again in an ever-widening movement, Bradley can not persuade himself that subjective experience alone—as either thought or sensation—provides the impetus for this advance.[4] Hence Bradley comes to the position that the only way to explain the relation between perspectival awareness and the greater reality that exposes its inadequacies is to postulate a larger experience of which our perspectival awareness (sensuous and intellectual) is but an aspect. And this experience, we have now seen, Bradley calls "feeling" in its fullest sense.

However, let us consider the matter in Bradley's own terms. The more usual view, and the one which he feels forced to modify, is described in *Essays on Truth and Reality*. According to Bradley this position holds that

> The whole reality is so immanent and so active in every partial element, that you have only to make an object of anything short of the whole, in order to see this object pass beyond itself. The object visibly contradicts itself and goes on to include its complementary opposite in a wider unity.[5]

But after telling us this Bradley is quick to point out that, although he accepts the general conception of dialectic described here, he cannot agree with one of its central assumptions.[6] And what Bradley rejects in this interpretation of inferential advance is the claim that the object of experience, as it appears within the experiential boundaries of a finite subject, is capable of *visibly* contradicting itself. To say that our finite experience does this "visibly" is, according to Bradley, to say that the ultimate criterion of knowledge is contained *within* the subjective and perspectival experience itself, and that any such experience will, if left to its own devices, ultimately betray an *internal* defect that, followed by a *self-generated* supplementation, will transform itself into something higher and more complete.[7] But Bradley is unwilling to accept this. Although such a theory might be plausible if we interpret finite experience in the broadest possible sense (that is, as including both perspectival and nonperspectival aspects), as normally construed, neither the explicit judgment nor the larger ideal experience that contains it, can do what the orthodox account asks of it.

But let us consider the various ways in which this account breaks down. When we assert, Bradley tells us, *what* we assert is believed to be an accurate formulation—that is, it is believed to be true of the reality that it articulates and develops. And, while there may be varying degrees of force with which any assertion is put forth, we cannot, Bradley believes, doubt the truth of what we assert in the moment we judge.[8] Of course, we may question our asserted truth an instant after it is made; but—as a judgment that is being asserted *as* true—its immunity from doubt is complete.[9] But, if this is the case, if all judgments are made on the assumption that they are accurate characterizations of reality, then we are forced to say that, whatever is consciously before our minds *in judgment* cannot visibly betray itself. (If it did, we would not put it forth as true.) But let us take this idea even further. The real claim we are examining here is not just that this or that focused assertion visibly betrays itself, but that *finite experience* does; and hence we must consider whether or not any finite perspectival experience (sensuous or intellectual) can contain the seeds of its own destruction.

Now, we should realize that when pushed even to this level, Bradley will deny that any persectival experience can function in this manner. The very fact that an experiential content (even a felt one) possesses a point of view, presupposes a *beyond* in which its fuller reality is found. But this forces us to recognize that the levels of significance behind any finite experience run deep, and that our perspectival apprehension (intellectual or sensuous) can only contain so much of the contextual web of meaning that fans out beneath our circumscribed existence. Hence, for Bradley, it is not just the nexus of interconnected conditions that fall *within* my boundaries as a finite centre (and that have not been included in my conscious assertion) that undermines my experience, it is the *entire structure of reality* that is ultimately the source of this destabilization. As we should recall from chapter 3, when I assert the content of my assertion cannot be said to have rigidly prescribed boundaries;

rather it appears to point beyond itself to other contexts that, although they are partially located within my experience as a finite centre, extend beyond to the reality within which my limited experience falls. Thus we may say that overt assertion carries with it (or initiates) *reverberations* within the larger domain of meaning-fact.

At first these reverberations are found in the larger sensuous, intellectual, and volitional sphere Bradley calls "immediate experience." However, these rumblings cannot be said to stay within the boundaries of myself as an experiential centre. Given the complete continuity of content between what constitutes "my" universe and *the* universe, at some level, a felt disparity arises. And, it is just this deeper disturbance— a disturbance that can be legitimately said to reside neither within the judgment nor the fuller perspectival experience of a finite centre—that, for Bradley, initiates the inferential advance. Put differently, as we become increasingly aware of the limits of our judgment we begin to recognize that what we have asserted (perhaps only an instant earlier) is not precisely true. And the awareness that what we have asserted requires qualification is one that is at first neither explicit nor precise. We assert—and *then* there is a felt uneasiness that develops. In many cases this uneasiness may result merely from the pressure my immediately experienced world places upon my assertion. However, in some cases the process is slower. Though an assertion may initially strike me as wholly plausible—indeed, even as indubitably true—as the fuller significance of what I have judged filters down to the deepest recesses of feeling (recesses that transcend my boundaries as a finite centre) a subtler form of tension may develop. And, as a result of this process, I may be eventually forced to transform (perhaps radically) my entire sensuous-intellectual universe.

I would summarize these points, then, as follows: First, since this fuller realm of meaning that is required in order for dialectical tension to arise is external to both my explicit assertion and any larger sense of myself as a circumscribed experiential centre, we cannot say that it is the "visible" assertion or any perspectival subjective state that contradicts itself. Rather, the source of this dismantling must come from the deeper level of meaning that, although it belongs to and is continuous with merely finite experience, cannot be said to reside wholly therein. And second: this "larger domain of experience" comprises, as we have already seen, not only my immediate experience. For Bradley, that which ultimately undermines any judgment's claim to complete truth is the *totality* of experience—feeling in the very fullest sense. Thus, not only is it impossible for any sort of "thought" to visibly contradict itself, *any* ideal experience (thinking, perceptual, or otherwise) must also fail to have this capacity. Ideal (i.e., limited) experience can develop these dialectical transitions, then, only because it participates in a form of experience larger than itself. Although we may legitimately say that these deeper conditions of dialectical advance are *continuous* with and *immanent* in my merely finite existence, it is much more accurate to say that they are found in the larger presupposed (i.e., "felt") world that is sustained beyond my finite boundaries; and that it is in this world that the fuller significance of what I have actually managed to think or sense is found.

> The object before me [we are told] is not the whole of Reality, nor is it the whole of what I experience. The Universe (I must assume this here) is one with my mind, and not only is this so, but the Universe is actually now experienced by me as beyond the object. For, beside being an object, the world is actually felt, not merely in its general character but more or less also in special detail. Hence, *as against this fuller content present in feeling, the object before me can be experienced as defective.* . . . The important point [to be made though] is that with the object there is present something already beyond it, something that is capable both of demanding and of furnishing ideal suggestions, and of accepting or rejecting the suggestions made.[10]

Here we have a concise statement of the metaphysical vision behind Bradley's understanding of inference and the dialectical progress of knowledge. But, in considering this quotation we must always bear in mind that "the object before me" is the content as it falls within my boundaries as a merely finite being; and, that the same content that exists within these boundaries is understood as continuing *beyond* my experiential finitude. Still, in this beyond it is somehow experienced. Somehow, in an area of feeling that is no longer perspectival, I am one with it. And it is only within the deepest recesses of the feeling base where the fuller significance of an experienced object is to be found. We may put this otherwise by saying that the content that exists within perspectival experience (here and now) is continuous with itself in other spaces and other times and thus beyond the present assertion and the finite centre's circumscribed world. Even though my experience of this "elsewhereness" remains vague and inchoate, it is, nevertheless, there—present in the furthest reaches of feeling.

FINITUDE AND THE ABSOLUTE

With this statement, though, we are again forced into the most difficult (some would say "ridiculous") aspect of Bradley's thought. And I would begin here by repeating what we have just considered: "the Universe is one with my mind" and "the Universe is actually now experienced by me as beyond the object." These are strong words that cannot, I think, be dismissed as mere metaphors. And to put the matter very directly, Bradley seems to be claiming that the content of feeling must encompass—at some level—the content of the universe, which, though it partially appears within my sensuous and intellectual experience, is not wholly contained there. Utterly rejecting the idea that "my experience" can be *merely* mine, Bradley is presenting to us a metaphysical vision in which finite experience is not understood as a self-enclosed and isolated, but rather as a surface manifestation of the *one experience* in which he believes the universe ultimately consists.[11] However, to follow him on this difficult point we must remember some critical distinctions of which we have already spoken.

The Limits of Experiential Finitude

First, we must be aware that there is, for Bradley, no sharp boundary between the focused awareness that constitutes judgment proper and the broader experience—the feeling base—out of which we select when we assert. And thus there appears to be underlying the explicit awareness that exists in judgment levels of feeling that, as they move away from the surface level of experience (conscious judgment), become progressively less focused and gradually overcome the finitude of the conscious experiential centre. Now, we have already considered how immediate experience—so far as its contents are perspectival—is subject to disruption by what lies beyond it. And we have also learned that these contents of my immediate experience reach beyond themselves at a level of feeling that can no longer be seen as merely mine and the private possession of a finite centre. It cannot be insisted on too strongly that Bradley sees the deepest reaches of feeling (which obviously can't be identified with sensation) as beginning to lose its focus as "my" experience; at *some* point this feeling must be construed as "experience in general." And, although this experience certainly belongs to "me-not-you" at its surface, this division between "my experience" and "yours" (and "everyone else's") must eventually break down.[12]

There is, of course, an obvious objection here that one might make. And that is that "experience must always be *someone's* experience." But, although Bradley is willing to concede this point he would qualify his response by saying that this is only a partial truth that quickly degenerates into the grossest error should we fail to see it in the proper light. Even though every content that appears in judgment must be experienced by "me" and must exist as part of the perceptual-conceptual content of "my universe," to say that this content is merely mine is, Bradley insists, to begin the process that inevitably results in a self-refuting scepticism. Certainly that *aspect* of the content that is present in my judgment is "mine" in that it is being directly experienced by "me" in the "here and now." And so, too, must we say that any merely felt content—any perspectival sense experience—is merely "mine." However, it is central to Bradley's conception of experienced phenomena that the present content reaches beyond its appearance in my felt experience into reality itself.[13] And if we look deeply enough into this felt experience we shall discover that the perspective that belongs to the level of experiential finitude and that makes the experience of, for example, the red rose "mine not yours" must be abandoned. *Feeling—at least at its deepest levels—is no one's feeling in particular.*[14]

But why is Bradley committed to such a view? The answer is (again) that if the contents of my judgment are construed as merely "mine" then ultimately they must be viewed as *mental-states* that bear a contingent relation to both the objective universe and every other knowing subject. Or to state the matter differently, unless Bradley acknowledges that what a finite centre experiences is at some level common property with other finite centres, he has re-erected the chasm between experience and its object that it has been his primary objective in his logic and metaphysics to overcome. And if philosophical theory takes seriously such a divide between thought and its object then there exists, he tells us, no justifiable basis upon which we can move forward in the inferential development of the world. If the link is broken between the content as it exists "in the world" and as we find it "in my mind" (which the claim that experience is merely "mine" entails) then we have effected a division that, Bradley believes, cannot be repaired. In his *Essays on Truth and Reality* he tells us that

> The notion of my self as a thing standing over against the world, externally related to it in knowledge, and dividing with it somehow unintelligibly the joint situation or result, must once for all be abandoned. This point of view rests on the ideal construction which we call the soul or the mind, and it assumes this construction to be an absolute fact. But . . . such a position is untenable. To take my self or soul as a separate thing, and to regard everything that happens to it as its psychical states, is, in its own place, proper and necessary. For certain purposes we are right, and we are even compelled, to adopt such a attitude. And not to realize this necessity is to fall into dangerous error. On the other side to rest in this position as ultimate is fatal. It is to turn a relative truth into a

ruinous falsehood. And, if we are to understand knowledge
and judgment, we must discard the doctrine of a self which
by itself is or could be real.[15]

Although this might be seen by some as an extreme doctrine, it
has, I would suggest, positive and far reaching consequences. By postulating such a unified vision of thought, feeling, and reality Bradley
has handled in a fell swoop the two central problems (as discussed in
the previous chapter) that any theory of knowledge must face. By
viewing thinking as but an aspect of a larger experience—a feeling
experience with which it is continuous—and by viewing this felt experience as itself continuous with the objective universe, Bradley has
overcome what we have referred to as the "problem of distance"
between the knowing mind and its object. And further, by locating the
precise structure of the differentiated universe within the content of
this feeling experience Bradley has provided the individual knower
with something that can not only provide suggestions as to how inference should develop, but also a standard that would allow him to
grasp the success or failure of any inference after it has been made. By
viewing all experiencable contents as themselves interpenetrating and
continuous—as a single identity-in-difference—and by making this
structured whole continuous with the larger (felt) experience of every
finite knower, Bradley has provided a theoretical mechanism by which
a nonarbitrary ideal development of the object (inference) may proceed. Indeed, Bradley tells us that

> We must view the Reality in its unbroken connexion with
> finite centres. We must take it as, within and with these cen-
> ters, making itself an object to itself and carrying out them
> and itself at once ideally and practically. The activity of the
> process is throughout the undivided activity of the Realty and
> of the centre in one. There is in the end no "between," nor
> any external relation. The striving of one side or the other
> merely for itself is impossible, and to seek to verify such a
> striving, for instance, in selfishness or its opposite, is futile.
> And in knowledge the impression by the object, and the will
> to experiment in fact with the object or to grasp it ideally, all
> belongs to the single activity at once of myself and the whole
> Universe. For certain purposes (if I may repeat this) the divi-
> sion of subject from object, and the relation taken as existing
> between them, are ideas which are requisite. But beyond these
> purposes such ideas are fatally false. They are directly
> opposed to our immediate consciousness of the whole rela-
> tion in one, and, if you start from them as premises, you are
> inevitably entangled in a network of dilemmas.[16]

I would summarize our discussion by saying that there is only one universe for Bradley. And at the deepest levels of our being we are each identified with it. Indeed, his claim is that it is only progressively, as we move from the depths of our unconscious experience into the light of conscious awareness, that the experience of distinct and separated identity emerges. Hence, in the end, Bradley would reject entirely not only any suggestion that my felt experience is my exclusive possession but also that my knowledge (in its continuity with the feeling base) can be wholly private. He would insist that at one level my knowledge, as it reaches into the depths of felt experience, and your knowledge (also as felt experience) are one. And they are one because the contents of both must at some point in our individual experiences escape from the idiosyncrasies of subjective viewpoint and submit themselves to the tribunal of the *totality* of experienced contents: a totality within which ideas like "me," and "mine," and "you," and "yours" have no privileged status.[17] That "I" exist, and that "I" have experiences that are different from "yours," these are all, Bradley claims, *ideal constructions* whose very intelligibility presupposes an objective universe of experienced contents that transcends and includes every distinction within it. And, the vindication of this claim, he believes, rests with its denial. Assume at any point, Bradley tells us, an ultimate divide between thought and feeling, feeling and the object of thought, or the objects of thought and feeling from one another and you bring down in one "ruinous mess" the legitimacy of any and every inference.[18] As Bradley tells us:

> At bottom the Real is what we feel, and there is no reality outside of feeling. And in the end the Reality (whatever else we say of it) is experience. Our fundamental fact is immediate experience or feeling. We have here a many in one where, so far, there is no distinction between truth and fact. And feeling again is mine, though of course *it is not merely my feeling. It is reality and myself in unbroken unity.* We in a sense transcend this unity; that is clear, for we could not otherwise speak of it. But that we should ever in any way reach a reality outside of it, seems impossible. And if this is so . . . then experience is Reality. For in attempting to deny this thesis, or to assert something else, we find on experiment that we have asserted this thesis or nothing.[19]

We see with this quotation once more, then, the transcendental argument that underlies Bradley's project. And, as outrageous as this metaphysical vision might appear to some, it is Bradley's belief that even the philosopher who most vociferously denies this continuity of experience must yet presuppose it in the denial (the presupposition being unconscious, of course). *If* we assert, then at some level a commitment to this interconnected universe is inevitable. And those who would reject this have failed, according to Bradley, to reflect deeply enough upon what sorts of conditions power the activity of judgment.

Solipsism

That Bradley's solution to the problem of scepticism is at a great remove from our ordinary conception of things is, perhaps, obvious. However, we must not forget that this solution is not one that Bradley undertakes lightly. And, as has been suggested by others, he seems, indeed, to be a man who is forced to adopt such a view because all other theoretical constructs seem to him grossly inadequate.[20] But there are immediate problems that arise with such a doctrine, and the first and most obvious of these is the problem of solipsism. Might it not be asked here if Bradley's doctrine of "one experience" is just another description of the solipsistic universe? Is not the claim that at the deepest levels of feeling there exists a "commonality of experience" one that destroys the idea of individuated, finite subjects?

These, I think, are not unreasonable questions. And I would briefly reconstruct Bradley's reply as follows.[21] Solipsism asserts the existence of the entire universe within an individual mind or consciousness. Somehow, or in some way, there is to be but one experience, but this single experience possesses all the characteristics of the finite consciousness. The existence of "other minds" is, on the solipsistic view, a mere appearance. And therein lies its objectionable nature. The beliefs that we all hold about the nature of experience, the belief that there are many conscious beings who experience the same universe, seems on the doctrine of solipsism, to be an impossibility. And thus we resist.

But it should be clear by now that Bradley's doctrine of feeling does not do this. Our ultimate identity with the universe is, for Bradley, never one that can fully come into the conscious assertive awareness or the subjective conative experience of any finite centre. And, in addition, Bradley's doctrine allows for—indeed, demands—other selves that must be understood as finite centres who possess their own viewpoint and individual self-awareness. As he puts it, these finite centres are in their finitude "not directly pervious to one another."[22] We must not forget that, while Bradley sees the deepest recesses of feeling as belonging to an experience that cannot be legitimately identified as "mine-not-yours," as soon as this experience is made either sensuously perspectival or the object of conscious assertion, it becomes *my* possession—and in one sense, my possession only. Although Bradley will insist on the continuity of content as it exists within my experiential boundaries and the feeling base (which, again, at some level becomes common property), he will equally insist that the precise perspectival grasp of the universe that we individually possess within our boundaries as finite centres is something that is *not* shared. Solipsism, on the other hand, does not allow for the exclusivity of finite perspective that Bradley's doctrine demands. Solipsism rather reduces all experience to the perspectival view of a *single* consciousness. And, while Bradley's solution to scepticism argues that at some level experience must be one, his own account of this intersubjective unity is completely opposed to the sorts of considerations that power the solipsistic metaphysic.[23]

THE GOAL OF THOUGHT

We may legitimately say that, for Bradley, the ultimate goal of thought is to bring into conscious awareness that which is already experienced at an unconscious (or at least preconscious) level.[24] At the level of feeling we are somehow in possession of a whole of experience that is, although internally differentiated, united throughout. And it is just this vague and inchoate sense of a perfect, integrated whole that provides both the motivation for and the standard against which any assertion is measured. As Bradley tells us:

> That on which my view rests is the immediate unity which comes in feeling, and in a sense this unity is ultimate. You have here a whole which at the same time is each and all of its parts, and you have parts each of which makes a difference to all the rest and to the whole. This unity is not ultimate if that means that we are not forced to transcend it. But it is ultimate in the sense that no relational thinking can reconstitute it, and again in the sense that in no relational thinking can we ever get free from the use of it. And an immediate unity of one and many at a higher remove is the ultimate goal of our knowledge and of every endeavor. The aspects of coherence and comprehensiveness are each a way in which this one principle appears and in which we seek further to realize it. And the idea of a whole something of this kind underlies our entire doctrine of judgment.[25]

Two points that I would immediately make here are that (i) no relational thinking (and *all* thinking we should recall is relational) can get free from the use of this whole of feeling; and (ii) no relational thinking can perfectly reconstitute it. And, although we have already considered in some detail why relational thought cannot duplicate what appears in feeling we should, I think, say something more about the fact that all thought must "use" or "presuppose" this felt whole, because it is here that we find that which tempers Bradley's harsh pronouncement on the cognitive powers of the human mind.

I think that what Bradley is trying to tell is here is simply this. If there is to be what we call "conscious experience," then there must be a criterion that provides us with a sense of value and direction. Or to use what has become a somewhat abused term, Bradley is trying somehow to "ground" our experience. And, without such a grounding he believes we would be left with (if we are left with anything at all) an incoherent cacophony of differences. But what we must be continually sensitive to is that, for Bradley, there is just no sense in looking for what grounds and stabilizes our experience in finite, conditioned experience. When we look *there* we find nothing that can function as a foundation for experience. We find nothing there because there *is* nothing that is self-sufficient within its domain.

But Bradley is equally convinced (and he is following both Kant and Hegel here) that the explicit limitation and dependency that characterize the contents of both our assertive knowledge and our sensuous finitude cannot exist in the absence of that which is without limit and fully self-sufficient. Put otherwise, the contingent cannot exist without the necessary, and the contradictory is meaningless if it is not accompanied by a sense of the noncontradictory and complete. And since when Bradley looks to our perspectival apprehension of reality as it is found in thought and sense and is invariably confronted by the finite, the contingent, and the contradictory, he is forced to postulate their necessary correlates as existing somewhere else. But, as stated so many times now, he cannot put these necessary aspects of coherent experience entirely outside of our experience or they could not do the work that is required of them. Hence, he is compelled to adopt the view that says humankind must necessarily have one foot in finite and conditioned temporality while the other is firmly rooted in what, despite its lack of popularity with "hard-nosed" philosophers, we can only call the "infinite." And it is Bradley's belief in the necessity of a ground of experience that transcends and includes this distinction that has led him to develop his doctrine of feeling as Absolute experience.

There is, Bradley tells us, an undeniable fact that the theory of knowledge (or more accurately metaphysics) must face up to. We begin with *experience*—experience that we cannot get outside of or beyond.[26] And this experience, no matter what we do to it or with it, remains throughout. And, it is just this fact that we cannot get outside our experience that demands that we treat it—or at least part of it—as ultimate.[27] Should I refuse to do so then I have merely cordoned off one aspect of the feeling base, identified it as the domain of "my" experience, while simultaneously experiencing something that (on my own principles) I should not be entitled to experience. But this, as we have already considered, is precisely what Bradley means by being in a state of "self-contradiction." And the reason why Bradley can call it a state of self contradiction is because the self (finite knower) who is denying the presence of this larger all-inclusive experience, must presuppose—that is, *feel*—it as a condition of his or her denial.

IMPLICATION AND THE IMMANENCE OF THE REAL

I would like to bring this discussion of feeling to an end with a few comments regarding Bradley's vision of Absolute experience as a necessary condition for the existence of true assertion and justifiable inference. And as a first step we must remind ourselves of the nature of the object of truth as understood by Bradley. Put bluntly, we may say that the object of truth is reality; and that this reality is (ultimately) one. In short, the object of truth is nothing less than the eternal order of objects and events that Bradley calls the "Absolute." And this Absolute is for him that which is most real and the ultimate subject in any judgment. Now, it has also been pointed out that any truth is true for Bradley just so far as it captures or becomes its object. And since the nature of the object of truth is itself understood to be timeless and eternal, so too must truth (so far as it *is* true) possess these characteristics. As we read:

> Every truth is eternal, even, for instance, such a truth as 'I now have a toothache'. Truth qualifies that which is beyond mere succession, and it takes whatever it contains beyond the flux of mere event. To be, it must appear there, but, to be truth, it must also transcend that appearance. The same thing holds again without exception of all beauty and goodness, and of everything in short, however mean, which is apprehended as an object. . . . Though revealed in time and in our 'mortal world', they are not subject to its chance and change, and though in this world they remain something which never is of it.[28]

Here we have before us the all-important point that occupied so much of our attention in chapter 3. The judgment is not (and cannot be) for Bradley any mere event in time. Although one aspect of its being may be said to rise and fall in the temporal series and to have a specific spatial location, we cannot reduce judgment to these conditions lest we fall into a radical scepticism. (The importance of this point cannot be overemphasized.) But this brings us back to what is the central metaphysical claim of Bradley's philosophy. For Bradley, we can make no sense of our experience, and philosophy has failed in its mission, if we do not acknowledge the dual nature of human existence.

Although we are in one sense finite beings who are bound to extinction and whose provincial knowledge is largely determined by the historical circumstances into which we are thrown, we are also a great deal more. Bradley is utterly committed to the principle that "the truth is the whole" and it is this vision that motivates him to say that every finite thing receives its significance only through its participation in this whole. Any intelligible apprehension of any thing requires, Bradley tells us, that we experience our object as not only a "this" but also a "not-that"; as not only "here and now" but also as "there and then." That is, any object of experience can be intelligibly grasped only to the degree that we see it as participating in the timeless nexus of events that is the universe-as-a-whole. And without the penetration of the finite object by the complete universe (making it what it is), and without a precise structure to this penetration, our experience would become both unmeaning and arbitrary.

For Bradley, then, the ultimate condition of any intelligible experience is the Absolute, which, although it manifests itself in a disappearing time series, cannot be reduced to this series. But with this we are led to yet another result. Bradley's Absolute is not some mere thing-in-itself that lay forever hidden from human experience. The whole as understood by Bradley just *is* experience (one aspect of which manifests itself in human form). And, when Bradley speaks of the real unity between content and existence that we sense in feeling he is speaking of nothing other than that sense of the whole that lies at the deepest depths of our being and that both nourishes and motivates all of conscious awareness. But this whole that experience presupposes and that is (in its inchoate form) one with feeling must not be understood as some empty and unstructured realm of pure being. Bradley's Absolute is one that possesses a precise and articulate structure; it is an identity-in-difference with (so to speak) "sinews and joints." And it is only for this reason that there can exist a legitimate transition from one judgment to another.[29]

The point I care to make here is the simple one that unless what is before our mind in conscious awareness possesses a precise identity of content with the whole—that is to say, unless the whole is immanent within what we actually apprehend—there is no legitimate and justifiable basis upon which we may proceed to develop our object in inference. And if you take away this structure you have not only blown to the winds the threads along which thought must travel, but with it goes the very idea of truth and falsity and intelligible assertion. It is for this reason, then, that Bradley insists that reality is one. And if it were not—if it were truly plural in the sense that the empiricist and realist so often claim—then all implication of one thing by another would disappear. But Bradley also believes that at some level of our being we already are aware of this (even though we do not always consciously grasp it and incorporate it into our philosophy). For many, though, this is not the claim of Bradley's that they find so unreasonable. Far more difficult to accept is the idea that this unified whole must be understood as *experience*. And before ending this chapter I would like to offer one last observation on this point.

When (and if) we manage to see the necessity of a unified and structured universe for the existence of any legitimate movement within thought (i.e., inference), and when (and if) we are willing to grant to Bradley this point, it is not such a great leap to grasp his idea of the real as experience. And in an effort to better understand this notion let us consider the following: If it is true that in my present judgment I have a knowledge of X that can be "ideally developed" into a larger (and hence new) judgment that now contains knowledge of Y, it is only because, in some sense, Y was *immanent* in X. That is, only because Y was part of the "hidden inside" of X (or vice versa) may the inferential transition from X to Y be seen as legitimate. However, we must not assume that Y is an isolated fact. Y too must contain differences internal to itself and be part of a larger system of which it is an internal difference. And let us call these hidden differences (or larger system) Z. Now, the point to be insisted on is this: While we assume in all our inferences that such relations of implication exist, we are certainly not consciously aware of them. However, on Bradley's view, the relation of immanence that exists between the different aspects of the world is essentially the relation that exists between conscious awareness as it exists in judgment and in the deeper recesses of the feeling base. But both, we must remember, *we experience*. We may not experience Z's immanence in X *consciously*; but this is just the point that forces us to postulate some other type of experience that extends beyond conscious, knowing assertion. And we *must* postulate this immanence (the implication) of Z in X if we are legitimately to move forward in thought. This presence of something that is below the surface but that permeates and colors everything we do consciously grasp in judgment is, then, Bradley's "feeling-base."[30] And it is, I think, only the prejudice that what constitutes "experience" must be consciously apprehended (and exclusively "mine") that prevents us from more easily accepting Bradley's language here.

But, one last point: If the Absolute is experience, and if, as we are told, the Absolute contains nothing other than the unified and integrated experiences of the multitude of finite centres, then the depths of our own being must consist in not just a vague sense of identity with material existence, but a brotherhood with all sentient beings. And although such a vision can at times stretch the limits of credulity, we would do well to give our most sincere attention to Bradley's claim that it is "this or nothing."

Chapter 10

TWO CRITICS: RUSSELL AND JAMES

Up to this point we have, for the most part, entertained objections to Bradley's doctrine in the abstract. However, I would now like to become more specific in my consideration of complaints. And hence in this chapter I shall examine some of the criticisms of Bradley's views that were developed by two of his most forceful contemporaries: Bertrand Russell and William James. Although Bradley certainly came under attack by others (a number of these have been included in the chapter notes), I think it has been the reproach of Russell and James that have had the greatest influence on twentieth-century philosophy. And it is my hope that through a direct consideration of some of their concerns we shall arrive at a fuller sense of Bradley's actual position.

RUSSELL'S ATTACK ON MONISM

When reflecting upon his philosophical career, Bertrand Russell tells us that, while G. E. Moore saw as his target the general epistemological thesis of "idealism" (the "mind-dependence" of objects) it was his own concern as a young man to refute what he saw as the harmful effects of philosophical "monism."[1] And, to this end, Russell raised a number of objections to Bradley's "monistic" doctrine of relations and truth (or at least what he believed to be Bradley's doctrine). However, before going on to examine some criticisms, I would like to consider Russell's own words on the relation between what he calls the "monistic theory of truth" and the "axiom of internal relations"—the closely related theories he was so concerned to refute. Russell writes:

> The doctrines we have been considering may all be deduced from one central logical doctrine, which may be expressed thus: "Every relation is grounded in the natures of the related terms." Let us call this the *axiom of internal relations*. It fol-

lows at once from this axiom that the whole of reality or of
truth must be a significant whole. . . . For each part will have
a nature which exhibits its relations to every other part and
to the whole; hence, if the nature of any one part were completely known, the nature of the whole and of every other
part would also be completely known; while conversely, if
the nature of the whole were completely known, that would
involve knowledge of its relations to each part, and therefore
of the relations of each part to each other part, and therefore
of the nature of each part. It is also evident that, if reality or
truth is a significant whole . . . the axiom of internal relations must be true. Hence the axiom is equivalent to the
monistic theory of truth.[2]

Based upon the discussion of the previous chapters, I think we must
acknowledge that Russell, at least in this passage, accurately portrays
two central ideas behind Bradley's logic and metaphysics.[3] As already
considered, Bradley understands our judgments—*all* of which are "relational"—to sit somewhere on a scale of adequacy. The least adequate
are those that exhibit the greatest degree of "externality" between their
terms; the most adequate are those that show the greatest "internality"
(by which is meant here "all-inclusive systematicity"). But we should
not forget that, for Bradley, both the completely external and completely internal relation are creatures of philosophical theory.[4] Every
judgment, Bradley believes, exhibits a precise *degree* of systematic interpenetration between its terms and their conditioning context; and every
judgment, due to the externality of the conditions that provide the ultimate ground of union between these terms, exhibits "mere conjunction"
(or "externality") as well. Now, we shall return to these issues further
down. But, since these are ideas that we have already discussed in some
detail, I shall now move on to consider more closely what were the problems Russell saw as arising from these "monistic" doctrines.[5]

Objection (a)

The first objection I shall consider is a somewhat technical one.
However, it has been widely discussed, and I think we should consider
it closely. I would add, though, that it is here in his detailed account of
Bradley's logical doctrine that Russell's misunderstanding begins to
manifest itself. Although I shall be forced to expand on this point below,
I would begin with a brief paraphrase of the argument as follows:

The axiom of internal relations (which is found on every page
of Bradley) leads to a hopelessly inadequate account of relations. And this is because the "monistic" theory sees all relations as consisting in a relational property *R* being predicated

of a complex and individual whole (*a, b*). Further, the monistic theory views the relation of both *a* and *b* to the whole (*a,b*)
as exactly the same. Hence, the idealist (or "monistic") theory
of relations treats all relations as "symmetrical." (For example, in "Jones is the same age as Smith," "same age as" is
symmetrical because we may use it in "Smith is the same age
as Jones" without altering the meaning.) However, many
relations of which we have knowledge are asymmetrical.
(Consider: "Jones is older than Smith" and "Smith is older
than Jones"; here "older than" is asymmetrical.) The "distinction of sense, i.e. the distinction between asymmetrical
relation and its converse, is one which the monistic theory of
relations is wholly unable to explain." Therefore, this inability to handle asymmetrical relations forces us to conclude that
the monistic doctrine of relations is false.[6]

In order to better understand this condensed statement we should
realize that Russell deploys here a threefold classificatory scheme
through which he views the history of relations. First, there is what he
calls the "monadistic" account; second, the "monistic" theory
(Bradley's); and lastly his own. The monadistic account, Russell tells us,
is characteristic of most of traditional philosophy. It is found in syllo-
gistic logic, in classical empiricism, and in the philosophy of Leibniz—
the figure from whom Russell takes the theory's name. And, though
Russell believes that Bradley's theory is an advance over the monadistic
account, he still thinks that the monistic account of relations (Bradley's)
shares with the monadistic a fundamental error.

Russell's argument against the monadistic and monistic theories
turns on his belief that they see all propositions as analyzable into subject-predicate form. But unfortunately, Russell claims, this does not
cover all the judgments we actually make. While many of our assertions
can be seen as attaching a predicate to a subject (e.g., "This pan is hot"),
there exist, Russell argues, *relational* propositions (e.g. "Bill is taller
than Sally") which are not of the subject-predicate variety, and whose
actual meaning is often distorted when analyzed into this form. This
error is particularly evident Russell argues when we consider propositions containing "asymmetrical relations." Although the monistic theory
can provide a plausible account of propositions containing symmetrical
relations (like "same age as" or "equal to"), the same cannot be said for
its ability to handle asymmetrical relations.

But in order to follow these differences, let's consider one of Russell's own examples: "A is greater than B." Russell claims that the traditional or "monadistic" account (to consider it first) would analyze this
proposition as a conjunction between two simpler subject-predicate

propositions each of which attributes a magnitude to their respective subjects (a and b). But, Russell tells us, mere differences in magnitude is not all that is involved. We shall have to say that, on any intelligible analysis, one magnitude is *greater* than the other, and thus we shall have to say that, in the monadistic account, we have failed to get rid of the relation "greater than."[7] Although the monadistic account tries to explain "greater than" by reducing it to the properties (in this case "magnitude") of the two terms, this, Russell tells us, will not do. "Greater than" could never be generated by these magnitudes alone, or any subsequent analysis. And hence this relation shows itself to be both irreducible and ineliminable.

Now, Bradley's doctrine, as understood by Russell, recognizes the irreducibility of relations to mere properties of the related terms. And for this reason, Russell tells us, Bradley's theory is superior to the traditional doctrine. But, as mentioned above, Russell also understands Bradley as committed to the notion that there is an individual whole—in "a is greater than b" that whole would be (a,b)—that functions as the logical subject, and that has attached to it the predicate "greater than." The difficulty with this analysis, though, is that it fails to disclose *which aspect* of the whole (a,b) attaches to which "end" of the relation. And, Russell claims, therein lay the problem. By seeing the whole (a,b) as subject and the relation R as predicate, the relation R is entirely stripped of its "sense" or "direction." It must be, Russell tells us, "indifferently" predicated of any whole to which it is attached. Hence, the monistic account, through its unquestioned commitment to the subject-predicate analysis of judgment, cannot differentiate between aRb, and bRa. However, this distinction is crucial; and any theory that fails to recognize it must be condemned.

Response to Objection (a)

I shall not enter here into historical questions here regarding the "monadistic" theory of relations and the reliability of Russell as a historian of logic.[8] I would merely point out that anyone who actually held this view would, indeed, be open to the objection Russell raises. Of far greater concern for our purposes, however, is Russell's belief that Bradley has committed the error just described. But is this really the case?

Russell's charge that the "monistic" theory of relations cannot handle the sense of asymmetrical relations proceeds, I suggest, upon a simple misunderstanding of Bradley's view. Whereas Russell sees Bradley as claiming that a judgment like "Jones is older than Smith" has as its subject the complex whole consisting of "Jones" (a) and "Smith" (b), with the predicate "older than" (R) indifferently attributed to both (a,b), this is hardly Bradley's position. As we have already seen, for Bradley, the ultimate subject of any assertion is reality-as-a-whole. And the predicate term that attaches to this whole is the complex unity-in-diversity that the grammatical proposition "Jones is older than Smith" describes (albeit in limited form). Hence, given that this is Bradley's understanding of the predicate in judgment it seems clear that Russell is arguing against a view that Bradley does not hold.[9] I would further add that, even if we consider the judgment in terms of its "limited" (or "special") subject and predicate (see chapter 2), we must realize that, according to Bradley's theory, the limited predicate is not "older than" but rather "*older than Smith.*"[10] Hence, the claim that the monistic theory of relations does not take into account the "sense" or "direction" of asymmetrical relations is simply false. But what would lead Russell to so completely misinterpret Bradley's position here?

This is not an easy question to answer. Russell apparently takes scattered comments made by Bradley to suggest that (i) since reality-as-a-whole is "individual"; and (ii) since any content identified in judgment is internally related and thus dependent upon that whole, this content too is entirely individual. This, it would seem, is why Russell takes the "whole" (a,b) as subject in "a is larger than b." But, since we have in our earlier discussion (see chapter 6) considered why these limited wholes are, for Bradley really only abstract systems that are *predicates* of the one whole, and the one individual (the Absolute), we can quickly recognize the error in Russell's account.[11] Russell also takes Bradley's comments that all predicates—including what Russell calls "relational predicates"—are "adjectives" of this one reality to indicate Bradley's commitment to the subject-predicate analysis of judgment.[12] And, in one sense, Russell is right. Bradley does believe that all asserted contents function as properties of (in the sense of "belonging to") reality-as-a-whole. But we must take care to understand the import of this statement.

For Bradley, we must remember, experience begins as a felt many-in-one. And as feeling begins to become conscious and explicit, certain differences are referred back to the larger whole from which they have been taken. Some of these differences can be seen as, in Russell's sense of the term, "properties" (e.g., "green," "hot," "heavy," "opaque," etc.); and some can be seen, again in Russell's sense, as "relations" (e.g., "to the left of," "same age as," "larger than," "older than," etc.) However, Bradley does not place much logical stock in this distinction. For him, both what Russell calls "properties" and "relations" are *universals*— real universals that are present in the given universe (and not just fabricated by the mind).[13] And what makes both "properties" and "relations" universals is the fact that they always *point beyond themselves* to their other instantiations. We should recall (see chapter 2 again) that any experienced universal is, for Bradley, a "what" or "content" divorced from its "that" or "existence"; and that the present instantiation of any universal content forms a continuous bond with other instantiations of itself not presently given to sense. Hence, on Bradley's account, every such content transcends the given datum and thereby *relates* other "thats" (existences) which share in the identical "what" (content).

But what can be the said of a Russellian relation like "older than"? We must realize here that Bradley understands the difference between relation-contents like "older than" and property-contents like "yellow" to be simply that universals-*qua*-properties are (usually) immediately sensuous and universals-*qua*-relations (usually) are not. And, while a relation-content like "larger than" or "over" may not possess the sort of *sensuous* instantiation that a property-content like "red" or "hot" would, relation-contents are still universals in that they bind together differences and have instances. For example, when I assert "Jack is older than Jill" the universal relation-content "older than" is understood by Bradley as being present both *here* between this Jack and Jill, and *elsewhere* between other limited subjects. And in this it functions for Bradley no differently than a sensuous property-content like "red" or "hot." Recognizing, then, that both Russellian "properties" and "relations" are, on Bradley's theory, universals that, through an identity of content, bind together differences, we may indifferently view them as elements, some sensuous and some not, within systems. And since all predicates-*qua*-propositions are really limited systems, they may, in this sense, be seen as relational through and through. Of course, on this view, all predicates-*qua*-propositions may also be seen as properties—including ones like "Jack is older than Jill."

But what, then, does Bradley mean when he uses the terms "relations" and "relational"? Bradley's relations—the ones that, for example, come under such heavy attack in *Appearance and Reality*—might be seen as the *defective* bond between limited subject and special predicate in assertion. According to Bradley, it is a necessary presupposition of all experience that the actual ground between limited subject, special predicate, and reality is both perfect and complete. However, it is also an unavoidable fact that in any assertion we make this complete ground cannot be made explicit. There is, for Bradley, always something missing from our understanding of how the components identified in the predicate-*qua*-proposition relate both to one another and to the rest of reality. And it is just this *im*perfect grasp of what we assume is a perfect bond that constitutes for him the "relational form." And this point is

quite significant when we consider the usual charge made against
Bradley's theory of relations. Russell, along with many others, claims
that Bradley specifically denies the "reality of relations," and that for
this reason alone we have sufficient reason to dismiss his theory. What
I would care to point out here, though, is the following: Bradley does *not*
deny—at least in Russell's sense—the reality of relations. What he denies
is the *ultimate* reality of relations. And there is a very great difference
between these two statements. Indeed, when Bradley tells us that relations are incapable of conveying to us "ultimate reality" he is claiming
that the actual unifying bond between the components (limited subject,
special predicate, and conditioning context) of any assertion is, in reality, so complete—so continuous and all-inclusive—that any apprehension of this perfect unity made by finite beings will necessarily fail to
capture its full extent. What this really means, then, is that, for Bradley,
the connective tissue between the diverse elements of the universe is
greater than we are at any one time capable of explicitly grasping. But
this point demands, I think, our attention. What has struck so many as
"absurd" about Bradley's position is the alleged denial of the unifying
bond that Russell refers to by the term "relation." But, from both our
previous discussion and the comments above, it should now be clear that
if what we mean by the term "relation" is this actual bond between
diverse elements within reality then Bradley is the proponent of a *super-
relational* reality.[14] This is, of course, not how Bradley himself uses the
terms "relations" and "relational." As mentioned above, for Bradley,
"relation" just means the falsifying act of abstraction in which this unity
fails to make its complete appearance. But, if we bear in mind these distinctions, I think we can better understand just how far from Bradley's
actual position Russell's characterization of it is.

Objection (b)

Russell claims that all relational statements are, on Bradley's theory,
ultimately about a single whole—the Absolute. And this whole contains
all of reality within it. Hence, Russell argues, in order to know any truth
on this view, one must grasp this individual totality, the Absolute itself.
But, by Bradley's own admission, it is impossible for anyone to grasp
fully this one true subject of predication. Thus, Russell claims, Bradley's
theory of relations and his doctrine of truth leads to a radical scepticism.
As Russell writes:

> Assuming that we are not to distinguish between a thing and
> its "nature," it follows from the axiom [of internal rela-
> tions] that nothing can be considered quite truly except in
> relation to the whole. For if we consider "A is related to B,"

the A and the B are also related to everything else in the universe. When we consider merely that part of A's nature in virtue of which A is related to B, we are said to be considering A *qua* related to B; but this is an abstract and only partially true way of considering A, for A's nature, which is the same thing as A, contains the grounds of its relations to everything else as well as to B. Thus nothing quite true can be said about A short of taking account of the whole universe; and then *what is said about A will be the same as what would be said about anything else*, since the natures of different things must, like those of Leibniz's monads, all express the same system of relations.[15]

There are actually two charges here. First is the claim: (i) since no truth is quite true, no truth is true at all; and second, (ii) since all truths are ultimately about the same object, all truths are equivalent. But let us take these in turn.

Response to Objection (b-i)

As for the first charge, I think the point to bear in mind this: While Bradley always insists that no judgment is perfectly true (including the judgment "No judgment is perfectly true") he does not deny that for *practical* purposes judgments can be (and are) treated as entirely true or false. (And certainly Bradley believes that for practical purposes the judgment "No judgment is perfectly true" is true.) Hence, when Bradley tells us that no judgment is perfectly true and that truth is a matter of degree, he is merely pointing out that any judgment stands at greater or lesser distance from what it ultimately seeks—perfect identification with its object. So far as the knowing mind has grasped its object in its actual being, it has, Bradley claims, judged truly; to the degree that the knowing subject has failed to effect this identity between mind and its object it has judged falsely. (See chapter 7.) Thus, while practically "No judgment is perfectly true" is taken by Bradley as wholly true, he insists that anyone who understands the meaning of the terms of the assertion is in possession only of a relative grasp of their meaning. But to make this point clearer, I would ask you to recall here the account of "degrees of truth" as found in chapter 6. There it was asked whether or not a judgment like "Caesar crossed the Rubicon" is, when uttered by a schoolboy, the same when put forth my a mature scholar who is an expert in Roman history? And the answer we found in our previous discussion was "Of course not."

I would reiterate here the point made in our earlier examination this matter: Bradley always sees entities like "Caesar," "the Rubicon," and "crossing" as *complex* entities-ideas. For example, "Caesar" was who he was, that is, he had a certain "nature," because he was the son of specific parents at a specific time in Roman history that entailed quite specific political circumstances. What this means, however, is that the significance of the term "Caesar" (and every other term in the judgment) contains references beyond itself to other entities and other meanings. The "nature" of Caesar cannot, for Bradley, be self-contained—at least not in the sense advocated by Russell. And, given this depth of meaning, not only must we say that there is "more to know" (in the sense that any judgment we make is incomplete), when we make utterances about Caesar, what we actually do understand carries with it an element of untruth in that what we actually manage to get into our judgment is, to some degree, distorted. (See, again, chapter 3.) And this distortion is present just so far as we fail to make explicit the larger web of meaning that penetrates and conditions our terms. Since for Bradley the terms of any judgment are infinitely related to other terms, no proposition can actually be self-contained; and this simply tells us that the depth of meaning of any proposition itself is never capable of being exhausted. Hence, Bradley's claim that truth is coextensive with the apprehension of this larger meaning complex.

These are (or at least should be) by now familiar ideas. And I would end my discussion of Russell's charge here by saying that "not perfectly true" is equivalent to "not true at all" only if one presupposes the either-or conception of truth and falsity that Russell favors. But, bearing this in mind, we may say that Russell's argument against Bradley on this issue just begs the question. And unless Bradley's idea of the systematic interrelation of all meanings can be shown to be incoherent, Russell's objection carries no force. Now, I shall have more to say on this point further down, however, let us first consider the second charge that is made in this passage.

Response to Objection (b-ii)

While Bradley would certainly admit that "Caesar" is an entity who stands in precise relations to all else in the universe, this hardly makes a judgment like "Caesar crossed the Rubicon" equivalent to "The Blue-Winged Teal winters only on the American Gulf coast." We must remember that, for Bradley, every judgment expresses a precise continuity of content, both between its named elements and the reality "beyond the act." When I judge "Caesar crossed the Rubicon" I am asserting an intimate and immediate connection between the concrete universal idea-objects "Caesar," "Rubicon," and "crossing." And I cannot, on Bradley's theory, just arbitrarily put together experiential contents in my judgments. My judgments must exhibit the same structure as the reality on which they are focused (or more accurately, with which they strive to become identical).

Russell is quite fond, however, of blurring distinctions Bradley makes. And, when Bradley insists upon the ultimate unity of all predicates in the Absolute, Russell twists this to mean that this unity is indifferent. But this is not Bradley's view. Some experiential contents, let's say "bananas" and "yellow," possess on Bradley's theory a *proximity* that is lacking between other contents; let's say "milk" and "purple." Another way of putting this is to say that all judgment reflects a "point of view." And in possessing a point of view the judgment always has a special or limited subject. However, special subjects (which, we must remember, are themselves parts of the complex predicate), though they *ultimately* connect to everything else, bear relations to other predicates in a precise and structured manner. Some of these predicates are near, some are far; some are closely related; others are distant. And to say that, since all assertions are aspects or moments of the one reality, the moments are equivalent, is like saying "Since the trunk, ears and feet all belong to one elephant, they too are equivalent." But on Bradley's view, the only way two assertions could be so "equivalent" would be if they managed *per impossibile* to apprehend the Absolute itself. However, such a perfect act of apprehension would entail both the abandoning of a point of view and thought's becoming identical with reality. But if thought has become reality then there exists neither thought nor judgment. Hence if viewpoint and judgment persist then the judgments made can never be "equivalent." All judgment on Bradley's theory can be said to *strive* for equivalency; but this is something that, even in the higher reaches of knowledge, can only be partially achieved.

Objection (c)

I would now like to consider a lengthy passage that contains several objections. While this passage is somewhat complex, I think we might understand its larger import to be that philosophical monism is itself an incoherent notion. And, to make matters worse, this doctrine is, Russell suggests, inconsistent with one of the principles of which it purports to be an expression. Consider the following quotation from Russell's "The Monistic Theory of Truth." There Russell writes:

> The axiom of internal relations is incompatible with all complexity. For this axiom leads . . . to a rigid monism. There is only one thing, and only one proposition. The one proposition (which is not merely the only *true* proposition, but the *only* proposition) attributes a predicate to the one subject. But this one proposition is not quite true, because it involves distinguishing the predicate from the subject. But there arises

the difficulty: if predication involves difference of the predicate from the subject, and if the one predicate is *not* distinct
from the one subject, there cannot, even, one would suppose,
be a *false* proposition attributing the one predicate to the one
subject. We shall have to suppose, therefore, that predication
does not involve a difference of the predicate from the subject,
and that the one predicate is identical with the one subject.
But it is essential to the philosophy we are examining to deny
absolute identity, and retain "identity-in-difference." The
apparent multiplicity of the real world is otherwise inexplicable. The difficulty is that "identity-in-difference" is impossible if we adhere to strict monism. For identity-in-difference
involves many partial truths, which combine by a kind of
mutual give and take, into the one whole of truth. But the
partial truths, in a strict monism, are not merely quite true,
they do not subsist at all. If there were such propositions,
whether true or false, that would give plurality. In short, *the
whole conception of "identity-in-difference" is incompatible
with the axiom of internal relations; yet without this conception, monism can give no account of the world*, which suddenly collapses like an opera hat. I conclude that the axiom is
false, and that those parts of idealism which depend upon it
are therefore groundless.[16]

Response to Objection (c)

It is hard to know where to begin with a passage like this; indeed, it
seems to miss Bradley's actual position by such a wide mark that it is difficult to imagine that Russell meant all of this to be taken seriously.
However, since Russell appealed to this passage at both early and late
stages in his career, and since his statements have provided the basis for
many subsequent attacks by other writers, I think we must take him at
his word.[17] I shall identify in this passage, then, the following claims
(some of which we have already examined): (i) there is, according to
Bradley, ultimately only "one proposition" and "one truth"; (ii) the one
proposition is "not quite true"; (iii) but the one proposition must be
true, hence there can be no false propositions; and finally (iv) the axiom
of internal relations is incompatible with complexity—the claim in this
passage with which Russell both begins and ends.

Response to Objection (c-i). As for Russell's first claim—that Bradley's
monism entails only "one proposition"—I would only say the following:
Bradley insists time and again that the very act of predication assumes a
certain distance between subject and predicate in judgment. And, while
I don't want to belabor a point already considered in previous chapters,
I would reiterate here that all acts of judgment (predication) in assum-

ing a "reality beyond the act" postulate a *surd*—an unknown condition that we must presuppose as providing the ultimate ground of union between subject and predicate. Hence, if there exists an act of judgment at all, there exists the assumption (if not the conscious recognition) that there is *more to be known*. If, *per impossibile*, there existed an act of awareness that grasped the totality (the Absolute), this would entail the absence of judgment and the absence of thought. Hence, the condition that Russell describes could, on Bradley's theory, never obtain. But recognizing this we must also recognize that there is not for Bradley "one proposition" and "one truth only." Wherever there are propositions and truth *there must be something left unthought*, which means that there is necessarily more than one truth and one proposition.

Response to Objection (c-ii). The claim that "no truth is quite true" has already been dealt with in section (b).

Response to Objection (c-iii). This brings us to the next charge. Russell attributes the following (inconsistent) claims to Bradley: (1) all predication involves a difference or distance between subject and predicate. (This is true for reasons given in [c-i] and elsewhere); and (2) the doctrine of "identity-in-difference" will not tolerate a *real* difference between subject and predicate. Russell's reasoning here seems to be as follows: On the one hand, things are said by Bradley to be different; and yet, on the other hand, his monism demands that they somehow be the same. But, if they are truly the same, then there is no real difference between subject and predicate; hence the "one proposition" (as discussed in section [c-i]) must exist and must be true. And this apparently follows because all false propositions are false in that they improperly attach a predicate to a subject—something that the sameness of subject and predicate precludes. Of course, the suggestion here is that this absurd result can be avoided only by admitting a true difference between subject and predicate. But if there is *true* difference, and not an identity-in-difference, then monism is false, and Russell has made his point.

Now, the problem with these charges is that they equivocate on the terms "identity" and "difference." At times Russell uses these terms as does Bradley; but, all too often, Russell tries to get the upper hand on Bradley by forcing upon him an understanding of these terms that he simply would not accept. For example, Bradley never countenances Russell's idea of absolute identity. But this is just what Russell often tries to make Bradley's statements about identity mean. Hence, such that we can call these charges "arguments" at all, we must see them as wholly question-begging.

I think that we must acknowledge here that, to Russell, Bradley's conception of identity-in-difference just doesn't make sense. And to Bradley, Russell's notion of absolute identity and absolute difference is equally incoherent. But is there no way to settle the issue? In my concluding remarks on the Russell-Bradley exchange I shall offer what I understand as Bradley's general argument for the truth of monism (identity-in-difference) against radical pluralism (absolute identity). However, let us first return to this passage and attend to another aspect of what is the same problem.

Response to Objection (c-iv). Directly related to Russell's general attack on philosophical monism is his claim that the axiom of internal relations is incompatible with complexity. And Russell's argument here is simplicity itself. He reasons that "if things are different, they can't be the same; and if they are the same, they can't be different." However, Bradley insists continually that "the universe is one," and that "in the Absolute all distinction is transmuted."[18] Clearly, claims like these emphasize the sameness of things at the expense of difference. But, Russell reasons, if Bradley is to insist that they are the same, let us force upon him the full implication of his claim. If truly the same, then not different—difference and complexity are, then, mere illusions. But, equally clearly, there *is* difference in the world. Hence Bradley's position must be rejected; not only because it contains an internal inconsistency, but because it flies in the face of given fact.

Such, it would appear, is the logic that Russell employs against Bradley throughout his "Monistic Theory of Truth" and in the several articles in which he addresses these issues. But the question remains: Is this a valid criticism? Certainly Bradley would say No. And to understand why we should recall here that the fundamental ontological claim of Bradleian idealism is not that there exists "one thing" only. There exists—by necessity on Bradley's analysis—many things. The Absolute could not be unified unless it had differences internal to it that it could somehow hold together. And the point made by the monist (or at least by Bradley) is simply that it is a presupposition of all experience that the diverse phenomena we experience are *au fond* unified into a single coherent *system*. Bradley's Absolute is *not* a contentless "night in which all cows are black." It is, rather, a multiplicity of entities that possess—in and through this multiplicity—a ground of union that, though in its completed form can never be fully grasped by finite consciousness, is presupposed in every moment of our conscious existence, and is that which all judgment strives to comprehend. Simply put, the conception of "monism" that Russell assumes in this passage is one that Bradley just does not embrace.

RUSSELL OR BRADLEY?

When one reviews either Russell's account of Bradley or Bradley's of Russell, there arises the sense that the most fundamental issues are ones on which neither is willing to make any concessions. Russell, convinced of the complete independence of the constituents of the world, argues forcefully for a radically pluralistic universe in which each thing is what it is in a manner that is essentially unaffected by what is external to it. Bradley, on the other hand, remains equally convinced of the ultimate unity of all things, a unity so strong that to change one aspect of the universe is, if only to an infinitesimal degree, to change every other aspect. And, though some have argued that it is, in the end, a matter of philosophical "taste" as to which of these competing worldviews one cares to embrace, certainly neither Bradley nor Russell thought that the question could be settled so easily. Hence, before ending my brief consideration of Russell, I would like to say something more about why Bradley felt he had to take the position he did, and why Bradley felt that his own doctrine was better equipped to meet the challenge of empirical scepticism. And to this end, let us consider once more the question of relations.

When both Russell's and Bradley's views on relations are understood, I think we must acknowledge a greater similarity between them than is usual. As I have argued, both accounts see relations as, in one sense, fundamental aspects of experience, and both doctrines manage to preserve the asymmetry of certain relations. But, once both theories are understood, I think it must be admitted that Bradley's doctrine has a distinct advantage over Russell's. While both doctrines—properly understood—capture the immediate asymmetry of certain relations, only Bradley's, I suggest, captures the *ultimate* asymmetry, and thereby preserves the unity of experiential contents that a theory of inference demands. Simply put, while Russell agrees that certain relations are asymmetrical, it is Russell, and not Bradley, who fails to appreciate the depth of this asymmetry. And I say this because Russell's asymmetrical relations are ones that are *isolated*. Although Russell certainly wants to insist that relations always have a "sense" and a "direction," he has, from Bradley's perspective, a profoundly limited notion of this direction. For example, "older than" is a relation with a sense and, in Russell's system, this sense can, up to a point, be illustrated and preserved. However, given that Russell's relational complexes are wholly external to other relational complexes (as well as non-relational ones), Russell's view presents these relations to us as brute facts. That is, the "older than" that exists between, let us say,

Michael and Henry is essentially no different than the "older than" that characterizes the relationship between Susan and Sally.

This relation, in being externally related to both its relata and other relations, cannot therefore provide us with any suggestions as to how the mind, once it has apprehended these brute facts, is to proceed to extract any further significance from the situation. (See chapters 8 and 9.) And, though Russell's concept of the external relatedness of subjects, predicates, and relations might allow him to confidently declare that a judgment like "Susan is older than Sally" is true or false *tout court*, this capacity to completely capture truth and falsity leads to an *independence* of the judgments within which these terms and relations appear; but this in turn makes any inferential transition problematic. Not so, however, for Bradley. Since all relations—asymmetrical and otherwise—are for him conditioned by *further* relations that are not brought into the explicit assertion, but that make a difference to the terms, nonetheless, Bradley's theory preserves the rational ground not just within, but also *between* relational wholes (or more accurately, parts of *the* whole); and for this reason alone the theory is better equipped to meet the challenge of scepticism. And it is better equipped precisely because it maintains the route or pathway that can justify the inferential transition from one item of knowledge to another. Take away this route, a route that Bradley's holistic ontology preserves, and inferential transition becomes, if not tautological and vacuous, then informative in a sense that is open to sceptical dismissal.

Of course, Russell is himself quite sensitive to these difficulties. And, though he is never persuaded by rationalist attempts to meet them, neither can he ever bring himself to endorse a strict empiricism. Still, realizing that he must postulate *something* that can make legitimate the inferential transitions between atomic facts, he is forced to acknowledge "principles of inference" that are neither logically demonstrable nor inductively derived.[19] And, in the end, Russell adopts the view that simply says "it is more reasonable to believe in the principles upon which our inferences are based than to disbelieve in them."

Now, though Bradley would certainly agree that it is more reasonable to assume the truth of principles by which our inferences are justified than deny them, he certainly would not accept this move as an adequate *philosophical* defense. Simply put, though we might assume the truth of a principle like "the future will resemble the past" (to mention the most notorious) because it appears to us "reasonable," the mere assumption of such a principle hardly guarantees its truth. And, though *we* might see it as "reasonable"—perhaps only because it is in harmony with our previously assumed idea of what it means to be "reasonable"—the sceptic need not be concerned with such a response. What is required to stop the sceptic is not the mere assumption of principles that seem, by our lights, "reasonable"; rather, what is required is a *demonstration* that we have no choice but to assume them, because in their absence not even the minimum of experience would be possible. And, though Bradley does not attempt to "transcendentally deduce" such principles in the manner of his idealist predecessors, he does argue that there are ultimate assumptions about reality that are ineluctable. We can rely on them absolutely (even if we cannot not fully understand them) because in their absence "there is nothing." Either, Bradley claims, the universe exhibits a law-governed reciprocity between its elements (which for him is far stronger than mere regularity) and perfect internal consistency or there could be no experience—at least as it is conceivable by us. And he would, of course, add here that it is sheer nonsense to discuss things that we cannot conceive. We must treat, on pain of self-contradiction, he believes, such unavoidable assumptions about the nature of reality as being both epistemologically and onto-logically valid.

It might be further observed here that Russell's own doctrine, though in a highly roundabout fashion, seems to admit much of this. As suggested above, Russell never has a problem with appealing to *some* sort of "principle" by which his collections of bare and externally related facts can be used as evidence for further inferences. But when comparing the Bradleian and Russelian ontologies, there arises the question: What is the real difference between a metaphysic that sees every-thing related in a systematic and interpenetrating fashion (Bradley's), and one that sees the universe as a collection of externally related enti-ties that are, nevertheless, governed by lawlike principles (Russell's)? It has always seemed to me, and certainly this idea is found throughout Bradley's work, that with the admission of lawlike principles there also comes the tacit admission that things are *not* indifferently related and merely external to one another. But if this is true, why, we must ask, would one persist in one's commitment to the externality and indiffer-ence of all phenomena?

This is not a question for which I have any answer. However, I do think that, in the end, Russell's "pluralism" and Bradley's "monism" are not quite as distant as is sometimes thought. In the final analysis, both writers are committed the idea that there are rational principles that guide our factual inferences and daily conduct. But, in saying this I would add that, compared to Russell's, Bradley's realization of this idea seems, to my thinking, far less susceptible to sceptical dismissal.

WILLIAM JAMES ON BRADLEY'S "INTELLECTUALISM"

One recent commentator has claimed that it is not Bertrand Russell but William James who provides, in many cases, the most profound criticism of Bradley's idealism.[20] And, while I do not care to pursue at this point questions about whose criticism is the most insightful, I must agree that James must be taken into account in any critical appraisal of Bradley. This is, I think, particularly important given the apparent agreement between these thinkers on so many issues. Both believe that the universe is, in its actual nature, a seamless "unity-in-diversity." And both think that there exists a mode of experience that allows us to directly grasp this fact. A further point on which both agree is that each understands "thought" as somehow introducing an element of distortion into our apprehension of what is most truly real.

However, I must emphasize here the word "apparent" when discussing the issues upon which James and Bradley agree. And I do this because I think we need not look too far in order to find some serious, and perhaps irreconcilable, differences. But let me begin to explain these differences by considering a passage from Timothy Sprigge's *Bradley and James*, as it sets the stage nicely for the issues I now want to examine. Focusing on how both James and Bradley see thought as, in some sense, inadequate to ultimate reality, Sprigge writes:

> For James the most basic way in which concepts cannot do justice to reality lies in their inability to deal with its flux. Concepts are static and sharply distinct from one another. In concrete reality, in contrast, one item flows into another without their being either sharply distinct from or identical with each other. Again, concepts cannot capture the kind of continuity which pertains to real change. . . . For Bradley it was not so much the flux of reality which eludes our conceptual grasp as the combined togetherness and variety of things. Conceptual thought divides things up into separate units, each intelligible apart, and cannot put them together again it its own terms. . . . Here then is a major difference: For James concepts of flux and becoming bring us nearer to the reality which concepts distort than do concepts of eternity and being, while with Bradley the opposite is true. Thus for James the solution is to quit conceptual thinking and plunge oneself in some more intuitive way into the sensory flux. Then when one starts thinking again one will have a better sense of what one is talking about, even if one can never adequately capture its nature in talk. For Bradley, in contrast, it lies rather in a determination to think harder, while recognizing that thought

must fail to give any final understanding. It is this aspect of
Bradley's approach which James thought so unsatisfactory,
and from which he turned with relief to Bergson, whom he
thought had seen further than anyone else on this.[21]

Now, I have turned to this summary because I think it concisely
states what James himself never in one place makes so clear. However,
I think that of the several differences noticed here, we must first ask ourselves which is the most important.

On the surface the differences between the two thinkers appear to
consist largely in their preferred ways of characterizing ultimate reality.
James always describes this reality as a "flux" or "ever-changing continuum." Bradley, on the other hand, emphasizes the "timeless" and
"eternal" aspects of the Absolute. However, as important as these pref-
erences may be, I think we may best appreciate their differences by considering how each tells us we are to *access* this fundamental reality. As
mentioned in the above passage, while both believe that there is a sort
of experience (James usually calls it "perception," Bradley "feeling")
that conveys to us a fuller sense of reality than can mere concepts, their
ideas of how we come to apprehend it are, as Sprigge remarks, in dra-
matic opposition. Hence, let us attempt to understand this opposition by
considering the views of each on the closely related subjects of perception and thought.

James on Perception and Concepts

For James, we must always realize, *perception* is the source—ultimately, the only source—of all that our intellect craves. Indeed, for
James, it is in direct and conceptually uncontaminated perception that
we encounter the "many-in-one," or the "unity-in-diversity" of which
both he and Bradley speak.[22] Consider, for example, James's words in
Some Problems of Philosophy:

Concepts . . . being thin extracts from perception, are always
insufficient representatives thereof; and, although they yield
wider information, they must never be treated after the ratio-
nalistic fashion as if they gave a deeper quality of truth. *The
deeper features of reality are found only in perceptual experience.* Here alone do we acquaint ourselves with continuity, or
the immersion of one thing in another, here alone with self,
with substance, with qualities, with activity in its various
modes, with time, with cause, with change, with novelty,
with tendency, and with freedom.[23]

Consider also the following passage in which James enthusiastically
endorses the advice of his philosophical hero, Henri Bergson:

> Bergson *drops* conception—which apparently has done all the
> good it can do; and, turning back towards perception with its
> transparent multiplicity-in-union, he takes its data integrally
> up into philosophy, as a kind of material which nothing else
> can replace. The fault of our perceptual data, he tells us, is not
> of nature, but only of extent; and the way to know reality
> intimately is, according to this philosopher, to sink into those
> data and get *our sympathetic imagination to enlarge their
> bounds. Deep* knowledge is not of the conceptually mediated,
> but of the immediate type.[24]

Here, then, we begin to discover why James admonishes us to sometimes *quit thinking* and directly intuit that enduring flux that constitutes
for him the bedrock of experience. We should intermittently quit thinking, he tells us, because after we have contacted this most basic level of
perception we shall come back to our ordinary experience both
refreshed and inspired. James also suggests that as a result of direct contact with the continuous and enduring perceptual reality, we shall find
ourselves capable of constructing more adequate conceptual representations. Crucial for James, though, is the idea that our conceptual representations of reality are just that—representations. And, as such, they
lack the fullness and vigor of the more fundamental experience that they
attempt to portray. Our concepts "carve and cut" the perceptual continuum, but since "the [intellectual] cuts we make are *purely* ideal" they
lose in this carving, all the detail and life that our direct perceptual experience provides.[25] And it is the gravest of errors, James tells us, to take
the "map for the reality." As we read:

> The [conceptual] map remains superficial through the
> abstractness, and false through the discreteness of its terms;
> and the whole operation, so far from making things appear
> more rational, becomes the source of quite gratuitous unin-
> telligibilities. Conceptual knowledge is forever inadequate to
> the fullness of the reality to be known.[26]

And consider further this contrast between perception and thought:

> Perception is solely of the here and now; conception is of the
> like and unlike, of the future, of the past, and of the far away.
> But this [conceptual] map of what surrounds the present, like
> all maps, is only a surface; its features are but abstract signs
> and symbols of things that in themselves are concrete bits of
> sensible experience.[27]

The map—our conceptual approximation of concrete perceptual experience—is, then, not only emptier and more abstract, but it contains

distortions and "unintelligibilities" that are not to be found in perceptual experience itself. And, for any philosophy that mistakes the map for the terrain (both rationalism and idealism) James reserves the epithet "intellectualism."

Bradley's "Prejudice"

Of course, anyone familiar with the Jamesian corpus is well aware of the charge of "intellectualism"—it is a recurring theme. Indeed, what at times approaches contempt for both the rationalist and idealist traditions cries out on many pages. (This is especially true of James's later works.[28]) Hence it might at first seem surprising that James lavishes so much attention on his "intellectualist" contemporary, F. H. Bradley. But this more generous treatment is not without reason. Though Bradley's status in the philosophical community must have had a good deal to do with his receipt of so much of James's notice, there exists between himself and Bradley— or so James believes—a certain kinship that he thinks he does not share with others beset by this philosophical disease (intellectualism). As already mentioned, both Bradley and James believe (contra Russell and other realist critics) that reality, in its truest nature, is a "many-in-one" or a "unity-in-diversity." And both philosophers also argue that there exists some sort of primitive experience whose presence assures us that reality has just such a character. (The precise nature of this experience will soon become an issue of great concern for us.) It is for these reasons, then, that James sees Bradley as having at least grasped the most important truth: the presence of the many-in-one in feeling. And, indeed, it is for this reason that James also sees Bradley as not only a "traitor to orthodox intellectualism," but as a philosopher who, in some important respects, is very near to the higher truth of his own "radical empiricism."[29]

But still, James believes that Bradley is unable to shake off the most serious of idealist dogmas. And the one aspect of Bradley's doctrine that James finds the most objectionable is his idea that if perception is to have any real value for us it must be somehow "worked over" by thought. That is, the idea that abstract thought somehow *participates in* and is *part of* the our deepest perceptual intuitions is, for James, an anathema. Hence we read:

> Mr. Bradley preserves one [intellectualist] prejudice uncriticized—perception 'untransmuted' must not, cannot, shall not, enter into final 'truth.' Such loyalty to a blank direction in thought, no matter where it leads you, is pathetic: concepts disintegrate—no matter, their way must be pursued; percepts are integral—no matter, they must be left behind. When anti-sensationalism has become an obstinacy like this, one feels that it draws near its end.[30]

We have found here, I suggest, an epistemological difference between James and Bradley of fundamental importance. Bradley's doctrine is, to James, not only "intellectualist" in that it sees thought as somehow participating in the structure of reality itself, it is also "antisensationalist" in its refusal to acknowledge the presence of the unity-in-diversity that immediate perception—indeed, sensation—provides.[31] But, as suggested above, James apparently finds all of this terribly confusing. Does not Bradley believe with him that in "feeling" the highest truth is to be found? And if this is truly Bradley's belief (he seems to have said it many times), how can he continue to worship at the "altar of the intellect"? Consider now the following passage in which James tells us what Bradley, given his *partial* insight into philosophical truth, should have done in order to maintain something like intellectual consistency.

> The wise and natural course [for Bradley, James tells us, would be] . . . to drop the notion that truth is a *thoroughgoing* improvement on reality, to confess that its value is limited, and to hark back [to immediate perception, i.e. feeling]. But there is nothing that Mr. Bradley, religiously loyal to the direction of development once entered upon, will not do sooner than this. Forward, forward, let us range! He makes the desperate transconceptual leap, assumes *beyond* the whole ideal perspective an ultimate 'suprarelational' and transconceptual reality in which somehow the wholeness and certainty and unity of feeling, *which we turned our backs on forever when we committed ourselves to the leading of ideas*, are supposed to be resurgent in transfigured form; and shows us as by only authentic objects of philosophy, with its 'way of ideas' an absolute which, 'can be' and 'must be' and therefore 'is'.[32]

The complaint here as I read James is simply that Bradley—after acknowledging that *feeling* is the actual source of our awareness of unity-in-diversity—tries to combine in his philosophical conception of the Absolute that which cannot be combined. That is, Bradley attempts to preserve the role of the intellect in the highest sort of experience we can possess. Dissatisfied with the limited immediacy that feeling provides, Bradley seeks to "have his philosophical cake and eat it too" by arguing that the limitations of perceptual immediacy can, through the participation of the intellect, be progressively, if not perfectly, overcome. But this is, of course, precisely what James (along with Bergson) denies. While James is willing to concede that perceptual apprehension of the many-in-one is limited in its extent, to claim that our *intellectual* augmentation of this direct and noncognitive experience can adequately overcome this feature of perceptual experience strikes him as sheer folly. The limited extent of immediate intuition is to be overcome, James argues, both through the use of our noncognitive "synthetic imagination" and the continual reimmersion of our awareness in the perceptual flux. And, though we must acknowledge that the intellect can be of *in*direct service to us in achieving this intuition, to pursue the course suggested by Bradley—to try to grasp ultimate reality through thinking—James sees as positively counterproductive, and as an indication of serious confusion on Bradley's part. But the question that forces itself upon us here is "How can two philosophers who, in some areas, agree about so much have such opposed views on the nature and function of the intellect?'

THE FUNDAMENTAL TENSION

I think we can best grasp the essential difference between Bradley and James here by examining two assumptions made by James but rejected by Bradley. These assumptions I would describe as follows: (*a*) primitive perception—perception uncontaminated by thought—provides the most adequate mode of apprehending reality; and (*b*) thought is of a fundamentally different nature than perception. Of course, Bradley rejects these assumptions because, to his thinking, they are both phenomenologically unjustified and theoretically incoherent. And, though we shall be traversing ground already considered, let us consider once more the reasons for his taking this view.

The Noncognitive Apprehension of Reality

We have just considered how for James it is only in immediate perception that we apprehend the true nature of reality. But what can we say about Bradley's doctrine here? We might first recall our discussion of "mere feeling." There we learned that, for Bradley, mere sensuous immediacy is our most defective form of experience, and that it is in an effort to repair its shortcomings that we are led to assert in the first place. Hence, it should be clear that Bradley does not believe that sensuous immediacy provides us with an awareness of a many-in-one. But what of perception?

Throughout this essay I have tried, whenever the subject of perception has arisen, to emphasize two aspects of Bradley's theory. These are: (i) perception is never "bare," or "pure," or otherwise uncontaminated by thought; and (ii) perception is always, to some degree, *ideal*. I would stress here that by calling perception "ideal" Bradley wants to claim that there does not exist in given perceptual experience either the pure particular or the perfectly seamless reality that is understood to reside there by James and other "radical empiricists." It cannot be emphasized too strongly that, for Bradley, there just is no concept-free perceptual given.[33] And we should recall the discussion of the earlier chapters where we learned that, on Bradley's view, both the distinct particular and the unifying bond—the "continuities" seen between those particulars—are the *result* of thought's working over the intractable experiential contents we identify as perceptual. Hence, what for James is complete and pure only in the absence of conception, for Bradley, comes at the end of what can, at times, be the arduous process of thinking. And, while it is true that Bradley agrees with James that the intellect distorts what we must assume (but never, on Bradley's view, fully perceive) to be ultimate reality, the intellect also plays for him a crucial role in our apprehension—both perceptual and conceptual—of that reality. No matter how far thought has elevated perception, the given experiential contents of a perceptual complex, they will still exhibit, Bradley claims, a degree of generality and hence can be said to be, at least partially, "ideal." And when and where this ideality is (partially) overcome it is only with the assistance of the intellect.

Bradley, it is true, believes thought to be capable of making an advance from lower to higher, from the less concrete to the more concrete, only if it allows itself to be guided by feeling and will. But, as we have spent so many pages considering, Bradley's "feeling"—the guiding light of thought's inferential advance—can hardly be equated with either sensation or mere perception. (See chapters 8 and 9 again.) Feeling, construed in the broadest sense, is, for Bradley, the totality of our experiential being. And perception per se, we must remember, is but the tip of this experiential iceberg. While perceptual contents convey for Bradley a sense of their concrete particularity, that particularity as it consciously manifests in this or that perceptual experience is only a partial and relative realization of the complete particularity that exists only as a "feeling" (i.e., an experiential assumption) behind the explicit and given perceptual data. And, though we have yet to consider the question as to whose theory of perception is the least problematic, it should be very clear by this stage of the discussion, that Bradley's "feeling" and James's "perception" stand at what we must acknowledge as a great distance from one another.

Thought as Different from Perception

But let us consider next some further differences between James and Bradley on the relation between thought and perception. And I would begin by appealing again to James's own words:

> The great difference between percepts and concepts is that
> percepts are continuous and concepts are discrete. Not dis-

crete in their *being*, for conception as an *act* is part of the flux
of feeling, but discrete from each other in their *meanings*.
Each concept means just what it means, and nothing else.[34]

There are two points here that demand our notice. First, we should
realize that James sees concepts as that which essentially sever and
divide the more primitive experiential continuum; that is, concepts are
essentially distinct from one another in that they rigidly isolate various
aspects of the perceptual flux, and hold the result of this act of abstraction apart from what, in the flux itself, is continuous. Although James
insists that there exists a plurality of elements within the flux, the respective individuality of these elements can be grasped only by directly *intu-
iting* them in the seamless experiential continuum.[35] But it is just this
experience of a seamless unity-in-diversity that, for him, thinking
destroys. Second, concepts, on this view, have a limited referential
capacity. That is, for James any "meaning," any intensional content (or
relation to other intensional contents), is subjective in origin and
remains fixed unless and until we revise it. While James believes that the
perceptual flux itself contains given experiential complexes that flow
naturally into other such complexes, thought itself functions, as we shall
consider below, essentially as described by the nominalist-empiricist.
That is, thought is an *arrest* of what is perceptually fluid; and whatever
meaning a term has, we, in our intellectual act of arrest, have put it
there—often with disregard for the given continuities that perceptual
experience provides.

Now, James does not want to deny that we can and, indeed, must
make an effort to revise and rehabilitate our concepts. He always tells
us that it is the philosopher's special task to turn back to perception so
as to expose the abstract and inadequate nature of conception, and then
to correct that inadequacy by employing ideas that are more closely
adjusted to given sensuous reality (so far, anyway, as conception will
allow such correction). But, no matter how far we might go in the reha-
bilitation of our concepts they will always be, James claims, a poor show
when compared to the perceptual basis from which they are taken.

There is, of course, an air of familiarity to all of this. Bradley, too,
advises us to let feeling expose the abstract and general nature of our
intellectual vision of reality; and Bradley also claims that we should
allow feeling to provide "suggestions" as to how we should proceed in
our inferential advance. However, we must not be led astray by the
superficial similarity of view between these writers. We must remember that, whereas James sees thought as capable of analysis only, for
Bradley, thought is simultaneously analytic *and* synthetic. (See chap-

ter 3.) While James sees thought as only "brutalizing" and "distorting" the intrinsic continuity and seamlessness that pure perception
provides, Bradley sees *both* the moments of specification (analysis) and
unification (synthesis) as arising from the combined activity of feeling,
will, and intellect.

Bradley, we must not forget, sees thought as, amongst other things,
a "running through" or "unifying" activity amongst differences.
Thought is "divisive" and "analytic" in the sense that it must always
select out of a larger experiential continuum this or that limited subject
(and that which it unites in judgment always falls short of its presupposed ideal). But we should recall that, on Bradley's theory, as the
abstractive or selective function of thought increases, that is, as we begin
to notice differences, we simultaneously begin to grasp—at the level of
both thought and perception—points of *identity* between those differences. (See chapter 4.) And the converse is also true: as we find sameness
or universality, we simultaneously begin to experience difference and
particularity. Hence, for Bradley, it just is not true that either a pure
"continuum" or a "unique particular" is given *prior* to thought's activity. We possess, Bradley argues, a relatively vague and undefined sense
of both the seamless unity and unique particularity of all that exists at
the level of feeling. But that vague sense of reality that we posses at the
level of feeling becomes capable of explicit apprehension in perception
only *after* thought has "synthetically analyzed" the experiential contents
that at any moment are before it.[36] But this difference may be illustrated
by also considering the contrasting views of these writers on how our
concepts are formed.

For James, all concepts are generic mental representations of qualitative differences supplied by immediate perception. They are, we may
say, intellectual extracts from the given flux; and as such they may be
simple or complex in nature. And while some concepts show themselves
to be devoid of differentiated internal content (an example might be
"red"), others possess an internal complexity of sorts. (The concept
"man" would be an example here.) But a complex concept like "man"
must still be understood, on James's theory, as an abstract and hollow
grouping of marks. Concepts are the products of thinking; and thinking
always begins with perception—a perception that is infinitely richer and
more detailed than the thoughts (concepts) that arise out of it.

In complete agreement with traditional empiricism (on this point,
anyway), James claims that we come to possess concepts through an act
of eliminative abstraction. That is, beginning with the richness of pure
perception we (i) focus on points of sameness; (ii) ignore the differences
that fall under those points of sameness; and (iii) fix this result through

language.[37] And thus the concept is really nothing more or less than an abstract and hollow "map" that we have extracted from the perceptual given.[38] Of course, given the independence between thought and perception that James postulates, it is not surprising that he sees the results of concept formation to be capable of great variation. Given the same set of perceptual data, you might generate one set of concepts while I abstract from it ideas that are quite different. And there is nothing wrong with this, we are told, so long as the concepts we each employ help us to achieve our individual goals and purposes. Although James claims that to rest satisfied with our merely abstract concepts—that is, to not bring them into greater harmony with the perceptual flux—is the greatest sin we can intellectually commit (as it will ultimately be counterproductive in our effort to realize our goals), he remains committed to the view that the more we think about reality (in the sense of employing broad and widely denotative concepts) the further away from the richness of primitive perception we get.[39]

But, as should by now be clear, this is not Bradley's understanding of the act of selective abstraction. We should recall that selective abstraction, while it must choose from an experiential base that is infinitely rich, involves in its choice both the separation *and* the unification of the given contents. Although it is true that thinking severs the "what" from the "that," it is, on Bradley's theory, the special provenance of thought to take the orphaned "what" and to find for it further and fuller "thats." And these further "thats," we must remember, are *not* to be found in any "preconceptual" perceptual experience. (See chapter 2 again.) Indeed, it is only thought that, for Bradley, overcomes the sheer immediacy (mere feeling) and limited extent that the sensuous moment provides.

This is, of course, a highly condensed statement of a point that we have spent several chapters developing. However, I think it important to point out here that Bradley's understanding of thought as a "synthetic-analysis" (or "analytic-synthesis") is something that James apparently does not see in Bradley. And to illustrate this point I would like to turn to a passage from James's short article of 1910 "Bradley or Bergson?" There we read:

> Bradley's first great act of candor in philosophy was his breaking loose from the Kantian tradition that immediate feeling is all disconnectedness.[i-a] In his *Logic* as well as in his *Appearance* he insisted that in the flux of feeling we directly encounter reality, and that its form, as thus encountered, is the continuity and wholeness of a transparent much-at-once.[ii] This is identically Bergson's doctrine.[iii-a] In

affirming the 'endosmosis' of adjacent parts of 'living' experience, the French writer treats the minimum of feeling as an
immediately intuited much-at-once. The idealist tradition is
that feeling, is aboriginally discontinuous, are [sic] woven
into continuity by the various synthetic concepts which the
intellect applies.[i-b] Both Bradley and Bergson contradict
this flatly; and although their tactics are so different, their
battle is the same. *They destroy the notion that conception is
essentially a unifying process.*[iii-b] For Bergson all concepts
are discrete; and though you can get the discrete out of the
continuous, out of the discrete you can never construct the
continuous again. Concepts, moreover, are static, and can
never be adequate substitutes for a perceptual flux of which
activity and change are inalienable features. Concepts, says
Bergson, make things less, not more, intelligible, when we use
them seriously and radically. They serve us practically more
than theoretically. Throwing their map of abstract terms and
relations round our present experience, they show its bearings
and let us plan our way. Bradley is just as independent of [the]
rationalist tradition, and is more thoroughgoing still in his
criticism of the conceptual function.[iv-a] When we handle
felt realities by our intellect they grow, according to him, less
and less comprehensible; activity becomes inconstruable, relation contradictory, change inadmissible, personality unintelligible, time, space and causation impossible—nothing survives
the Bradleyan wreck.[iv-b] [40]

Now, I have included in this passage bracketed Roman numerals
(just after the claim) so as to indicate the various points that I wish now
to discuss. And I believe that this passage does need some discussion
because, if there is one thing it shows, it is how thoroughly James
appears to misunderstand Bradley on both the subject of "feeling" and
"conception." But let us take these points it turn.

(i) First, let us consider the historical points made in [i-a] and [i-b]
above. To these I would say that it is difficult to understand precisely
which "idealist tradition" James is referring to here. While there is *a*
reading of Kant that takes him as saying that there exists a given manifold of disconnected perceptual contents that we can somehow consciously experience prior to the application of the categories, this is not
the reading that gave rise to any subsequent "idealist tradition" [i-b].
Certainly those writers who are ordinarily characterized as "idealists"
took Kant at his word when he said that the categories were conditions
of "any possible experience."[41] But this means, to the writers in this
tradition, anyway, that *all* phenomenal experience is unified by both
the categories and the transcendental unity of apperception of which

the categories are an expression or manifestation. Indeed, so committed were these thinkers to the idea of the complete *unity* of primitive experience that they made it one of their primary complaints against Kant that, through the postulation of a realm of "things-in-themselves," he held open the possibility that this unity was only the form of the mind.[42] Now, I do not want to want to enter into here questions of James as a historian of philosophy except so far as it applies to Bradley. However, Bradley does make a special point to question James on this issue. And, in direct response to this characterization of the "idealist tradition" and "absolutism," Bradley insists that, if there is one thing that he clearly took from Hegel and the "idealist tradition" it is that experience, at its most primitive and fundamental level, begins as a unity.[43]

(ii) The point to be emphasized regarding James's comments here is that Bradley's primitive experiential unity is not "transparent." (Feeling is, for Bradley, problematic in all the ways described in the previous chapter.) And, in direct response to James, Bradley comments on this issue.[44] While both writers agree that immediate experience, as either feeling or perception, is the *beginning* of experience, they disagree profoundly as to the *end* of that experience. For James, all that we intellectually desire is to be found in this immediate perceptual foundation. However, for Bradley, as we have now seen, the end can only come about, and even then never fully, *after* thought has done its work.[45]

(iii) While I do not care to recount the discussion of previous chapters, I think it beyond doubt that Bradley's doctrine is most emphatically not Bergson's, and their battles are not the same. And, based on our discussion, we may say that there are two fundamental points (at least) on which Bradley disagrees—and disagrees strongly—with the Jamesian-Bergsonian account of knowledge. First, there is the complete lack of equivalency between James's understanding of perception and Bradley's idea of feeling. (As suggested above, feeling for Bradley is only the beginning of what would bring complete satisfaction.) And second, there are their differing views on the synthesizing nature of thought. It is simply false that Bradley has "destroyed the notion that conceptualization is essentially a unifying process." Though Bradley admits that in selective abstraction we "sever" and "divide," and even "mutilate," in every word he writes he holds to the view that *unification* is also a result of thought's analytic and divisive habits.

(iv) The last point marked in the passage above is closely related to what we have just considered. However, it is more focused on the idea of thought's intelligibility (or lack thereof). Time and again, James tells us that thinking introduces "unintelligibilities" into our experience.[46]

And he attributes to Bradley a similar doctrine. What needs to be pointed out here, however, is simply this: Though James tries to attribute to Bradley his own view that thought, while practically unavoidable, does nothing but make less intelligible that which is transparent and coherent in immediate perception, this is not Bradley's view. While Bradley certainly does claim that the activity of thought precludes "ultimate" or "complete" intelligibility, this can hardly be taken to assert that thought only obscures and makes unintelligible something that is, prior to thinking, wholly coherent. Bradley's actual position holds that it is only through the synthesizing and unifying activity of judgment that there exists intelligible experience at all. And his admission that this activity must, even with the assistance of feeling and will, always fall short of its ultimate goal must not be taken to mean that it is directly antagonistic to that end.

I would conclude my brief discussion of James's analysis of Bradley simply by saying that every criticism that James has put forth here has been a criticism, perhaps of some philosopher, but certainly not of F.H. Bradley. And if there is in these brief comments one point I have hoped to make, it is that Bradley's account of both feeling and thought are in no way equivalent to James's views on perception and conception. They are expressions of different philosophical traditions; and any effort to reconcile them is, I believe, doomed to failure.

JAMES OR BRADLEY?

Thus far I have argued that, in terms of their theories of knowledge, James and Bradley stand much further apart than is sometimes thought. James clearly endorses some species of empiricism; Bradley, equally clearly, does not. In spite of his commitment to feeling as supplying our deepest sense of reality, Bradley, I suggest, stands firmly rooted in the idealist tradition of which James is so unceasingly critical. And he stands in this tradition for (at least) the following reasons: First, Bradley believes that when we think, the mind, to greater or lesser degree, participates in the being of the object(s) known. And though Bradley always insists that thought and its object cannot become entirely identical, there exists for him always a partial identity between thinking and reality. The second basis of Bradley's idealism has to do with his commitment to a categorial structure within both thought and reality. While Bradley always rejects any "bloodless ballet" of categories in which there is no difference between categorial concepts (as they are apprehended by us) and a reality beyond our conceptual apprehension, he still remains committed to the notion that some concepts are—despite our imperfect grasp of them—unavoidable. And, while acknowledging fully that our understanding of any categorial structure must be flawed, Bradley still insists that those things that we must think have to be seen as both epistemically and ontologically necessary.

Bradley's commitment to the epistemic necessity of certain ideas we have already considered. But I would point out here that he claims ontological status for these same ideas simply because we have no perspective or viewpoint outside of our thoughts from which we could criticize such concepts as mere ideas. And finally, we may place Bradley within the idealist tradition because he argues that the primitive unity of feeling is coextensive with any subsequent philosophical conviction we might come into that reality itself must be unified and one. While previous idealist writers were inclined to say that we must "presuppose" this unity, Bradley prefers to say that we "feel" it. But since this is a "feeling" that on his theory we must have, these ideas seem to come largely to the same thing. And, though there may be some agreement between James and Bradley on this last point, certainly there is none on the first two. Their ultimate understanding of the relation between thought and reality seems, to my thinking, so distant that there is little chance of bringing their views together. And, if we bear in mind the results of the previous chapter and recognize that our sense of the perfect unity of content and existence is a feeling that cannot even be called "mine-not-yours," the distance at which Bradley's idealism stands from James's empiricism becomes even more evident. But it is to this point that I want to return in my final comments.

As should now be apparent, whereas Bradley sees conception as an integral component in our experience of the real universe (including our direct perceptual experience), for James things are very different. Indeed, I do not think that it is going too far to say that, at least when compared to Bradley, James sees conception as a second-class citizen whose offerings are always suspect. And we may better grasp this idea, I think, by considering what it is about thinking experience that James sees as being of value. As I understand James, he wants to say that, while "thought" and "conception" (I use the terms interchangeably here) are fundamentally opposed to perception, they assume, nevertheless, a dual function within our larger experience. On the one hand we must see the value of thought as resting with its ability to convey to others, albeit in defective form, our primitive, and ultimately private, perceptual experience. (Our individual experience of the "flux" itself, is ultimately ineffable for James.) Nevertheless, our concepts allow us to approximate its nature and to share this approximation with our fellow language users. Hence we may say that thought (or conception) is the primary means by which we communicate with one another. And without it, not only would we be unable to convey our experiences to others, neither we should know how others experience the universe.

But conception, it would appear, has another equally valuable function in our lives. And we may say that, in addition to allowing us to communicate (more or less) to others our individual perceptual experiences, concepts somehow motivate or assist us in getting more of what we ultimately crave—a direct and uncontaminated intuition of reality. Indeed, we should recall here that James sees immediate perception, though not faulty "in nature," defective "in extent."[47] Although James tells us that it is in direct and unmediated perception that we apprehend the "many-in-oneness" (the "native state") of reality, he is also forced to admit that, in spite of the riches this immediate intuition provides, there is present therein a defect of sorts. And the defect is simply this: While we seek to experience directly all of reality, immediate perception—in being immediate—does not allow this. That is, it does not give to us the entirety of the real. But two questions arise here. First, we must ask, how on James's theory do we recognize this defect? And second, how, on the same theory, can essentially empty concepts assist us in overcoming it?

As for the first difficulty, though James insists that perception unmediated by thought is the absolute bedrock of experience, it remains, on his view, difficult to explain why we should crave a fuller experience than that which unmediated perception provides. And it would appear that, in order to explain our dissatisfaction with given immediacy, we must admit the existence of a criterion—a form of experience *superior* to unmediated perception—that allows us to recognize the shortcomings of mere immediacy. But what could this experience be? Bradley, of course, can appeal to his larger doctrine of feeling here. But what does James have? If he tells us that it is immediate perception *along with thought* that discloses perception's defect and limitation, then immediate perception can not be seen as ultimate; and neither can it be said that it discloses the "nature" of reality in an undistorted (i.e., nonconceptual) fashion. Indeed, if James takes this route his position would be very close to Bradley's. But, while he sometimes feels forced into something very much like this, his own conception of thought does not allow him to carry this idea forward with any consistency. Committed to the view that thought is completely derivative and in no way capable of directly grasping the deepest structure of reality, James is forced into a quite awkward position. Perception, he insists, is the only source of "deep knowledge." But perception, in overcoming its intrinsic limitation, must rely on thought.

If, as James says, concepts are fundamentally "other" than the immediate perceptual experience they work upon, then the assistance they provide would seem to consist largely in their reminding us that immediate perceptual experience is not the totality of perceptual experience that is available to us. Hence, thinking—somehow possessed of a fuller sense of reality than perception—admonishes us, over and again, it seems, to quit thinking and throw ourselves into the intellectually unmediated perceptual flux. But what a curious state of affairs this is. The intellect, consisting in empty abstract concepts, has as its saving grace, its capacity to remind us that we must not use it if we are to experience reality in its "purity." But in order to know that the given purity is not all there (remember, its extent is limited) we must appeal to a fuller experience than this pure perception can provide; and this is an experience that would appear to be completely mediated by the intellect.

But let us consider some further aspects of perceptual immediacy as described by James. First we must notice that the perceptual mechanism itself, in limiting the extent of reality available to us, cuts and carves the larger experiential continuum in a manner not unlike those described by James when discussing the activity of thought. And, though James would insist that there is a profound difference between the divisive activity of the intellect and the way in which the perceptual mechanism truncates the unified experiential continuum, the question that forces itself upon the careful reader here is simply "What could this difference be?" If both thinking and the human perceptual mechanism cut short the continuity of the real, both it would seem must, to some degree, introduce distortions into experience. And, indeed, if it is claimed that the truncated and limited perceptions we have are not in their nature distorted by this process, it would seem that James has tacitly admitted that the given contents of experience are radically plural. But if radically plural then not the many-in-one he often claims is to be found there.[48]

But to illustrate this point let us consider the following. If there is a complex whole a,b,c,d that is a system of interpenetrating and mutually conditioning terms, yet conditions c and d fall within our direct perceptual awareness while a and b remain external to it, how can we say that our awareness of c and d is "undistorted"? If a and b truly make a difference to c and d then their absence is not a *mere* absence; it is an absence that can only lead to a corrupted impression of c and d. And this can be denied, it would seem, only through the admission that a and b are somehow *unessential* to the being of c and d. But again, if what is absent is unessential to what is present, then it can hardly be said that what is present to immediate perceptions is a "seamless flux." (It could only be a group of objects whose actual natures were disconnected and external to that which is absent.) And, if the explicit absence of conditions *a* and *b* does make a difference to our apprehension of the nature of the perceptually given, then the distorting influence that is attributed to thinking by James seems to belong *equally* to the very perception which, he insists, provides the sole route to the many-in-oneness of reality. And in his discussion of James's theory, Bradley is quick to point this out: the limited *extent* of perceptual experience entails, no matter how much James denies it, its incapacity to accurately convey the true *nature* of reality.

Indeed, Bradley drives this point home when he argues further that James's acknowledgment of perception as limited in extent, also makes of it a partially abstract—and hence *ideal*—experience.[49] (This is something James continually denies.) And this results because the given nature of immediate perception, by James's own admission, "leads to" its fuller extent. Put differently, James wants to suggest that, while limited in extent, we somehow grasp *in the given perception* the fact that it is continuous with the rest of perceptual experience. But, Bradley asks, what could this "leading to" or sense of "continuity" be? If perception really does lead us anywhere (and Bradley agrees that it does), it is because it "points beyond itself" and in so pointing is "self-transcendent." But a self-transcendent perception, in not being self-contained, is just a "what" torn from its "that." It is a relatively abstract content that can only overcome its abstractness through being reattached to the perceptually absent *through an act of thought*. And, as we have now learned, it can, for Bradley, only partially (and never fully) overcome this limitation.

Bearing all of this in mind one must, I think, question the final coherency of James's position on these matters (certainly, Bradley did). And thus I would end my discussion here by saying that it strikes me as far more reasonable to simply acknowledge, as have the "intellectualist" traditions of rationalism and idealism, that the intellect's true value is that it discloses to us—at least at its best—the nonimmediate and hence nonperceptible structure of reality. And certainly any good "intellectualist" must further point out that, (i) since finite experience is always perceptually focused on the immediate "here" and "now," and (ii) since we unavoidably strive to experience more than what any perceptual "here" and "now" is capable of providing, we are (iii) philosophically ill-advised to reduce our conceptual grasp of the nonimmediate real to the status of a mere representation. It would seem that, given our undeniable reliance upon conceptualization (James admits this over and again), it would be a far more satisfying philosophy that could show that in thinking we do not necessarily move further away from the real (though through *bad* thinking we certainly might). Certainly it is a far better philosophical world that can show that such thinking is, in some sense, a participation in reality's deepest structure. And, while, in the end, it might be simple self-delusion to embrace such notions, certainly Bradley thought that philosophy must at least attempt to bring about this result.

CONCLUSION

OUR examination of Bradley's theory of knowledge is now complete; and, in our discussion we have covered a good deal of philosophical territory. At the very least I hope I have managed to convey to the reader a sense of the subtlety of Bradley's thought on these matters. But I hope to have also done something more. As stated in the introduction, I believe that Bradley's philosophy, despite the metaphysical distance at which some of his views stand from our ordinary manner of viewing things, still provides an extremely reasonable account of both judgment and inference. And if I have managed to communicate that reasonableness to the point that the reader has been motivated to explore further Bradley's writings then I must rest satisfied with the result this essay has brought about. However, this work was written with more in mind. It was written in the belief that a good deal of contemporary philosophy remains, not only misinformed about its own recent history, but confused on some very fundamental epistemological and metaphysical issues, and that a reconsideration of Bradley might help us to clarify some of this confusion. Hence, in my concluding comments I would like to offer a few observations on Bradley's idealism in light of some of the tendencies of recent philosophy.

I would begin by saying that I think anyone who tries to find in Bradley philosophical antecedents for one of the currently popular programs—realism or antirealism, foundationalism or antifoundationalism—will be disappointed. And I say this simply because the theory we have now considered in such detail resists classification under one or the other of today's philosophical slogans. But let us consider why.

While it is the persisting tendency of some interpreters to see Bradley as a realist, such an understanding (I hope it is clear after these many pages) would be mistaken.[1] Even though it is true that Bradley believes that—if it could exist—there would be only "one true description" of the world, and, even though he is the first to admit that finite minds do not in any significant sense create the reality they experience, we must never forget that for Bradley thought and reality are—while never reducible to one another—still aspects of the same ontological cloth. (Reality is, we must recall, completed thought; thought is but incomplete reality.) Whatever does exist—if it is to make a difference to our experience at all—must have been (or be) *experienced* by someone or something at some time or other. And when we add to this Bradley's complete rejection of what we call today "bivalence" (the either-or of truth and falsity), there seems to be little left in common with contemporary realism.[2] Hence we must consider how antirealism and Bradley might coexist.

If we take as fundamental to all forms of antirealism that there are no "evidence transcendent" facts—facts that could make a proposition true or false irrespective of our grasp of them—then the "antirealist" label seems equally inappropriate. If we are to say that "so long as the meaning of each sentence [in a language] is given by specifying what is to be taken as conclusively establishing a statement made by means of it" or "conclusively falsifying such a statement . . . in terms only of conditions which a speaker is capable of recognising" there seems to be little here that Bradley could embrace.[3] As we have already seen, for Bradley, the meaning that any sentence (judgment) possesses is both "real" and "ideal." The "ideal" meaning—the meaning that the speaker *is* capable of recognizing at any moment—is what exhausts the notion of meaning for the antirealist. However, Bradley's "real" meaning must to some extent always consist in more than this and thus remain "evidence transcendent"—at least this is true if we mean by *evidence accessible* "being either thought or perceived." (For Bradley, we must remember, experience is not exhausted by thought and perception.) And if what appears in thought or perception is understood as comprising the *complete* domain of meaning, then clearly Bradley cannot endorse such a view. We must remember that Bradley's conception of real meaning is nothing other than the structure of reality itself. It is that which all judgment seeks, but can only partially obtain. And, since there is for Bradley a domain of meaning that is in excess of (and forever beyond) what any finite mind can cognitively or perceptually apprehend, Bradley's own conception of truth and meaning hardly seems compatible with those doctrines described as "antirealist."[4]

But there is, perhaps, a more general way in which to cast the tendencies of contemporary philosophy. And I refer here to the divide between what is sometimes called "objectivism" (closely aligned with realism and foundationalism) and "relativism" (often, but not always, aligned with antirealism and antifoundationalism).[5] The former is obsessed not only with isolating certain foundations upon which all further knowledge can be based, but also with developing an invariable "procedure" or "method" that if followed will allow us to adjudicate without error disputes between rival knowledge claims. The latter is the philosophical tendency that says that no such foundations exist and that the attempt to isolate any method as *the* method is a hopelessly deluded project. And, in the hands of its more extreme proponents, it asserts that whatever knowledge we possess is utterly defeasible and completely provisional. Knowledge, so it is argued, is determined solely by its cultural conditions and in no way can be understood as providing any sort of universal and necessary truth.

But it should be clear by now that Bradley must reject the central theses of both these philosophical camps. Bradley cannot embrace the isolated noninferentially derived "given" in experience that purportedly provides an indubitable foundation for all knowledge claims. As we have now seen in some detail, if it were the case that such certain foundations existed (at least as they are described by the foundationalist) these "basic truths" could not do the work that is required of them. And neither can Bradley accept the notion of an invariable algorithm by which certainty may be achieved. In his philosophy there just are no clearly defined paths. The road to knowledge is one which, as Bradley puts it, is "clearly experimental"; and any effort to rigidly prescribe this experimental approach is doomed to failure.

But we should also be very clear that Bradley cannot embrace the alternative that is offered by so much of contemporary philosophy. Bradley does not believe that the rejection of the foundationalist's isolated and certain truths (or method) commit him to the sort of relativism that the modern "pragmatist" would believe inevitably follows.[6] Even though Bradley is the first to admit that all our knowledge is culturally and historically conditioned, he asks that we reexamine what such conditioning means. For Bradley, a correct understanding of the historical consciousness entails that we see it as supported by the whole. But this is precisely what contemporary pragmatic-relativism has missed.

Mired in a subjectivism from which it cannot escape, contemporary relativism believes that the fact that we are conditioned by our historical context means that we are stuck there. It has failed to grasp the deeper conception of history that sees that truly to be "in the present" entails that we simultaneously be "at one with our past." Or put differently, it has not seen that any understanding of the "now" constitutes an understanding of "then"; and that a grasp of the "temporal" demands a co-originating apprehension of the "eternal." Of course, from the perspective developed in these pages, if we have understood what it means to be a human being living in the twentieth century, we have at the same time grasped what is common to all human forms of life; and this because the particular can only be known relative to the universal, the part to the whole. But for the modern relativist who can conceive of history only as the brute unfolding of some mere material universe such claims must remain unmeaning.

The central claim of Bradley's philosophy can be summed up in the phrase "the truth is the whole." And when this is understood so too is the claim that "the relative presupposes and demands the Absolute"—even if that Absolute must remain incapable of being fully and explicitly formulated in human knowledge. But to say that we cannot grasp the Absolute fully is not to say that we cannot grasp it at all. And here the importance of Bradley's doctrine of degrees of truth—his notion that our knowing penetration of the whole can be more or less adequate because more or less complete—shows its importance. And it is only on this basis, Bradley believes, that either the ideas of truth and falsity or of value can arise. But, I would emphasize here what was left only partially said in the body of the text. Not only for Bradley is any truth valuable as a truth insofar as it embraces the whole, but the truest truths are those that bring to us an understanding of value.

We must not forget that Bradley sees the "mere fact" as a rather low-level abstraction; and any "truths" in which such facts appear (the strictly categorical judgment) are amongst the flimsiest and most easily falsified. As we have already considered, our facts become much truer and more stable as they incorporate themselves into broader and more expansive systems. But with increased systematic insight come the notions of higher and lower, and better and worse. Thus we find that as our breadth of vision expands, the criteria of coherence and comprehensiveness begin to assign the various contents of our experience to their proper hierarchical space. We can then begin to say that "x is truer than y," "p is more beautiful than q," and "a is more morally correct than b."

But I would call upon Bradley's own words one last time, as I think that the essence of what he believes his philosophy to be about are aptly summed up here. On the concluding pages of *Appearance and Reality* we read:

> The positive relation of every appearance as an adjective to Reality, and the presence of Reality among its appearances in different degrees and with diverse values—this double truth we have found to be the centre of philosophy. It is because the Absolute is no sundered abstraction but has a positive character, it is because this Absolute itself is positively present in all appearance, that appearances themselves can possess true differences of value. And, apart from this foundation, in the

end we are left without a solid criterion of worth or of truth or reality. This conclusion—the necessity on one side for a standard, and the impossibility of reaching it without a positive knowledge of the Absolute—I would venture to press upon any intelligent worshiper of the Unknown.[7]

Bradley's point is, I believe, the simple one that unless we have access to reality and unless that reality that we access has a determinate structure that is capable of manifesting itself in our knowledge, then *every* claim we make about value—*every* assertion about right and wrong, the beautiful and the ugly, and truth and falsehood—is worthless. And I raise this issue because it has been the tendency of twentieth-century philosophy to reject just that point upon which Bradley is here insisting. We have been told time and again by contemporary philosophy that either we have no access to the real or—if we do have access—we shall find no actual, no universal value there. However, the question I would like to leave with the reader is simply this: At what cost has the denial of such a universal criterion been made?

Appendix: Associationism

F.H. Bradley believed that *the* empiricist theory of inference was to be found in what is called the "theory of the association of ideas" or more simply "associationism." Given its first complete statement by Hume, it underwent development at the hands of a number of writers including: David Hartley, Jeremy Bentham, James and J. S. Mill, and, in Bradley's own day, Alexander Bain.[1] It was (and is still today) considered by many to be the philosophical ally of "scientific" theories of reasoning in that it does not postulate the existence of doubtful nonmaterial "ideas" or problematic entities such as "universals."[2] And, while proponents of the theory have usually admitted that its truth could be ascertained only through an act introspection, in treating thought as consisting in nothing other than factual "psychical states" it believed itself to be keeping the study of inference on a basis that was, if not rigorously experimental, at least devoid of "armchair metaphysics."[3]

However, the idea that a meaningful thought could be reduced to a factual, psychical state is precisely what Bradley found objectionable. That the fundamental "furniture of the mind" might consist in nothing more than disconnected, discrete sensa and a set of psychological habits developed out of them Bradley was unwilling to accept. And whether they are called "impressions" or "ideas" the belief that *psychical states* (i.e., states that have some sort of existence in time and that are the possession of an isolated perceiving subject) could be the essential constituents of significant thought was an anathema to him. But what was the doctrine of associationism that both Bradley and empiricism saw as the logical development of such an understanding of ideas?

Briefly put, associationism is the account of judgment and inference that sees ideas (psychical states) as establishing psychical bonds or dispositional connections with one another on the basis of the "contiguous relations" in which they appear. And for associationism the inferential process is one that unfolds essentially on the basis of these contiguously established psychical bonds. One of the most succinct statements of the theory has been supplied by J. S. Mill who briefly states the "laws of associationism" as follows:

> (i) Similar phenomena tend to be thought of together. (ii) Phenomena which have either been experienced or conceived in close contiguity to one another, tend to be thought of together. The contiguity is of two kinds; simultaneity, and immediate succession. (iii) Associations produced by contiguity become more certain and rapid by repetition. When two phenomena have been very often experienced in conjunction, and have not, in any single instance, occurred separately either in experience or in thought, there is produced between them what has been called Inseparable, or less correctly, Indissoluble Association. . . . (iv) When an association has acquired this character of inseparability—when the bond between the two ideas has been thus firmly riveted, not only does the idea called up by association become, in our consciousness, inseparable from the idea which suggested it, but the facts or phenomena answering to those ideas, come at last to seem inseparable in existence.[4]

But let us examine the mechanism that Mill describes more closely. It appears that condition A (which first comes to us as a sensuous impression) will become associated with condition B (also directly sensed) through the repeated experience of their simultaneous or successive conjunction. And somehow through this repeated contiguity a "mental bond" will develop between the preserved impressions (which in their "less lively" and preserved form have usually been called "ideas"). Indeed, the theory tells us that it is *only* through this repeated contiguous experience of conditions A and B, let us say "fire" and "heat," that we have formed in us any mental habit or disposition to see these terms as belonging together at all. And the strength of any association that so develops is entirely dependent, Mill tells us, upon the frequency and regularity of their prior contiguous appearance.

Hence, because of the previous regularity of their conjunction in my experience, whenever I think of "fire" I shall also think of "heat." But what is of great significance here is that when I am presented with the isolated impression of "fire" this impression will trigger or restimulate or cause to associate the idea of "heat" even though there is no impression of "heat" presently given to sense, and even though there is nothing in the content of the experienced impression "fire" that itself implies, or in any way necessitates, that of "heat." It is solely on the basis of the psychic bond that has been established through their prior conjunctive regularity—and not because of any intrinsic connection of content—that what Mill calls their "inseparable" or "indissoluble" association comes about.

We find, however, that there is a further condition that is required for the theory of associationism to work. Although we must have first developed through the repeated contiguity of conditions a dispositional "psychic bond," we must also have before us the relation of *resemblance* or *similarity* (I treat them as synonymous here) between a present impression (or idea) and a previous one. We must not forget that the theory of the association of ideas is supposed to be a theory that explains how it is we can *reason* given that the fundamental nature of an idea is to be a psychical image or mental fact. And it is only through the doctrine of resemblance that one idea (or impression) is said to bring before the mind another that can then bring forth a further idea on the basis of the dispositional bond existing between contents. But let us develop this central notion by considering an example.

I am presently smelling cod liver oil; this is the impression before my mind. And according to the associationist, it is the result of the relation of resemblance (similarity) that exists between my present impression of cod liver oil and previous impressions (now, less lively "ideas") that sets the inferential process in motion. I smell cod liver oil and I think of orange juice. Why? Because, let us suppose, invariably in my youth when my mother forced me to take cod liver oil she also insisted that I wash it down with a glass of orange juice. And, since every time I smelled cod liver oil I experienced the taste of orange juice immediately thereafter, the appropriate bond developed between the two conditions.

So, the present impression of cod liver oil "calls up" the idea (the preserved, less lively impression) of cod liver oil which in turn is attached to the idea of orange juice. We have first, a relationship of resemblance or similarity between the present impression of cod liver oil and a previous one, and we have next an associative bond (approaching indissoluble association) between cod liver oil and orange juice based upon their prior contiguous relation. Of course, the idea of orange juice could itself call up a further idea (either through resemblance or prior conjunctive regularity) which could in turn call up yet another. For example, it could be the case that after my present impression of cod liver oil calls up the idea of orange juice, it in turn might call up the impression of grapefruit, which, since I always ate grapefruit on the porch of my beach-front summer cottage, calls to mind the smell of the sea and salt air. There is, of course, virtually no limit to the associative connections that could develop, and to give further examples would be redundant. But, always at work is this twofold mechanism of contiguous relation and resemblance. Although both the psychical ideas and the associative bonds that develop between them may become quite complex, reduced to its essentials we are left with only these mechanisms. And, in the end, virtually all of our thinking can, according to the associationist, be understood to follow this pattern.

As mentioned above, Bradley saw the theory of associationism as the logical consequence of empiricism's greatest sin—the reduction of significant ideas to psychical states. I would mention at the outset, though, that in criticizing empiricist associationism Bradley did not deny that our ideas do "associate" or that the thinking of one idea somehow "calls up" or "brings to mind" further ideas that are similar. Bradley was completely willing to grant to the empiricist—indeed, insist along with him—that presented with one idea another with a similar content would develop out of it. What Bradley did object to, however, was the *theory* used by empiricism to explain this phenomenon.[5] And it is what Bradley saw as the shortcomings of the associationist's explanation that we must next examine.

Now, though he believed that the theory fails for more general reasons, Bradley does draw our attention to two immediate difficulties entailed by associationism, both of which, he thinks, should arouse our suspicion. First, he claims that, although the theory demands that our ideas be somehow *preserved*—that they exist in a "storehouse" of such ideas in order that they might be called up by a present impression or idea—no intelligible account can be provided of how this might occur. And second, he tells us, the theory rests upon an problematic account of the relation of similarity (or resemblance).

As for the first claim, Bradley argued that the "School of Experience" (his mocking term for empiricism) could provide absolutely no evidence that its idea-*qua*-image could—after its initial occurrence—preserve itself so that it can be called up again at a later date. Bradley argued that not only was there no empirical evidence of such a collection of stored image-ideas, but that the very notion fails to appreciate the nature of determinate existence that must characterize these psychical particulars. Although Bradley admits that psychical images can (and often do)[6] succeed one another in our consciousness as the inferential process develops, he utterly rejects the claim that the image that is before the mind at any time is one that has somehow been "revived"—that it is in any way the same (albeit weaker) image as the one originally experienced. In the *Principles of Logic* we read:

> The particular fact is made particular by an elaborate context
> and a detailed content. And this is *not* the context or content

which comes back. What is recalled has not only got different
relations; itself is different. It has lost some features, and some
clothing of its qualities, and it has acquired some new ones. If
then there is a resurrection assuredly what rises must be the
ghost and not the individual.[7]

According to Bradley, any imaged content that comes before the
mind as a result of the inferential process always reflects its new circumstances and the development of experience since its original appearance. Try as I may to recover the same sensuous impression of, for
example, my first taste of vanilla ice cream I cannot. My present image,
we are told, must necessarily contain both more and less than the original. Although I may be able to bring before my mind the *ideal conception* of my first taste of vanilla ice cream, the present image that accompanies this conception, is entirely new and it cannot fully recover the
intense nature of the varied data of sense as they originally occurred; nor
can it divest itself of the awareness of subsequent experiences. No matter how hard I try I shall be unable when thinking about my first taste
of vanilla ice cream to fully suppress the fact that when I had my second
taste it was covered with chocolate topping. And this new development,
Bradley claims, will always manage to infiltrate any subsequent image or
idea I might possess. But, if Bradley is right about this and if an image is
not capable of being recalled in its original particularity, then the traditional theory of associationism fails. And it fails because one if its central tenets is that *what* is associated just *is* the prior impression (now an
idea, of course) itself. And, should this be shown to be impossible then
the theory betrays itself as incoherent.[8]

The empiricist doctrine of "resemblance" (or "similarity") as it is
employed within the theory of associationism is, Bradley tells us, also
unintelligible. And, simply put the problem is that one of the resembling
psychical particulars must, on this account, be both present *and* absent
at the same time in order to do the work required of it. But let us consider this point in greater detail.

Bradley claims that for there to be any relation of similarity both
terms that stand in this relationship must be *simultaneously* before the
mind. But, then he asks whether or not it makes any sense for a *present*
and existing impression to stand in the relation of resemblance or similarity to an *absent*—yet to be associated—idea? Let us consider Bradley's
own words here.

Similarity [we are told] is a relation. But it is a relation
which, strictly speaking, does not exist unless both terms are
before the mind. Things may perhaps be the *same* in certain
points although no one sees them; but they can not properly

resemble one another, unless they convey the impression of resemblance; and they can not convey it unless they are both before the mind.[9]

It would appear, Bradley tells us, that the associationist has an insoluble problem here. If two ideas are said to resemble one another (or be similar) then they must both be before the mind at once in order to stand in this relation.[10] But, if they are both before the mind how is it that the relation of similarity (or resemblance) can "call up" an absent idea via resemblance? It would seem that the idea—in order to resemble—must already be present as an aspect of the existing impression. But, if it is already present then certainly the relationship of resemblance cannot explain how it is that one idea calls-up or restimulates the next. Hence, besides conjuring up the nonexistent past particular and placing it alongside the present impression the theory presupposes, Bradley claims, the very fact it was put forth to explain; and, in the end, it is "utterly bankrupt" as an explanation of the inferential process.[11]

But (and this really takes us to the heart of Bradley's opposition to the theory), even if both of these objections were met, Bradley believed that associationism should still be rejected as an accurate account of the inferential process. And this, we are told, is because it results in a vicious sceptical subjectivism which must ultimately appeal to the arbitrary frequency of conjunction between psychic particulars as that which effects the associative bonds between ideas. Even if it be granted that there exists a "natural affinity" between certain ideas due to their resembling content, that one idea might come into contact with another so as to let this natural "chemistry" work is, for associationism, a wholly contingent matter that could in no way preclude radically different word-world associations between judging subjects.[12]

> Association [Bradley tells us] implies chance; that is, it depends on circumstances external to that which is conjoined. And so, when we use the term, we must be taken to suggest that, if A and B had not been associated, they would nevertheless have been A and B. For the conditions, which happened to bring them together, do not follow in fact, nor are deducible in idea, from the existence or character of mere A and B.[13]

The point here is, I think, the simple one that the train of association that is set in motion by the relations of resemblance and contiguity is one that ultimately contains no necessity—no intrinsic connection—between the phenomena themselves; and, this account (if true) describes a process of "reasoning" that reflects only the idiosyncrasies of the individual's own experience.[14] For the associationist, it is entirely possible that when I smell cod liver oil I immediately think of orange juice as its necessary accompaniment; but when Smith smells cod liver oil he has called up before his mind the taste of mashed potatoes; and when Jones is exposed to this same fishy aroma she becomes overwhelmed with grief. And, since it is the frequency of previously experienced conjunctions between conditions that determines the *force* of this associative bond, it is—given that I have experienced few if any contiguous relations between the odor of cod liver oil and the image of a fish—all but impossible that when I smell or taste cod liver oil I should ever think of fish before orange juice.

But this, according to Bradley, is just the problem. Since these idea-*qua*-images are seen as intrinsically disconnected there is nothing about the content of the one that would demand the content of the other; and neither for associationism can there exist any real criterion that would make the thought of gilled creatures swimming in the ocean a more appropriate—a more rational—inference from the smell of fish oil than the taste of mashed potatoes or orange juice. Although the real universe may ultimately falsify my associative bonds, it would be (on this theory) not only impossible, but also *irrational* to think of fish as being more intrinsically connected to the aroma of cod liver oil than the taste of orange juice, if my own experience did not already have developed within it the appropriate psychical bond between these elements. Hence, rationality just *is* what our arbitrarily established associative habits dictate. And there can thus be as many "rationalities" as there are diverse, idiosyncratic experiences of the universe. For Bradley, though, such a result was unacceptable.[15]

NOTES

1. INTRODUCTION

1. A sense of Bradley's influence in the early part of this century is provided by J. H. Muirhead who, writing in 1924 (the year of Bradley's death), says: "Mr. F. H. Bradley has been by general acknowledgment the foremost figure in British philosophy (perhaps in the philosophy of our time in any country) for the last generation." Muirhead also calls Bradley the philosopher "to whom British philosophy owed the impulse that gave it new life in our time." *Contemporary British Philosophy* 1 (1924), 9. Better known on the Continent at that time was Höffding who referred to Bradley as "the most important English representative of the tendency which may be described as the *New Idealism*." *Brief History of Modern Thought* (English translation, London, 1915), 284.

2. And, I would suggest, his literary style as well. T. S. Eliot said of Bradley that his was "the perfect style"; and he attributed to Bradley's writing a major influence on his own intellectual development. See "Francis Herbert Bradley," *The Times Literary Supplement*, 29 Dec. 1927. Also see reprints in *For Lancelot Andrewes* (London, 1928), and *Essays Ancient and Modern* (London, 1936).

3. See, for example, Cook Wilson's *Statement and Inference*, ed. A. S. L. Farquharson (Oxford, 1926), 280–94.

4. *F. H. Bradley* (first edition London, 1959), 18.

5. The quotation here is taken from F. C. S. Schiller—one of Bradley's harshest critics—who wrote in the pages of *Mind* 34 (1925), 215, that Bradley was "admittedly the most eminent philosopher Oxford has ever produced." As for the revival of interest in Bradley we may notice that recent years have seen many works. For a complete listing of articles, books, and dissertations on or about Bradley (through 1991), see Richard Ingardia's *F. H. Bradley: A Research Bibliography* (Bowling Green, Ohio, 1991). Also see the bibliography at the end of selected issues of *Bradley Studies* (Manchester College, Oxford, W. J. Mander, editor).

6. The terms "judgment" and "predication" can be seen as all but synonymous. Predication is usually understood as the *act* of judging. Judgment is usually understood to be the *result* of that act.

7. *Essays on Truth and Reality* (Oxford, 1914), 252.

8. As we shall see, the statement "at least as it is understood by us" is an important qualification. Bradley certainly believes that some judgments are "necessary" in the sense that we cannot deny them without simultaneously assuming their truth. However, he is equally insistent that the full ground or basis of this necessity can never be fully grasped by finite knowers.

9. Ibid., 253.

10. *Ethical Studies* (Oxford, 1876; second edition, 1927).

11. It is for this reason (at least) that it is ill advised to locate Bradley's "idealism" within the tradition of realism. See, for example, the comments of W. J. Mander in his introduction to *Perspectives on the Logic and Metaphysics of F. H. Bradley* (Bristol, England, 1996), i–xxvii.

12. In response to the appearance of such views in the *Principles of Logic* (Oxford, 1883; second edition, 1922), Bosanquet wrote in 1885 "Only a rich man may wear a bad coat and only a philosopher of Mr. Bradley's force could escape suspicion of a crude dualistic realism." *Knowledge and Reality* (London, 1885), 18.

13. This is essentially the criticism made by both H. H. Joachim and J. H. Muirhead. See Joachim's *Logical Studies* (Oxford, 1948), 278–92. Also see Muirhead's *The Platonic Tradition in Anglo-Saxon Philosophy* (London, 1931), 245–304.

14. *Ethical Studies*, 323–4 note. My emphasis starting "If the ultimate. . . ." The complete note begins as follows: "People find a subject and object correlated in consciousness; and having got this *in* mind, they at once project it outside the mind, and talk as if two independent realities knocked themselves together, and so produced the unity that apprehends them; while all the time, to go out of that unity is for us literally to go out of our minds. And when the monstrous nature of their position dawns on some few, and they begin to see that without some higher unity this 'correlation' is pure nonsense, then answering to that felt need, they invent a third reality which is neither subject nor object but the 'Unknowable' or the Thing-in-itself (there is no difference). But here, since the two correlates are still left together with, and yet are *not*, the Unknowable, the question arises, How does this latter stand to them? And the result is that the Unknowable becomes the subject of predicates . . . and it becomes impossible for any one who cares for consistency to go on calling it Unknowable. So it is necessary to go a step further, and, giving up our third, which is *not* the correlates, to recognize an Identity of subject and object, still however persisting in the statement that this identity is *not* mind. But here again, as with the Unknowable, and as before with the two correlated realities."

15. Consider also: "The mind is *not* finite, just because it knows it *is* finite. 'The knowledge of the limit suppresses the limit.' It is a flagrant self-contradiction that the finite should know its own finitude; and it is not hard to make this plain. Finite means limited from the outside and by the outside. The finite is to know itself as this, or not as finite. If its knowledge ceases to fall wholly within itself, then so far it is not finite. It knows that it is limited from the outside and by the outside, and that means it knows the outside. But if so, then it is so far

not finite. If its whole being fell within itself, then, in knowing itself, it could not know that there was anything outside itself. It does do the latter; hence the former supposition is false." Ibid., 75.

16. See *Appearance and Reality* (Oxford, 1893; 2nd edition 1897), 64–104; *Essays in Truth and Reality*, 409–27.

17. This is also found in the *Collected Essays* (Oxford, 1935), 630–76.

18. For a different view see Stewart Candlish's "The Truth about F. H. Bradley," *Mind* 98 (1989), 331–48.

19. Consider, for example: "The proceeds of experience are contradictory, and the mind is a principle of unity. It feels the contradictions and, without knowing it, is more or less alienated from its contents, but comes to no downright breach with the world. On the contrary it imagines itself to be bringing all new details faithfully under the old world or old self; and it does not know that *itself* is the active principle of subsumption, and that it no longer is one with the former self. From that old self it separates itself more and more, develops and partially solves its contradictions, critically corrects its one-sidedness, rules out its inconsistencies with unconscious but incessant activity. . . . [And further down on the same page:] 'What necessity is there for the given world to be self-contradictory?' . . . The universe seems to be one system; it is an organism (it would appear) and more. It bears the character of the self, the personality to which it is relative, and without which for us it is as good as nothing. Hence any portion of the universe by itself cannot be a consistent system; for it refers to the whole and has the whole present in it. Potentially the whole (since embodying that which is actually the whole), in trying to fix itself as itself, it succeeds only in laying stress on its character of relativity; it is carried beyond and contradicts itself. Or more briefly thus. Evolution is necessary because the mind is actually limited, virtually unlimited; and the object lives in the life of the mind and varies with it." *Collected Essays*, 68–70.

20. These comprised twelve essays, along with over a hundred pages of notes, which were appended to the original 1883 edition.

21. It should be remembered that Bradley felt that, with the exception of some of what was said in the first edition of the *Principles of Logic*, his philosophical thought *did* constitute a consistent body of work.

22. We might also see Bradley's theory of predication as, in the end, an effort to restate the distinction between "reason" and "understanding"—a distinction of fundamental importance for post-Kantian idealism. And, as we shall see, Bradley effects this restatement in a manner that does not disguise the difficulties one encounters when considering the subject-object distinction and the generally abstract character of articulate thought. Although the language in which Bradley puts forth his interpretation of this doctrine might be seen by some as idiosyncratic, his analysis provides, I believe, an original development in the history of idealism in that it contains a highly self-conscious effort to avoid what has been called "panlogism" (the doctrine that sees reality itself as constituted by just those abstract universal contents, or "categories," that characterize logical thought). Often attributed to Hegel, the theory was harshly criticized by

Notes to chapter one

subsequent German writers. For criticisms familiar to Bradley, see Lotze's *Kleine Schriften*, 4:453–54; or *Mikrocosmus* (English translation, Edinburgh, 1888), book II chap. iv and book V chap. iv. For an account of Lotze's philosophy and its relation to English idealism, see H. Jones, *The Philosophy of Lotze* (New York, 1895). Also see G. R. G. Mure's discussion of this point in his *Idealist Epilogue* (Oxford, 1978), 147–66.

23. This was the phrase that Bradley used (*Principles of Logic*, 591ff.) to describe those idealist systems that never confronted the difficulties entailed by the fact that all thought—even the categorial thought of a "transcendental subject"—must remain abstract while its object is utterly concrete. This Bradley felt to be the great weakness of most idealist systems.

24. And this "pushing" the question was, for Bradley, the essential feature of metaphysical enquiry. "By metaphysics," he writes, "I do not mean the doctrine of any one school, but I include under that term all speculation which is at once resolved to keep its hold upon all sides of fact, and upon the other to push, so far as it can, every question to the end." *Essays on Truth and Reality*, 444.

25. For the reader who must know more in advance, let me say the following about how Bradley's doctrine of feeling fits into his larger theory: For Bradley, there are certain assumptions or presuppositions about Reality that we cannot help but make. And, while we may never explicitly *think* through these presuppositions, we always *feel* them. That is, although our understanding of them may always be partially unconscious (and always limited), there exist, on Bradley's theory, judgments that, if they were made fully conscious, could not be denied. And we may know that these judgments could not be denied because there is no experience conceivable by us in which they could be consistently rejected or otherwise avoided. Now, it is just this set of presuppositions that are included within what Bradley calls the "feeling base" of experience. (There is, of course, much more to feeling than this.) And it is what we may refer to as the *felt* "a priori belief structure" that, in the end, assures us that our "coherent system" is also a *true* system. Through a series of transcendental arguments, Bradley attempts to establish what he believes the ultimate conditions of knowledge must, at least in general terms, look like.

26. M. J. Cresswell's "Reality as Experience" appears to do just this. See *The Australasian Journal of Philosophy 55* (1977), 169–88. Interestingly, Stewart Candlish, in his criticisms of Cresswell, sees no problem with the idea that the "idealist tradition" is found in the works of Berkeley, Hume, Mill, Ayer, and Carnap. See "The Status of Idealism in Bradley's Metaphysics," *Idealistic Studies* 11 (1981), 242–53; also see "Idealism and Bradley's Logic," *Idealistic Studies* 12 (1982), 251–59.

27. Many recent commentators have wanted to see Bradley's conception of feeling as echoing the views of Bergson and James. See, for example, Leemon McHenry's *Whitehead and Bradley: A Comparative Analysis* (Albany, N.Y., 1992), 79–85; and, although much more qualified, Timothy Sprigge seems to push Bradley in a similar direction. See *James and Bradley: American Truth and British Reality* (La Salle, Ill., 1993), 434ff. See also James Bradley's "F. H.

Bradley's Metaphysics of Feeling and Its Place in the History of Philosophy,"
The Philosophy of F. H. Bradley (Oxford, 1984), 227–43. Also see Peter Hylton's *Russell, Idealism, and the Emergence of Analytic Philosophy* (Oxford,
1991), 44–71.

28. Recent authors who press this interpretation are Leslie Armour in
"F. H. Bradley and Later Idealism: From Disarray to Reconstruction," and
William Sweet in "F. H. Bradley and Bosanquet." Both are found in *Philosophy
after F. H. Bradley* (Bristol, England, 1996).

29. See, for example, the late Anthony Manser's *Bradley's Logic* (Blackwell,
1983). While much in this work is enlightening, there is also much that must be
treated with caution.

30. A notable exception is Guy Stock. See, for example, his "Bradley's Theory of Judgment" in the *Philosophy of F. H. Bradley*, 131–53, for a careful comparison. See also "Negation: Bradley and Wittgenstein," *Philosophy* 60 (1985).

31. The most significant being the wholesale identification of thought with
language. On the importance of this identification to mainstream philosophical
analysis, see M. Dummett's *Logical Basis of Metaphysics* (Cambridge, Mass.,
1993), 3ff; see also his *Frege: Philosophy of Language* (London, 1973), 5.

2. THE DIFFERENTIA OF JUDGMENT

1. See *Essays on Truth and Reality*, 29.

2. Some recent writers have, I believe, made far too much of Bradley's
claim that logic can be pursued largely independently of metaphysics. (See, for
example, Manser's *Bradley's Logic*.) And, while Bradley certainly does make
some effort to distinguish logic from metaphysics, the reader must not be led to
believe that this effort represents any philosophical principle (as it does, for, say,
the logical positivists). The distinction, if it has any basis at all, would seem to
be one which is determined by (*a*) explicit subject manner; that is, the discussion
of "ideas," "judgment," "inference," "meaning," and "truth"; these are all
"logical" subjects; and (*b*) lack of direct ontological enquiry. If these topics can
be discussed without directly bringing in questions about ultimate reality then
the discussion is, for Bradley, merely "logical."

3. See *Principles of Logic*, 32–34.

4. As we shall see, though, this indifference is not complete. Finite thought
will always make some difference to its object.

5. I have treated this issue at length in "Bradley's Attack on Associationism." See *Philosophy after F. H. Bradley*, ed. James Bradley (Bristol, England,
1996).

6. *Principles of Logic*, 2. The "strict sense" was, however, to change somewhat. Whereas in 1883 Bradley sometimes reserved the term "judgment" for
those acts that were elevated to the level of *reflective* awareness, the mature
Bradley viewed this as unnecessary and far too strict a criterion. In the first edition of the *Principles of Logic* Bradley writes: "Not only are we unable to judge
before we use ideas, but . . . we can not judge till we use them *as* ideas. We must

have become aware that they are not realities, that they are *mere* ideas, signs of existence other than themselves." Bradley footnotes this passage twice and specifically claims that it is "wrong." Ibid., 39.

7. There is a danger here to which the reader should be alerted. The universals whose existence we assert as real must not be thought of as the abstract qualities that are attributed to the popular account of Platonism. The world that we apprehend in judgment is for Bradley (ultimately) as particular as one pleases—even though its complete particularity escapes us at the level of conscious assertion. What he is claiming, however, is that in this wholly individual universe there exist identities of content and bonds of connection *between* particulars that on many theories are ignored.

8. Ibid., 11. My emphasis. Bradley also tells us in a note to the second edition that "floating" should be read here as "loosened."

9. I must qualify what I say here regarding perception. We must take care to understand that, although the real comes to us *through* perception, *mere* perception cannot be its locus. As we shall see in chapters 3, 4, 8, and 9, perception is, for Bradley, *ideal*. That is, it is an integral part of the judgment that (because it is not identical with the completely real) can be falsified.

10. Although this idea is abstract in one sense (in that it has left out a great deal of the content of sense), in another it is more concrete. Being "purified" of the explicit content of sense the judgment can envisage a broader expanse of reality. See *Principles of Logic*, 474.

11. This we shall consider in greater detail in chapter 3. For the present, however, I would mention that Bradley sees this perceptual "facticity" as consisting in (*a*) "sensuous infinitude," which is a felt sense of its uniqueness; and (*b*) "immediacy," the fact that it is *here* before us *now*.

12. Perhaps some care is in order here. "Limitless" only because capable of indefinite determination; "indefinite" only because open ended.

13. What makes for such "merely subjective" assertion is just that the subject's own idiosyncrasies—rather than the content of the object itself—are allowed to dominate the ideal elaboration.

14. It is important to realize that this given is not something that is "nonintellectual" in the sense that it is an experience of a naked particular (or manifold of particulars). Bradley insists that universals are present in our experience from the beginning; that is, we are, at the level of feeling, capable of experiencing identities that bind differents together so as to have, in some sense, an awareness of these objects. These felt contents *would* be intellectual, we are told, if made the object of our explicit, focused assertion. And, indeed, the act of judging is essentially the bringing together these given and merely felt contents into conscious and articulate awareness.

15. But actually more concrete. Sensuous content is, in one sense, a hindrance to concrete experience.

16. Useful here is James Allard's discussion in his "Introduction to the *Principles of Logic*" in *Writings on the Logic and Metaphysics of F. H. Bradley*, 3–16.

17. *Principles of Logic*, 11. Bradley also appends to this paragraph a footnote in the second edition in which he informs us that it needs "correction." He tells us that, although the ideal content certainly is unified and one, there is nothing objectionable in our treating it as containing a logical subject and predicate—or two ideas—as long as we do not forget that these ideas are not mental images. This would be, again, to confuse the symbol with the symbolized. See also p. 477 where Bradley writes: "The content which it has selected is complex; it involves elements in relation, which the joint selection binds together in our minds; and this is synthesis."

18. Ibid.

19. The grammatical proposition, however, even if it accurately indicates the logical (limited or special) subject, always fails to indicate the level or extent of systematic understanding which accompanies the utterance of the sentence. To some minds the significance of a sentence is very low; to others the same sentence can convey tremendous significance.

20. It should be obvious, I hope, that predication could not, for Bradley, be the inclusion of a particular into a class. Although such a view bears a superficial relation to Bradley's it is only superficial. A class is, on the theory we are considering, ultimately a fiction. It involves the degradation of an identity-in-difference into a mere collection. Even though we might say that in judgment we are bringing the particular "under a concept" when we ideally extend the "what," the particular is not itself seen as some hard "fact" which is brought into the relation of "class inclusion" (whatever that is) in a merely external manner. The theory of class inclusion, although it approximates the idealist doctrine, is quite different in that its universals and particulars are fundamentally distinct from one another and externally related.

21. Although he largely disregards the topics of "special" subject and predicate, very helpful on this topic is W. J. Mander's discussion in *An Introduction to Bradley's Metaphysics* (Oxford, 1993), 57–83.

22. Timothy Sprigge is one of the few commentators to address this issue. See *James and Bradley*, 305ff.

23. For example, "Hot!" or "Fire!" expresses (if they are significant at all) complete judgments.

24. I think it also important to notice here that this complex predicate idea ("The wolf eats the lamb") is one that both presupposes and ignores a good deal of given content. Certainly there are given sensuous contents that are not consciously grasped and hence cannot be said to be part of the content *as asserted*. Of course, the same thing can be said of the overtly ideal elements. The intension of the term "wolf" is certainly not exhausted by "lamb eatingness." And, even though the remainder of the intension is not consciously before the mind, certainly we must acknowledge that the meaning of "wolf" must include further notions like "carnivore," "mammal," "four-legged," etc. But the point to be emphasized here is that the assertion of a predicate ("The wolf eats the lamb") of the subject (reality-as-whole) presupposes just this complex structure. We must not forget that this "wolfness" that is explicitly before us is understood as

existing in continuity with the "wolfness" that is merely implicit (i.e., contained in the larger reality). Not only that, the whole wolf (both inside and outside perception) is understood as being continuous with the class (system) of wolves of which it is a member. And, to carry this line of thought further, all of these wolves are themselves seen as being part of the systematic complex that extends both above and below it (e.g., "vertebrates," "the animal kingdom," etc.). In short, when we judge we are declaring that our ideal predicate-*qua*-sentence is part and parcel of the *one* reality that provides the context of the assertion and that functions as its ultimate subject. And, though this complex predicate idea is recognized as "ideal," we declare reality to consist (partially) in this ideal content that we affirm as true. I treat this topic in greater detail in "Bradley on the Intension and Extension of Terms," *Perspectives on the Logic and Metaphysics of F. H. Bradley*, ed. W. J. Mander (Bristol, England, 1996).

25. While it is certainly not wrong to suggest that for Bradley the ultimate subject (reality-as-whole) is "particular" (it is the only true particular on his account), it is an error of some significance to suggest that the special subject in judgment (that which is represented by the grammatical subject) is apprehended by us as fully particular. (See Cresswell's "Bradley's Theory of Judgment," *Canadian Journal of Philosophy*, 1979, 576–78.) For Bradley both special subject and predicate are, within our judgments, systematic universals (and as such they exhibit only a relative degree of particularity). And both are components in a larger systematic universal—the judgment *qua* predicate idea.

26. And, as we shall see, the only real difference (in the end) between judgment and inference will be that in judgment the (R) remains largely implicit and unnoticed whereas in inference this becomes open and explicit. See my "Why the Idealist Theory of Inference Still Matters," Coates and Hutto, *Contemporary Idealism*, for a fuller discussion of this point.

27. *Principles of Logic*, 3.

28. *Appearance and Reality*, 143.

29. There could exist on this theory, I suppose, a state of inactive or suspended judgment, where sensuous contents do not (or at least do not forcefully) exhibit this split; however, that we consciously perceive a sensuous content at all is possible because of the previous judgments that have occurred and that have made it what it is. In this sense, then, we can say that if we are conscious we are judging, because consciousness itself is only understood as the maintenance of a world for ourselves in the act of judgment. Indeed, our unified conscious experience can, in fact, be understood as a single conscious assertion.

30. Ibid., 146.

31. Ibid.

32. "Thought," writes Bradley, "has to accept, without reserve, the ideality of the 'given,' its want of consistency and its self-transcendence. And by pushing this self-transcendence to the uttermost point, thought attempts to find there consummation and rest." *Appearance and Reality*, 146. This point is treated in detail in chapters 8 and 9.

33. See W. J. Mander's *Introduction to Bradley's Metaphysics*, 32–37.

34. For a very different view—a view that sees the judgment as incapable of significantly improving its lot—see David Holdcroft's "Holism and Truth" in *The Philosophy of F. H. Bradley* (Oxford, 1984), 192–209.

35. The idea of "intellectual satisfaction" cannot be fully considered until the later chapters. For now, though, I would say that it is both a psychological and logical condition that is realized only to the degree that the content of any overt assertion begins to approximate the standard of perfect comprehensiveness and coherence that the feeling base of experience provides.

36. For a different reading of this point, see Timothy Sprigge's *James and Bradley*, 295–302.

37. *Principles of Logic*, 474.

3. SYMBOL AND SIGNIFICANCE

1. The term "reactionary" was Bosanquet's. See, for example, "Mr. F. H. Bradley on Fact and Inference," *Mind*, o.s., 10, 256–65.

2. Fortunately, Bradley footnoted most of these points in the 1922 edition.

3. *Principles of Logic*, 2. Also consider: "No fact ever *is* just that which it *means*, or can mean what it is; . . . wherever we have truth or falsehood, it is the signification we use, and not the existence. We never assert the fact in our heads, but something else which that fact stands for." Ibid., 8.

4. Ibid., 10.

5. Ibid., 6.

6. With the use of the term "subsistent" we are again confronted by one of the peculiarities of the first-edition *Logic*: the theory of floating ideas. As we shall see, although all significant ideas might be understood as being mediate (and hence "ideal"), all ideas as affirmed will also show themselves to possess some sort of existence.

7. Ibid., 3–4. It might be noted here that there is really little that is lost when a fact becomes a symbol. This is because as a "mere fact" or "psychical existent" it has no stable individuality. When Bradley speaks of "loss" he must be understood as appealing to the common notion. See R. F. A. Hoernlé's comments in *Mind* 16, 70–100.

8. Although it is accurate to say that, for Bradley, some imagery accompanies all our thinking, the problem is that the imagery that accompanies some thinking is so removed from what would to appear to be its actual significance that it is hard to say that the imagery "belongs" to that idea.

9. *Principles of Logic*, 9.

10. I would emphasize here that the "symbol" is just that aspect of the larger meaning within which it is an element. When, for example, a scientist holds before his or her mind some law—let us say that "water boils at 100 degrees Celsius under one atmosphere of pressure"—he or she may symbolize this understanding by an image of the kettle full of boiling water as it appeared that morning at breakfast. Now, the actual event that this image portrays (the

boiling of water at breakfast that morning) is only one of what is, in fact, an indefinite number of times that water has or will boil according to the principle that the law cites. What is *meant* is this larger nexus; that is, all the occurrences of water boiling (and more) that have or will come about. And this nexus—which is what the judgment actually *means*—we represent to ourselves by perceptually focusing on only a fragment of its content. In this case, the boiling of the water for that morning's tea.

11. *Principles of Logic*, 8. I would add, however, that this way of putting things will require some modification when we consider the thought of the mature Bradley who was to claim that *all* ideas have existence of a sort. The nonexistence of which he speaks here is primarily that sort of existence that is attributed to the psychical image or immediate perception.

12. Ibid., 470–71. My emphasis. We must be careful here. For Bradley it most emphatically is *not* the case that either the identity we apprehend through synthesis or the differences we grasp via analysis are the mere result of *our* activity as judging subjects. Both differences and identity have to be there (in reality) before we judge; and hence every such act is both an act of creation *and* discovery.

13. Ibid., 487.

14. I have considered this issue in "Perceptual Ideality and the Ground of Inference," *Bradley Studies* 1.2 (1995), 125–38.

15. *Principles of Logic*, 2:478–79. My emphasis. Also see the entire chapter from which this is taken, "The Final Essence of Reasoning."

16. And consider this: "The content which it has selected is complex; it involves elements in relation, which the joint selection binds together in our minds; and this is synthesis." *Principles of Logic*, 477.

17. And, as we shall see, as Bradley's philosophy matured, any doubts he had about the intrinsic continuity between given reality and ideal reconstruction in judgment disappears. See, for example, the 1922 edition of the *Principles of Logic*, 625ff.

18. One writer who apparently takes very seriously these statements is Stewart Candlish. In his "The Truth about F. H. Bradley," (*Mind* 98, 331–48), he attributes to the author of the first edition *Principles of Logic* (*a*) a correspondence theory of truth; and (*b*) the rejection of a theory of "degrees of truth and reality." For a helpful discussion of these issues, see James Allard's "Degrees of Truth in F. H. Bradley," in *Perspectives on the Logic and Metaphysics of F. H. Bradley* (Bristol, England, 1996), 137–58.

19. In language that he would later regret, Bradley writes "The subject cannot belong to the content or fall within it, for in that case it would be the idea attributed to itself." *Principles of Logic*, 14. Words such as these (taken along with the doctrine of the floating idea) led Bosanquet to comment that—were one not entirely familiar with the larger argument of the *Principles of Logic*—such language would cause one to suspect Bradley of a "crude dualistic realism." Bradley soon came to insist that the special subject of any judgment be both inside and outside at once.

20. See David Holdcroft's "Holism and Truth," *F. H. Bradley*, 191–211, for a development of this interpretation.

21. In this work Bosanquet directly attacked some inconsistencies—or at least apparent inconsistencies—in the *Principles of Logic* (the floating idea, the exaggerated importance of perception, Bradley's discussion of negation, the separation of content from affirmation in judgment etc.). However, in the preface to his *Implication and Linear Inference* (London, 1920) many years later, Bosanquet acknowledged that he had overreacted to some of Bradley's statements and that the mature position was, to a large degree, already articulated in the 1883 discussion of inference.

22. His most concise statement of this solution is found in his essay "Floating Ideas and the Imaginary." This essay, while first published in *Mind* (April 1908), is most easily found today in Bradley's *Essays on Truth and Reality*, 28–64.

23. Ibid., 28–64. Bradley's essay "Floating Ideas and the Imaginary" addresses this point. Again, I have not followed this convention in the text.

24. See Bosanquet, *Implication*, chapter 2, for a full discussion of this issue. Bradley makes concessions to Bosanquet's criticism at many points in the second edition of the *Principles of Logic*. See, for example, the notes to "The Modality of Judgments," 236–42.

4. CLASSIFICATION OF JUDGMENT

1. A rich source of information on the historical divisions within logic from an idealist perspective is provided by H. W. B. Joseph's *Introduction to Logic* (Oxford, 1906; 2nd edition 1916). Having entirely missed the point of its analyses, however, later writers dismissed it as "anachronistic"; see, for example L. S. Stebbings *Introduction to Modern Logic* (London, 1930; 6th edition 1948), 42, 285, 416, 471.

2. Bradley was persuaded, largely by Bosanquet, that a better way to put the matter was to say that all judgments were "conditional." He (like Bosanquet) preferred to reserve the term "hypothetical" for a certain species of conditional assertion—those which were lawlike and overtly universal. However, his point that all conditional assertion (and all assertion *is* conditional, for Bradley) could be construed as an "if-then" statement still holds.

3. This was also the same year in which Lotze's *Logik* was published in Germany. This work appears to have been quite influential on the young Bradley.

4. However, since the singular affirmative judgment was seen as having its subject taken in its full extent—that is, *all* of the subject is qualified by the predicate—it was generally included under the heading of "universal" on the traditional scheme.

5. The disjunctive was often analyzed into two hypotheticals. See for example, Mill's *System of Logic* (London, 1843; 8th edition 1872), 49–55. Also see Mansel's *Prolegomena Logica* (Oxford, 1851), chapter I; also Bosanquet's *Essentials of Logic* (London, 1910), 123–24.

6. Ibid., 112–23.

7. Although the active pursuit of this project was begun by T. H. Green (see his "Logic of the Formal Logicians," *Works*, 2:158–94, "Mill's Logic," 2:195–306, and "The Philosophy of Aristotle," 3:46–92). Bosanquet's "Logic as the Science of Knowledge" in *Essays in Philosophical Criticism* (London, 1883) became something of a logical manifesto for the younger idealists.

8. The difference here can be illustrated by "All the papers have been looked over" (enumerative), and "All triangles have their three angles equal to two right angles" (universal).

9. See Bosanquet's *Essentials of Logic*, 116–17. We read, "[the particular affirmative] . . . is an unscientific Judgment, in which the mind cannot rest, because it has an undefined limitation imposed upon the subject." Bosanquet here means that if the judgment is examined with an eye to its concrete content it will tend toward an interpretation that is either singular or universal. Consider the example: "Some engines can drag a train at a mile a minute." On one interpretation this means trains of a certain (although unspecified) *type* possess the ability to drag a train at a mile a minute. In this case it is equivalent to "All X-type trains can. . . ." This, however, is analyzable into "If X-type then capable of pulling a train at a mile a minute." And the implication of existence is much weaker here. Even if there were no presently existing cases of X-type engines we still might be inclined to call the judgment true (depending on the exact relation between subject and predicate). The other interpretation would be to view a judgment like "Some men can run a mile in under four minutes." Here we mean "John Jones can run a mile in under four minutes." Or perhaps, "John Jones and Jerry Smith can run a mile in under four minutes." Here the hypothetical aspect—the connection between attributes—is weak, but the implication of existence is very strong. If there were no actually existing men who could run a mile in under four minutes we would be quite inclined to call the judgment false; and this because there appears to be no necessary relation between subject and predicate (as there might be in our other example).

10. Bosanquet probably states the position more clearly than anyone when he writes: "A categorical judgment asserts an actual fact absolutely. A hypothetical judgment asserts only the consequence that follows on a supposition. The distinction between the two seems clear. It is the difference between 'There is a bad smell in the house' and 'If there is an escape of gas there will be a bad smell'." *Logic or the Morphology of Knowledge* (Oxford, 1910), 1:88.

11. There appear to be many judgments that, although we must assert their truth, do not at all state "fact" in the sense described above. Indeed, sometimes their explicit content is such as to completely preclude their actual existence; nevertheless, such judgments are made, are believed to serve a useful purpose, and still exhibit the characteristic of truth. Consider for example: "If there were a 20 power microscope 1/1000 of an inch in length, then its front and rear lens elements would have to be of such and such a diameter." It is obvious in this case that it not only doesn't exist, it could not exist. Nevertheless, the judgment is put forth as true; and in some sense it must be about the real to which it is referred.

12. *Principles of Logic*, 47.

13. Ibid.

14. Another way to describe this is to say that a latent condition is a disposition. "If you strike the glass with a hammer then it will break" does not claim that one has or will strike it; but there is still an actual claim being made about an existing state of affairs.

15. And thus the present existence or nonexistence of its explicit elements is irrelevant to its truth.

16. As Bradley puts it in *Appearance and Reality*, 479: "Finite truth must be conditional. No such fact or truth is ever really self-supported and independent. They are all conditioned, and in the end conditioned all by the unknown. And the extent to which they are so conditioned, again is uncertain. But this means that any finite truth or fact may to an indefinite extent be accidental appearance."

17. Bradley sometimes uses the term "logical" to refer to what he at other times calls the "special" or "limited" subject and predicate as discussed in the previous chapters.

18. In providing these examples the assumption is that the grammatical form is indicative of the logical form, which (we should recall) may not always be the case.

19. *Principles of Logic*, 58.

20. Explicitly, in this case, all "bird-things" and "yellow-things"; implicitly, *all* things. It should also be emphasized that this pointing beyond itself constitutes a synthetic construction. This is why the distinction between analytic and synthetic must be understood as one of emphasis.

21. Again, what is being ideally extended here is the same content as is explicitly present to perceptual experience. This is why it is better seen as analytic and not synthetic.

22. The first example assumes, of course, that "London" is not part of our explicit perceptual experience. The latter two judgments—since necessarily made from the perspective of "today"—preclude the possibility of being construed as analytic judgments of sense.

23. "Constructing" is a dangerous word to apply here; but as it is consistent with the tone of Bradley's discussion it will be used. However, as we shall see further down, if we merely "construct" (as opposed to "discover") we are not judging, according to Bradley; we are only "imagining."

24. *Principles of Logic*, 75. My emphasis.

25. Ibid., 73.

26. Although one might be able to find a few scattered comments in the first two books of the 1883 *Logic* where Bradley ignores this point and where he speaks of an "arbitrary synthesis" of an ideal content with perception, in the later books (on Inference) this notion of arbitrary synthesis is entirely absent. These occasional statements are, of course, instances of the floating idea raising its head. Fortunately for the reader of the second edition the majority of cases where this

occurs are noted. See also Bosanquet's *Knowledge and Reality*, chapter 3.

27. *Principles of Logic*, 48.

28. Ibid., 49. No matter what we think about the truth or falsity of such judgments, Bradley tells us that they *are* made and thus logic must deal with them.

29. Which is, of course, not the case with hypothetical assertion.

30. Of course the analysis of this judgment could be many levels down, and thus we could say that there is a whole series of synthetic judgments that function as links in a chain. However, such a mode of description seems quite misleading when we bear in mind that all third class judgments still ultimately consist in an analysis of what is perceptually given.

31. As Bradley was to later insist, perception is the "anchor" for our assertions only so far as it is the medium through which the felt unity of content and existence appears. This point is examined in some detail in chapters 8 and 9.

32. Ibid., 72.

33. It should be remembered, too, that this "presupposed nexus" is, at the time of assertion, largely unconscious and outside the sphere of active attention. Hence, although we are effecting a synthetic construction that is, perhaps, many steps removed from the given, this synthesis is one that is justified by the fact that it constitutes a precise analysis of the actual (even though hidden or implicit) nature of its perceptual content

34. This doesn't really become clear until the second book where Bradley deals with inference. Its most precise statement, however, is to be found only in the "Terminal Essays" where the "inferential construction" is seen as the "ideal self-development of the object."

35. Despite this, the *Principles of Logic* would remain largely unintelligible to the reader who did not have a precise grasp of these distinctions. Thus their discussion here.

36. According to Bradley it would be entirely wrong to say that we "make" inferences, if by that term we imply some sort of arbitrary and unrestrained act of creation in our ideal expansion of given fact. (That's what Bradley understands "pragmatism" to assert.) Again, to merely "make" is to imagine; to actually infer is to both make and "discover." See *Essays on Truth and Reality*, 48–49.

37. *Principles of Logic*, 598.

38. See, for example, *Essays on Truth and Reality*, 363.

39. And, I would also remind the reader that for Bradley there is ultimately only *one* context—the universe-as-a-whole.

40. As we shall see, there exists a great deal more "in the mind" for Bradley than the system of our prior judgments and the intellectual world that they have articulated. Ultimately—that is, at the deepest level—we are forced to say that the "mind" contains (and is in one sense identical with) the Absolute. This point is discussed in chapters 8 and 9.

41. This type of theory, we must remember, was understood by Bradley to be the only alternative to the atomistic theories of both traditional empiricism

and rationalist-essentialism. The inferential development of thought cannot be coherently explained, Bradley insisted, if the world is broken up or fragmented into a diversity of particulars each of which is external to the other. Bradley argues that reality must be an integrated whole lest the entire process of inference become a wholly contingent and irrational affair.

42. It is tempting to use the word "knowledge" instead of "experience" here. However, the term "knowledge" is, I think, more easily misinterpreted than "experience." "Knowledge" would be correct so long as we do not forget that, for Bradley, this knowledge is both within and beyond the explicit cognitive grasp of any subject. That is, "knowledge" is not to be understood as comprising only of what finite subjects have actually thought. The contents in "knowledge" extend beyond into a larger base of experience.

43. It is the shared submeanings that would constitute the element of truth here. We can say that it is not entirely false because part of what we asserted does hold. By identifying what is before us as "this tree" we have correctly synthesized this perception with the universal meaning "tree." It is only when we go on from there and try to be more precise in our synthetic-analysis that reality repels the assertion. The *general* analysis, we might say holds; it is only the more refined aspect of the predicate that reality will not accept. We shall deal with this point in detail in chapter 7.

44. See *Appearance and Reality*, 323.

45. As we shall see in the next chapter, every judgment bears some point of connection with this nexus of meaning or we would not be prompted to assert it as true; and since possessing some identity of content, every judgment is—at least partially—true.

46. This logical force is also referred to by both Bradley and Bosanquet as "implication." This notion of implication must, of course, be differentiated from that which attaches to the term in modern logic. Again, see my "Why the Idealist Theory of Inference Still Matters," Coates and Hutto, *Contemporary Idealism*, for a further discussion of this point.

47. *Principles of Logic*, 87.

5. SEARCHING FOR CATEGORICAL TRUTH

1. Before we consider the attack on the individual judgment I should mention that Bradley selects the analytic judgment of sense as the most appropriate target for criticism. Since it is in the strongest position to maintain its claim to categorical status it will be here, if anywhere, that a defense might be made. But if *it* fails, there is no hope to maintain categorical status of either the synthetic judgment of sense or the third class.

2. See Appearance and Reality, 320–21.

3. The modified assertion would, of course, be subject to the same attack.

4. See ibid., 478–94.

5. *Principles of Logic*, 97–98.

6. Ibid.

7. Ibid.

8. Ibid., 71.

9. Ibid., 94.

10. Ibid., 95–96.

11. We should understand that the term "fuller experience" refers to something more inclusive than mere sense or perception.

12. See *Appearance and Reality*, 205.

13. *Principles of Logic*, 94.

14. While we are not yet in a position to appreciate this point fully, the complete interpenetration of content and existence—their seamless continuity—does not reside in mere perception. Rather Bradley will place them in the deepest recesses of feeling; and though this feeling underlies (and contains) perception, it is not the same as it.

15. Ibid.

16. In 1922 (Terminal Essay V) Bradley writes: "In the present work I clearly gave an undue importance to the 'this' of *external* perception. Even if there is no actual error, there certainly has been here an undue emphasis. For the 'this' is present just as much in mere internal fancy, since it belongs everywhere to that which is immediately experienced. An act of attention, for instance, is 'this,' 'mine,' and 'now,' even if we hesitate to add 'here'. 'This,' 'my,' 'now,' and 'my,' and 'here' must (in short) be regarded each as a special aspect of 'this'; and 'this,' belonging essentially to the felt, can not be confined merely to that which comes as an external perception." *Principles of Logic*, 659.

17. I am thinking here of both William James and Henri Bergson. See chapter 10 for a fuller discussion of this issue.

18. See *Appearance and Reality*, 145. While Bradley sometimes speaks of different "time series," we must realize that these are all united in the one experience—the Absolute.

19. *Principles of Logic*, 66.

20. For example, see *Appearance and Reality*, 208.

21. *Essays on Truth and Reality*, 262.

22. We must not forget that it is through the activity of judgment—through thinking—that we get progressively closer to our object. As Bradley tells us: "the further an individual is removed from designation, the *more* unique (the less of a mere 'sort') it becomes, though it never becomes unique entirely." *Essays on Truth and Reality*, 264.

23. See *Principles of Logic*, 63–66 on this point.

24. Ibid., 99.

25. *Appearance and Reality*, 347.

26. As we shall see in chapters 8 and 9, even this statement is in need of qualification. The true locus of our sense of the uniqueness and specificity of all that exists—a sense that is wholly concrete and non-ideal—is a level of feeling

that can be seen as even more primitive than what is usually understood as my "immediate experience."

27. Ibid., 351–52.

28. Since the reliability of any purely inductive inference rests upon the uniformity and repeatability of phenomena in the physical world, and since these characteristics of phenomena are only known via induction, all inductive inference (on this theory) is circular and wholly unjustified. The classic statement comes, of course, from Hume, *Treatise of Human Nature*, part III, section II; also part IV, sections I and II; see also *An Inquiry Concerning Human Understanding*, chapters IV and VI.

29. For a very different reading, see James Allard's "Bradley's Argument against Correspondence," in *Idealistic Studies* 10 (1980), 236–40.

30. Although this argument is primarily directed against empiricist theories of knowledge, it is interesting to note that what would count as contemporary versions of "Platonism" would—although possibly capable of avoiding the charge of (*a*)—still be faced with the problem posed by (*b*). As long as one's universals remain abstract and externally related (as they do on most modern theories) the justification of nontautological inference remains problematic.

31. We should be aware that, for Bradley, if the isolated perceptual base that exists within any moment is self-contained and characteristically unique, then all of thought's activity must be seen as hopelessly abstract in the sense that the activity of thinking will never get us any closer to our object. If *complete* individuality is wholly given in any distinguishable perceptual "now" (which can stand alongside of other such "nows") then the activity of thinking becomes somewhat superfluous. On such a view the idea of systematically reconstructing (in thought) the unique individuality of the one real must be seen as a wholly deluded project. If the perceptually given fact is whole and unique within its own four corners then *all* thought must be seen as inferior to what is given in perceptual intuition. This would follow because the given percept, being wholly unique (while thought and language are necessarily abstract and general), must always stand closer to the goal of thought than thought itself. On this point see *Appearance and Reality*, 480–85.

32. On the traditional empiricist interpretation universal judgments become either collective judgments or tautologies. For example, "All men are mortal" means, in fact, "The man Jones has been examined and found to be mortal, The man Smith has been examined and found to be mortal," and so on. That is, it merely states that "All men experienced thus far have been found to (contingently) possess the characteristic of "mortality." If there is a necessary relation between being a man and being mortal then it is the result of a "nominal definition"; in other words, it is "analytically true" that "man" entails "mortal." This interpretation of the universal affirmative judgment is diametrically opposed to Bradley's. See *Principles of Logic*, 82–85.

33. And, if it is protested that the truth about these facts resides in their relations to other facts, then the following question must be asked: "Do these relations *belong* to the facts so as to constitute their essential character or not?" If

they do then the facts cannot appear in their completely determinate (unique) character. If they do not then the "truth" that the protester has in mind cannot be any *objective* condition of these facts. This dilemma, Bradley believes, is inescapable.

34. *Absolute* independence can never be allowed. All identifiable objects must overreach themselves (display ideality) or both judgment and inference would disappear. *Principles of Logic*, 611–21.

35. I have also discussed this topic in "Perceptual Ideality and the Ground of Inference," *Bradley Studies* 1.2, 125–38.

36. See again, *Principles of Logic*, 659; and Terminal Essay V, "The 'This'").

37. *Appearance and Reality*, 335.

38. Ibid., 208.

39. Ibid., 204, 206.

40. And a content *must* extend beyond the "that" or it would not be a content. The very differentia of content is that it exists in more than a single "that" or existence.

41. It is only by stepping out of the incessant flow of temporal change that anything approaching consciousness of an experienced world could arise. And it is the act of judgment that effects this elevation from mere feeling into something higher. See *Appearance and Reality*, 202–6.

42. If immediate presentation weren't defective why would we assert at all? Consider, for example: "And there is no 'what' which essentially adheres to the bare moment. So far as any element remains involved in the confusion of feeling, that is but due to our defect and ignorance." Ibid., 206. Also, "The 'this' . . . is a unity below relations and ideas; and a unity, able to harmonize all distinctions, is not found till we arrive at ultimate Reality. Hence, the 'this' repels our offered predicate, not because its nature goes beyond, but rather because that nature comes short. It is not more, we may say, but less than our distinctions." Ibid., 204.

43. Ibid., 204, 206.

44. See, for example, *Collected Essays*, 653–54.

45. A concrete universal contains as its elements other concrete universals that—since they are elements within that universal—function as concrete particulars. See *Essays on Truth and Reality*, 297.

46. Only the Absolute (the universe-as-a-whole) would be a perfect system; and thus only the apprehension of the universe-as-a-whole would constitute a nondefective judgment. And that such a judgment is (*ex hypothesi*) impossible for finite knowers lies at the heart of Bradley's philosophy. See *Appearance and Reality*, 332ff.

47. See, for example, *Essays in Truth and Reality*, 114–15.

48. It must be remembered first, that every significant perception is—if not itself an active component in judgment—the result of a judgment. And second, we must remember that perception is always mediated in that it involves the binding together of sensations within its unified grasp. It just *is*, we might

say, the systematic integration of these sensations. But what holds these differences together is, we should recall, the act of selective abstraction. It is an act that identifies *these* contents as belonging together (and as being opposed to *those*). But this selective act of abstraction that unifies perceptual contents, since it *is* selective, must ignore some of what is given in feeling. And (as we have already considered in chapter 3) the very act that differentiates these elements from those also constitutes a bond of identity between them. (To analyze, we must recall, is always to synthesize as well.) But, even though perception contains an integrated unity of differences, this systematic and concrete experience is not self-contained. It is not self-contained because the conceptual "running through" of the differences internal to the perception (the result of which provides us with an enduring percept) is of such a character that it cannot confine itself to the content as judged. What endures through a series of changing "thats" must be understood as—not only holding these "thats" together so as to enable us to experience them as an object—but also as going beyond them in a manner that is "loose at the edges" so to speak. When, for example, I assert "This bird is yellow" I am isolating from the changing flux of sensuous experience an identity of content on at least two counts ('birdness" and "yellowness"). And in so extracting these characteristics from the presented experience I am rescuing them from the disappearing "now" and asserting that they are universals; I am acknowledging the content of *this* experience as somehow continuous with *other* experiences that constitute the context of this present series. Thus, in recognizing the existence of universals (through the simultaneous analysis-synthesis of judgment), I am acknowledging the existence of a timeless nexus of events that is not contained in the given "now" but that is the very condition of there being any "now" at all. And this is essentially what Bradley means when he claims that every judgment has "ragged edges." The edges of our assertion are ragged because they cannot be pinned down to this moment. The content that makes our judgment what it is an essentially timeless content that depends for its meaning upon the entire system of contents that necessarily extends beyond what is contained within the explicit content as judged.

49. Only a complete unity of content and existence could avoid this generality. See, for example, *Appearance and Reality*, 337–38.

6. Contradiction and Thought

1. It must remembered that the ultimate subject is reality-as-whole and the complex predicate "John is honest" is what we are attaching to it. However, discussing the issue in these terms need not obscure the issue (and indeed may help to elucidate it). The real issue is that of the abstract and general character of our thought in relation to the unique character of its object. See, for example, *Appearance and Reality*, 521–22. I would note again that the terms "limited" and "special" are interchangeable.

2. I have used here (as does Bradley) the term "predicate" to refer to both special subject and special predicate in judgment. This is because the special sub-

ject is not really the ultimate subject. This, we should recall, is always reality-as-a-whole. The special subject and special predicate are both elements within the larger predicate-*qua*-proposition. And when we judge we are asserting the continuity of one aspect of this larger predicate (the special subject) with another (the special predicate); and we are declaring that these form a continuous tissue with the larger reality that conditions and supports them.

3. *Appearance and Reality*, 509.

4. And, since the claim that reality (as opposed to appearance) is "noncontradictory" or "self-coherent" is so fundamental in Bradley's philosophy, we should, perhaps, augment our discussion by providing some defense of its two principle assumptions. These are: (*a*) the law of contradiction is undeniable; and (*b*) that it applies to reality and not just thought. Regarding the first claim we must offer some defense against the "conventionalist" view that claims that all logical laws and standards of rationality are themselves arbitrary and the result of cultural agreement rather than forced upon us by the nature of things. The standard objection to the relativist-conventionalist position (and the one that can be found in various forms throughout Bradley's works) points out that the conventionalist himself must assume the falsity of conventionalism in order to assert it as true. That is, by putting forth the claim that all laws of logic—including (and perhaps especially) the law of contradiction, are conventional, the exponent of this position is implicitly asserting on an *absolute* (nonconventional) basis that conventionalism is true; or that its denial is false. However, by putting this claim forward as *true* (and by denying that conventionalism might under different conditions be false) the conventionalist has accepted the very principle his theory rejects. If he did not accept the law of contradiction as universally applicable, he would have no basis upon which to make his claim. In other words he must assume the non-conventional truth of the law of contradiction in order to assert the truth of conventionalism (which denies the universal applicability of the law). Hence, according to Bradley, the conventionalist is ensnared in a hopeless contradiction.

In defense of the claim that the law of contradiction is not just for mere thought, we might consider the following. There are many philosophers who would argue that reality—that is the universe of objects to which our terms refer—is in itself neither contradictory nor noncontradictory. This they would argue is because such things as "consistency" and "inconsistency," "contradiction" and "contrariety" are conditions that exist between sentences or propositions; hence it is absurd to speak of the objects of thought as being contradictory or contrary to one another. Further, it has been claimed, any attempt to prove that the law of contradiction applies not just to thought, but to things as well, can only be a circular (and hence ineffective) proof. This (so they argue) is because any "proof" that reality is logical must assume the law of contradiction in order to proceed as a proof at all. However, since what we must assume in order to argue is precisely the issue in question, the "proof" is question begging.

There is to such an argument, however, a forceful response. (This argument actually comes from H. W. B. Joseph. *Introduction to Logic*, 2nd edition, 13.) What would happen, we might ask, if the law of contradiction held for thought only. Consider, for example, that if this were the case then, although we could not *think* that the page before us both is and is not white (at the same time and in the same space, of course), still we could *know* (or somehow apprehend) that it (the page) doesn't have to be as we think it must. Thus in the act of saying that we cannot *not think* in terms of violating the law of contradiction—but that we can know or otherwise grasp that things themselves need not obey this law—we have, in fact, done precisely what we have said we cannot do; that is we have "thought" the "unthinkable." On the one hand we say that we cannot think noncontradiction but (nonetheless) that we *can* "think" it (in terms of knowing that the law doesn't apply to objects). Hence, we are involved in a blatant contradiction that if true would undercut the validity of the law—even for thought. In addition to this, such a view assumes certain important metaphysical theses that Bradley is unwilling to concede. Namely that the real exists in a manner that is external and indifferent to our experience as it comes to us in the basic act of thought (which is conjoined with a larger realm of "experience") with which logic is concerned—the judgment. Bradley's argument against such an assumption is often made by putting forth the simple (but highly effective) question "How do you know of a reality external to your experience?" It is Bradley's claim that if reality did exist in such a purely external manner to experience then we could neither know about nor be influenced by it. Any reality that is *totally* external to our experience could make no difference to it. Knowledge and reality cannot—as the above view assumes—be separated. We are not in possession of a single shred of evidence that there exists a nonexperiential reality that exists separate from the various knowledge claims of judging subjects; hence it is utterly unjustified to claim that logical notions such as "contradiction" or "contrariety" have no place in a discussion of reality.

5. The fact that the irrational connection (conjunction) is *our* shortcoming and not a characteristic of reality is emphasized throughout Bradley's works. For example, in *Appearance and Reality* (511) we read: "Bare irrational conjunctions are not given as facts. Every perceived complex is a selection from an indefinite background, and, when judged as real, it is predicated both of this background and of the Reality, which transcends it. Hence, in this background and beyond lies, we may believe, the reason and the internal connexion of all we take as a mere external 'together'. Conjunction and Contradiction in short is but our defect, our one-sidedness, and our abstraction and it is appearance and not Reality."

6. Although Bradley often speaks of our "intellectual need" and "intellectual satisfaction" it should be pointed out that both need and satisfaction presuppose something more than mere intellect. The need to know can arise only because there is a felt discrepancy between explicit intellectual apprehension and the implicit sense of unity and completeness that characterizes the feeling base of experience. And "intellectual satisfaction" can be said to result just so far as this discrepancy is overcome.

7. We must remember that the special (or limited) subject and special (or limited) predicate combine as elements within a larger predicate concept that is referred to reality-as-a-whole.

8. *Essays on Truth and Reality*, 227, note.

9. We should always bear in mind that, for Bradley, the law of contradiction is ultimate. And by this is meant that the law of contradiction functions as a condition of any possible conscious experience. To be conscious at all is to judge and to judge is to assume a criterion of reality. And if we examine this criterion we shall see, Bradley tells us, that it consists in the presupposition that reality is a noncontradictory whole. There is for Bradley nothing derivative about this notion. It is the most inescapable and fundamental characteristic of the conscious apprehension of even the barest sense-datum.

10. According to Bradley, the connection between predicates is perfect and complete in the Absolute. We must bear in mind that Bradley sees every unique subject as possessing its further predicates in a manner that is ultimately determined by the entire universe. See *Essays on Truth and Reality*, 261–67; also *Appearance and Reality*, 337–39.

11. Reality cannot have, at the same time and in the same point, predicates that both are and are not. This is the presupposition of any coherent experience. And, according to Bradley, even in its denial we must assume its truth. If we consider the proposition "It is false that reality cannot both be and not be something in the same point and at the same time" we see that this demands that reality possess a definite characteristic—namely that which excludes the truth of "reality is such that it cannot both be. . . ." In other words, in order to be in possession of a meaningful judgment that denies of the real that it must obey the law of contradiction we must assume that reality operates upon the basis of that which we deny.

12. *Appearance and Reality*, 506.

13. Ibid. Also see, for example, 170.

14. Although I have not directly treated of the negative assertion in my discussion, what follows in the text may be understood as a commentary on Bradley's understanding of negation. Whenever we say (for example) "Unicorns don't exist" or "The sky is not red" we do so, Bradley insists, only upon the basis of a positive (even if vague) experienced content. See, for example, *Essays on Truth and Reality*, 286–87; also *Principles of Logic*, 662–67.

15. Ibid., 123.

16. As Bradley tells us, "This positive ground, which is the basis of negation, is not *contradictory*. It is merely discrepant, opposite, incompatible. It is only contrary." *Principles of Logic*, 123. And also, "Thus the notion of a 'contradictory' as a mere opposite does no work."

17. *Appearance and Reality*, 500.

18. We might also consider: "Nothing in itself is opposite and refuses to unite. Everything again is opposite if brought together into a point which owns no internal diversity. Every bare conjunction is therefore contradictory when take up by thought, because thought in its nature is incapable of conjunction and has no way of mere 'together'. On the other side no such conjunction is or possibly could be given. It is itself a mere abstraction, useful perhaps and so

legitimate and so far valid, but taken otherwise to be condemned as the main root of error." *Appearance and Reality*, 510–11.

19. Ibid.

20. Ibid., 500–501. We might also consider the following from the same text: "Contradiction is appearance, everywhere removable by distinction and by further supplementation, and removed actually, if not in and by the mere intellect, by the whole which transcends it. On the other hand contradiction, or rather what becomes such, as soon as it is thought out, is everywhere necessary." Ibid. 511.

21. Although for us the intension is complex it cannot be said to be unambiguous. The full precision of the terms's meaning can only be understood to exist in reality. Certainly as *we* understand the term its intension is not stable at all. See my "Bradley on the Intension and Extension of Terms," Mander, *Logic and Metaphysics* for a fuller discussion.

22. Ibid., 505.

23. For a different reading see W. J. Mander's *Introduction to Bradley's Metaphysics*, 50–55.

24. But does this mean that "the real is the rational" for Bradley? It all depends what one means by "rational." For Bradley, reality contains an intelligibility that outstrips anything that mere thought could (on its own) ever hope to duplicate.

25. In *Appearance and Reality* Bradley most often discusses "qualities" and "relations." However, "terms" should be considered synonymous for the purposes of our discussion. Although a broader term than "quality" the mechanism is the same. See, for example, *Appearance and Reality*, 502–12.

26. This was Bradley's final work. It was incomplete when he died in 1923. H. H. Joachim edited it into the form that it finally took when it was published in the *Collected Essays*. See 628–76.

27. Ibid., 642.

28. Bradley goes on to say: "To find qualities without relations is surely impossible. In the field of consciousness, even when we abstract from the relation of identity and difference, they are never independent. One is together with, and related to, one other, at the least—in fact, always to more than one. Nor will an appeal to a lower and undistinguished state of mind, where in one feeling are many aspects, assist us in any way. I admit the existence of such states without any relation, but I wholly deny there the presence of qualities. For if these felt aspects, while merely felt, are to be called qualities proper, they are so only for the observations of an outside observer. And then for him they are given *as* aspects—that is, together with relations. In short, if you go back to mere unbroken feeling, you have no relations and no qualities. But if you come to what is distinct, you get relations at once." *Appearance and Reality*, 22.

29. See, for example, *Principles of Logic*, 470–72.

30. *Appearance and Reality*, 517.

31. Ibid., 507.

32. See Guy Stock's "Introduction" in *Writings on Logic and Metaphysics*, esp. 105–14.

33. It is interesting to note that this theory was well developed by the time the first edition of the *Principles of Logic* appeared. There Bradley writes: "If the units have to exist together, they must stand in relation to one another; and, if these relations are also units, it would seem that the second class must also stand in relation to the first. If A and B are feelings, and if C their relation is another feeling, you must either suppose that component parts can exist without standing in relation with one another, or else that there is a *fresh* relation between C and AB. Let this be D, and once more we are launched on the infinite process of finding a relation between D and C-AB; and so on forever. If relations are facts that exist between facts, then what comes *between* the relations and the other facts? The real truth is that the units on one side, and on the other side the relations existing between them, are nothing actual. They are fictions of the mind, mere distinctions within a single reality, which a common delusion erroneously takes for independent facts." *Principles of Logic*, 96.

34. *Collected Essays*, 644.

35. And, we must remember that *all* thinking is, for Bradley, "relational."

36. And let us consider the notion of a "merely internal" relation. "What . . . [Bradley asks] should, on the other hand, be meant by a relation viewed as absolutely and merely internal? You, I presume, still in this case would continue to take the terms each one as, so far, in and by itself real, and as independent absolutely of any whole that could be said to contain them. And you would go on to attribute to the particular character of the terms, as so taken, some actual relation or relations which you find, as you say, to fall between them. Something like this, I suppose is or ought to be meant by a relation which is asserted to be real ultimately and internal merely. . . . Relations would be merely internal if, the terms taken as real independently, each in itself, the relations between them (as a class, or in this or that particular case) in fact arose or were due merely to the character of the terms so taken." And Bradley also writes: "The idea, I would add, that I myself accept such a doctrine as the above seems to myself even ludicrous. And to whom, if to anyone, it should be attributed in fact, I will not offer to discuss. In any case, to assume, it as the necessary alternative, when the mere externality of relations is denied is (I submit) an obvious and perhaps natural mistake." *Collected Essays*, 642.

37. I must disagree with the analysis of internal relations provided by W. J. Mander in his *Introduction to Bradley's Metaphysics*. There Mander tells us that it is one of the "commonest misconceptions" that Bradley held a theory of internal relations. And when he encounters claims on Bradley's part that all relations *are* (to some degree) internal, Mander tells us that we "should not take seriously" such statements. Mander's justification for all of this turns on Bradley's comments (see 104–5 of Mander's *Introduction*) that a relation that is placed wholly into its terms disappears, and hence cannot be seen any longer as a "together and between." But let me reiterate a point made in the text: the problem with internal relations is not that they are relations absorbed by their

terms. (That would be no relation at all.) Bradley's difficulty is that the "together" and "between" of the internal relation is always infected by an *external* Other whose difference to the related terms's being it cannot include. Put differently, anything short of an *all-inclusive* awareness of the universe (the universe-as-a-whole) must assert the relation of terms within that awareness as subject to an unknown condition, and are hence "disrupted from without."

38. To say that two terms, let us say subject term A and predicate term B in "A is B," are internally related is to say that to some degree they have shed their mere indifference to one another and have (again, to some degree) brought into their explicit content a sense of that felt many-in-oneness that exists at the level of felt experience and which provides the impetus to judge. In other words, we have managed to view A and B as elements in a systematic whole. We view them as forming a continuous tissue with one another and as being continuous with the real that lay beyond the purview of explicit judgment.

39. See, for example, *Appearance and Reality*, 332.

40. Although we must always bear in mind that the terms as they exist within the grammatical proposition are much more complete as they exist in the perceptually laden judgment, to a certain extent they can never fully shed their abstract linguistic form; and that linguistic form is (ultimately) merely relational and hence merely conjunctive. We might go so far as to say that, to the extent that the actual judgment (as thought) retains its merely linguistic form, it remains a mere aggregate of terms held in external relation.

41. Bradley writes: "Mere internal relations, then, like relations that are merely external, are untenable if they make a claim to ultimate and absolute truth." *Collected Essays*, 645. However, I would emphasize here the "mere" and the "ultimate." Recent commentators have, to my thinking, given far too little attention to the fact that—while still defective—the internal relation is one that conveys greater truth than the external relation. See, for example, Mander's *Introduction to Bradley's Metaphysics*, 96–111; see also Sprigge's *James and Bradley*, 430ff.

42. *Appearance and Reality*, 50.

7. COHERENCE AND ERROR

1. See *Appearance and Reality*, 320–21.

2. *Essays on Truth and Reality*, 223.

3. "Truth, in other words, content with nothing short of Reality, has, in order to remain truth, to come short forever of its own ideal and to remain imperfect." *Essays on Truth and Reality*, 251.

4. *Appearance and Reality*, 319.

5. We should notice that the Bradleian idea of coherence is far stronger than the sort of formal definition that is often bandied about. A formal definition of coherence—and perhaps the weakest one that could be provided—is that if two propositions are not inconsistent then they "cohere." There are, however, two important reasons why Bradley cannot accept a definition of coherence that

revolves around the notion of "lack of inconsistency between propositions." Such a definition, we must notice, both does not go far enough on one side while going entirely too far on the other. The formal notion of consistency essentially assumes that there are such things as clear and unambiguous meanings for our terms. And the only sort of "implication" that can exist is the sort of formal implication that results from the tautological relations between those terms. It should be evident that this notion of implication is far weaker than the sort envisaged by Bradley. However, where the formal notion of coherence goes too far is in claiming that a mere lack of inconsistency between propositions constitutes coherence. We should recall that, for Bradley, all propositions (judgments) when considered in relation to other judgments (or reality) are always—to some extent—external and thus partially inconsistent.

6. As we have already considered, the "merely subjective" just *is* the irrelevant. See *Essays on Truth and Reality*, 328.

7. See *Appearance and Reality*, 351–52.

8. But what could the real meaning actually be in a case like this? We must be aware that, for Bradley, there is always a real meaning that functions as the implicit ideal and standard of objective reference in every assertion. And this ideal is the Absolute—that is, the totality of intersecting and interpenetrating objects and events that *all* (directly or indirectly) bear upon one another and, in this case, the question of Mary's relative disability vis-à-vis her recent car accident.

9. See *Essays on Truth and Reality*, 177.

10. Ralph Walker notes that "F. H. Bradley . . . who is often described as a coherence theorist—and who often writes like one—is in the last resort not one, because what determines reality for him is ultimately not belief but feeling." *The Coherence Theory of Truth* (London, Routledge, 1989), 39. While Walker's remark is certainly true, we must not be mislead by it. As we shall see in chapters 8 and 9, the feeling base *is* ultimately that with which a proposition coheres or doesn't. However, we must realize here that this feeling is, at one level, permeated by our belief structure. And even where feeling outstrips my system of belief, the structure that it contains there is still one that Bradley characterizes as "intelligible."

11. One further point which we must always keep in sight when discussing coherence is that the context of our explicit assertion is understood as being *continuous* with its presupposed world. As we have considered before, although we might justifiably employ a concept-percept distinction, it is one that is wholly relative. That is, every perception is shot through with what may be called conceptual content; and, every concept has a perceptual base of some sort. We would do well to remember that there just are no "concept-free" perceptions for Bradley. Every percept is tightly bound up with the greater conceptual nexus that forms our "world"; and thus the relation between *this* judgment (the one presently asserted) and our world is a relation that exists between elements of the same order. And it is for this reason that Bradley (and those who held similar views) were inclined to call this relation one of "coherence."

12. We should notice that the judgment cannot escape system entirely. "This" presupposes "not-this" (or space); "red" presupposes "not-red" (and the system of color); and "now" presupposes "not-now" (or the stream of time). But, although the bare perceptual judgment reaches beyond itself to a larger reality, only a minimal amount of that reality makes its way into our consciousness. And it is precisely this narrowness, the limited scope and comprehension, that makes our judgment true at one moment and false the next. This (we may recall from chapter 3) is one of the primary defects of the categorical judgment.

13. Although all truths can be understood as going beyond the temporal present, we must realize that some judgments do this more than others. If, while my attention is narrowly focused on a red patch, I judge "This red now," I am engaged in an analytic judgment of sense that to only a slight degree explicitly reveals the timeless nexus of meanings that Bradley calls the "Absolute." See *Essays on Truth and Reality*, 344ff.

14. The claim "water boils at 100 degrees Celsius or 212 degrees Fahrenheit under one atmosphere of pressure" also has a great number of conditions that are necessary (but unstated) to its truth; but we should see that they are far fewer than the number of conditions that must hold in order for "This hurts my mouth" to be true. We should also point out that when we say "Water boils at 100 degrees . . ." we do not mean only *some* water; this is not a claim about the water that is now before us, or even about just the water we have perceptually encountered. It is a claim about *all* water whenever and wherever it may exist. It is an assertion that announces a fact about the universe and that is intended to illustrate an aspect of its essential structure.

15. Of course, there is no explicit perceptual content here. But, as Bradley says, to become more concrete in one sense is to become less concrete in another. The broad comprehension of scientific assertions precludes their containing much in the way of perceptual content. When such an assertion is actually made the individual making the judgment may have before his mind an image of this or that water boiling. However, this image is but an infinitesimal fragment of the assertion's fuller comprehension.

16. The topic of disjunction is a complex one that we can only touch upon here. And, Bradley's own views on the subject underwent a great deal of modification, so much so that in 1922 he writes: "On the subject of Disjunction the reader is referred to Dr. Bosanquet's *Logic*. I fully accept his main view; but before proceeding in consequence to point out some errors made in this volume, I will add a few remarks which may perhaps assist the reader." *Principles of Logic*, 137. And the main points that Bradley goes on to make are that, although disjunction is a higher stage than the mere conjunctiveness that is represented in categorical judgment, and the limited display of necessity that the hypothetical assertion provides, it is not ultimate. The strength of disjunction rests with the fact that—in its highest form—it shows exclusive and exhaustive determination of universals in their concrete manifestation. It attempts to say that "Here are all the various manifestations which these predicates can take and they can only take one of them at a time." For example, "Being an Oxford man he is either a University College man, or a Balliol man, or a Merton man etc." systematically

presents how the "He is an Oxford man" realizes itself in fact. (The example is suggested by Bosanquet; see his *Logic*, 1:325.) The suggestion is always—at least if our disjunctive judgment is of the highest form—that the disjunction is both exclusive and exhaustive. It says that our Oxford man must be one—and only one—of these things and that these are all the choices. And in expressing this it has reached to a high level of systematicity—at least for the universal predicates it is considering. (Disjunction is "higher" only relative to the hypothetical and categorical expression of the same predicates.) Bradley tells us, though, that disjunction is not really the most expressive form of system. "But we are led none the less to look beyond it [disjunction] to a higher and more ultimate stage, where we return to Conjunction in a different sense and at a higher level. In a complete and perfect system, where all conditions were filled in at once, all as connected and each as qualifying the others and the whole. And here negation would disappear except as one aspect of positive and complementary distinction. But for us this ultimate stage of the intellect remains an ideal, in the sense that it can not in detail and everywhere be attained completely." *Principles of Logic*, 138.

17. I am using my terms here according to the conventions that both Bradley and Bosanquet came to adopt. When I say "categorical" I am referring to the narrow type of categorical assertion as discussed in chapter 3. When I say "hypothetical" I am talking about the universal affirmative of traditional logic. What is confusing here is that even the categorical is "hypothetical" in that it is conditional. And thus it can be translated into an "if-then" proposition. But, some means of differentiating between this "low-level" hypothetical is required. And thus Bradley elected (following Bosanquet) to reserve the term "hypothetical" for the broad-based universal affirmative assertion.

18. But, this lack of "expanse" or "range" illustrates an important condition of any truth. With a narrowness of comprehension comes a certain *externality* to the greater system that the assertion presupposes. There are innumerable instances where the denial of "My mouth is burning" would in no way create friction or tension with my intelligible world. However let us consider what would occur if I were to assert "It is not the case that water boils at 100 degrees Celsius under one atmosphere of pressure." What sort of intellectual havoc would result if under controlled laboratory conditions instances of what was certifiably H_2O failed to boil when heated to the requisite temperature under the appropriate pressure? The different reactions that these two denials would prove are, of course, intimately tied to the fact that in the one case the denial impeaches much (if not most) of my intellectual universe whereas in the other little is at stake. The meanings of "water" and "boils" etc. are—when used in a lawlike assertion—so broad in comprehension and tied into so many other significant experiences that an exception to the truth of the assertion would require a considerable reworking of my entire system of knowledge. However, the analytic judgment of sense "My mouth is burning" is one whose denial lacks this degree of engagement with the larger universe. In saying this, though, we must bear in mind following. The *actual* judgment (and not the grammatical form) must truly be a categorical (and thus narrowly focused) judgment. We could imagine the

utter terror that might result should I encounter my mouth to burn every time I put a bit of food into it. However, such upset could only occur as a result of a far more sophisticated judgment than "My mouth is burning." If I were to become alarmed at the fact that whenever I tasted a piece of chilled fruit I experienced a burning sensation in my mouth it would be because I was engaged in the denial of a more comprehensive universal assertion. (Perhaps something like "If one is healthy one should experience sensations of hot and cold in the mouth in a manner that reflects the temperature of the food that is tasted" or some such thing.) The mere awareness that my mouth was hot could in no way cause discomfort, intellectual or otherwise. It is only upon the recognition that something was "wrong" that my upset would result. But, this recognition would entail the presence of a comprehensive and far-reaching assertion (usually disjunctive) that proclaimed some standard or norm to which I subscribed.

19. Another way of viewing this is to understand that the conditionality of any judgment increases as the comprehensiveness decreases. Indeed, we might say that a judgment is comprehensive just to the degree that its conditions are made internal to the judgment itself.

20. To the objection that a false scientific assertion is "more comprehensive" but not very coherent we must reply that this fails to understand Bradley's notion of comprehensiveness. We are talking about actual comprehensiveness here. The false scientific assertion *attempts* to bind together in a unified vision a great mass of experience, but largely fails. Failed comprehension is—in the end—*non*-comprehension.

21. We must remember that a tautology can not really exist as a judgment for Bradley. If we truly assert then there is a difference between limited subject, special predicate, and the reality beyond.

22. I insert "ideal" in parentheses to emphasize that the meaning that *we* possess, which is based on *our* experience, is not entirely coextensive with what I have referred to as the "real meaning."

23. *Appearance and Reality*, 333–34.

24. See *Essays on Truth and Reality*, 344–45.

25. See *Appearance and Reality*, 336–37. To complement the discussion of degrees of truth and reality in the text, I would like to offer the following metaphor. And, though it is only a metaphor, it may aid in understanding what Bradley is driving at here. I have on an earlier occasion referred to the system of reality to which judgment relates (and which is always present as its condition) as the "atmosphere" within which all judgment takes place. We might imagine this atmosphere to be a thick fog that—although we are aware of it in some sense—remains vague and inchoate until we consciously reflect upon it. Now, to further develop this metaphor we might think of a fog-lamp whose beam is capable of varying in both intensity and range. Sometimes the lamp emits only a weak and short-reaching glow into the atmosphere; at other times, however, it can be very intense and far-reaching. We might also think of it as capable of a varying range of focus. At times there might be present a very intense but still narrowly focused beam; at other times, though, this narrow focus would relax

and the beam would transform itself into a more spherical or omnidirectional light. We might consider the various ways in which the lamp illuminates the fog as being equivalent to the forms of judgment that we are capable of making. The very dimmest light would represent the low level categorical assertion; the very bright but narrowly focused would be analogous to the hypothetical assertion of science, while the bright and omnidirectional illuminator would be in our example representative of the disjunctive judgment. Although the ultimate goal of experience would be the complete illumination of the atmosphere within which it finds itself, we can say that the judgment (like the beam of light) has truth and is compresent with the real just so far as it can illuminate—that is, make transparent to itself or *be*—that universe from which it arose.

26. Ibid., 322–23.

27. Ibid., 321–22.

28. Ibid., 169–70.

29. I should mention here that when Bradley calls all predicates "real" he does not mean that they necessarily have a place in the world of *physical* objects. For Bradley, *all* predicates do have their place in the real universe—even "unicorns," "martians," and "time-machines." This is because Bradley's ultimate notion of the "real universe" is one that is far more expansive than the merely physical. Although all "worlds" are continuous and interrelated, for Bradley, ultimate reality is not exhausted by the spatiotemporal flow of events. See, for example, *Appearance and Reality*, 323–32; and "Floating Ideas and the Imaginary," in *Essays on Truth and Reality*, 28–64.

30. The point here is that, considered as a concrete universal (and not as an empty abstract concept), the idea of "dying in ones sleep" contains the identity of all those people who actually have died in their sleep.

31. *Appearance and Reality*, 171.

32. Ibid., 323–32; also *Essays on Truth and Reality*, 28–64, passim.

33. See *Appearance and Reality*, 172ff.

34. For a concise discussion of these standard objections, see Laurence BonJour's *Structure of Empirical Knowledge* (Cambridge, 1985), 107–10. See also his earlier "The Coherence Theory of Empirical Knowledge," *Philosophical Studies* 30 (1976), 281–312. And, while I can not fully agree with his analysis, see, too, David Crossley's "Justification and the Foundations of Empirical Knowledge," in *Philosophy after F. H. Bradley*, 307–29.

35. I might also add here the following: For Bradley, every assertion is grounded in—not just the fleeting contents of momentary perception—but in the feeling base that supports and conditions them. (I shall much more to say about this point in the next chapter.) Judgments (or beliefs) are not just "mental phenomena" that can stand in external and indifferent relation to their objects. The object is *in* the belief (to some degree) and the belief is *in* the object (again, at least to some degree). And more than this, when we judge we do so upon certain *presuppositions* (which are at first largely unconscious). Were these presuppositions not made, there could be no conscious assertive experience at

all. And, while Bradley does not try to explicitly "deduce" a series of categories (as did both Kant and Hegel), he *does* identify certain "general features of reality" whose denial, he believes, ensnares one in a state of self-contradiction. Now, amongst these presuppositions are beliefs about the noncontradictory, and coherent nature of all that is real. Bradley further claims that, not only is it a necessary condition of any experience that we believe that the universe is coherent and unified, we also believe—indeed, must believe—that its contents are permeated by necessary connections. By claiming first that any possible experience demands that it be construed in certain ways, and that the forms under which we must construe even the minimal experience carry with them reverberations that condition all further experience, we can be assured that—in the end—we shall all agree as to the nature of truth and reality. Since for Bradley the given contents of experience (the sense data) are themselves permeated by conceptual relations to other contents, to correctly follow out the lines of sense is also to develop within one's conscious experience the *one* true conceptual system.

36. We should also consider that Bradley would be completely unwilling to concede the point that there can exist two different theoretical interpretations that do equal justice to the facts. Since the nexus of meaning that underlies both theories is ultimately the same, one theory or the other will, in one place or the other, better capture their common presupposed ground.

37. See *Appearance and Reality*, 460ff.

38. I am not referring here to ordinary conceptions of correspondence. And it is a serious error to attribute to Bradley a garden-variety correspondence theory of truth in the first edition of the *Principles of Logic*. As James Allard has pointed out, the argument against "degrees" in the 1883 *Logic* concerns itself with Bradley's view (at that time) that a judgment was either put forth as true (i.e., asserted) or it wasn't. See Allard's comments in "Degrees of Truth in Bradley," *Perspectives on the Logic and Metaphysics of F. H. Bradley*, 140–42.

39. See Stewart Candlish's comments in the pages of *Mind* 98 (1989), 331–48. For another valuable discussion of these problems, see Thomas Baldwin's "The Identity Theory of Truth," (*Mind* 100, 35–53). As Baldwin states, "a coherence theory of truth can be derived from the identity theory and the further premise that reality is the coherent system." Also see W. J. Mander's *Introduction to Bradley's Metaphysics*, 27–39; and Julian Dodd's "Resurrecting the Identity Theory of Truth: A Reply to Candlish" (*Bradley Studies* 2.1, 42–50).

40. While there are many such statements, see *Essays on Truth and Reality*, 343ff., for a particularly strong example.

8. Feeling and Knowledge (i)

1. *Essays on Truth and Reality*, 178. My emphasis on the words "comprised within."

2. Ibid., 179ff.

3. What is important to note here, though, is that the product or result of thought's advance is one that permanently alters the character of immediate experience.

4. It is to my thinking a serious interpretive error to deny this point. If Bradley were to claim that immediate experience is a wholly noncognitive level of experience he would be (a) denying the continuity of asserted contents as they exist in judgment and as they exist in reality; and (b) turning our thinking awareness into a mental representation of something that—in its most primitive nature—is wholly other than our thoughts.

5. *Essays on Truth and Reality*, 177.

6. It should, perhaps, be emphasized that much of that significance may have never entered into my explicit relational awareness.

7. The word "intuitively" is used here with caution. See Bradley's comments in *Collected Essays*, 688.

8. *Essays on Truth and Reality*, 160.

9. And in order to illustrate the necessity of such immediate experience we may turn for a moment to the doctrine of a philosopher whose views Bradley often rejects—David Hume. Even Hume, we should recall, realized that he had to postulate something like "immediate experience" in order to provide his impressions and ideas with meaning or significance. And we may easily grasp this point by reminding ourselves that, on the Humean account, all impressions and ideas ("less lively impressions") possess significance only because they "lead to" or "cause to come before the mind" *other* ideas. I think of "fire" and I next think of "heat" (even though no impression of "heat" is given to sense). But why is this? As is well known, for Hume this occurs only because there exists an "associative bond" between the ideas of "fire" and "heat." And it is only because this bond has formed (through the mechanism of repeated contiguity) that the idea of "fire" can be said to be significant at all. Of course, on Hume's theory, this associative bond resides in our experience as a "mental habit." And as such, it is definitely not the object of our explicit awareness. However, Hume assumes its existence nevertheless; and he does so because he realizes (as does Bradley) that unless *some* such mechanism exists, the significance of explicitly apprehended impressions remains inexplicable.

10. Bradley tells us: "Object and subject and every possible relation and term, to be experienced at all, must fall *within* and depend vitally on such a felt totality. . . . Everything, therefore, no matter how objective and how relational, is experienced only in feeling, and so far as it is experienced still depends on feeling." *Essays on Truth and Reality*, 176. My emphasis.

11. *Essays on Truth and Reality*, 159–60.

12. See, for example, *Appearance and Reality*, 356–57, 365–70, and 410–14.

13. Bradley's commitment to this idea can be found in numerous passages. Consider the following: "On their side the wills of finite centres, though real, are never the mere wills of these several centres. Experienced volition is always the will of the Whole in one with my own. What therefore is carried out into existence in and by my will is always more than any content which is merely mine. The content carried out belongs also and, in one sense, just as much to the Whole. And not only is this so, but some content is realized in and by my will,

though the content goes beyond that of which in willing I was aware. To some extent this realization beyond what I have consciously willed seems evident in fact, and how far it conceivably might go, we seem unable to say. My will thus carries out into existence, and into the external world, more than in one sense was actually contained in my will." *Essays on Truth and Reality*, 350 note.

14. To my thinking, Bradley's most interesting discussion of this point is to be found in the final chapter of his *Ethical Studies*. See the "Concluding Remarks," 313–44.

15. I shall leave it to the reader to think through such thought experiments, and to judge how convincing they are.

16. *Essays on Truth and Reality*, 176. My emphasis.

17. Consider also: "We cannot [Bradley writes] speak of a relation between immediate experience and that which transcends it [relational awareness] except by a licence. It is a mode of thinking found convenient in our reflective thinking, but it is in the end not defensible. A relation exists only between terms, and those terms, to be known as such, must be objects. And hence immediate experience becomes so far a partial object and ceases so far to keep its nature as a felt totality." Ibid., 177.

18. Ibid.

19. *Appearance and Reality*, 407. My emphasis.

20. See, for example, *Appearance and Reality*, 199.

21. *Essays on Truth and Reality*, 161. My emphasis.

22. For a non-idealist account of this problem, see Roderick Firth's "Coherence, Certainty, and Epistemic Priority," *Journal of Philosophy* 61 (1964), 545–47; and Roderick Chisolm's *Theory of Knowledge*, 3rd edition (Englewood Cliffs, N.J., 1989). For a brief overview of more recent conceptions of the criteria of knowledge, the reader might profitably consult Bruce Hunter's article "Criteria and Knowledge," in Blackwell's *Companion to Epistemology*, ed. Dancy and Sosa (Oxford, 1992), 82–86.

23. *Essays on Truth and Reality*, 189.

24. For example, to understand the content "yellow" *perfectly*, we would (*per impossibile*) have to simultaneously apprehend all manifestations or instantiations (in "this world" and beyond) of yellow.

25. Historically sensitive readers may notice a similarity here between Bradley's problem and that confronting Kant in his discussion of "pure" and "schematized" categories. See Kemp Smith's translation of the *Critique of Pure Reason*, 180–87.

9. Feeling and Knowledge (ii)

1. By "discursive" I do not mean here "linear." The notion of discursive thought is one that, in this context, implies, an incompleteness on thought's part. And this incompleteness can only be overcome through the elaboration and extension of the discursus itself. "Linear" thinking, on the other hand, would be discursive thought that moves in a straight line and that is essentially unsystem-

atic. (The sorities might be the best example.) This idea of discursive thinking should, however, be differentiated from Bradley's; for him the discursus consists in the expanding and contracting apprehension of system.

2. Curiously, Bradley's position *verbally* exhibits a complete reversal of view of some of his idealist predecessors. For some writers it was *only* in thought that reality could be reached. "Feeling" (which was identified with sensation) was understood as that which kept us earth-bound and tied to our merely subjective perspective. It was for this reason, more than any other, that Bradley was sometimes treated with reserve by the more orthodox idealist writers (e.g., Caird, Haldane, Joachim, and Muirhead). By restricting "thought" to that element of our experience that is essentially discursive Bradley seemed to be challenging one of the fundamental theses of the more traditional forms of idealism—namely, the ultimate unity of thought and reality.

3. The "final form" to which I refer here is the mature doctrine of feeling. In *Appearance and Reality* Bradley talked about the "principle of non-contradiction" and "the Whole" as supplying the criterion of truth and reality. However, when he came to mere closely consider how we as finite beings *access* these criteria he was forced to develop the notion of "felt experience" more fully than he had done previously.

4. The terms "inference" and "dialectic" are used below in a largely synonymous manner. However, technically speaking, not all inferential movement can be construed as dialectical movement *if* we mean by "dialectic" a movement that involves the major advance from one categorial form to another. But all inference can be understood as "dialectical" if we realize that in every inference we are developing the *inner content* of a category; and this local development is crucial to the larger movement that might be called "dialectical" in the more precise sense.

5. *Essays on Truth and Reality*, 225.

6. I must disagree here with the analysis provided by Wollheim. See his *F. H. Bradley*, 149–52 (1st edition). And while W. J. Mander seems to portray Bradley's view accurately, his comments on the differences between Bradley and Hegel are, I suggest, to be treated with caution. For an interesting commentary on this difference see Bernard Bosanquet's *Principle of Individuality and Value*, 223–34.

7. This is, of course, the orthodox interpretation of the Hegelian *aufhebung*. And, again, Bradley's problem rests only with the suggestion that finite experience itself—*as* either thought or sensation—can generate the contradiction or supply that which is needed to overcome it once it exists.

8. See *Appearance and Reality*, 454.

9. While it is true that we cannot doubt in the moment we judge, we may say that the force with which we put forth any assertion is itself based upon the degree to which its evidential support has been integrated into the judgment. I would add, however, that this statement would apply only to Bradley's work after 1883. In the first-edition *Logic* Bradley still seemed to believe that assertion was essentially independent of content and that there was no sense in which

we could *logically* identify varying degrees of assertiveness. However, under the criticism of Bosanquet (who in his *Knowledge and Reality* argued that the force of any assertion varied with its necessitation by the larger system) Bradley recanted his earlier statements, which he saw as but another example of the doctrine of the floating idea creeping into his work. See Bosanquet's *Knowledge and Reality*, 114ff.

10. And continuing: "We have not only connexions in the object-world, temporal, spatial and other relations, which extend for us the content of a partial object. We have also another world at least to some extent actually experienced, a world the content of which is continuous with our object. And, where an element present in this world is wanting to our object, dissatisfaction may arise with an unending incompleteness and an endless effort at inclusion. The immanent Reality, both harmonious and all-comprehending, demands the union of both its characters in the object." *Essays on Truth and Reality*, 225–26.

11. *Appearance and Reality*, 453–89.

12. Bradley writes, "Thought can form the idea of an apprehension, something like feeling in directness, which contains all the character sought by its relational efforts. Thought can understand that, to reach its goal, it must get beyond relations. Yet in its nature it can find no other working means of progress. Hence it perceives that somehow this relational side of its nature must be merged and must include somehow the other side. Such a fusion would compel thought to lose and to transcend its proper self. And the nature of this fusion thought can apprehend in vague generality, but not in detail; and it can see the reason why a detailed apprehension is impossible. Such anticipated self-transcendence *is* an Other; but to assert that Other is *not* a self-contradiction." Ibid., 160. Also 140–43 for Bradley's discussion of this point. And, *Essays on Truth and Reality*, 246–47.

13. See *Appearance and Reality*, 153–54 and 464–65.

14. See Sprigge's *James and Bradley* for a somewhat different view. Especially 441–57.

15. *Essays on Truth and Reality*, 326–27.

16. Ibid., 327–28.

17. Bradley writes: "A finite experience already *is* partially the universe. Hence there is no question of stepping over a line from one world to another. Experience is already in both worlds; and is one thing with their being; and the question is merely to what extent this common being can be carried out, whether in practice or in knowledge." *Appearance and Reality*, 465.

18. As Bradley says: "It is both possible and necessary to transcend what is given. But this same transcendence at once carries us into the universe at large. Our private self is not a resting place which logic can justify." *Appearance and Reality*, 221. Also consider: "And what I repudiate is the separation of feeling form the felt, or of the desired from desire, or of what is thought from thinking, or the division—I might add—of anything from anything else. Nothing is ever so presented as real by itself, or can be argued so to exist without demonstrable fallacy. And in asserting that the reality is experience, I rest throughout on this

foundation. You cannot find fact unless in unity with sentience, and one cannot in the end be divided from the other, either actually or in idea. But, to be utterly indivisible from feeling or perception, to be an integral element in a whole which is experienced, this surely is itself to *be* experience. Being and reality are, in brief, one thing with sentience; they can neither be opposed to, or even in the end distinguished from it." Ibid., 129.

19. *Essays on Truth and Reality*, 316–17. My emphasis.

20. I am thinking of Richard Wollheim again here. See *F. H. Bradley*, 18ff.

21. Bradley explicitly addresses the idea of solipsism in *Appearance and Reality*, 218–30.

22. Ibid., 464; but also see *Essays on Truth and Reality*, 248–49.

23. See Sprigge's *James and Bradley*, 522–32, for a different interpretation.

24. See *Essays on Truth and Reality*, 329–30; also 256.

25. Ibid., 230–31.

26. Bradley asks us to, "Find any piece of existence, take up anything that any one could possibly call a fact, or could in any sense assert to have being, and then judge if it does not consist in sentient experience. Try to discover any sense in which you can still continue to speak of it, when all perception and feeling have been removed; or point out any fragment of its matter, any aspect of its being, which is not derived from and is still not relative to this source. When the experiment is made strictly, I can myself conceive of nothing else than the experienced. Anything, in no sense felt or perceived, becomes to me quite unmeaning. And as I cannot try to think of it without realizing either that I am not thinking at all, or that I am thinking of it against my will as being experienced, I am driven to the conclusion that for me experience is the same as reality. The fact that falls elsewhere seems, in my mind, to be a mere word and a failure, or else an attempt at self-contradiction. It is a vicious abstraction whose existence is meaningless nonsense, and is therefore not possible." *Appearance and Reality*, 127–28.

27. See Tom Sorrell's discussion of this point in "Idealism, Realism, and Rorty's Pragmatism without Method," in *Issues in Contemporary Idealism*, ed. Coates and Hutto (Bristol, England, 1996), 1–21.

28. *Essays on Truth and Reality*, 340–41.

29. Inferential validity cannot exist in the absence of soundness for Bradley. I discuss this relation in "Why the Idealist Theory of Inference Still Matters," *Contemporary Issues in Idealism*, ed. P. Coates and D. Hutto (Bristol, England, 1995), 235–66.

30. *Appearance and Reality*, 403–4.

10. Two Critics

1. See *My Philosophical Development* (London, 1959), 42.

2. *Philosophical Essays* (New York, 1966), 139–40. This passage is specifically directed at H. H. Joachim's *The Nature of Truth* (Oxford, 1906). But Russell applied the same arguments to Bradley further down in the text.

3. I mention this here because there have been some writers who have tried to deflect Russell's attack by claiming that Bradley did not subscribe to the "axiom of internal relations." But, as I have already suggested, this is indefensible. See note 41, chapter 6.

4. As Bradley writes: "With regard to externality and mere fact I should first explain that, in my opinion, these are things which are not and cannot be observed. To have bare A in bare external relation to B is not possible in any observation or experiment. The supposed fact is really an inference reached by vicious abstraction." *Essays on Truth and Reality*, 290.

5. There has appeared in recent years a series of articles by Fred Wilson in which the Russellian attack on Bradley is vigorously defended. These articles are: "Bradley's Impact on Empiricism," in *Philosophy after F. H. Bradley*, ed. James Bradley (Bristol, England, 1996); "Moore's Refutation of Idealism," in *Current Issues in Idealism*, ed. P. Coates and D. Hutto (Bristol, England, 1995); "Burgersdijck, Bradley, Russell, Bergmann: Four Philosophers on the Ontology of Relations," in *The New Schoolman* 72, 282–310; "Bradley's Critique of Associationism," in *Bradley Studies* 4.1, 5–60. Readers looking for a more sympathetic reading of Russell are urged to consult these papers.

6. *The Principles of Mathematics*, 225. The full passage begins on page 224 and runs as follows: "The monistic theory holds that every relational proposition aRb is to be resolved into a proposition concerning the whole which a and b compose—a proposition which we may denote by (ab)r. This view, like the other, may be examined with special reference to asymmetrical relations, or from the standpoint of general philosophy. We are told, by those who advocate this opinion, that the whole contains diversity within itself, that it synthesizes differences, and that it performs other similar feats. For my part, I am unable to attach any precise significance to these phrases. But let us do our best. The proposition 'a is greater than b', we are told, does not really say anything about either a or b, but about the two together. Denoting the whole which they compose by (ab), it says, we will suppose, '(ab) contains diversity of magnitude.' Now to this statement—neglecting for the present all general arguments—there is a special objection in the case of asymmetry. (ab) is symmetrical with regard to a and b, and thus the property of the whole will be exactly the same in the case where a is greater than b as in the case where b is greater than a. . . . In order to distinguish a whole (ab) from a whole (ba), as we must do if we are to explain asymmetry, we shall be forced back from the whole to the parts and their relation. For (ab) and (ba) consist of precisely the same parts, and differ in no respect whatever save the sense of the relation between a and b. 'a is greater than b' and 'b is greater than a' are propositions containing precisely the same constituents, and giving rise therefore to precisely the same whole; their difference lies solely in the fact that *greater* is, in the first case, a relation of a to b, in the second, a relation of b to a. Thus the distinction of sense, i.e. the distinction between an asymmetrical relation and its converse, is one which the monistic theory of relations is wholly unable to explain."

7. Ibid., 223.

8. Nicholas Rescher is highly critical of Russell's account of Leibniz here. See Rescher's *The Philosophy of Leibniz* (Tottowa, N.J., 1979), 21ff. However, see also Nicholas Griffin's remarks regarding Rescher's analysis. See *Russell's Idealist Apprenticeship* (Oxford, 1991), 325.

9. It should be noted that this response was made by Timothy Sprigge as early as 1979 in his essay "Russell and Bradley on Relations" (*Bertrand Russell Memorial Volume*, ed. George W. Roberts, London, 1979), 150–70. The same material is also found in his *James and Bradley*.

10. We should recall that Bradley employed the language of "special" (or "limited") subject and predicate only to emphasize that reality-as-a-whole (the ultimate subject in any proposition) reached into or appeared within individual assertions. However, reality's appearance therein was never complete. The special subject, while it might be more of a focal point for the whole that lay beyond than special predicate, was always understood to be (more or less) abstract. It was never an individual in any complete sense.

11. Nicholas Griffin has remarked on the inapplicability of the subject-predicate analysis when one takes, as Bradley did, the subject to be reality-as-a-whole, and the predicate to be the complex proposition. See his "Bradley's Contribution to the Development of Logic," in *Philosophy after F. H. Bradley* (Bristol, England, 1996), 195–230. See also Peter Hylton's remarks in *Russell, Idealism, and the Emergence of Analytic Philosophy* (Oxford, 1990), 60–62, 154–55.

12. Consider Russell's words in his work on Leibniz: "In the belief that propositions must, in the last analysis, have a subject and a predicate, Leibniz does not differ either from his predecessors *or from his successors*. Any philosophy which uses either substance or the Absolute will be found, on inspection, to depend upon this belief. . . . Philosophers have differed, not so much in respect of belief in [the theory's] truth, as in respect of their consistency in carrying it out." *The Philosophy of Leibniz* (Cambridge, 1897), 15. My emphasis. Quoted by Hylton in *Russell, Idealism*, 154.

13. It is a persisting "Bradley myth" that he subscribes to some species of nominalism, and thus sees universals as existing "only in the mind." See, for example, Wilson's "Bradley, Russell, Bergmann," and his "Bradley's Critique." See also William Winslade's "Russell's Theory of Relations," in *Essays on Bertrand Russell*, ed. E. D. Klemke (Urbana, Ill., 1971), 81–102. The claim has been made, however, by numerous writers.

14. See, for example, *Appearance and Reality*, 522–24.

15. *Philosophical Essays*, 140. My emphasis.

16. Ibid., 145–46. My emphasis.

17. Ibid. The passage is also used, many years later, in *My Philosophical Development*, 47.

18. See, for example, *Appearance and Reality*, 124ff. 152–53, 403–12, 460ff., 494.

19. "Pure empiricism," Russell writes, "finally is believed by no one, and if we are to retain beliefs that we all regard as valid, we must allow principles of

inference which are neither demonstrative nor derivable from experience." *An Enquiry into Meaning and Truth* (London, 1950), 305.

20. See Sprigge's *James and Bradley*, 430.

21. Ibid., 434.

22. James writes that "The many-in-oneness that perception offers is impossible to construe intellectually." *Some Problems of Philosophy*, 51.

23. Ibid., 97. My emphasis.

24. And continuing: "Bergson thus allies himself with old-fashioned empiricism, on the one hand, and with mysticism, on the other. His breach with rationalism could not possibly be more thorough than it is." *Essays in Philosophy*, 152.

25. *Some Problems of Philosophy*, 32.

26. Ibid., 45.

27. Ibid., 43.

28. The most concise statement of James's view is to be found on 48–60 of *Some Problems of Philosophy*.

29. Ibid., 52.

30. Ibid., 53.

31. James's charge against T.H. Green is, on this count, even stronger. See, for example, *The Meaning of Truth*, 17–18, 245; and *A Pluralistic Universe*, 124ff.

32. James continues: "It *shall* be is the only candid way of stating its relation to belief; and Mr. Bradley's statement comes very near to that." *Essays in Philosophy*, 154; cited by Sprigge, 190. My emphasis appears in the line: "which we turned our backs on forever. . . ."

33. Scattered comments in the first-edition *Principles of Logic* that suggest such a nonconceptual given must be seen as manifestations of the doctrine of the "floating idea."

34. *Some Problems of Philosophy*, 32. Consider also from the same page: "The perceptual flux as such . . . *means* nothing and is but what immediately is; and no mater how small a tract of it be taken. It is always a much-at-once, and contains innumerable aspects and characters which conception can pick out and isolate and thereafter intend."

35. Ibid., 36–38.

36. As Bradley tells us: "It is said that according to me 'the whole development of thinking consciousness resolves itself into an endeavour to reconstitute the unity which it has destroyed.' But this, I have tried to point out, is not my view. *The unity at which thought aims lies beyond that from which it starts* [my emphasis]. Otherwise the consequence would follow that, the more you think, the more you remove yourself from reality." *Essays on Truth and Reality*, 275.

37. See *Some Problems of Philosophy*, 32. Also, 56–57.

38. See chapter 3. I also consider the difference between abstract and eliminative abstraction in "Bradley on the Intension and Extension of Terms." *Perspectives*, 223–42.

39. See James's chapter "Abstractionism and "Relativismus'," 134–45, in his *The Meaning of Truth*. (This is found on pages 300–11 in the Harvard edition.) James wants to claim here that our concepts as originally taken from reality should be "flexible" and willing to mold themselves according to subsequent experience. Apparently he believes that it necessary to say this because, according to him, the "intellectualists" believe otherwise.

40. "Bradley or Bergson?" *Journal of Philosophy, Psychology, and Scientific Methods*, 1910, 7, 29–33. My emphasis in the line "They destroy the notion. . . ."

41. I think it uncontroversial that writers like Jacobi, Fichte, Schelling, and Hegel (in the German tradition), and Green, Caird, and Bosanquet (in the British) all saw primitive experience as unified throughout.

42. I discuss this point in "Caird on Kant and the Refutation of Scepticism." See *Idealism: 1865–1927* (Westport, Conn., 1999), ed. W. J. Mander. (This is a collection of essays based on the conference of the same name that took place at Harris Manchester College, Oxford University, July 3–6, 1997.)

43. Consider, for example, the following: "Prof. James's teaching presents another and a very diverse aspect. It suggests to my mind that in a great measure he really shared that view of the world which in the main I, for instance, inherited from Hegel. . . . And in short the radical opposition which Prof. James took to exist throughout between his own doctrine and that of monistic Absolutism, rested, I venture to think on what I must call his partial ignorance about the latter." *Essays on Truth and Reality*, 144–45. Consider also: "The doctrine which Prof. James, would, I think, have preferred is the view that given experience is non-relational, that it is an unbroken totality containing in one 'now' an undivided lapse, and it is foreign to any terms and relations as such. This I also have taken to be the true account of the matter; and what I would notice here is the fact that while urging this view as a fatal objection ignored by Absolutism and idealism, Prof. James might, like others, have himself learnt it at the very source where according to him it is unknown. . . . [T]hat I myself derived it from Hegel is perfectly certain. If I had ever been asked if it was Hegel's teaching, I should have replied that so much at least was indubitable." Ibid., 152–53.

44. Ibid., 153ff.

45. Ibid.

46. Consider, for example, the following: "Conceptual treatment of perceptual reality makes it seem paradoxical and incomprehensible; and when radically and consistently carried out, it leads to the opinion that perceptual experience is not reality at all, but an appearance or illusion of it." *Some Problems of Philosophy*, 46.

47. Consider also from *Some Problems of Philosophy*: "The full nature, as distinguished from the full amount, of reality, we now believe to be given only in the perceptual flux." 61.

48. Bradley suggests that James alternates between these views at his convenience. See *Essays on Truth and Reality*, 151.

49. For example, ibid., 154–56.

CONCLUSION

1. See, for example, the comments of W. J. Mander in his introduction to *Perspectives on the Logic and Metaphysics of F. H. Bradley* (Bristol, England, 1996), i–xxvii.

2. This is especially true if we accept Dummett's definition of realism. The primary tenet of realism, as applied to some given class of statements, is that each statement in the class is determined as true or not true, independently of our knowledge, by some objective reality whose existence and constitution is independent of our knowledge. *The Interpretation of Frege's Philosophy* (Cambridge, Mass., 1981), 434. See also James Allard's comments: "Degrees of Truth in F. H. Bradley," in *Perspectives on the Logic and Metaphysics of F. H. Bradley*, ed. W. J. Mander (Bristol, England, 1996), 137–58.

3. Michael Dummett "What Is a Theory of Meaning (II)," *Truth and Meaning*, ed. Evans and McDowell (Oxford, 1976), 110. However, I would still echo Strawson's well-known comment that there is much here that remains to be clarified. Strawson writes: "We need to know *at least* what is to count as falling within the range of 'recognisable situations'; what is to count as conclusive verification; *whose* capacity in fact or in principle to do the recognising is in question; what importance, if any, to attach to the disjunction: in fact or in principle; and what 'in principle' means." See "Scruton and Wright on Anti-Realism," *Proceedings of the Aristotelian Society*, 1976–77, 17.

4. Surely James Allard is right when he rejects the interpretation of Bradley as a realist. However, his own reading of Bradley as an antirealist, is, I suggest, equally problematic. See his comments in *Writings on Logic and Metaphysics* (Oxford, 1995), 12.

5. I take these terms from Richard S. Bernstein. See his *Beyond Objectivism and Relativism* (Philadelphia, 1983).

6. Perhaps the most currently influential statement of this position is found in the work of Richard Rorty. See his "Pragmatism, Relativism, and Irrationalism" for a concise statement of this view. *The Consequences of Pragmatism* (Minneapolis, 1982), 160–75. Most interesting in this context, though, are his final comments on the possibility that pragmatism itself might presuppose the "Platonic means" it so openly deprecates.

7. *Appearance and Reality*, 488.

APPENDIX

1. Certainly in the writings of Hobbes and Locke there are intimations of the theory. And, while his account was wholly inadequate, the Rev. John Gay is often acknowledged as providing the first explicit statement of "associationism." Although he published his *Preliminary Dissertation* (1731) some nine years before Hume's *Treatise*, it appears that Hume was unaware of Gay's work. See Albee's *History of English Utilitarianism*, 69–113 on this point. Also of value is D. B. Klein's *A History of Scientific Psychology* (New York, 1970), 638–759.

2. That associationism is not dead is evidenced by the recent appearance of Fred Wilson's *Psychological Analysis and the Philosophy of John Stuart Mill* (Toronto, 1990). Wilson provides a spirited, if unconvincing, defense of Mill's theory. See also note 5, chapter 10 for a further listing of Wilson's articles.

3. See E. G. Boring's *A History of Experimental Psychology* (New York, 1950), esp. 219–46 and 459–501, for an account of this development.

4. *Examination of the Philosophy of Sir William Hamilton* (London, 1865; 6th edition 1889), chap. xi, 190–91.

5. *Principles of Logic*, 300.

6. I say "often" here but not "always." See ibid., Chapter I, note 8 (38). In the second edition of his *Logic* Bradley claimed that, although there must always be a "psychical event" that accompanies our having a significant idea (and the event is not the idea), there is not necessarily an *image*.

7. Ibid., 306

8. We should be aware that impressions turned into ideas and present impressions (part of which is the felt dispositional bond between present impression and preserved idea) is all that the theory sees as belonging to our thinking experience.

9. Ibid., 320

10. Ibid., 320–21.

11. Ibid., 321.

12. It should be noted, perhaps, that on some statements of the theory even this "natural affinity" is the result of contiguous (and wholly contingent) relations between particulars that are themselves entirely distinct and that have no content in common with another.

13. Ibid., 300–301.

14. Ibid., 302.

15. This discussion is taken from a longer article entitled "Bradley's Attack on Associationism." It is found in *Philosophy after F. H. Bradley*, ed. James Bradley (Bristol, England, 1996), 283–306.

SELECTED BIBLIOGRAPHY

The most complete bibliograpy on Bradley is Richard Ingardia's *Bradley: A Research Bibliography* (Bowling Green, Ohio: Philosophy Documentation Center, 1991). More recent bibliographic information may be obtained by consulting Bradley Studies, W. J. Mander (ed.).

BOOKS BY BRADLEY

Bradley, Francis Herbert:

—— (1876) *Ethical Studies*. London: H.S. King.

—— (1883) *Principles of Logic*. London: Kegan Paul, French and Co.

—— (1893) *Appearance and Reality*. London: Swan Sonnenschein.

—— (1897) *Appearance and Reality*, 2nd edition. Oxford: Clarendon Press.

—— (1914) *Essays on Truth and Reality*. Oxford: Clarendon Press.

—— (1922) *Principles of Logic*, 2nd edition. 2 vols. Oxford: Clarendon Press.

—— (1927) *Ethical Studies*, 2nd edition. Oxford: Clarendon Press

—— (1930) *Aphorisms*. Oxford: Clarendon Press.

—— (1935) *Collected Essays*. 2 vols. Oxford: Clarendon Press.

ARTICLES AND PAMPHLETS BY BRADLEY

Original place of publication is given. Those articles that also appear in *Collected Essays* or *Essays on Truth and Reality* have either *CE* or *ETR* after them.

—— (1874) *Presuppositions of Critical History* (pamphlet). Oxford: J. Parker and Co. (*CE*).

—— (1877) "*Mr. Sidgwick's Hedonism*: An Examination of the Main Argument of the 'Method of Ethics'" (pamphlet). Oxford: H. S. King. (Also *Mind*, o.s., 2, and *CE*).

—— (1877) "Mr. Sidgwick on 'Ethical Studies'." *Mind*, o.s., 2, 122–25 (*CE*).

—— (1883) "Is Self-Sacrifice an Enigma?" *Mind*, o.s., 8, 258–60 (*CE*).

—— (1883) "Is There Such a Thing as Pure Malevolence?" *Mind*, o.s., 8, 415–18 (*CE*).

—— (1883) "A Note on *The Principles of Logic*." *Mind*, o.s., 8, 454.

283

—— (1883) "Sympathy and Interest." *Mind*, o.s., 8, 573–75, (CE).

—— (1884) "Can a Man Sin against Knowledge?" *Mind*, o.s., 9, 286–90 (CE).

—— (1885) "The Evidences of Spiritualism." *Fortnightly Review*, n.s., 38, 811–16 (CE).

—— (1886) "Is There Any Special Activity of Attention?" *Mind*, o.s., 11, 305–23 (CE).

—— (1886) "On the Analysis of Comparison." *Mind*, o.s., 11, 83–85 (CE).

—— (1887) "Association and Thought." *Mind*, o.s., 12, 354–81 (CE).

—— (1887) "On a Feature of Active Attention." *Mind*, o.s., 12, 314 (CE).

—— (1887) "Why Do We Remember Backwards and Not Forwards?" *Mind*, o.s., 12, 579–82 (CE).

—— (1888) "On Pleasure, Pain, Desire and Volition." *Mind*, o.s., 13, 1–36 (CE).

—— (1888) "Reality and Thought." *Mind*, o.s., 13, 370–82.

—— (1893) "On Professor James' Doctrine of Simple Resemblance." *Mind* 2, 83–88 (CE).

—— (1893) "Consciousness and Experience." *Mind* 2, 211–16.

—— (1894) "A Reply to Criticism." *Mind* 3, 232–39 (CE).

—— (1894) "On the Failure of Movement in Dream." *Mind* 3, 373–77 (CE).

—— (1895) "What Do We Mean by the Intensity of Psychological States?" *Mind* 4, 1–27 (CE).

—— (1895) "In What Sense Are Psychological States Extended?" *Mind* 4, 225–35 (CE).

—— (1895) "On the Assumed Uselessness of the Soul." *Mind* 4, 176–79 (CE).

—— (1896) "The Contrary and the Disparate." *Mind* 5, 464–82.

—— (1899) "Some Remarks on Memory and Inference." *Mind* 8, 145–66, (ETR).

—— (1900) "A Defense of Phenomenalism in Psychology." *Mind* 9, 26–45 (CE).

—— (1901) "Some Remarks on Conation." *Mind* 10, 437–54 (CE).

—— (1902) "On Active Attention." *Mind* 11, 1–30 (CE).

—— (1902) "On Mental Conflict and Imputation." *Mind* 11, 289–315 (CE).

—— (1902) "The Definition of Will, I." *Mind* 11, 437–69 (CE).

—— (1903) "The Definition of Will, II." *Mind* 12, 145–76 (CE).

—— (1904) "The Definition of Will, III." *Mind* 13, 1–37 (CE).

—— (1905) "Note by A.F. [sic] Bradley." *Mind* 14, 148.

—— (1905) "Reply to Knox." *Mind* 14, 439 (CE).

—— (1906) "On Floating Ideas and the Imaginary." *Mind* 15, 445–72 (ETR).

—— (1907) "On Truth and Copying." *Mind* 16, 165–80 (ETR).

—— (1908) "On Memory and Judgment." *Mind* 17, 153–74 (ETR).

—— (1908) "On the Ambiguity of Pragmatism." *Mind* 17, 226–37 (*ETR*).

—— (1909) "On Our Knowledge of Immediate Experience." *Mind* 18, 40–64 (*ETR*).

—— (1909) "On Truth and Coherence." *Mind* 18, 329–42 (*ETR*).

—— (1909) "Coherence and Contradiction." *Mind* 18, 489–508 (*ETR*).

—— (1910) "On Appearance, Error, and Contradiction." *Mind* 19, 153–85, (*ETR*).

—— (1911) "On Professor James's Meaning of Truth." *Mind* 20, 327–34 (*ETR*).

—— (1911) "Reply to Mr. Russell's Explanation." *Mind* 20, 74–76 (*ETR*).

—— (1911) "On Some Aspects of Truth." *Mind* 20, 308–37 (*ETR*).

—— (1911) "Faith." *Philosophical Review* 20, 305–37 (*ETR*).

—— (1912) "A Reply to Criticism." *Mind* 21, 148–51 (*CE*).

ARTICLES BY OTHERS

Acton, H. B. (1967) "Bradley, Francis Herbert." In Edwards (ed.), *The Encyclopedia of Philosophy*. London: Collier Macmillan, 359–63.

Adamson, R. (1884) "Review of the *Principles of Logic*." *Mind*, o.s., 9, 122–35.

Allard, James (1984) "Bradley's Principle of Sufficient Reason." In A. Manser and G. Stock (eds.), *The Philosophy of F. H. Bradley*. Oxford: Clarendon Press, 173–89.

—— (1985) "Bradley's Intensional Judgments." *History of Philosophy Quarterly* 2, 469–75.

—— (1986) "Wollheim on Bradley on Subjects and Predicates." *Idealistic Studies* 16, 27–40 .

—— (1989) "Bradley on the Validity of Inference." *Journal of the History of Philosophy* 27, 267–84.

—— (1994) "Introduction to the Principles of Logic." In J. Allard and G. Stock (eds.), *Writings on Logic and Metaphysics*. Oxford: Clarendon Press, 3–16.

—— (1996) "Degrees of Truth in F. H. Bradley." In W. J. Mander (ed.), *Perspectives on the Logic and Metaphysics of F. H. Bradley*. Bristol, England: Thoemmes Press, 137–58.

Albee, E. (1909) "The Present Meaning of Idealism." *Philosophical Review* 18, 299–308.

Armour, L. (1995) "F. H. Bradley, Duns Scotus, and the Idea of a Dialectic." *Bradley Studies* 1.1, 6–27.

—— (1996) "The Summum Bonum and Idealist Ontology" In P. Coates and D. Hutto (eds.), *Contemporary Issues in Idealism*. Bristol, England: Thoemmes Press, 203–34.

—— (1996) "Bradley's Other Metaphysics." In W. J. Mander (ed.), *Perspectives on the Logic and Metaphysics of F. H. Bradley*. Bristol, England: Thoemmes Press, 107–36.

Austen, A. (1995) "Bradley and Feminist Ethics." *Bradley Studies* 1.1, 30–44.

Ayer, A. J. (1935) "Internal Relations." *Proceedings of the Aristotelian Society*, supplementary vol. 14, 173–85.

Baldwin, T. (1991) "The Identity Theory of Truth." *Mind* 100, 35–52.

Bakewell, C. M. (1907) "The Ugly Infinite, and the Good for Nothing Absolute." *Philosophical Review* 16, 136–43.

Baxter, D. (1996) "Bradley on Substantive and Adjective: The Complex-Unity Problem." In W. J. Mander (ed.), *Perspectives on the Logic and Metaphysics of F.H. Bradley*. Bristol, England: Thoemmes Press, 1–24.

Bayliss, C. A. (1929) "Internality and Interdependence." *Journal of Philosophy* 26, 373–79.

Bedell, G. L. (1971) "The Relation of Logic and Metaphysics in the Philosophy of F. H. Bradley." *Modern Schoolman* 48, 221–35.

Bell, D. (1984) "The Insufficiency of Ethics." In A. Manser and G. Stock (eds.), *The Philosophy of F. H. Bradley*. Oxford: Clarendon Press, 53–76.

Benecke, E. C. (1898) "On the Logical Subject of the Proposition." *Mind* 7, 34–54.

Bertolotti, G. (1995) "Ghosts and Parasites: Some Remarks on Bradley's Theory of Signs." *Bradley Studies* 1.1, 45–56.

Bird, G. (1996) "Sprigge's Account of William James." *Bradley Studies* 2.1, 64–71.

Blackburn, S. (1984) "Is Epistemology Incoherent?" In A. Manser and G. Stock (eds.), *The Philosophy of F. H. Bradley*. Oxford: Clarendon Press, 155–72.

Blanshard, B. (1925) "Francis Herbert Bradley." *Journal of Philosophy* 22, 5–13.

——— (1984) "Bradley on Relations." In A. Manser and G. Stock (eds.), *The Philosophy of F. H. Bradley*. Oxford: Clarendon Press, 211–26.

Bode, B. H. (1910) "Objective Idealism and Its Critics." *Philosophical Review* 19, 597–609.

Bosanquet, B. (1885) "Mr. F. H. Bradley on Fact and Inference." *Mind*, o.s., 10, 256–65.

——— (1915) "On a Defect in the Customary Formulation of Inductive Reasoning." *Proceedings of the Aristotelian Society* 15, 29–40 (also in Science and Philosophy).

——— (1915) "Science and Philosophy." *Proceedings of the Aristotelian Society* 15, 1–21 (also in Science and Philosophy).

——— (1915) "The History of Philosophy." In *Germany in the 19th Century*, 2nd series. Manchester, England: University Press.

Bradley, J. (1979) "Hegel in Britain: A Brief History of British Commentary and Attitudes." *The Heythrop Journal* 20, 1–24.

——— (1984) "F. H. Bradley's Metaphysics of Feeling and Its Place in the History of Philosophy." In A. Manser and G. Stock (eds.), *The Philosophy of F. H. Bradley*. Oxford: Clarendon Press, 227–42.

—— (1985) "'The Critique of Pure Feeling': Bradley, Whitehead, and the Anglo-Saxon Metaphysical Tradition." *Process Studies* 14, 253–64.

—— (1996) "The Transcendental Turn in F. H. Bradley's Metaphysics of Feeling." In W. J. Mander (ed.), *Perspectives on the Logic and Metaphysics of F. H. Bradley*. Bristol, England: Thoemmes Press, 39–60.

Broad, C. D. (1914) "Mr. Bradley on Truth and Reality." *Mind* 23, 349–70.

Brown, W. H. (1907) "The Pragmatic Value of the Absolute." *Journal of Philosophy* 4, 459–64.

Candlish, S. (1978) "Bradley on My Station and Its Duties." *Australasian Journal of Philosophy* 56, 155–70.

—— (1981) "The Status of Idealism in Bradley's Metaphysics." *Idealistic Studies* 11, 242–53.

—— (1982) "Idealism and Bradley's Logic." *Idealistic Studies* 12, 251–59.

—— (1984) "Scepticism, Ideal Experiment, and Priorities in Bradley's Metaphysics." In A. Manser and G. Stock (eds.), *The Philosophy of F. H. Bradley*. Oxford: Clarendon Press, 331–48.

—— (1995) "Resurrecting the Identity Theory of Truth." *Bradley Studies* 1.2, 116–24.

Carr, H. W. (1910) "Mr. Bradley's Theory of Appearance." *Proceedings of the Aristotelian Society* 2, 215–30.

Church, R. (1942) "Bradley's Theory of Relations and the Law of Identity." *Philosophical Review* 51, 26–46.

Cresswell, M. J. (1977) "Reality as Experience in F. H. Bradley." *Australasian Journal of Philosophy* 55, 169–88.

—— (1979) "Bradley's Theory of Judgement." *Canadian Journal of Philosophy* 9, 575–94.

Crossley, David J. (1996) "Justification and the Foundations of Empirical Knowledge." In James Bradley (ed.), *Philosophy after F. H. Bradley*. Bristol, England: Thoemmes Press, 307–29.

Cuming, Agnes (1917) "Lotze, Bradley, and Bosanquet." *Mind* 26, 162–70.

Dawes Hicks, G. (1925) "Mr. Bradley's Treatment of Nature." *Mind* 34, 55–69.

Delaney, C. F. (1971) "Bradley on the Nature of Science." *Idealistic Studies* 1, 201–18.

Dewey, J. (1906) "Experience and Objective Idealism." *Philosophical Review* 15, 470–78.

—— (1907) "Reality, and the Criterion for the Truth of Ideas." *Mind* 16, 317–42.

Dodd, J. (1996) "The Identity Theory of Truth." *Bradley Studies* 2.1, 42–50.

Duprat, E. (1926) "La Metaphysique de Bradley." *Philosophical Review* 102, 31–69.

Eliot, T.S. (Dec. 1927) "Francis Herbert Bradley." *The Times Literary Supplement* 29.

Fawcett, E. D. (1911) "The Ground of Appearance." *Mind* 20, 197–211.

——— (1912) "Truth's Original Object." *Mind* 21, 89–92.

Ferreira, P. (1995) "Perceptual Ideality and the Ground of Inference." *Bradley Studies* 1.2, 125–38.

——— (1996) "Why the Idealist Theory of Inference Still Matters." In P. Coates and D. Hutto (eds.), *Contemporary Issues in Idealism*. Bristol, England: Thoemmes Press, 235–66.

——— (1996) "Bradley on the Intension and Extension of Terms." In W. J. Mander (ed.), *Perspectives on the Logic and Metaphysics of F. H. Bradley*. Bristol, England: Thoemmes Press, 223–42.

——— (1996) "Bradley's Attack on Associationism." In J. Bradley (ed.), *Philosophy after F. H. Bradley*. Bristol, England: Theommes Press.

——— (1998) "Contradiction, Contrariety and Inference." *Bradley Studies* 4.2, 123–44.

——— (1999) "Caird on Kant and the Refutation of Scepticism." In W. J. Mander (ed.), *Anglo-American Idealism: 1865–1927*. Westport, Conn.: Greenwood Press (forthcoming).

Findlay, J. N. (1984) "Bradley's Contribution to Absolute-Theory." In A. Manser and G. Stock (eds.), *The Philosophy of F. H. Bradley*. Oxford: Clarendon Press, 269–84.

Fortier, E. (1996) "Was the Dispute between Russell and Bradley about Internal Relations." In W. J. Mander (ed.), *Perspectives on the Logic and Metaphysics of F. H. Bradley*. Bristol, England: Thoemmes Press, 25–38.

Foster, M. B. (1930) "The Contradiction of 'Appearance and Reality'." *Mind* 39, 43–60.

Gibson, J. (1923) Review of the second edition of "The Principles of Logic." *Mind* 32, 352–56.

Griffin, N. (1983) "What's Wrong with Bradley's Theory of Judgement?" *Idealistic Studies* 12, 199–225.

Haldar, H. (1899) "The Conception of the Absolute." *Philosophical Review* 8, 261–72.

——— (1918) "The Absolute and the Finite Self." *Philosophical Review* 27, 341–91.

Hammond, A. (1921) "Appearance and Reality in the Theory of Relativity." *Philosophical Review* 30, 602–15.

Harris, Errol E. (1985) "Bradley's Conception of Nature." *Idealistic Studies* 15, 185–98.

Hicks, G. D. (1925) "Mr. Bradley's Treatment of Nature." *Mind* 34, 35–69.

Hoernlé, R. F. A. (1905) "Pragmatism vs. Absolutism, I." *Mind* 14, 297–334.

Holdcroft, D. (1984) "Holism and Truth." In A. Manser and G. Stock (eds.), *The Philosophy of F. H. Bradley*. Oxford: Clarendon Press, 191–210.

——— (1995) "Parts and Wholes: The Limits of Analysis." *Bradley Studies* 1.1, 57–68.

Ingardia, R. (1996) "Bradley and Aquinas: Empirical Realists." In *Perspectives on the Logic and Metaphysics of F. H. Bradley*, W. J. Mander (ed.). Bristol, England: Thoemmes Press, 75–106.

—— (1905) "Pragmatism vs. Absolutism, II." *Mind* 14, 441–78.

—— (1913) "Review of Rashdall, H.: The Metaphysics of Mr. F. H. Bradley." *Mind* 22, 598.

James, W. (1893) "Mr. Bradley on Immediate Resemblance." *Mind* 2, 208–10.

—— (1904) "Humanism and Truth." *Mind* 13, 457–75.

—— (1910) "The Absolute and the Strenuous Life." *Journal of Philosophy* 4, 546–48.

—— (1910) "Bradley or Bergson?" *Journal of Philosophy* 7, 29–33.

Johnson, (1984) "Bradley and the Nature of Punishment." In A. Manser and G. Stock (eds.), *The Philosophy of F. H. Bradley*. Oxford: Clarendon Press, 99–116.

Keen, C. N. (1971) "The Interaction of Russell and Bradley." *Russell: The Journal of the Bertrand Russell Archives* 3, 7–11.

Kenna, J. C. (1966) "Ten Unpublished Letters from William James, 1842–1919, to Francis Herbert Bradley, 1846–1924." *Mind* 75, 309–31.

Knox, H.V. (1905) "Mr. Bradley's Absolute Criterion." *Mind* 14, 210–20.

—— (1906) "Mr. Bradley and Self-Contradiction." *Mind* 15, 141.

—— (1907) "Remarks on a Footnote by Mr. Bradley." *Mind* 16, 475–76.

Lazarus, S.C. (1925) "In Memorium, F. H. Bradley." *Australasian Journal of Psychology and Philosophy* 2, 268–86.

MacKenzie, J. S. (1894) "On Mr. Bradley's View of the Self." *Mind* 3, 305–35.

—— (1909) "Edward Caird as a Philosophical Teacher." *Mind* 18, 509–37.

Maclachlan, D. L. C. (1963) "Presupposition in Bradley's Philosophy." *Dialogue* 2, 155–69.

Mallinson, J. (1996) "Eliot, Bradley, and Coleridge." *Bradley Studies* 2.1, 33–41.

Mander, W. J. (1991) "F. H. Bradley and the Philosophy of Science." *International Studies in the Philosophy of Science* 5, 65–78.

—— "Levels of Experience in F. H. Bradley." *The Southern Journal of Philosophy* 33, 485–98.

—— "Bradley's Philosophy of Religion." *Religious Studies* 31, 285–301.

—— "What's So Good about the Absolute?" *British Journal for the History of Philosophy* 4, 101–18.

—— (1996) "Introduction" to W. J. Mander (ed.), *Perspectives on the Logic and Metaphysics of F. H. Bradley*. Bristol, England: Thoemmes Press, ix–xxvii.

—— (1996) "The Role of Self in Bradley's Argument for Idealism." In W. J. Mander (ed.), *Perspectives on the Logic and Metaphysics of F. H. Bradley*. Bristol, England: Thoemmes Press, 61–74.

Manser, A. (1982) "Bradley and Internal Relations." In *Idealism Past and Present*, Royal Institute of Philosophy Lecture Series. Cambridge: Cambridge University Press.

―――― (1984) "Bradley and Frege." In A. Manser and G. Stock (eds.), *The Philosophy of F. H. Bradley*. Oxford: Clarendon Press, 303–17.

―――― (1984) "Introduction." In A. Manser and G. Stock (eds.), *The Philosophy of F. H. Bradley*. Oxford: Clarendon Press, 1–32.

Martin, R. M. (1977) "On Peirce, Bradley and the Doctrine of Continuous Relations." *Idealistic Studies* 7, 291–304.

McFee, G. (1996) "Bradley, Possibility, and a Question and Answer Logic." In W. J. Mander (ed.), *Perspectives on the Logic and Metaphysics of F. H. Bradley*. Bristol, England: Thoemmes Press, 269–88.

McHenry, L. (1996) "Bradley's Conception of Metaphysics." In W. J. Mander (ed.), *Perspectives on the Logic and Metaphysics of F. H. Bradley*. Bristol, England: Thoemmes Press, 159–76.

Montague, R. (1964) "Wollheim on Bradley on Idealism and Relations." *Philosophical Quarterly* 14, 158–64.

Moore, G. E. (1922) "External and Internal Relations." In *Philosophical Studies*. New York: Harcourt, Brace and Co., 276–309.

Muirhead, J. H. (1925) "Mr. Bradley's Place in Philosophy." *Mind* 34, 173–84.

Mure, G. R. G. (1961) "F. H. Bradley—Towards a Portrait." *Encounter* 16, 28–35.

Nicholson, P. (1984) "Bradley as a Political Philosopher." In A. Manser and G. Stock (eds.), *The Philosophy of F. H. Bradley*. Oxford: Clarendon Press, 117–30.

Passmore, J. (1969) "Russell and Bradley." In R. Brown and C. D. Rollins (eds.), *Contemporary Philosophy in Australia*. London: George Allen and Unwin, 21–30.

―――― (1976) "G. F. Stout's Editorship of *Mind* (1892–1920)." *Mind* 85, 17–36.

Perry, Ralph Barton (1925) "The Cardinal Principle of Idealism." *Mind* 34, 322–36.

Pritchard, H. A. (1906) "Appearances and Reality." *Mind* 15, 223–29.

Pugmire, D. (1996) "Some Self: F. H. Bradley on the Self as 'Mere' Feeling." *Bradley Studies* 2.1, 24–32.

Ridley, A. (1995) "F. H. Bradley: Relations and Regresses." *Bradley Studies* 1.2, 107–15.

Robinson, J. (1980) "Bradley and Bosanquet." *Idealistic Studies* 10, 1–23.

Rogers, A. K. (1903) "The Absolute as Unknowable." *Mind* 12, 35–46.

Royce, Josiah (1894) "Review of *Appearance and Reality*." *Philosophical Review* 3, 212–18.

Russell, B. (1910) "Some Explanations in Reply to Mr. Bradley." *Mind* 19, 373–78.

—— (1906–7) "On the Nature of Truth." *Proceedings of the Aristotelian Society* 7, 28–49.

Sabine, C. H. (1915) "The Social Origins of Absolute Idealism." *Journal of Philosophy* 12, 169–70.

Sayers, S. (1991) "F. H. Bradley and the Concept of Relative Truth." *Radical Philosophy* 59, 15–21.

Schiller, F. C. S. (1904) "In Defence of Humanism." *Mind* 13, 525–42.

—— (1906) "Is Absolute Idealism Solipsistic?" *Journal of Philosophy* 3, 85–89.

—— (1906) "Idealism and Dissociation of Personality." *Journal of Philosophy* 3, 477–82.

—— (1907) "Mr. Bradley's Theory of Truth." *Mind* 16, 401–09.

—— (1908) "Is Mr. Bradley a Pragmatist?" *Mind* 17, 370–83.

—— (1910) "Absolutism in Extremis?" *Mind* 19, 531–40.

—— (1915) "The New Developments of Mr. Bradley's Philosophy." *Mind* 24, 345–66.

—— (1917) "Mr. Bradley, Bain, and Pragmatism." *Journal of Philosophy* 14, 449–57.

—— (1925) "The Origin of Bradley's Scepticism." *Mind* 34, 217–23.

Sidgwick, H. (1876) "Review of Ethical Studies." *Mind*, o.s., 1, 545–49.

—— (1894) "Mr. Bradley and the Sceptics." *Mind* 3, 336–47.

—— (1904) "On a Note of Mr. Bradley's." *Mind* 13, 59.

—— (1905) "Mr. Bradley's Dilemma." *Mind* 14, 293–94.

—— (1908) "The Ambiguity of Pragmatism." *Mind* 17, 368–69.

—— (1909) "Notes on a Note of Mr. Bradley's." *Mind* 18, 639–40.

Sievers, K. (1991) "Bradley's Theory of Judgment and Ideas." *Idealistic Studies* 21, 135–50.

—— (1996) "Inference and the Criterion of System." In W. J. Mander (ed.), *Perspectives on the Logic and Metaphysics of F. H. Bradley.* Bristol, England: Thoemmes Press, 243–68.

Silkstone, T. W. (1974) "Bradley on Relations." *Idealistic Studies* 4, 160–69.

Spaulding, E. G. (1910) "Structures of Self-Refuting Systems II: Ontological Absolutism." *Philosophical Review* 19, 610–31.

—— (1912) "Defense of Analysis." In *The New Realism.* New York: Holt and Co.

Sprigge, T. L. S. (1979) "Russell and Bradley on Relations." In G. Roberts (ed.), *Bertrand Russell Memorial Volume.* London: George Allen and Unwin, 150–70.

—— (1984) "The Self and its World in Bradley and Husserl." In A. Manser and G. Stock (eds.), *The Philosophy of F. H. Bradley.* Oxford: Clarendon Press, 285–302.

—— (1988) "Personal and Impersonal Identity." *Mind* 97, 29–49.

—— (1995) "Bradley and Christianity." *Bradley Studies* 1.1, 69–85.

—— (1996) "Idealism, Humanism, and the Enviornment." In P. Coates and D. Hutto (eds.), *Contemporary Issues in Idealism*. Bristol, England: Thoemmes Press, 267–304.

Stanley, M. (1996) "The Paradox of the Individual." *Bradley Studies* 2.1, 51–63.

Stern, R. (1993) "James and Bradley on Understanding." *Philosophy* 68, 465–76.

—— (1994) "British Hegelianism: A Non-Metaphysical View?" *European Journal of Philosophy* 2, 295–321.

Stock, G. (1984) "Bradley's Theory of Judgment." In A. Manser and G. Stock (eds.), *The Philosophy of F. H. Bradley*. Oxford: Clarendon Press, 131–54.

—— (1984) "Introduction" to A. Manser and G. Stock (eds.), *The Philosophy of F. H. Bradley*. Oxford: Clarendon Press 1–32.

—— (1985) "Negation: Bradley and Wittgenstein." *Philosophy* 60, 465–76.

—— (1993) "Introduction" to *The Presuppositions of Critical History and Aphorisms*. Bristol, England: Thoemmes Press.

—— (1994) "Introduction to the Argument of Bradley's Metaphysics." In J. Allard and G. Stock (eds.), *Writings on Logic and Metaphysics*, 103–14.

—— (1996) "The Plurality of Worlds, Historical Time, and Uniqueness." In P. Coates and D. Hutto (eds.), *Contemporary Issues in Idealism*. Bristol, England: Thoemmes Press, 179–203.

Stout, G. F. (1898) "Review of Appearance and Reality." *Mind* 7, 117.

—— (1901–02) "Alleged Self-Contradiction in the Concept of Relation: A Criticism of Appearance and Reality." *Proceedings of the Aristotelian Society* 2, 1–24.

—— (1902–3) "Mr. Bradley's Theory of Judgment." *Proceedings of the Aristotelian Society* 3, 1–27.

—— (1925) "Bradley on Truth and Falsity." *Mind* 34, 39–55.

Strange, E. H. (1911) "Mr. Bradley's Doctrine of Knowledge." *Mind* 20, 457–88.

Sturt, H. (1907) "Mr. Bradley on Truth and Copying." *Mind* 16, 416–17.

Swabey, W. C. (1919) "Mr. Bradley's Negative Dialectic and Realism." *Journal of Philosophy* 16, 404–17.

Tacelli, R. K. (1991) "Cook Wilson as a Critic of Bradley." *History of Philosophy Quarterly* 8, 199–205.

—— "Bradley on Relations: A Defense." *Proceedings of the Catholic Philosophical Association* 66, 149–61.

—— (1927) "The System of Bradley." *The Monist* 37, 226–37.

Taylor, A. E. (1921) "Philosophy." In F. S. Marvin (ed.), *Recent Developments in European Thought*. London: Oxford University Press, 211–31.

—— (1924–25) "Francis Herbert Bradley." *Proceedings of the British Academy* 11, 458–68.

—— (1925) "F. H. Bradley." *Mind* 34, 1–12.

Trott, E. (1996) "Watson, Bradley and the Search for a Metaphysical Metaphor." *Bradley Studies* 2.1, 5–23.

Walsh, W. H. (1964) "F. H. Bradley." In D. J. O'Connor (ed.), *A Critical History of Western Philosophy*. Basingstoke: Macmillan and Co.

—— (1984) "Bradley and Critical History." In A. Manser and G. Stock (eds.), *The Philosophy of F. H. Bradley*. Oxford, 33–52.

Ward, J. (1887) "Mr. F. H. Bradley's Analysis of Mind." *Mind*, o.s., 12, 564–75.

—— (1925) "Bradley's Doctrine of Experience." *Mind* 34.

Watson, John (1909) "The Idealism of Edward Caird." *Philosophical Review* 18, 147–63, 259–80.

Wilson, F. (1995) "Moore's Refutation of Idealism." In P. Coates and D. Hutto (eds.), *Current Issues in Idealism*. Bristol, England: Thoemmes Press, 23–59.

—— (1995) "Bradley's Conception of Ideality: Comments on Ferreira's Defense." *Bradley Studies* 1.2, 139–54.

—— (1996) "The Demise of Classical Psychology." In W. J. Mander (ed.), *Perspectives on the Logic and Metaphysics of F. H. Bradley*. Bristol, England: Thoemmes Press, 177–222.

—— (1996) "Bradley's Impact on Empiricism." In James Bradley, ed., *Philosophy After F. H. Bradley*. Bristol, England: Thoemmes Press, 251–281.

—— (1996) "Burgersdijck, Bradley, Russell, Bergmann: Four Philosophers on the Ontology of Relations." In *The New Schoolman* 72, 282–310.

—— (1998) "Bradley's Critique of Associationism." *Bradley Studies* 4.1, 5–60.

Wollheim, R. (1970) "Eliot and F. H. Bradley: An Account." In G. Martin (ed.), *Eliot in Perspective: A Symposium*. London, 169–93.

—— (1995) "Bradley in the Fifties: Some Philosophical Reflections." *Bradley Studies* 1.2, 98–106.

Wright, C. (1984) "The Moral Organism." In A. Manser and G. Stock (eds.), *The Philosophy of F. H. Bradley*. Oxford: Clarendon Press, 77–98.

BOOKS BY OTHERS

Ayer, A. J. (1970) *Metaphysics and Common Sense*. San Francisco: Freeman, Cooper and Co.

—— (1982) *Philosophy in the Twentieth Century*. London: Weidenfeld and Nicolson Ltd.

Benn, A. W. (1906) *A History of English Rationalism in the Nineteenth Century*. London: Longmans, Green and Co.

Bernstein, Richard (1983) *Beyond Objectivism and Relativism*. Philadelphia: University of Pennsylvania Press.

Blanshard, Brand (1939) *The Nature of Thought*, 2 vols. London: George Allen and Unwin.

—— (1962) *Reason and Analysis*. La Salle, Ill.: Open Court.

Bonjour, Lawrence (1985) *The Structure of Empirical Knowledge*. Cambridge, Mass.: Harvard University Press.

Bosanquet, Bernard (1885) *Knowledge and Reality*. London: Kegan Paul, French and Co.

—— (1888) *Logic or the Morphology of Knowlyedge*, 2 vols. Oxford: Clarendon Press, 2nd edition 1911.

—— (1897) *The Psychology of the Moral Self*. London: Macmillan and Co.

—— (1910) *The Essentials of Logic*. London: Macmillan and Co.

—— (1912) *The Principle of Individuality and Value*. London: Macmillan and Co.

—— (1913) *The Value and Destiny of the Individual*. London: Macmillan and Co.

—— (1920) *Implication and Linear Inference*. London: Macmillan and Co.

—— (1923) *Three Chapters on the Nature of Mind*. London: Macmillan and Co.

—— (1924) *The Meeting of Extremes in Contemporary Philosophy*. London: Macmillan and Co.

—— (1927) *Science and Philosophy*. London: George Allen and Unwin.

Bosanquet, Helen (1924) *Bernard Bosanquet: A Short Account of His Life*. London: Macmillan and Co.

Broad, C. D. (1933) *An Examination of McTaggart's Philosophy*. Cambridge: Cambridge University Press.

Caird, Edward (1877) *A Critical Account of the Philosophy of Kant*. Glasgow: Maclehose and Sons.

—— (1889) *The Critical Philosophy of Kant*. Glasgow: Maclehose and Sons.

Campbell, C. A. (1931) *Scepticism and Construction: Bradley's Sceptical Principle as the Basis of Constructive Philosophy*. London: George Allen and Unwin.

Coates P., and D. Hutto (eds.) (1996) *Current Issues in Idealism*. Bristol, England: Thoemmes Press.

Collingwood, R. G. (1924) *Speculum Mentis: or the Map of Knowledge*. Oxford: Clarendon Press.

—— (1934) *An Essay on Philosophical Method*. Oxford: Clarendon Press.

—— (1940) *An Essay on Metaphysics*. Oxford: Clarendon Press.

Church, Ralf Whitington (1942) *Bradley's Dialectic*. London: George Allen and Unwin.

Dancy, J. (1985) *Introduction to Contemporary Epistemology*. Oxford: Basil Blackwell.

Creighton, J. E. (1925) *Studies in Speculative Philosophy*. New York: Macmillan and Co.

Cunningham, G. W. (1967) *The Idealistic Argument*. New York: Books for Libraries Press, 1st edition 1933.

Dewey, J. (1916) *Essays in Experimental Logic*. Chicago: University of Chicago Press.

—— (1929) *Experience and Nature*, revised edition. New York: Norton and Co.

Eliot, T. S. (1964) *Knowledge and Experience in the Philosophy of F. H. Bradley*. London: Faber and Faber.

—— (1936) *Essays Ancient and Modern*. London: Faber and Faber.

Ewing, Alfred C. (1934) *Idealism: a Critical Survey*. New York: Humanities Press.

—— (ed.) (1957) *The Idealist Tradition*. Glencoe, Ill.: Free Press.

Fairbrother, W. H. (1896) *The Philosophy of Thomas Hill Green*. London: Meuthen and Co.

Forsyth, T. M. (1910) *English Philosophy*. London: A. and C. Black.

Green, Thomas Hill (1883) *Prolegomena to Ethics*. Oxford: Clarendon Press.

Griffin, N. (1991) *Russell's Idealist Apprenticeship*. Oxford: Clarendon Press.

—— (1885, 1890) *Works of T. H. Green*. London: Longmans, Green and Co.

Haldane, R. B. (1903) *The Pathway to Reality*. London: John Murray.

—— (1929) *Richard Burdon Haldane: An Autobiography*. London: Hodder and Stoughton.

Haldar, H. (1927) *Neo-Hegelianism*. London: Heath, Cranton Ltd.

Harris, Errol E. (1954) *Nature, Mind and Natural Science*. London: George Allen and Co.

—— (1970) *Hypothesis and Perception: The Roots of Scientific Method*. London: George Allen and Co.

—— (1987) *Formal, Transcendental and Dialectical Thinking*. Albany: State University of New York Press.

Hegel, G. W. F. (1832–40) *Werke*, 18 vols. Berlin: Dundar und Humblot.

—— (1931) *Hegel's Phenomenology of Mind*, J. B. Baillie, trans. London: George Allen and Unwin.

—— (1959) *The Science of Logic*, A. V. Miller, trans. London: George Allen and Unwin.

—— (1892) *Encyclopaedia of Philosophical Sciences: Logic and Philosophy of Mind*, W. Wallace, trans., 1892, revised by A. V. Miller 1975. Oxford: Oxford University Press.

Hobhouse, L. T. (1896) *Theory of Knowledge*. London: Meuthen and Co.

Hoernlé, R. F. A. (1924) *Idealism*. London: Hodder and Stoughton.

—— (1952) *Studies in Philosophy*. London: George Allen and Unwin.

Hume, David (1874–75) *Hume's Philosophical Works*, 4 vols. T. H. Green and T. M. Grose, eds. London: Longmans, Green and Co.

Hylton, Peter (1990) *Russell, Idealism, and the Emergence of Analytic Philosophy*. Oxford: Clarendon Press.

James, William (1907) *Pragmatism*. New York: Longmans, Green and Co.

—— (1909) *A Pluralistic Universe*. London: Longmans, Green and Co.

—— (1911) *Some Problems of Philosophy*. Cambridge, Mass.: Harvard University Press edition 1979.

—— (1912) *Essays in Radical Empiricism*, R. B. Perry, ed. Expanded and republished in 1943. New York: Dutton and Company.

Jevons, W. Stanley (1895) *Elementary Lessons in Logic*. London: Macmillan and Co.

Joachim, H. H. (1939) *The Nature of Truth*. Oxford: Oxford University Press, 1st edition 1906.

—— (1948) *Logical Studies*. Oxford: Clarendon Press.

Jones, Henry (1895) *A Critical Account of the Philosophy of Lotze*. Glasgow: Maclehose.

—— (1921) *The Life and Philosophy of Edward Caird*, with J. H. Muirhead. Glasgow: Maclehose and Jackson.

Joseph, H. W. B. (1916) *An Introduction to Logic*. Oxford: Clarendon Press, 1st edition 1906.

Kant, Immanuel (1902–55) *Kants gesammelte Schriften*, 23 vols. Berlin: Preussischen Akademie der Wissenschaften.

—— (1929) *Critique of Pure Reason*. Norman Kemp Smith, trans. London: Macmillan and Co.

Kagey, Rudolph (1931) *The Growth of Bradley's Logic*. New York: Macmillan and Co.

Lazerowitz, M. (1955) *The Structure of Metaphysics*. London: Routledge and Paul.

Lofthouse, W. F. (1949) *F. H. Bradley*. London: Epworth Press.

Lotze, H. (1894) *Microcosmus, E. Hamilton and E. E. C. Jones*, trans., 4th edition. New York: Scribners, orignal German edition 1856.

—— (1888) *Logic*, 2 vols., B. Bosanquet, trans. and ed. Oxford: Oxford University Press, original German edition 1874.

—— (1887) *Metaphysic*, 2 vols., B. Bosanquet, trans. and ed. Oxford: Oxford University Press, original German edition 1879.

Mander, W. J. (1993) *An Introduction to Bradley's Metaphysics*. Oxford: Clarendon Press.

—— (ed.) (1996) *Perspectives on the Logic and Metaphysics of F. H. Bradley*. Bristol, England: Thoemmes Press.

Mansel, H. (1851) *Prolegomena Logica: An Inquiry into the Psychological Character of Logical Processes.* Oxford: Graham.

Manser, Anthony (1983) *Bradley's Logic.* London: Basil Blackwell.

Manser, A., and G. Stock (eds.) (1984) *The Philosophy of F. H. Bradley.* Oxford: Clarendon Press.

McHenry, L. B. (1992) *Whitehead and Bradley: A Comparative Analysis.* Albany: State University of New York Press.

McNiven, Don (1987) *Bradley's Moral Psychology.* Lewiston, N.Y.: Edwin Mellen Press.

McTaggart, J. M. E. (1896) *Studies in Hegelian Dialectic.* Cambridge: Cambridge University Press.

——— (1934) *Philosophical Studies.* Freeport, N.Y.: Books for Libraries Press.

Mill, John Stuart (1872) *A System of Logic* (8th edition). London: Longmans, Green and Co., 1st edition 1843.

——— (1889) *An Examination of Sir William Hamilton's Philosophy* (6th edition). London: Longmans, Green. 1st edition 1865.

Moore, G. E. (1922) *Philosophical Studies.* New York: Harcourt, Brace and Co.

Morris, C. R. (1933) *Idealistic Logic.* Port Washington, N.Y.: Kennikat Press.

Muirhead, J. H. (1931) *The Platonic Tradition in Anglo-Saxon Philosophy.* London: George Allen and Unwin.

——— (ed.) (1935) *Bernard Bosanquet and His Friends: Letters.* London: George Allen and Unwin.

Mure, G. R. G. (1958) *The Retreat from Truth.* London: Basil Blackwell.

——— (1978) *Idealist Epilogue.* Oxford: Clarendon Press.

Nettleship, Richard Lewis (1897) *Philosophical Lectures and Remains.* London: Macmillan and Co.

Nicholson P. (1990) *The Political Philosophy of the British Idealists.* Cambridge: Cambridge University Press.

Passmore, John (1957, 1966) *One Hundred Years of Philosophy.* London: Duckworth.

Putnam, Hilary (1981) *Reason, Truth and History.* Cambridge: Cambridge University Press.

Rashdall, H. (1912) *The Metaphysics of Mr. F. H. Bradley.* London: H. Frowde.

Rescher, N. (1973) *The Coherence Theory of Truth.* Oxford: Clarendon Press.

Rorty, Richard (1979) *Philosophy and the Mirror of Nature.* Princeton, N.J.: Princeton University Press.

——— (1982) *The Consequences of Pragmatism.* Minneapolis: University of Minnesota Press.

Royce, Josiah (1901–2) *The Word and the Individual* (1st series). New York: Macmillan.

——— (1919) *Lectures on Modern Idealism.* New Haven: Yale University Press.

——— (1951) *Logical Essays*, D. S. Robinson, ed. Dubuque, Iowa: W. C. Brown Co.

Russell, Bertrand (1964) *The Principles of Mathematics*. London: George Allen and Unwin, 1st edition 1903.

——— (1910) *Philosophical Essays*. New York: Simon & Schuster.

——— (1974) *The Problems of Philosophy*. Oxford: Oxford University Press, 1st edition 1912.

——— (1974) *Our Knowledge of the External World*. London: George Allen and Unwin, 1st edition 1914.

——— (1956) *Logic and Knowledge*, R. C. Marsh, ed. London: George Allen and Unwin.

——— (1959) *My Philosophical Development*. London: George Allen and Unwin.

Saxena, Sushil Kumar (1967) *Studies in the Metaphysics of Bradley*. London: George Allen and Unwin.

Schiller, F. C. S. (1903) *Humanism*. London: Macmillan, 2nd edition 1912.

——— (1912) *Formal Logic*. London: Macmillan, 2nd edition 1921.

——— (1930) *Logic for Use*. New York: Harcourt, Brace and Co.

Seth (Pringle-Pattison), Andrew (1882) *From Kant to Hegel*. Edinburgh: Williams and Norgate.

——— (1885) *Scottish Philosophy*. Edinburgh: William Blackwood and Sons.

——— (1887) *Hegelianism and Personality*. Edinburgh: W. Blackwood and Sons, 2nd edition 1893.

——— (1892) *Man's Place in the Cosmos*. New York: Scribners.

Seth A., and R. Haldane (eds.) (1883) *Essays in Philosophical Criticism*. London: Longmans, Green and Co.

Sprigge, T. L. S. (1970) *Facts, Words and Beliefs*. London: Routledge.

——— (1985) *Theories of Existence*. London: Pelican Books.

——— (1983) *The Vindication of Absolute Idealism*. Edinburgh: Edinburgh University Press.

——— (1993) *James and Bradley: American Truth and British Reality*. La Salle, Ill.: Open Court.

Stebbing, L. S. (1948) *A Modern Introduction to Logic*, 6th edition. London: Meuthen and Co.

Stirling, J. H. (1898) *The Secret of Hegel: Being the Hegelian System in Origin, Principle, Form and Matter*, 2 vols., second edition. Edinburgh: Oliver and Boyd, 1st edition 1865.

Stout, G. (1896) *Analytic Psychology*. London: Swan Sonnenschein.

——— (1899) *A Manual of Psychology*. London: University Correspondence College Press.

——— (1931) *Mind and Matter*. Cambridge: Cambridge University Press.

Taylor, A. E. (1921) *Elements of Metaphysics*. London: Meuthen and Co. Ltd, 1st edition 1903.

Vander Veer, G. L. (1970) *Bradley's Metaphysics and the Self*. New Haven: Yale University Press.

Walker, R. C. S. (1989) *The Coherence Theory of Truth*. London: Routledge.

Ward, J. (1915) *Naturalism and Agnosticism*. London: A. C. Black, first edition 1899 (in 2 volumes).

—— (1918, 1920) *Psychological Principles*. Cambridge: Cambridge University Press.

Watson, J. (1881) *Kant and His English Critics*. Glasgow: James Maclehose.

—— (1898) *An Outline of Philosophy*. Glasgow: Maclehose and Sons.

—— (1908) *The Philosophy of Kant Explained*. Glasgow: James Maclehose and Sons.

Wilson, F. (1990) *Psychological Analysis and the Philosophy of John Stuart Mill*. Toronto: Univesity of Toronto Press.

Wilson, J. Cook (1926) *Statement and Inference*. Oxford: Clarendon Press.

Wollheim, R. (1959) *F. H. Bradley*. Harmondsworth, England: Penguin Books, 2nd edition 1969.

INDEX